IN THE DETAILS

Jessica Christ, Book 6

H. CLAIRE TAYLOR

FFS Media

ISBN: 978-0-9996050-8-0 (H. Claire Taylor)

FFS Media, LLC

www.ffs.media

contact@hclairetaylor.com

Contents

To everyone who's told the truth and wasn't believed.

And to everyone too scared to tell the truth because you know you won't be believed.

And especially to everyone who has told the truth, been believed, but discovered nobody cared.

Chapter One

May, 21 AGC

Jackhammers and the beeping of dump trucks blended with the purring of car engines in rush-hour gridlock. Marching down the sidewalk, oblivious to all the noise, thanks to the mighty-and-all-that voice in her head was a girl—no, a *woman*, dammit!—carrying an empty cash purse in a tattered Texas State University tote bag. She frowned meanly at the world, partially to warn those passing her against engaging her in conversation, but also because her Father was being especially chatty, and it was the last thing she needed after a long day of work that wasn't yet over.

I ought to report him to ... whoever regulates banks.

FOR WHAT, HONESTY?

No! You were there. You saw it. You see nothing wrong with him withholding my receipt until I smiled for him?

HE WAS RIGHT, THOUGH. YOU ARE MUCH

PRETTIER WHEN YOU SMILE. IT IS A UNIVERSAL LAW.

That's not the point! Ugh! Why do I even try with you?
BECAUSE I CREATED YOU THAT WAY.

A car horn honked right next to her on the congested street. She knew that honk. It wasn't a you-changed-lanes-without-signaling honk or a the-light-is-green-you-fucking-idiot honk or even an I'm-so-angry-I-just-need-to-be-loud honk. No, the precise duration of this one told Jessica McCloud it was directed at her. She knew that instinctually. However, the driver clearly hadn't thought it through, and now, as she glared at him in stand-still traffic where his anonymity was blown, he looked away from her quickly and slunk down in his seat.

See? I don't need to smile to be pretty enough for creeps.

The exchange with the bank teller was especially infuriating because, in the moment, her incredulity levels had been so extreme, she couldn't properly yell at him when he'd held the receipt for her It is Risen deposit just out of her reach, cocked his head coyly to the side and said, "Uh-uh-uh..." like this was a game they regularly enjoyed together. In her surprise, she'd resorted to her feminine default of placating the other person, of not rocking the boat. She'd even giggled! And when he'd named his price—a smile for the receipt—she'd actually done it. Because she needed the damn receipt so she could get on with her exhausting day and get back to work.

I could just smite him.
SEEMS A LITTLE EXTREME.

I don't literally mean it. It's just that ...

YOU'RE MAD AT YOURSELF. THAT IS CLEAR.

You're right. And that's so stupid! He's the one who was being a jerk.

IT'S NOT STUPID. IT WAS YOUR FAULT YOU SMILED.

Um. I think I'm done talking to you.

"Change, miss?" hollered a homeless man crouched on a narrow, partially shaded stoop, wearing way too many layers in the Texas summer.

Shit. She'd forgotten to bring a handful of change from the bakery with her. Or rather, she'd brought one with her, but she'd deposited it all without leaving anything for the walk back. Wendy Peterman wouldn't like that if she found out.

Jessica grimaced. "Sorry. I got nothing on me."

"Thanks anyway," said the man, and Jessica paused in her progress, one foot hovering above the ovenlike cement. She stared at him, observing the deep wrinkles of his sun-damaged skin.

"You're welcome." And now she really *did* feel sorry she couldn't help. There was no "you stupid whore" tacked on the end of the gratitude. And if she wasn't mistaken, this was the most polite interaction she'd had all day. She wanted to stop and speak with the man more, but she didn't for a couple reasons. First, she didn't want to push her luck with the niceties. But mostly, she didn't have the time to spare. Not today, when Wendy was driving all the way from Dallas to chat.

The publicist had been kind enough to allow Jessica some time to get the bakery up and running before requesting another meeting. Not that Jessica's overwhelm wasn't still at a ten out of ten. Running a business was so hard, it might be one giant mistake, though she wasn't ready to admit that yet. Instead, she told anyone who asked that it was "deeply gratifying."

Maybe it was for the best that Chris was—

Another car honked, and she flipped the driver the bird and kept walking.

Maybe it was for the best that Chris was all the way across the country. From their conversations, neither had much time for anything other than their new job and the bare minimum hours of sleep each night to remain lucid.

Granted, in the month and a half since her party at the bakery, her definition of lucidity had grown rather relaxed. Just the other day she'd sworn her miracled image on a sugar cookie had winked at her. She was so sure of it that she'd yelled at God for screwing with her when she was already on the edge. He'd denied the whole thing, of course, but for once, His denial sounded genuine.

The large metallic sign for It is Risen came into view down the block. A flash of pride at seeing her creation was quickly bludgeoned into the fetal position by her fear of failure, the never-ending list of responsibilities, and, getting its fair share of licks in, the knot of guilt in her stomach every time she remembered Miranda marching out of the party, having discovered Quentin's secret and the part Jessica played in the deception.

She still wasn't sure what the right course of action would have been. Should she have outed Quentin as an angel?

IT'S ALMOST LIKE YOU'RE TRYING TO DECIDE WHICH PATH YOU SHOULD HAVE TAKEN.

No. That's definitely not it. I'm done with paths. There are no paths. Life is just a random assortment of an infinite number of decisions that are in no way predetermined. Every moment determines the next, but none are set.

DID YOU JUST GET A LITTLE NAUSEATED THINKING OF ALL THAT RESPONSIBILITY?

No. She was lying.

AS THE LORD AND CREATOR OF ALL THINGS —EXCLUDING, YOU KNOW, THE REALLY AWFUL STUFF—I DO FEEL IT IS MY DUTY TO INFORM YOU THAT WHAT YOU JUST SAID MAKES NO SENSE.

That was because she'd made it up on the spot. She still wasn't sure how it might work philosophically to refuse to follow a path set out for her; she only knew that she was firmly anti-paths.

Opening the front door and meeting the blast of A/C with an appreciative moan, Jessica allowed herself a moment to simply enjoy the cool air she was paying so much for.

"There you are," came a nasally voice to her left.

She groaned, recognizing the speaker immediately. It was Dennis. Or maybe Darius? No, what was his name ...?

He'd awkwardly dropped it into their overlong exchanges enough times that she should remember it.

He grinned at her from his cafe table as she let the door shut behind her. His notably small hands clutched his coffee mug that he would probably refill three more times before they closed in two hours.

"Hi," she said, trying not to grow annoyed with how greasy he kept his stringy hair.

"I was wondering if I'd missed you today. What's a day without Jessica? Heh."

She forced herself to grin at him and promised that would be her last for the afternoon. Then she marched over to the register to tuck away the empty cash purse.

Destinee McCloud, who was perched on a tall stool behind the counter, indulging obscenely in a chocolate chip muffin while no customers needed her assistance, nodded at her daughter and spoke around a mouthful of mush. "Have a good walk?"

"Yep," said Jessica. "It was deeply gratifying."

* * *

Despite the many open chairs in the cafe of It is Risen Bakery, Wendy Peterman refused to sit. Instead, she stood straight in her high heels, shoulders back, arms crossed in front of her chest, hardly bothering to tilt her head down to properly glare at Jessica McCloud. "We had a plan, and everyone in this room has stuck to it except for you."

The everyone in this room was not as overwhelming a

majority as was implied. Outside of Wendy and Jessica, it included Destinee and Cash Monet, both of whom had taken a seat at one of the round cafe tables for the duration of the after-hours team meeting.

"And I've told you," Jessica said, acting more confident than she felt while confronting the formidable publicist, "I'm done with other people's plans. God's been stiff-arming me to do whatever he thinks is best, and I'm done. No more set paths, no more imposed plans from *anyone*."

"Wow." Cash, Jessica's genderless social media specialist, blinked lethargically at her, shaking their head slowly. "You're still on about that." They turned to Wendy. "Did you know she was still on about that? I thought she would have grown out of it by now."

Wendy's gaze attached itself to a ceiling tile as she inhaled deeply for patience.

"Yes, Cash," Jessica continued, "I'm sticking to this. If you'd had God and an egomaniacal hog-oil salesman and teachers and professors and the media nipping at your ankles your whole life to keep you going in the direction that best suits them, you'd be right where I am."

Cash rolled their eyes. "You're right. No one has ever told me to stay in my lane. Announcing that I was genderless when I was fifteen was instantly and universally accepted."

Jessica paused, sensing the sarcasm, but more importantly wanting to ask a question so badly she thought her head might explode. "So before that you were a ...?"

"A different person." Cash grinned petulantly.

Wendy uncrossed one of her arms to snap and bring the attention back to her. "Focus. I didn't call this meeting because I wasn't sure whose life was a bigger 'screw you' to society. I drove down from Dallas because Cash has been working their butt off, and still your social media follows have stagnated and your overall relevancy score hasn't increased in three weeks." She stepped closer, hovering over Jessica. "You, my dear, are in danger of becoming irrelevant."

"Hot damn," said Destinee. "That sure would be a relief, wouldn't it, baby?"

Jessica nodded but Wendy cut in with, "A relief for Jimmy Dean, sure. And a relief for any competing bakery in Austin. And a relief for Eugene Thornton and every other Jessica hater out there who mindlessly protects the status quo."

Destinee sank slightly in her chair, grumbling under her breath.

"What do you want me to do?" Jessica said. Time wasn't a luxury she had, and this meeting was dragging out already, meaning it was taking up any space at all on her already theoretically full schedule. Humoring her publicist was a much easier way to bring this meeting to a close than arguing with her.

"Anything," Wendy said. "Absolutely anything that isn't spending all day and all night in this bakery."

"But I like spending all my time in this bakery," Jessica said.

"First of all, no. You're suffering small business

Stockholm Syndrome. I've seen it a thousand times. You start a business, it takes over everything, and then you think you need it to rule you to keep on living. Second of all, and Destinee"—Wendy pointed at her—"don't come at me for what I'm about to say. I know you can fight, but so can I. You might beat me since I'm in a skirt and heels, but I'll get my blows in." She turned back to Jessica. "Second of all, your products are *okay*. They're not great. I can get a croissant as good as yours at the Starbucks a block over. Or the one two blocks over. Yes, yours are gluten-free and they have that going for them. What I'm saying is that your success, the reason you *have* a business is entirely because of who you are, not your baking skills. If you don't keep building your personal brand, your business will stall, and you'll be stuck in the lifestyle you're in right now indefinitely. Or worse, your star will fall, and your business will go with it."

"You have a point," Jessica said quickly to lower her mother's hackles, "but that seems lame. Shouldn't my business be able to stand on its own legs without me exploiting my curse?"

Wendy shrugged. "No. Not necessarily. Every successful business has something memorable about it. McDonald's has a clown and has spread across the world like antibiotic-resistant syphilis. Its food isn't great, but you see a sign and you trust it because, hey, if the rest of the world embraces it, maybe it's not that bad. Their thing is clowns and yours is Christ. Not that different."

Jessica glanced at the large clock above the front door.

She needed to be back here in five hours to start her day all over again. But more importantly, Destinee needed to be back in eight. If her mom didn't get enough sleep, the customer service skills she'd developed over years of working at a pharmacy went out from under her in a flash. Jessica wasn't looking to spend all the next day soothing over tensions by giving away free food.

"What's your proposed solution?" she said.

Wendy smiled. "I'm glad you asked. Because I spent quite a long time asking myself the same question until I had a stroke of genius. Remember at that party you had before you opened, where everyone got a little too drunk and some pictures surfaced that resulted in my canceling multiple dates with important and sexy men to fix it?"

"I didn't know that was a part of it, but yes, I know which party you're talking about." How could she forget anything from that night? It was the last time she'd spoken to her best friend and the first time she'd met her half-brother in the flesh. Those sorts of things lodged themselves in your memory.

"And do you remember the *single* silver lining that came from those pictures?"

Jessica's eyes darted to Cash, whose pleasant smile hinted at murder. "Uh, no, but I think Cash might."

They smiled. "Oh, I do. I remember it vividly because it was the clearest sign of a divine being I've ever encountered. From the mounds of social media shit rose this one gem that I like to call the Holy Trinity."

Wendy nodded. "And as sacrilegious as that is, that's a great way to think of it."

"You're still worried about sacrilege?" Jessica asked.

"Constantly," said Wendy. "But I'm not going to let that stop me from doing my job."

"Noted," said Jess. "Enlighten me: what's the Holy Trinity?"

Cash was ready for it. They flipped open their laptop bag, pulled out a tablet, and woke it from sleep mode with the touch of a button. The picture was already cued up.

"Ah yes," Jessica said, glancing at it disinterestedly, as if that precise moment hadn't planted a seed of a fantasy that she'd let grow and bloom in the weeks since.

Cash and Wendy called it the Holy Trinity, but Jessica had always thought of it as a Yes Please Sandwich.

It was a kind of picture that most people had taken with friends at some point. Except most people's didn't include Jameson Fractal.

And, admittedly, most people's didn't include Chris Riley. Not that she knew about, at least.

In it, the two men were seated on either side of her at a table only a few yards from where she sat now. Each one was a little red in the nose and planted a kiss on Jessica's cheek. Her face was scrunched up like a chipmunk, which she regretted immensely. If she were ever going to take a good selfie, this should have been the one. But as it was, she usually placed her thumb over her face when she stared at the picture, which she did more often than she would ever admit.

"You think I should have a threesome?" she asked, slathering sarcasm over her words to disguise the burning hope. Chris would never go for it unless she had a signed order from someone like Wendy. Of course, with God's overprotectiveness, it would have to be a non-penetrative threesome, which seemed okay all the same.

"No," Wendy said. "But I do believe stoking the flames of Team Jameson might be a quick and easy way to land you as a trending topic for a while."

Cash jumped in. "We would probably end up with multiple trending topics. Hashtag Team Jameson, hashtag Jessica Christ, maybe even hashtag Jessison. Or Jamica?" They shrugged. "We'll have to see how it plays out. Celebrity couple names are best when they form organically."

Jessica cringed. A threesome was one thing, but being a trending topic with another man was just plain cyber-cheating.

Jessica turned to her mother for backup, and Destinee shrugged. "I'd go with Jamica myself."

Okay, she was no help here. "You forget that I'm Team Chris all the way."

Cash put a hand over their heart. "Oh, that's tragic."

Wendy cringed. "Yeah, you probably shouldn't go around saying that. The depressed ex thing is not going viral like it used to."

"Depressed ex thing?" Jessica paused, trying to get her feet under her. "Chris isn't my ex. We're still together."

Wendy and Cash caught each other's eyes, then the publicist said, "Really? That's still going on?"

"Yes!" Jessica bristled. How dare they assume that just because Chris lived in Philadelphia now and had his own whirlwind life to attend to and the two of them almost never spoke in real life outside of a few daily texts that it meant their relationship was over. It wasn't over! It was just long-distance. They still had plenty of time together in their dreams, anyway. And, now that Jesus wasn't there to interrupt and Moses was back in retirement, their dream sex life had never been so ... bountiful? Eh, that wasn't quite the word.

"I apologize," said Wendy. "I don't know why, but for some reason I was sure that whole thing was over. Well, hey, even better! The continued possibility of a Team Chris will only invigorate Team Jameson."

Jessica held up her hands. "No thanks. I'm out. I don't have time for drama in my life."

"It's not like you actually have to sleep with the guy, which is the first time I've ever had to reassure someone they won't *have* to sleep with Jameson Fractal. Just be seen in public with him a few times. Chum the water. He'll be in between projects in September, so you have a few months to think it over. In the meantime, we can find a way to get the rumor mill started, right Cash?"

Cash nodded. "Just give me the word, Jessica. I beg of you. Give Team Jameson the room it needs to spread its wings and I will have your social media ranking flying into the stratosphere." They clasped their hands together in a greedy prayer.

"Sorry, but no. Chris isn't going to like that."

"Give him a heads up," said Wendy. "Let him know why the rumors will be flying around. Hell, I'll call him myself."

Chris had always had a soft spot (or hard spot) for Wendy and her form-fitting A-line skirts. It was entirely possible the publicist could convince him this was a good idea via video chat, but Jessica still didn't want to go there.

And not because her relationship was holding on by a thread. No, of course not that.

"Still no," she said, watching as Cash rolled their eyes and Wendy's jaw tightened. "We'll find another way. Maybe something that involves the bakery. I know I'm going about everything the hard way, but I want to be known for something I created, not who created me. No offense, Mom."

Destinee pooched out her lips and waved it off. "Totally get it."

"I don't," Wendy said curtly. "But you're technically my boss, so I guess I gotta roll with it. Just do me a favor, and before you reach total burnout and do that thing your generation does where you decide it's time for a small lifestyle shift so you scorch literally everything you have, write long social media posts explaining why you're leaving social media, and then move to Portland, give me a call and we'll try the Team Jameson tactic."

"Yeah, fine."

Wendy checked her rose gold wristwatch. "One more thing before I head home. Have you heard from Jimmy Dean lately?"

Ugh. This was about the ongoing law suit, wasn't it? Initially, the idea of suing Jimmy for falsely claiming she'd written the foreword to his book felt like sweet revenge, but now it just meant the two of them were tied together in a new way.

Meanwhile, the news had rediscovered its love affair with the reverend after he'd won the primary for Texas Railroad Commissioner. The tail of that was only just ending and now Jessica was asked to think about him again? "No. He's left me alone. Guess he's too busy rallying support for November."

Wendy crinkled her nose and chewed her bottom lip. "Jimmy would never be too busy to harass you, Jessica. He lives for it."

"It's true," said Destinee.

Wendy continued. "Perhaps his lawyer has advised him against making contact with you until the suit is settled. But my educated guess is that he's up to something."

"No shit," Jessica said. "When has Jimmy ever not been up to something? Never, that's when. So, while I know that him leaving me alone just means he's going to show up on my doorstep with an extra helping of horseshit later on, I'm not going to let that ruin the fact that *he's leaving me alone*. It's called being present in the moment."

"Suit yourself," said Cash. "But so you know, I've been

keeping data on him—his resurgences in your life and their effect on your online mentions—and he's well overdue for a disruption." When Jessica narrowed her eyes at them, they said, "What? It's just data science. Don't look at *me* all skeptical when it's you who can raise the dead."

Jessica leaned back in her chair, kicking out her legs, which was something she'd learned to do in a listicle called *Ten Ways to Harness the Power of Manspreading* that she'd read on her phone on the toilet the night before. "Here's what I'm going to do: the same thing I've been doing. I'm going to keep working my ass off at this bakery because I want to do things the hard way for a while. Maybe I'll change my mind later, but for now, I'm enjoying the grind. The next time I'm a trending topic, it'll be alongside hashtag It is Risen or hashtag self-made, not hashtag Team Jameson or hashtag Jimmy Fucking Dean. That's what I'm giving you to work with. If you two want to push some coverage of my bakery, I'd be all for it."

"Ooh," Cash said dramatically. "Bakery exclusives? Internet, prepare to be broken!"

Wendy bit back a smile. "Hear you loud and clear, Jessica." She grabbed her clutch from the table. "We'll be in touch whenever Jimmy Dean drops another bomb. Let us know if you change your mind."

"Will do."

Once they'd left, Destinee sighed loudly and pushed herself up to standing. She walked to the tray of the day's remaining goods and made quick work of a cheese danish. "Think you'll change your mind on this?"

"Maybe," Jessica replied. "Who knows? I'm not on any single path anymore. I'm in a field that spreads out in all directions, and I get to follow my whims."

She'd been piecing together that metaphor during dough prep in the mornings.

Destinee licked her fingertips and shrugged. "Whatever you say, baby. Having that many decisions to make every step of the way sounds goddamn exhausting to me."

Chapter Two

Judith brought a tray of freshly baked sugar cookies out from the back and set them on the checkout counter for Jessica.

Was it already three pm? How had the time flown so quickly?

"Shall I ring the bell, my lord?" Judith mumbled, arching a mocking brow.

"Stop. You know I hate this as much as you do. Maybe even more."

Judith turned toward the bell, saying, "And yet, here we are."

Jessica reminded herself that having Judith on the team was a blessing. Her NAO sister had only been there a matter of a week since her college graduation and insisted that her English degree qualified her to work for minimum wage for the rest of her life. And because she had experience working with Jessica in the food trailer before it was burned to the ground, the former Nu Alpha Omega was perfect for the job.

Destinee hadn't complained about getting a few days off each week, either.

The bell echoed through the cafe, and Jessica felt the eyes of the few post-lunch-rush patrons shift her way.

When Wendy had first suggested this ritual should become part of It is Risen tradition, Jess had adamantly opposed. But then, Wendy did have a point. There was the brand to think of. Stoking Team Jameson flames went too far because it was focused only on Jessica's personal life. This, though, while exploitative of Jessica's unique position in the world, directly related to her bakery.

So she'd agreed to try it once weeks before. It proved to be too big of a success to ignore, and after word traveled throughout the city that at three pm every day, you could go witness a miracle being performed at It is Risen, the crowds had made the decision for her.

However, it appeared that even a miracle could lose its appeal after enough repetitions.

How many were there today, seven? She did a quick headcount. Nine. Nine people watching her. Nine people *sitting* and watching her. Three weeks ago, it'd been standing room only, and now there were nine people sitting and watching.

Oh, no, now there were only eight. One of them had turned back to her phone.

Better get to it before anyone else loses interest.

She closed her eyes, and summoned the miracle from deep within.

Not that deep, though. This particular set of miracle muscles was toned from use. She didn't need to close her eyes and focus anymore to draw forth her heavenly ability to turn any baked good gluten-free. She didn't even need to focus to make sure the burned imprints of her face weren't doing anything awkward like blinking or sneezing. It just came naturally, and when she performed this in the back without an audience, she could do it with her eyes open while scrolling through her secret Instagram, double-tapping her favorite wildlife photos.

But out here, people wanted a show.

Well, eight people—she cracked an eyelid—seven now, seven people wanted a show.

The miracle pulled free of her without much resistance, and she opened her eyes and said, "Come and get 'em."

Three of the customers bothered to get up and grab their free miracle.

"Nobody else?" she held up the tray. "Last call before they go in the case for sale."

The girl on her phone looked up. "What's that?"

"Free cookie," Jessica said.

The girl blinked a few times. "Oh, cool. I'm good, though." She returned to her phone.

Jessica smiled, grinding her molars as she did, and then carried the tray over to the display.

Judith helped her transfer the cookies. "You can probably stop doing this."

"It's a fucking miracle," Jessica whispered. "How has the novelty already worn off?"

"Don't take it personally," Judith said. "I'm sure you'll discover a new miracle soon enough and it'll be all the rage."

As Judith carried the empty tray into the back, a presence at the counter tugged at Jessica's attention while she arranged the last few cookies so that her brand was clearly visible.

She dusted the sugar granules from her hands and stood, intending to tell the customer she'd be there in just one minute. But then she saw who it was.

"Mrs. Thomas?"

Jessica's former teacher and current business partner grinned back at her from in front of the register. "Did I miss the free cookies?"

"Never. Should I grab you some free coffee to go with it?"

"Ooh, yes please!"

"Have a seat and I'll bring it over."

Jessica carried out a small stack of sugar cookies and two coffees on a tray and set them out at the table in front of Mrs. Thomas. "I could use a coffee break myself. Caffeine and sugar. That's the ticket."

"I agree," said Mrs. Thomas. She nibbled a cookie and moaned her satisfaction. It seemed a little put on to Jessica, but she appreciated it all the same. "I'm so proud of what you've done here, Jessica."

For a moment, Jessica thought she'd gotten a bit of cookie caught in her throat. But nope, just a hunk of emotion and overwhelm. She attempted to swallow it without choking.

"Thanks. That, um, that means a lot to me."

Don't cry! Don't cry!

She didn't understand why it mattered so much to have Mrs. Thomas's approval, but it did. Maybe it was that the woman didn't hand out praise she didn't mean. Or maybe it was that Mrs. Thomas had invested so much money in the business that Jessica lived with a constant rattle of anxiety in the back of her mind that would be there until she could repay Mrs. Thomas. Or maybe she was overtired or hormonal or not as grown up as she pretended to be or ...

"I'm sure you're wondering what brings me to Austin today," said the teacher.

Jessica nodded.

"I'm here on a specific mission. I need to find a place to live." She brought her coffee cup to her lips, grinning coyly.

After the initial ludicrous question of *Is she homeless?* flitted its way through Jessica's brain, she asked, "Seriously? You're moving to Austin?"

Mrs. Thomas nodded. "Yes. Just accepted a job here. Same school as Brian Foster, actually. Didn't realize it at the time. I'm sure he won't be too excited to see me. Never liked me. Don't understand it." She shrugged. "Part of being an assertive woman, I guess. Just rubs some men the wrong way. You're learning that lately, I'm sure." She winked.

Jessica hadn't comprehended the sheer weight of responsibility on her shoulders until Mrs. Thomas appeared and unintentionally lightened the burden by half. Doing things the hard way was fine. But if she confined herself to making sure she always did things the hard way, wasn't she, in essence, turning her big open field of possibility into yet another narrow path? Her eye twitched. It was too much to think about until she had another cup of coffee. "I've always rubbed men, and women, the wrong way, so I don't know that anything has changed."

"And how's everything going lately?" Mrs. Thomas sipped her coffee. "I haven't heard from you, so I assumed no news was good news."

"For the most part, yes. It's, um, a lot more than I thought it would be."

"Ah." Mrs. Thomas nodded slowly then nibbled more of her cookie before speaking. "You can ask for help, Jessica. You know I'm always here for you. Is it more money you need?" She smiled.

"No, no. Actually, I've been meaning to talk to you about that. Chris and I discussed it, and he's ready to pay back investors, starting with you. He can pay you in full next month." Jessica had hoped it would come as good news, after all, consolidating her personal debt to a single man who loved her was something she'd looked forward to for months now.

What she wanted more than anything in the world was financial independence for herself and the bakery, but she couldn't get there all at once. Narrowing down her obligations was the first step. No more loan repayment, no more mortgage—she would be free and clear outside of owing Chris. And deep down, she knew he would never accept repayment. And if they ended up getting married— a consideration they'd agreed to put on hold until they settled into their new careers—would it even matter?

So, yes, she wanted to do things the hard way, but if an easy way presented itself and it didn't put out anyone too much, she wouldn't turn her nose up at it.

But Mrs. Thomas's smile faded, and the corners of her mouth stretched down into an apologetic cringe. "I hate to remind you of this, but the contract we both signed doesn't allow for early repayment."

Jessica almost laughed, but controlled herself before she did. "What do you mean?" That was the most insane thing she'd ever heard. Who didn't want their money back sooner?

"It was at the bottom. It might seem silly, but I've had enough people try to empty their life savings to pay me back, so desperate to be debt free that they don't think straight, and then some unexpected cost comes up—a health scare, a car breaks down—and they're unable to handle it because they no longer have anything in savings. I usually only find out about it after the fact because they were too embarrassed to ask me for another loan, so they go and take one out with a bank or open a new credit card instead, which is much more costly in the long run thanks to compounding interest. Long story short, I now include it as a way to protect the borrower from a similar fate."

It made a strange kind of sense, the same way most of Mrs. Thomas's altruism did. Years of being a teacher had clearly made the woman a pro at saving people from themselves.

"Okay, but we're not going to run out of money anytime soon. Chris signed a four-year contract, and what I owe you is only a tiny portion of one year of his salary."

"I understand that," said Mrs. Thomas. She inspected Jessica thoughtfully, tilting her head to the side as a faraway look came into her eyes. "You haven't actually read the contract yet, have you?"

Jessica felt the heat rush through her neck to her face. She *should* have read it by now. Add it to the list of things she should have done but hadn't yet. In her deepest bouts of overwhelm, the blood pulsing in her ears often sounded like *should, should, should …*

"Um. Did … did you ever send it? I don't remember seeing it in my inbox."

Mrs. Thomas straightened. "Of course I sent it! I sent it the morning after your get-together here. Although I understand if you had a little too much fun that night with

Chris *and* Jameson and it got lost in your inbox the next morning."

Jessica's face was on fire. "No, it's not like that with Jameson."

Mrs. Thomas shrugged. "It could be and that wouldn't change the way I feel about you one bit. He's a handsome young man." She nibbled the cookie and said, "If it's not financial help you need, what are you looking for?"

Jessica dunked her sugar cookie into her coffee, swirling it around. "I dunno. Guidance?" She took a bite before it became too soggy. "Dr. Bell thinks I should hire more people to help me, but I've never been a boss before. You have."

A wide grin dawned on Mrs. Thomas's face. "Dr. Bell. That's your old business professor, right?" Jessica nodded. "She's absolutely correct. And hiring people *is* a big step. I can see why you would feel nervous about it. Hiring is what makes or breaks a business."

Jess knew Mrs. Thomas would understand. "I don't even know where to start. Where do I find people? Do I have to write job descriptions? What if I don't know how to do a job myself? How do I interview? What don't I know about discrimination laws? The list goes on."

Mrs. Thomas cleared her throat and cupped her hands around her mug on the table. "It is a lot, which is why some corporations hire someone to be in charge of hiring!" She chuckled. "And I imagine you're overwhelmed with all the things you've already learned and are beginning to implement. My husband has always had a knack for hiring people for his campaigns and staff. I know plenty of good people you could hire. In fact, many would probably be thrilled to find a job outside of the amoral world of politics!"

"I wish I could just make you my hiring manager," Jess mumbled halfheartedly.

"I would if I didn't already have a job lined up in town. But how about this: you send me a list of things that need doing, and I can whip it up into a few separate positions you'll need to fill. Then I can recommend candidates for each one." She held up a hand to manage expectations. "Not forever. Just to get you started."

Once again, Jess felt like crying. "Thank you. And, you know, I would just hire whoever you told me to at this point. If you know someone's the right person for the job, I trust your judgment more than I do mine. You can just give me their name and I'll tell them they're hired."

Mrs. Thomas chuckled. "Probably not the wisest approach in general, but seeing as how it's me we're talking about, and I do know you better than just about anyone, and, of course, I trust myself implicitly"—she winked —"I'm happy to go along with it. Especially if I can lighten the burden for you." She leaned forward and placed a hand on Jessica's forearm. "I hope this doesn't come off the wrong way, but you look like you've been through it lately."

"Do I?"

Mrs. Thomas nodded. "Yes. Dark circles under your eyes, and it looks like you've lost some weight in your face, which isn't too unusual for someone entering their mid-twenties, but *is* of note for someone entering their mid-twenties who works at a bakery." She leaned back in her chair and sipped her coffee as she continued inspecting Jessica closely. "I know you mentioned Chris a bit ago, but are the two of you doing okay? I just mean, is the relationship still serving you?"

"Yeah, it's great," Jess answered quickly.

Rather than looking relieved, Mrs. Thomas's round face shined with even more sympathy. "Long distance is hard, especially when you have so much on your plate in your present location. You can't be two places at once, so to speak."

"We're making it work. Some Chris is better than none."

Mrs. Thomas's brows pinched together as a deep line appeared between them. "Jessica, dear, I wish you'd have a little more faith in your ability to make new friends and meet new lovers. I know you and Christopher go way back —I probably remember it better than you two, you were so young—but people change and drift apart, and that's perfectly okay, even if it is a little sad. If Chris left you, it wouldn't be the end, you understand that, right?"

"Why would Chris leave me?" The notion was ridiculous. Chris might cheat on her, sure. Everyone gave into temptation now and again. She knew that from personal experience. But the thought of Chris *leaving* her, that had never crossed her mind. *Could* he leave her? He was an angel and drawn to her by nature. She supposed he broke up with her that one time in college, but that was as a result of her actions, and they'd mended it later on. And when things had fallen apart with Mason, Chris had shown up for her in a heartbeat. He had always been around.

Leaving her?

Leaving her?

Like, what, just losing interest? Walking away? Pretending she didn't exist anymore? Would she become "one of my exes" in his stories to other women?

Mrs. Thomas brushed off the question with a wave of her hand. "Oh, I don't know. I'm just saying, were something unexpected to happen, I hope that you understand you would be fine. You're more resilient than you give yourself credit for. There are all kinds of men who would appreciate you for the bright, hardworking woman you are."

"No, I don't think so," she said honestly, still in a haze from the thought that Chris might someday leave her.

"How about Miranda?" Mrs. Thomas said. "You two keep in touch much?"

Talk about from bad to worse. Thinking about Miranda was even more painful than considering the possibility of Chris leaving her. Because Miranda actually *had* left her.

"No, we haven't talked since the party."

"Oh no," Mrs. Thomas breathed in between nibbles of her cookie. "What happened at the party?"

How did she explain it? Did Mrs. Thomas know she

herself was an angel? It might be unwise to broach that topic if the woman was unaware of her own situation.

But how could Mrs. Thomas get this far and *not* know? As Dr. Bell had explained it, angels either realized and accepted that they were angels after a certain age or they went a little batty. Case in point: Jeremy Archer, Jessica's across-the-hall neighbor and Jesus's new roommate.

Still, it seemed wise to work in broad terms. "Quentin hadn't told her everything he should have, and she found out. And then she found out that Chris and I knew about it the whole time and didn't tell her. She wasn't happy. She left, dumped Quentin, and we haven't heard from her since."

Mrs. Thomas tsked, and for a second, Jessica thought it was directed at her. "That's too bad. I could see ... Well, no, I shouldn't say it."

"No, what is it?"

Mrs. Thomas pressed her lips together on an inhale. "I never wanted to say anything, since the two of you were so close, but I've always felt like this is a long time coming. It's not your fault," she added hurriedly, "but it seems unlikely that her anger and resentment had anything to do with what happened at the party." Mrs. Thomas clasped her hands together on the tabletop, staring vaguely down at them before continuing reluctantly. "When the two of you were together, even as young children, all eyes were on you. And again, it's not your fault! But with you being who you are, she never could break through from being a very important person's friend to a very important person, could she? She is incredibly talented at a variety of things, as you know, and I imagine playing second fiddle to you no matter how much she achieved ... I believe her blow up was years in the making." She sighed, shaking her head and staring at her coffee cup. "I'm sorry that happened. And I'm sorry I said nothing before to warn you it might. I have to watch myself, you know. I feel incredibly protective of you, always have, but you're an adult now, and I can't keep intervening when I see someone trying to hurt you." She returned her attention to Jessica. "I can only imagine the abandonment makes everything harder. Starting a business is socially isolating enough. To have your best friend and your boyfriend leave you ..."

Jessica swallowed down the lump in her throat and dipped another cookie into her coffee, swirling it around. "Chris didn't leave me."

"No, no. Of course not. I just mean he *is* in another state now, so physically, he's gone. And Miranda will be leaving for grad school soon, if I'm not mistaken, so even if the two of you *do* make up ... I imagine this is terribly difficult for you."

When Jessica pulled the cookie from her coffee, the bottom half fell off, oversaturated, into her cup.

Shit, shit, shit, SHIT!

She gritted her teeth and held it together.

"And I'm glad I came by today," Mrs. Thomas added. "You don't always let on when you need help, you know. But there are people like me who are here for you over the long haul, who aren't going anywhere. You just have to let us know."

A man's voice interrupted from behind her. "Um. Can I get some service over here?"

She cast a glance back at the register, where a man in a red plaid shirt and skinny jeans raised his eyebrows at her curtly, like an invitation to fight.

"Yeah, Judith will be with you in a second."

When she turned back around, Mrs. Thomas was finishing the last of her coffee, as she crouched, midway out of her chair before standing upright. "I need to get a move on. You take care of yourself, okay, Jessica? You have decades of life ahead of you. Can't go burning yourself out yet." She grabbed her purse from the back of the chair. "Email me the list of things you want someone else to do, and I'll get to work right away on finding the right people for the job." She hitched her fuchsia purse up over her shoulder and inhaled deeply, adding on the exhale. "I'm so proud of you."

Jessica had taken the hint and stood as well. "Thanks, Mrs. Thomas."

"Dolores, please."

Jessica nodded, but, nope, still couldn't bring herself to use her first name.

After a quick hug, Mrs. Thomas turned to leave, pausing on her way out to add, "No matter *who* leaves you. I'll always be around."

Jess nodded, forcing a smile while fending off an incoming wave of fresh dread.

Why was she upset? Chris was still with her. And Miranda might come around.

Or maybe it was just the caffeine and carbs coursing through her digestive system providing a pop of hopeful optimism.

Baked goods really *were* a miracle, gluten-free or not.

Chapter Three

Jessica stared into the cosmos as she lay on her back in bed.

Not her real bed. Her dream bed. The one she shared nightly with Chris. Somehow, despite being concocted entirely from fantasy, the mattress on this one was never as comfortable as the memory foam one she actually slept on.

She could feel Chris's warm naked body next to hers, and though it didn't inspire the feelings it used to, it was still nice and welcome.

"I dunno," she said, "what do you want to try?"

"Umm ..."

Chris was drawing a blank tonight, too. So, she threw out the first suggestion that came to mind. "What about where one of us does a handstand? That was kind of cool."

He hesitated. "Do you want to do a handstand? Because I don't want to do a handstand."

She sighed. "Yeah, me neither. This mattress is really comfortable."

"Yeah, it is."

"Lady on top?"

"Sure."

Damn. That meant she had to do all the work. How was she so tired in her dreams? Had the exhaustion really seeped into her this deeply?

Lady on top was their go-to lately, and it was *okay*. It got a little boring unless they spiced up the surroundings a bit. So that's what she did once they got going.

"Are ... we ... in ... The Dead ... Sea?" Chris asked as Jessica went through the motions.

"Is that the one with all the salt?"

Chris nodded.

"Yeah, that's where we are."

"Can you ... bring ... back ... the mattress?"

"Sure." The buoyancy of the water wasn't as great as she'd imagine anyway.

And now they were floating on a mattress in the Dead Sea, and Jessica procured mild amusement out of seeing just how high up and down she could make it bob.

After a few minutes of refraining from asking him if he were close, she asked, "Are you close?"

Before he could respond, verbally or otherwise, a timer went off. Wait a second, she recognized that sound ...

"Is that ... the oven at ... your bakery?" Chris asked.

She cringed. "Yeah. Sorry."

He pushed her gently off of him and raised onto his elbows. "Did you put me on a timer?"

"What? No!"

"How am I supposed to get off when I know I'm being timed? It's not like I take longer than you. You have somewhere to be?"

Two sparrows flew overhead, one chasing the other, both squawking. "No, of course not. Sorry. I guess I still have work on my mind."

Chris sighed, his expression softening. "It's okay. Don't stress about it." He brushed the hair back from her face. "This is supposed to relieve stress, not create more."

"You're right. Another try?"

He nodded, grinning greedily. "How about gentleman on top?"

"I think it's called missionary, Chris."

"Let's not bring religion into this, okay? We just got Jesus and Moses out of here."

While she was grateful for it, now that the threat of being caught was gone, so was some of the thrill. She'd never admit to that, though.

Chris took over, and Jessica was glad to be able to enjoy the mattress for a while. This seemed a much better set-up for him, too, and the end of round one was well in sight when—

Beep-beep beep-beep beep-beep.

"Dammit!" Chris punched the pillow next to Jessica before grabbing it and biting it ferociously as he rolled off of her. He moaned and whimpered.

"Sorry!" she exclaimed. She propped herself up on one elbow, looking down at her writhing, frustrated boyfriend. "I'm not impatient, I swear!"

Movement caught her eye just beyond the edge of the mattress on the other side of Chris, and for a moment she thought Jesus was hurling across the surface at her at full speed.

Except Jesus couldn't land a tackle like this guy.

She was all limbs as she flew backward, tumbling off the mattress and into the salty sea. She surfaced and swam the short distance back to the mattress, blinking the water from her eyes. "Christopher Riley," she growled, climbing back onto their sex raft. "I swear to whoever ..."

Chris's expression was nothing short of horror. "I am *so* sorry, Jess. I guess my mind is stuck at work tonight, too."

"Yeah, I'd say." She glanced behind her where the massive man in a white and blue jersey with the number 94 on the back doggy paddled into the distance.

Chris added hesitantly, "You want to keep going, or—"

"No," she said, rubbing her banged up sternum and trying not to yell. "I'd say the mood is gone."

"At least he used good form. No helmet to helmet."

She glared at him. "Could that be because I don't wear a helmet while we screw?"

Chris bolted up into sitting. "You're angry. I get that. Although to be fair, the oven timer disruption was all you."

"How about we put a pin in this for now and come back tomorrow with fresh ideas?"

Chris looked around. "Yeah, the Dead Sea isn't the most romantic."

"And we could both clearly use some deep sleep," she added. "Busy day tomorrow."

He shot her a finger gun. "Good point."

After a quick kiss, Chris disappeared in a puff of powdery white, and Jessica, heaving a sigh, returned to a deep, dreamless sleep.

Chapter Four

The oven timer beeped, and Jessica pulled out the tray of kosher pigs in a blanket. These things went quick around lunchtime, which was coming up in a few short minutes. She hurried to miracle her mug onto each of them, then carried them out to the front. The line was three people deep. "I'll be right with you."

Destinee stood behind the display, chatting back and forth with a customer who pointed at various options with an overly serious expression. *Just pick one.* Why was it so hard? If you want another one, come back another time.

SOMEBODY ROSE ON THE WRONG SIDE OF THE TOMB.

I'm fine. Just didn't get great sleep last night.

BECAUSE YOU AND CHRISTOPHER SPENT HOURS LYING TOGETHER?

Not that. I mean we did. We just— Wait. No, I'm not talking about this with you.

SHALL WE SPEAK OF SOMETHING ELSE?

I already know you have something in mind. Just spit it out.

TODAY IS AN IMPORTANT DAY FOR YOU.

Why's that?

YOU'RE ABOUT TO FIND OUT.

Did you just drop by to fill me with foreboding? Again?

AND ONE PIECE OF ADVICE.

Oh, you're going to be helpful now! Is this God's love people keep talking about?

DO NOT LET HIM TOUCH YOU.

What the— She scanned the room all around her. *Are you* kidding *me? There isn't a creepier thing to whisper to a woman. You understand that, right? Don't let* who *touch me?*

JIMMY DEAN.

Jimmy Dean?

YES. JIMMY DEAN.

When would he even have a chance to ... oh for fuck's sake.

The door to It is Risen opened with a tinkle of the bell above it, and Jessica leaned her head back and groaned at the ceiling. "Not today," she murmured. "Or any other day."

Even dressed down in a tight black T-shirt and aviator sunglasses, Jimmy just couldn't let it go with the sleazy reverend thing. She saw through any attempt by him to go incognito, because if he'd actually wanted to, he should have left the red hog-hoof stole at home.

The hooves dangled by his waist, clopping together every few steps as he slid into the bakery. He kept his sunglasses on.

"No," Jessica said loudly. "Not today, Jimmy."

The name was a trigger for Destinee, who shoved a stuffed paper bag at the customer she was helping and hurried over. "Get my gun!" she said on impulse.

"There's no gun," Jessica announced to the anxious customers. She shot Destinee a warning look. "Don't make this worse. All we want to do is get him out of here without a scene."

"Jessica, my darling girl," Jimmy swooned. "Ah, but you're not a girl anymore." He held out his arms, palms raised. "You're a young woman now. It's so charming when women open a business in lieu of starting a family. The determination of the fairer sex is truly something." He clapped his hands together. "If only it could be harnessed for good. Aaaanyway."

"You need to leave," Jessica said firmly, taking pride in not yet having shouted "fuck."

"Or else I'll make you," Destinee said, standing just over Jessica's shoulder and glaring across the counter at Jimmy.

He sighed as he passed up those waiting in line, inserting himself between the woman at the front and the counter. "While I wholeheartedly support the right of small businesses to refuse to serve customers for any reason whatsoever, I ask that you allow me a moment of your time, old friend." He addressed Jessica directly.

"How about twenty seconds to leave, and I'm filing a criminal trespass notice this afternoon. That work?"

Jimmy's posture restricted, and she saw a muscle in his jaw tick. That got to him. Huh. Threats like that had never gotten to him before. He'd always thought he was above the law. What had changed?

He leaned closer, lifting his sunglasses so she could see his eyes. Whatever dark circles she might have under hers were nothing compared to his. "Please, Jessica," he whispered, "I need your help. I know you hate me, but if there's any mercy in you, please. Just a minute."

That wasn't Church Jimmy speaking. She could tell by the rushed, jagged cadence of his speech. This was Ice Cream Jimmy, the one who she'd seen as a surrogate father figure for two years of her young life. And boy did Ice Cream Jimmy look like he'd been put through the wringer.

It was almost enough to make her feel sorry for the guy and hear him out.

"You got a lotta gall," Destinee said. "You ain't got no right to come up in her business asking for favors. Not after that bullshit memoir, you lying sack of crap. If I had my shotgun with me—"

"Which you *don't*," Jessica said, mostly addressing the customers in the line. "So everyone is safe."

"Okay," Jimmy said, chopping the air with his hand and leaning as far as he could over the counter. "Just one quick thing. I just want to say one quick thing. And if you don't want other people to hear, I can just whisper it to you."

The line had doubled in size as the start of the lunch rush trickled in.

Jimmy was nothing if not a stubborn son of a bitch. "And then you leave?" asked Jessica. "You never step foot inside this bakery again?"

"Yes! Yes, I'll leave and you can file the criminal trespass if you want, or I can save you the effort by not coming back here ever again."

Jessica stepped forward. "Fine."

He motioned her closer with a wave of his hand.

Rolling her eyes, she leaned closer until his mouth was only inches from her ear. "You and me, Jessica, we're two sides to the same coin. You want to push me away, but you can't. When you rise, I rise. I'm a part of this business just as you are, and someday you'll realize it, and when you decide to thank me for all that I've sacrificed for you, I'll be the bigger man and let you have a place by my side."

Jessica's eyes went wide and she did the only thing she could: she laughed.

Jimmy was out of his gourd. He'd become completely unhinged. None of his words struck a chord with her. It was completely untethered from reality.

She continued laughing, partly because it remained funny, but also because she enjoyed laughing at Jimmy. After all the mud he'd dragged her through, hot damn, laughing at him felt liberating. It felt even better than yelling at him or fantasizing about his death, both of which felt pretty incredible.

When she straightened up to look him right in the

eyes, heightening the enjoyment of laughing in his face, he was laughing too.

Wait, why was *he* laughing?

It happened in a flash. Literally.

The phone's camera flashed, temporarily blinding her, and it was only after that shock wore off that she realized Jimmy had grabbed her hand and was shaking it.

Ohhh no...

She'd let him touch her.

When she yanked her hand free, Jimmy grinned and hollered, "Sooie!" before rushing from the bakery with the conspiring paparazzi close behind him.

From beside her came a grunt followed by Destinee saying, "I didn't want to tell you this before 'cause I knew you'd be mad, but I got a pistol out in my glove box. Want me to bring it in?"

Yes. Yes, she did want that. "No, Mom."

"It's only a Ruger thirty-eight," Destinee whined. "Hardly more than a nip at him. He'd survive, and if he didn't, you could bring him back and he'd owe you one."

"I wouldn't bring him back," Jessica said through gritted teeth.

Destinee put an arm around her daughter's shoulder. "I don't think I tell you enough how proud I am of the woman you've become."

As tempting as it was, Jessica shook her head. "No. I don't want you going to jail for him. I'd have to hire someone to fill your spot and that's the last thing I need on my plate."

Destinee nodded and gently moved Jessica away from the register, likely sensing that her daughter could use a minute.

And as Destinee greeted the customers, acting nicer than usual to compensate for the minor interruption, Jessica headed to the kitchen, wondering how many horrible outcomes could result from one simple picture of Jessica and Jimmy, laughing and shaking hands.

Would it effect her lawsuit against him? She'd better give Wendy a head's up.

Before she could take action, the oven timer beeped. Kolaches.

Chapter Five

"You ever wish that everything could just stop?" Jessica asked, staring up at one of the twelve nearby televisions showing ESPN. The bar was empty, but then again, it was a Tuesday during the summer, and baseball didn't draw the crowds it used to.

And that was why Judith had suggested this place, she supposed. Well, that and the fact that the drinks were so cheap she and Judith referred to it as Shithoused, rather than its actual name, which was Smashmouth.

When Jessica looked away from the screens and back at Judith, who sat across from her at the high-top table, her friend said, "Are we talking suicide or apocalypse here? I can't tell with you."

"Neither. More like a pause button."

"I think what you're talking about is overwhelm, and don't worry; everyone I know has it. For all intents and purposes, it's emotional HPV."

"Are you overwhelmed?" Jessica asked. She hadn't even stopped to think about how her stress might translate to those she worked with.

Man, I'm a terrible friend.

And an even worse boss.

"Yeah." Judith shrugged. "But not about work. Just, you know, overwhelmed with how terrible the world turned out to be."

Day by day, Judith was starting to sound an awful lot like someone else Jessica knew. "How are things going with Brian?"

Judith grinned coyly. "You know, good."

"It's just a one-bedroom, right?"

Judith nodded, sipping from her longneck.

"You're not driving each other up the wall?" Jess asked.

"No. We're doing other things against the walls."

Jessica's mind flashed to Jameson Fractal and the things she'd seen him do with women against walls in his films. No matter how many times Jessica had done the same sort of things with Chris, thinking back to Jameson made her feel confused, scared, and uncomfortably turned on. "All right, enough of that," she said. "I don't need to know the details."

"It's still weird for you?"

"Uh yes. He used to be my teacher."

Judith chuckled. "I truly don't know how you handled that. He was your college counselor, too, right?" Jess nodded. "And you never tried to bone him?"

"Jesus Christ, Judith."

"Not even once?"

"No! Not even once." Jessica flagged down a waiter as he passed. "Can we get some loaded fries over here?" When he nodded, she turned back to Judith. "I'm gonna need some food on my stomach if we're going to keep talking about banging Mr. Foster."

"Speaking of which, he wants to have dinner with you and Chris whenever Chris comes into town next. He said something about the last time the three of you went out, I dunno, something happened."

"I smote a fire hydrant. But only after some dick pulled a gun on us," she added hurriedly.

"Nice," Judith said, nodding approvingly. "When you finally gonna smite someone for real, Jess? You know there's a whole subreddit on you, and anything having to do with that gets upvoted like a motherfucker."

Judith had lost her attention, though.

"Jess?"

One of the screens behind the bar, the only one not tuned to a sports station, had been running on a 24-hour news channel. And on it appeared a familiar face. It was like Jessica knew that face would be on there before she ever saw the screen. She could feel it. She could feel *him*.

"Two sides of the same coin."

What did that even mean? What a load of gibberish.

She stood from the table and walked over to read the closed caption. "Hey," she called to the woman tending the square bar at the center of the room. "Can you turn this one up?" In the meantime, Jess read along.

Because of the lag, it was difficult to tell who the captions belonged to, but Jess thought it was the host, a stony-faced black man in a slate-gray jacket who looked incredible concerned and intrigued as his lips moved minimally.

The captions read, *"But does it matter that the payments came through White Light Church? The accusations are against Dean, and the payment came from a church that he started. It becomes quite difficult to separate out the man from the establishment. He's worked very hard for that to be the case, and now he wants to distance himself?"*

A redheaded woman on the panel began speaking animatedly. Jessica waited for the captions to catch up *"Fitzpatrick: People are asking the wrong question here. It's not a matter of did Reverend Dean pay the hush money or not. We know it came from him either directly or indirectly, which obviously raises questions for his campaign. No, the real question here is how many female victims have to come forward before we as a country decide to believe them? Two women claim to have been suckered into a mind-control doomsday cult with some suspiciously predatory rhetoric when they were only girls, and we can't stop talking about the payments to keep them quiet. We've seen this pattern time and again. When will we turn our focus to the moral misdeeds rather than asking what campaign finance rules might have been broken?"*

A large gray-haired man with beads of sweat glistening across his pale forehead followed up with, *"Jacobs: Of course we care about the victims. But with the money they claim to have been paid, they could have easily afforded some therapy or what have you. If they didn't do that, it's on them. Or maybe they never received any payments. We just don't know. It wouldn't be the first time in history two people conspired to take down a powerful man. Just look at Julius Caesar!*

"Fitzpatrick: You did not just compare two victims of mental and religious abuse to Brutus and Cassius.

"Jacobs: Frankly, I don't see how any of this is relevant to whether he can do the job or not. If you look at the man's record, it's clear that Reverend Dean has the experience and wisdom to faithfully execute the duties of the Texas Railroad Commission."

Judith's voice cut through. "What's going on?"

Jessica shook her head slowly. "Not sure. It looks like something's happening with Jimmy and White Light. Some sort of scandal."

The sound on the TV came on, but it was hard to hear over the music coming through the ceiling speakers. Jessica moved closer.

The host said, *"What do you make of Reverend Dean's refusal to speak publicly about this? Linda, we'll start with you."*

A matronly figure sat with her hands folded on the desk she shared with the other two panel speakers. Her expression was tight, her spine rigid. *"Campos: I haven't seen a guiltier man in power in, say, a week. It's getting a little cliché, to be honest. The sad thing is that we'll* probably never hear the conclusion of this because by the time it makes it to the courts, we'll have moved on to something far worse. After all, he didn't violently rape them, right? None of them got pregnant by him. He just manipulated them. Never got past the grooming and gaslighting stage, and after all, young women are gaslighted every single day by major news networks with guests like Mr. Jacobs, so why stop now?" She smiled and was clearly done. The shot cut back to the host, who looked uncomfortable and nodded to the redhead, saying, "Geneva?"

"Fitzpatrick: Linda nailed it. Reverend Dean won't make a public statement because he's nothing if not smart. He knows that if he doesn't say anything, we'll all move on, and our apathy will crush the strength and courage those women worked so hard to muster. It may even silence whatever other women had thought about speaking out, too. From a PR standpoint, he's making the right move here. He's not stupid, and that's the problem."

The sweaty gray-haired man scoffed.

"Keith?" said the host, "You feel differently about his refusal to comment?"

"Jacobs: No, Henry, I don't feel anything about this. I don't know why feelings are even involved here. This is a news show, right? We should be using our heads, not getting overly emotional about that one time our boss spoke over us at a meeting. These lovely ladies on this panel with me are projecting quite a bit of their own feelings onto a public figure who, for all we know, has done nothing wrong. We *must ask ourselves: do we want to live in a society where all it takes for our hard work to be toppled and all the good that we have done to be forgotten is a couple bitter schemers throwing around an unsubstantiated accusation?"*

"Campos: It's not unsubstantiated."

"Jacobs: It is." Keith wagged his winger at her. *"It is. There has been no evidence provided, no—*

"Fitzpatrick: What about the checks?" Geneva's rigid demeanor tightening even further as her voice rose. *"How do checks from White Light Church with a victim's name on them and the words 'hush money' in the memo not count as evidence to you?"*

Keith wagged his finger at Geneva now. *"Jacobs: You don't know what they were being asked to hush about, though. Could have been a surprise birthday party, for all we know."*

Before the screen cut back to the host, Jessica caught the shared glance between Geneva and Linda, and knew instantly they would be going out to drinks after this. Without Keith.

Linda addressed the host now, Keith clearly dead to her. *"Campos: It's just simple misogyny. That's all it is. And it's played out."*

"Jacobs: Misogyny? How do you explain that photo then? He's having a grand old time with Jessica McCloud in it. She's your gal, isn't she? She even wrote the foreword for his book!

"Fitzpatrick: She's suing him because she didn't *write it!*

"Jacobs: You can't tell me the supposed daughter of God is going to be such close friends with a misogynist."

As the host thanked his guests and took it to commercial, Jessica fell out of the trance and looked around to discover she was still in Smashmouth. Good. She needed another drink.

It was a lot to process, and Judith was kind enough to give her space.

Her last encounter with Jimmy made much more sense, now. The desperation, the strange behavior, the disturbing monologue. There was a lot to unpack there. And yet, there wasn't, because this was more of the same from him.

Their fries arrived, and Jessica tried not to sound too desperate as she ordered another round.

"What do you make of it?" Judith finally asked.

Despite having just packed her mouth full of potatoes, cheese, bacon, and who cared what that stuff sprinkled on the top was, Jessica replied, "Where do I even start?"

"You sure you haven't been spending time with Chris? You're starting to eat like him."

Jessica allowed herself a moment to chew. "The doomsday cult thing isn't a complete surprise. God showed me some flashes of Jimmy's past when I was eleven and got suckered into going to White Light Church"—Judith's nonchalance was nowhere to be found as her mouth hung in a little o—"Long story. Don't worry about it. Anyway, now that I think about it, it would surprise me if he hadn't done something like this. He's probably done it more than once."

"So, you believe the allegations?"

"Of course. I'll believe any allegations against Jimmy Dean."

Judith picked a less soggy fry from the side of the pile. "You think he molested them or something?"

She hadn't considered it yet. "If they say he did, then sure. I don't think they're saying that, though, right?"

"Who even knows at this point?"

"Well, he never molested me. He's a pain in the ass, but he's never been inappropriate. Not like that. Then again, there are a lot of ways to be inappropriate with children that don't involve the privates." She thought of Randy McAllister trying to touch her ears in the enclave next to the lion's den at the zoo and the way her mother had flipped when Jessica mentioned it.

"Yeah, I was about to say."

Jessica looked up at the TV where a pharmaceutical commercial showed a grinning woman inhaling deeply on a beach, her arms outstretched as she welcomed presumed good health and hefty copays. "Do you think this could be the beginning of the end for him? Like, what if more women come forward?"

Judith frowned. "It would have to be a lot of women. And if it's true that he did this, there *are* more women out there who will come forward. But like I said, it would have to be a lot of them, and even still, I just don't know."

"How many?" She'd never considered the critical mass required for such a thing.

"I don't want to rain on your parade, so I'll be modest and say two dozen."

"Two dozen? You think twenty-four women would have to have the same story before it would spell disaster for him?"

"Right. But don't get discouraged. There's always the possibility that a man could come forward claiming Jimmy did something inappropriate to him, and this state's lingering homophobia would put an end to Jimmy instantly."

"That's pretty damn cynical, even for you."

Judith waggled a fry at Jessica. "Doesn't mean I'm not right."

Chapter Six

Jessica closed the front door of her building behind her with some effort. The last week of work, if nothing else, had only made Jessica more excited to see who Mrs. Thomas had selected for her employees. She'd called Jessica the day before to say that she'd found some excellent candidates, and Jessica had reiterated that she didn't want multiple candidates for each position and that Mrs. Thomas ought to simply pick her favorite for each role and send them over for training. There was still a lot to prepare before the new hires arrived in a few days ... but it could wait.

For now, she was bone tired and agitated. It is Risen closed early on Sundays, the thought behind that being a moment for Jessica to catch up on inventory, pay bills, and possibly get more than five hours of sleep.

So, naturally, she'd spent most of the afternoon mindlessly staring at her phone screen, tumbling down one rabbit hole after the next. And just as naturally, that left her in a sour mood. Especially when a picture of her with her least favorite person in existence was all over the news.

AT LEAST YOU KNOW WHY I TOLD YOU NOT TO TOUCH HIM.

Could have been useful to have more notice or an explanation. Would've saved me quite a headache.

The photo of Jessica and Jimmy shaking hands was making the rounds after Thornton News published it the same day the first two women came forward.

"When you rise, I rise." Jimmy had said that. If there was any truth to IT, and that was a big fat if, did it also mean that if Jessica fell Jimmy would, too?

Doubtful. She'd fallen plenty of times, and Jimmy hadn't so much as stumbled during any of them. If it *were* true, though, she was nearing the point where it would be worth self-destructing just to see him suffer.

In the week since the breaking story, four more women had come forward and the number was expected to rise. Would it break two dozen—Judith's predicted threshold for it to make any difference?

Meanwhile, Jessica had been inundated with interview requests. She was, after all, a young woman who Jimmy knew. To some of the inquiring minds, that meant that if he'd never done anything untoward with Jessica, all the women must be liars. To others, it meant Jessica condoned whatever abuse might surface. And to others still, it meant something more nebulous and sinister about the state of the world.

IN MY INFINITE WISDOM, I HAPPEN TO KNOW THAT TELLING YOU SOONER OR EXPLAINING WHY WOULD NOT HAVE CHANGED THE OUTCOME.

Then why did you warn me in the first place?

SO YOU COULDN'T SAY I DIDN'T.

Nope. Not buying it. That's the predestination shit we've talked about. You know I'm done with it, right?

YES. AND I KNEW YOU WOULD SAY THOSE EXACT WORDS. I'VE KNOWN SINCE BEFORE I CREATED LIGHT.

Oh, bullshit. I know you don't think that far ahead. Otherwise you wouldn't have created Original Mistake.

She paused at the coke machine at the top of the open staircase to swipe a credit card and get herself a Dr. Pepper. She knew it was either that or a beer, and she could use an upper at the end of the day if she was going to get her finances into some semblance of an organized spreadsheet to present to her future accountant. He or she would see right through any attempt at organization, of course. So why did she bother?

Oh, who gives a fuck why. I feel the need to, so I'm gonna.

Twisting off the bottle top, she made her way down the hall toward the front door of her condo.

No, not *her* condo. Jameson Fractal's, which he'd bought for his gynecologist sister who didn't want it. Chris had offered to buy it outright with his football money so Jessica wouldn't feel like she owed Jameson anything (this was Chris's suggestion, and Jessica understood there was an ulterior motive to his not wanting his girlfriend to live in another man's house; she was okay with that degree of jealousy). She hadn't bothered to take the first steps toward actually making it happen, though. There was so much going on already. Next chance she got, though, she'd make him the offer. You know, whenever she stopped actively avoiding him to deprive Team Jameson of fodder.

She fumbled with her key ring, which had begun to look more like a metal pom-pom since she started the bakery. Unable to pluck out the correct one with her hands full, she paused, screwing on the lid to her soda and tucking it under her armpit.

Just as she did, the door behind her flung open, and she jumped. Why was she always so jumpy when she was tired?

She turned around to nod an exhausted hello to Jeremy. Except the man exiting was neither Jeremy nor her half-brother. Following after the first man was a small parade of others, mostly men but a few women, none of whom she recognized, and all of whom carried the distinct musk of the streets.

And at the end of the line was Jesus, waving dreamily. "So helpful, really. Stay safe out there, folks. Jesus sends his love."

"Get back to me when Jesus sends some heart medication," grumbled a man in way too many layers for the May heat.

"Jessica!" Jesus said excitedly.

"You two hosting parties now?" she asked, watching the woman at the back of the line check the coke machine's change dispenser on her way down the stairs.

Jeremy answered. "It's a focus group."

"Focus group?" She turned to him for further explanation, and Jesus provided.

"As you're aware, when I first took on this body, I was living on the streets. I quickly discovered that the treatment of homeless has gotten progressively worse over the last two millennia."

"I'm pretty sure Austin is one of the better locations in the country to be homeless."

"Even more horrifying!" Jesus said enthusiastically.

Jess paused, vacillating between curiosity and a deep desire to lie down. For the moment, curiosity won out. "You're a champion for the homeless now? Going to change the world ... again?"

He waved it off. "No, probably not. I find that your homeless—"

"Not mine."

"—are a bit more unruly than they were in my time. I've been attempting to help them find their way, and they ... they tell me to shut the H-E-C-K up."

"It *was* a party, then," she said, "not a focus group. Wish you'd invited me."

Jesus's mouth fell open, his eyes going wide as he placed a gentle hand on Jessica's shoulder. "My sister, have I upset you? Am *I* the meanie?" He pressed a hand over his heart.

Jessica cleared her throat. "No, no. I'm just kidding." No point spurring an existential meanie crisis in Jesus Christ. She nodded to Jeremy. "I'll let you two get back to it, then."

"Actually," Jeremy said, "we could probably use your help, right Joshua?"

Jessica rolled her eyes at Jeremy's continued refusal to acknowledge that he was living with Jesus Christ. Not only did the angel deny his own heavenly station, he maintained that Jesus was simply confused. And yet, he continued to allow "Joshua" to live in his condo. Seemed incredibly unwise from Jeremy's perspective.

Jesus nodded. "Oh yes! We would love your help, sister. We just spent the last four hours feeding the homeless while asking them a series of scientifically formulated questions about their daily treatment—"

"Mostly feeding them," Jeremy added factually.

"And the next step to our campaign is to repeat the process except with people who hate the homeless. We would love it if you were a part of that." Jesus grinned

"Oh, um, no. I don't *hate* the homeless."

"Your treatment of them says otherwise, sister."

"No way. Hating the homeless is just wrong. I don't hate them. Sure, I'm not *thrilled* when they call me a stingy whore or take their penis out in front of me, but, you know, it's just in-person practice for that rare occasion when I drunkenly log in to my Twitter account."

Jesus and Jeremy shared a patronizing glance.

"Sure," said Jesus.

"Ooh!" Jeremy snapped his fingers then pointed at his roommate. "Tell her the slogan you came up with."

Could she just slip inside midway through this conversation? Would that be okay? Except now her interest was piqued. "Let's hear it."

"Of course! That's the most important part of this awareness campaign. I've been studying what you call marketing, and it seems that the quality of a product matters much less than the slogan."

Jessica waved for him to get on with it.

Jesus bit his lip excitedly and planted his feet. "Treat every hobo like they might be Jesus."

OH, THAT'S NOT GONNA WORK.

Finally, we agree on something.

Jesus's exultation melted as his shoulders slumped. "Daaaad! Why can't you support me?"

"You heard that too?" Jessica asked, though it was clear from the level of moping that he had. "I hate to say it, but he's right. You'll see once you spend a little more time in today's world. But points for pronoun inclusiveness!" She thrust a forced grin at her brother.

He nodded, his spirits starting to lift with the compliment. "Thanks for noticing. We're all God's children."

"Some more than others," Jessica said. When Jesus looked up, she motioned to the two of them and he nodded.

"Ahh, right."

Jeremy jumped in. "We'd better go air out the condo if we don't want to suffer violent olfactory-induced nightmares. That's how Tupac went, you know. Of course, no one will admit it."

"Tupac?" said Jesus. "I'm not familiar. Sounds like some sort of a prophet, though."

The men headed across the hall, and Jessica found her key finally.

"He basically was," Jeremy said. "But the smellmares got him."

Chapter Seven

For someone who had never played quarterback, Quentin Jones could throw one hell of a spiral.

And for someone who played three years of high school football for the state champions, Jessica caught the football like a fucking idiot.

Despite being aware of that, the feel of the turf underneath her bare feet and the touch of the pigskin made her feel like she was miles away from the overwhelming and monotonous responsibilities of adulthood. Sure, being on the field meant work was simply going undone, but being on the field also meant she didn't care. Those were all problems for future Jessica to handle.

She caught Quentin's perfect pass by cradling it against her body and leaning her head away, just in case the ball bounced out and took an unfavorable angle into her face again. They'd been at it for a half-hour now, and just like the other few times they'd met up after dark to blow off some steam, Jessica wondered why they didn't make this a weekly thing.

She lobbed the ball back to Quentin, and he caught her wobbly attempt at a spiral effortlessly. "How many women is it now?"

He threw it back to her and she wrapped it up against her chest. "I think it's six or seven. Not sure."

"They still hounding you about the dumbass photo?"

She threw the ball and it soared over Quentin, even as it leaped into the air for it. "Sorry! No, Wendy, Cash, and my lawyer got that sorted out for me."

As he chased down the rogue throw, Jessica glanced over at the last two hopeful paparazzi on the bleachers, who stared, bored stiff, at their cell phones. One of them glanced up at her, but when it was obvious she wasn't about to kick field goals, he looked down at his phone again.

Quentin jogged over. "I think that's about it for me today. Stretch and go get a burger?"

"Sounds good. We easily burned like a hundred and fifty calories. Burgers are a little less than that, right?"

"Yeah, I'm pretty sure that's right."

They sat on the grass, facing each other and began to stretch.

Quentin reached for one of his feet and was only able to get a slight finger hold on his big toe.

"Not bad," Jessica said, unable to reach past her ankle as she attempted the same position.

Quentin nodded at her. "Damn, Jess. I'm surprised

you haven't pulled a muscle kneading dough or whatever the hell y'all do over there."

She decided not to mention that she *had* pulled a muscle in her forearm doing just that. "Stretching is the farthest thing from my mind lately."

"We need to do this more often or else you're going to end up in the hospital next time Chris comes in town."

"Is that why you're so limber?" she asked. "You been staying fit with a lady friend?"

It was clear, as the shadow moved across his face, that not enough time had passed for that. Quentin shook his head and fixed his attention on his outstretched leg. "Nah."

"Have you talked to her at all?"

He shook his head. "You?"

"Nope. She probably just needs a little time. Who knows? She could come around."

"She lives in the same city as us and she hasn't said a word. You think she'll come around once she's in another state surrounded by a bunch of people who *haven't* lied to her about me being an angel?" He whispered the last bit so the onlookers wouldn't hear, but it was unnecessary. No one was paying any attention. Amateurs.

"She loves you, though," Jess said. "She'll eventually understand."

Quentin moved into push-up position to stretch his calves. "I don't know why you assume that. Just because two people are in love doesn't mean it'll work out."

When she didn't respond, he looked up and added, "You and Chris are different."

"Of course we are," she said, staring at her hands as they clutched her touching toes in butterfly position. "I'm not worried about it."

"Right. You shouldn't be."

"Good, because I'm not."

"Okay then. When was the last time you hit him up?"

"You're an asshole," she said.

Quentin laughed and let his knees fall to the turf. "What?"

"You're trying to point out that Chris and I hardly ever talk anymore."

Rather than responding right away, Quentin sighed and pulled his knees through, leaning back on his butt. "You're right." He chewed his lips for a moment, avoiding her eye. "You got me." When he looked up, there was an uncharacteristic seriousness to his eyes.

She didn't trust it.

He continued, "I haven't been able to stop thinking about you ever since high school. Our fake break-up crushed me, and all I've wanted is to see you ditch that Riley creep so we can start fake dating again."

Jessica laughed. "God, you're an idiot."

Quentin jumped to his feet. "That's how I make the big bucks in tech."

"Can I ask you something?"

"I literally can't stop you from it without violence."

"Great. Do you think Miranda was just tired of being my friend and looking for an excuse to break up with me?"

He immediately squatted to be on eye level. "What?" He laughed as he said it.

"I mean, do you think she was tired of being overlooked because everyone was always focused on me?"

To his credit, he thought about it before answering, and Jessica waited in suspense. Then he said, "I could see a lot of people feeling that way, but not Miranda."

The relief was immediate. He was the only person who knew Miranda better than her. "Really?"

"Yeah. I guess some people need recognition from others to drive them, but that's not her. She does what she does because it matters to her, not because she thinks it'll please the right people. Have you been worrying about that?"

"Yeah."

"Shit. That's awful. No, I never sensed any genuine jealousy from her about you and your life."

Jessica laughed dryly. "Why would she? If anyone should be jealous of anyone else's life, it's me of hers."

"I agree. Your life sucks."

She snapped her head up to blink at him.

"What? Wasn't that what you wanted to hear? Hey, I got an idea. Let's give the paparazzi a new photo to circulate around instead of that one with you and Jimmy." He grabbed the football off the ground. "I'll hold."

She stood as well, wiping stray pieces of grass from her ass. "Sure. Start small or go big?"

He looked over at them. "They're not paying attention.

Go big. They'll near about poop themselves when they think they missed their one shot."

She laughed. "You're smarter than you look, Quentin."

"And act."

And the two of them jogged over to midfield to set up the field goal kick.

Chapter Eight

Jessica didn't bother to unhook her bra, and Chris didn't bother to do it for her. The mist of the dense and quiet forest was chilly, anyhow; not the best climate to bust out the nips.

Chris continued with his story. "After the morning workout, we were supposed to have lunch catered, but there was some mix-up and the food didn't arrive, so Coach called the place and they said they didn't have an order for a hundred and fifty cheesesteaks. It was such a disaster. So, I ended up going to burgers with Montopolis and Santino, but by the time we got there, the line was so long that—"

Beep-beep beep-beep.

The oven timer pulled Jess out of her bored stupor. "Sorry," she said. "My mind was wandering. You wanna have sex or ...?"

Chris shrugged. "We can, or you can tell me about your day."

Not a terribly difficult choice.

"We ran out of croissants about halfway into the lunch rush, and I had to put an SOS out to my mom to come bake more on her day off. Of course she did it without complaining. Rex helped too, since it's still his summer. Then another woman came forward about Jimmy's doomsday cult."

"Have you talked to God about that? Like, is it true?"

"Oh, I figure it is. God's shown me enough about Jimmy's past for me to know he's capable of it. And I believe the women. Being duped by a man you trusted is *humiliating*. I don't know why anyone would claim it if it hadn't actually happened."

"How many women does that bring it to?"

"Six? Ten? I can't keep track."

"Doesn't matter, does it? If even one went through that, Jimmy should have to answer for it."

She grinned, rolling onto her side toward Chris. "You're right."

"He should have to— Aw shit." Chris sat up quickly, pulling a shotgun from beside the mattress and taking aim at the giant jersey-ed man charging toward them, cutting through the dense ferns of the woods.

Jessica covered her ears to protect from the echoing blast of the gunfire. *Boom.* The man dropped like a bag of bricks.

Chris set down the gun and reclined again. "He should have to answer for what he's done to you, too, Jess. And I think he will, someday."

"I hope you're not talking about when he dies and faces judgment. That's too long to wait."

"I imagine God will have a word with him, though."

Jess chuckled. "Jimmy's been wishing he could actually speak to God his whole life. I don't think he'll like what God has to say when that day comes."

They lay there in the silence, which was peaceful. The lush canopy obscured the sky overhead, and the trees around them began to fade as the sun went down and the glow of the forest dimmed.

It would be a shame to ruin the peacefulness with our grunting.

"So," Chris cut in, "You wanna do it? If you don't, that's okay. But if you do, I'm down. You know I am."

"Maybe tomorrow," Jessica said.

"Good," said Chris. "That's what I would have picked."

"I have a long day tomorrow."

"Me too."

"And you know once we get started, it tends to go on for a while."

"I need some deep sleep if I'm going to step it up in practice tomorrow."

"Same. I'm training the new hires tomorrow. I have no clue who they are or what I need to teach them."

Beep-beep beep-beep. Beep-beep beep-beep.

Chris's head rotated as he scanned the surroundings again. "Good choice on the location. Much better than the Dead Sea or, where were we last time?"

Jessica cringed. "A tomb. I don't know why I thought that was a good idea."

"It's my turn to pick a place next time, I guess. I'll think of something good."

"Sure. When's next time?"

"End of the week? We'll be able to focus better if we don't have work."

"I work on the weekends, Chris."

"Damn. Me too."

"I still like Fridays, though. Just in general."

"Yeah, they have a good feel to them, don't they? Even when you have to work on Saturday."

She nodded, and he rolled over and held himself above her. He was shirtless—hard nipples weren't an issue for him—and she took in the sight of his chest and arms, growing stronger by the week as he bulked up for the job. She liked this new version of Chris. She hoped to one day rediscover the well of energy for having sex with him.

He kissed her softly on the lips, only breaking it to grab his shotgun and take out another charging linebacker. "See you Friday. Love you."

"Love you, too."

When Chris powdered his way out of there, Jessica let herself stick around for a while longer, listening to the silence. The pure, beautiful si—

Beep-beep beep-beep. Beep-beep beep-beep...

Chapter Nine

Jessica glanced across the bakery at her mom, who threw back the rest of her coffee like it was a shot of tequila. Grabbing the bus bin from beside the trash, Jessica snaked through the tables of breakfasters and dropped it off at the back (she would deal with it later, like she did with everything) before washing her hands. For months now, her skin had been a dry, brittle mess from all the washing, and no amount of moisturizer could offset it. She'd considered sleeping in lotion-filled gloves but wasn't ready to go there just yet; that seemed like a whole lifestyle.

"Tough night?" Jess asked her mother as they passed behind the display case.

Destinee yawned as if on cue. "Couldn't sleep. Dunno if it's hormones or Rex's libido. Or maybe I was just worried about today."

"Worried? Why are *you* worried?" Jessica's sleep had been fitful at best.

"The new hires. I want to make a good first impression."

"Again, why? I mean, beyond the usual reasons. If you don't get along with one, I'll just fire him."

"Oh, I don't want to cause any problems, baby. Besides, Dolores has gone to all the trouble of vetting. I can't stand the thought that I might run one off and it'd get back to her."

At least Destinee was warming to the idea. When she'd first heard that Jessica had left the scouting and hiring completely to Mrs. Thomas, she'd lost it, stopping just short of calling her daughter a moron. In the years since Jessica had moved away from Mooretown, she'd forgotten just how much mistrust existed between her mother and her former teacher, mostly from Destinee's end. Jess could understand it well enough, though. Mrs. Thomas was like a second mother to her, and Destinee obviously didn't appreciate the competition.

In the end, her mother had resigned herself to the fact that what was done was done. And perhaps the daily grind had started to wear her down, too, and the notion of having someone else handle a big responsibility seemed as enticing to her as it had to Jessica.

"How you feeling about it?" Destinee asked. "You ready to be a serious boss?"

"Nope. Not ready in the least."

"Eh, that's okay. Most folks aren't. Hard work comes natural to us McClouds. Leadership doesn't. But it's the right thing to do. Who's first?"

"Sampson Gauner."

"He the marketing guy?"

"No, he's the bookkeeper." He was also the one Jessica had been most nervous and most excited about bringing on. If she could get someone else to handle the finances, it would easily save her two hours of misery and frustration every night. That was two hours she could spend sleeping or—dare she say it?—doing non-work things.

I could make new friends.

Whoa, one thing at a time. She had to train Sampson before getting ahead of herself.

When he arrived two minutes ahead of schedule for his training, she took that as a good omen.

Granted, she was running behind herself and asked Destinee to bring him over a coffee and pastry while he waited, but still, it was nice to know *someone* might be punctual around there.

Sampson was pale-skinned, appeared to be somewhere in his forties with a short crown of bristly blond hair on his otherwise bald head. She couldn't tell if it were just his thick, frameless glasses or not that made his eyes appear uncomfortably close together on his face as he peered up at her from a small cafe table by the window when she approached.

"Sampson, I'm Jessica."

He stood and offered her his hand. As he shook, crushing her hand with unnecessary force, she wondered briefly why he was frowning. "Nice to meet you, Jessica. *You're* the owner?"

Ah. Right. Twenty-one-year-old business owner didn't sit right with some people. Sampson certainly wasn't the first to show surprise, and he wouldn't be the last. "Yep. That's me. Let's have a seat and I can walk you through some of the basics."

"I assume I'll already know the basics."

She paused, her ass hovering a foot above the chair as she stared at him. "Right. That's why Mrs. Thom— Dolores recommended you, I'm sure." Once she settled into her seat, she pulled out the file folder she'd tucked under her left armpit and opened it up. "I printed out some of the ledgers I've been using so you can take a look."

"I'll be doing it the proper way, of course," Sampson said, only briefly glancing down at the pages she'd stayed up late the night before perfecting and printing.

"Of course. I'm just showing you what I have so that if you have any trouble, I don't know, understanding what data is where, you can—"

"Did you study finance in college?"

Jessica blinked, stunned. "No. Why?"

"Oh, just that if you didn't, I'm sure whatever you came up with will be simple enough for me to understand without assistance. I've been a certified bookkeeper for twenty years, managing major political campaigns for the vast majority of it. I can save you the trouble of training and simply say that I can handle whatever you have going on in this"—he leaned back, surveying the bakery, his eyes sticking for a moment to the large tree of life mural on the wall—"little establishment of yours."

For the first time, Jessica realized that she'd never specified a budget with Mrs. Thomas. She'd assumed the woman would know to factor in affordability to the decision, but maybe she shouldn't have assumed. After all, in the last conversation they'd had in the bakery, where they'd discussed this harebrained arrangement, Jessica had mentioned how much money Chris had and how she wanted to pay Mrs. Thomas back in full.

Fuck. Sampson was going to cost a pretty penny, wasn't he? He'd better be worth it, or else.

OR ELSE WHAT?

Or else I'm screwed.

That tended to be the "or else" of her scenarios.

With Sampson's bold claims still lingering in the air, she said, "How about I email you what records I have, the logins and passwords so you can pay the bills, and then I get out of your way?" Yes, he was a bit rude, but it would be worth it if she could set it and forget it with him.

Sampson seemed pleased for the first time since he'd entered It is Risen. Well, not pleased, but not outright annoyed. "That works. Mind if I set up here to get started?"

Standing and pushing in her chair, Jessica smiled politely. "Not at all."

"And mind getting me a refill on the coffee and two more of those cheese danishes?"

She took the coffee mug he thrust at her. "Of course."

"On the house," he added, opening up his laptop.

"Was already planning on it," she mumbled.

She passed her mother on the way to the coffee dispenser and Destinee whispered eagerly, "How's it going?"

"Fantastic," Jessica lied.

* * *

Kumal Darinda was scheduled for his training right after Sampson's, but because Sampson's had been cut so short, it was another hour before Kumal arrived.

He approached the counter, and Destinee greeted him and began taking his order before Jessica noticed him, saw his confused expression, and realized he was not here to order a kosher pig in a blanket.

"Kumal Darinda?" she asked. He nodded.

Dressed in well-fitting dark jeans and a tangerine button down with a laptop bag slung over his shoulder, Kumal would have blended in easily on the streets of downtown Austin. If only he had gone with bright sneakers instead of dress shoes, he would have been virtually invisible walking down Sixth Street on a weekday.

But as it was, just ten minutes outside of the epicenter of town, Kumal in his jail-orange shirt stuck out.

"Nice to meet you," she said, and after a quick introduction to Destinee, she led her new marketing specialist over to a table in the corner, far enough away from Sampson that the accountant wouldn't be able to listen in.

He seemed like the type.

While Jessica already had a team managing *her* social media presence, that was quite different from the online marketing she knew the bakery needed.

After a few minutes of polite conversation, Kumal pulled out his laptop, popping it open, and as he typed in his password, he asked, "Let's see what your website looks like so far."

She cleared her throat. "It's more of just a landing page with the hours and phone number, but okay."

She provided the address, and a moment after he hit enter with some flourish, his eyebrows pinched together. Sitting opposite, she couldn't see his screen, and she wondered if maybe he'd typed the address in incorrectly and ended up with a 404 page or, if his expression was any indication, a website for animal husbandry.

Then he spun the laptop just enough for her to see. "This is your website?"

Shit. Yes. Yes, it was. "I know it's not much."

"It's nothing," he said plainly. "If I stumbled on this, I wouldn't even know you were the daughter of God. Where are all the crosses?"

"That's not really my thing," she said. Her sudden and intense dislike of Kumal reflected back onto the person who had selected him. What was Mrs. Thomas thinking? Was this really the right person for the job? Could Jessica's judgment really be this off? Because, at the moment, she wasn't sure she wanted to hand over her passwords to him.

She had a reason for hiring him. You trusted her over yourself. Give him a chance.

"What *is* your thing?" he asked. "Are you, like, a goddess? Oh, is it the chalice? I could make a kick-ass graphic where a priest is holding up the communion cup and then slowly it morphs into, well, you know." He chuckled, spinning the screen back toward him.

She blinked. "No, I don't know."

"The female chalice."

Jessica choked on her spit trying to say twelve different words at once. "You want to turn a communion cup into a vagina? On my website?"

"Hey, listen, the female anatomy is a beautiful thing. No reason to get all hung-up on it."

"That's not what I'm hung up on."

Wendy had always insisted Jessica play up the messiah thing a bit more, but what Kumal proposed seemed especially disrespectful. Also, not bakery related in the least.

"I'm just brainstorming here. Just spitballing," he said, not looking up from his screen as he typed and clicked rapidly. "You got a lot of potential. And if there's one thing I've learned, working in politics, it's that you have to go big. Subtlety is for the educated. But most people aren't educated, and if you want to run a successful business you can't discriminate against them."

"I also probably shouldn't offend the largest religion in the country."

He chuckled. "Too late for that, don't you think? Might as well stir up some controversy."

"I beg to differ."

His hands froze over the keyboard and he leaned his head back and groaned. "Okay, fine. You're not ready for that. Whatever. Just know that the longer you wait to pull the trigger on my ideas, the longer you'll wait to hit big-time success. I'm fine playing it your way. But we for sure need to update this website. Add a menu, maybe post some cool pictures of the place—we'll need to hire a photographer for that—get some testimonials, type up a sweet bio for you and a story of how this place got started."

Jessica's shoulders relaxed. "That sounds much closer to what I imagined."

"How cool is this?" Kumal asked to no one in particular. "I get to write the bio for God's daughter."

While Jessica was always intrigued when random people referred to her that way, her desire to dive into just how much they believed it had lessened over the years as she realized it didn't matter. People believed it as strongly as they needed to for the world to work out the way they wanted *in that moment*. Kumal's belief in her probably began the moment he'd been hired, because working for God's daughter looked great on a resume. And if she ever fired him, she assumed his belief would immediately cease, and he would either say she was a fraud or really commit to protecting his pride and jump on the antichrist bandwagon.

"Any expenses you incur for, I don't know, web hosting

or whatever, run it by me if it's over a hundred dollars, and be sure to send all your receipts to Sampson." She motioned over her shoulder at the friar-haired accountant. "That work?"

"Yuh-huh," he said, hunched over his computer.

She narrowed her eyes at him. That sounded like an autopilot answer if she ever heard one. Should she call him on it?

"And tell me when you're ready to launch so I can take a look at it first, okay?"

"Yep."

He definitely wasn't listening. "Sorry, but did you hear what I said?"

Finally, he tore his eyes from the screen and narrowed them scornfully at her. "Of course I heard you. I said yep, didn't I?"

She jerked her head back and resisted the impulse to fire him before he'd even signed the employment paperwork.

He must be some kind of savant. That was surely it. Mrs. Thomas would have known that when it came to Jessica's precious business, she cared more about results than whether everyone got along hunky-dory in the process.

"When do you think you can start on the website?"

"Huh?" He blinked and looked at her. "Oh, I'm already starting on it. I should have it ready to launch in a couple weeks."

"Oh. Um, okay. Just remember to let me review it before you launch."

"Yeah, I heard you the first time," he said without breaking from the screen.

She managed not to snap at him in her tired state, but only just. Then she made a note to keep Kumal away from Destinee as much as possible. Her mother wouldn't show such restraint. "Do you need anything else from me to get started?"

"Hmm?" He looked up again, and smiled. "Um. Yes. A mocha latte. Large. And if you have like a strudel muffin of some kind, I'll take that as well." Without a thank you, Kumal went to work, and Jessica went to fetch him his coffee and the stalest strudel muffin she could find.

* * *

"And when you shut the freezer, you kind of have to give it an extra tug to make sure it's secure."

"I know," said Dwayne Pogreska, the prep cook in training at It is Risen.

Jessica paused after demonstrating. "I mean, I know you know how to shut a freezer, it's just that this one's refurbished and it's got its own little quirk."

Dwayne, a stocky Croatian with forearms like thighs, nodded. "Yeah, they all do that."

Jessica wasn't sure they all did. If they all did, it seemed like a drastic design flaw that someone somewhere would have fixed by now. "Okay, then." She led him over to the ovens next. These were something she was admittedly quite proud of. When she'd been ordering all the appliances with Dr. Bell, they'd decided that one thing she couldn't scrimp on, given that baking wasn't something she was especially expert at, was top-of-the-line ovens. If Jessica wanted to reduce variance between her batches, the easiest way was to use equipment that was consistent each time, even if she was not. The ones they'd picked out were only used in five other bakeries around the world, and none of those were in the US. Bringing on Dwayne to get things started in the mornings was not only a thrilling prospect because it meant she could sleep two hours later and stroll in to grab some coffee and perform a baker's dozen miracles on the finished goods, it meant she would finally get to show off these goddamn ovens to someone who could appreciate them fully.

"So *these*," she said gesturing at the sleek chrome finish and the black matte knobs, "are the ovens. They're top-of-the-line and can only be found in five other bakeries around the world, none of which are in the United States."

Dwayne nodded once. "Yeah, I know."

A small squeak slipped from deep in Jessica's throat. "Oh, you know? How do you know?"

He shrugged unsatisfactorily. "Not sure. I just know about it. Do you remember how you know everything you know?"

She swallowed down the acid rising from her stomach. "No, I guess not." She paused. "Wait, you already know how to use these, or ...?"

"Yeah. I know. What I don't know, I can figure out."

She glanced down at his hands, which looked like they'd been stung by a hive of bees only minutes before arriving for his training. The thought of those absolute clubs pawing experimentally at the delicate and sensitive knobs and buttons made her want to shout or call the cops or blow a rape whistle—anything to keep that horrible scenario from coming to pass.

Anything, that is, except explain the panel to him after he'd already said he knew and would continue to say, "I know" with each new explanation.

"Okay, um, if you have *any* questions about it once you start using it, text me, okay? Day or night, just text me and I will help you out immediately."

He nodded, but if he couldn't stand to have something explained to him in a context that was created especially for explanation—training—there was little chance he would admit he didn't know something later on.

Mrs. Thomas sent him to me for a reason. He might really know his stuff. Maybe he's a genius and can intuit ... ovens? Goddamn, no, that isn't a thing.

"Last up before we go into the actual recipes," she said, leading him over to the cleanest countertop in the kitchen, the one by the telephone where she kept the paperwork and logs and spent late nights working, attempting to balance the books. At least Sampson would take care of that now. She grabbed a blank form off the top of a small stack. "This is an inventory request form. When you run out of an ingredient or a spoon breaks or whatever and you need a new one, just mark it down on one of these and put it in that metal basket so I know to take a look. That way—"

"Yeah, got it."

Jessica forced a smile. "You don't want me to show you what to put in each field?"

"Is each one labeled?" Dwayne asked.

"Yes, but—"

"Then I bet I can figure it out."

Jessica sighed. This was ridiculous. She glanced at the clock on the wall and said, "You sure? We still have a full two hours for your training, and baking prep won't take that long. We might as well use the time now. I'm just thinking that if I were starting a new job, I'd be more confident starting out if I'd been, you know, trained how to do the stuff."

He bounced on his toes as he said, "Nah, I'm plenty confident. You have all the recipes written down somewhere, right?"

Jessica nodded. It was one of the few things she'd taken the time to do right.

"Great. Maybe you can just point me to them rather than showing me how to do all of it."

"I wasn't going to show you how to do all of it, just point out where the ingredi—"

"Yeah, see, I actually told this chick I'd meet her at the gym in twenty minutes, and I don't want to disappoint her."

Jessica almost laughed. "Are you joking?"

"Nope. So you mind if I just use your bathroom then head over there?"

Twenty minutes? He told a *chick* he'd ...

Jessica glared at him, hardly able to believe what she was hearing.

How? How was every single person Mrs. Thomas had sent her disagreeable? Was this how people behaved in politics?

Am I PMSing?

She remembered the date and realized that she probably was. Maybe that was all that was causing this annoyance. She took a deep breath and said, "Yeah, sure. Here, let me give you a key." She reached in her pocket and pulled out the spare she'd made the day before. "You'll need to be in by four thirty tomorrow morning. The recipes will be all laid out for you. Text me if you have any questions."

"Yeah, I know," he said, taking the key. But before he hustled off, he said, "You mind making me a coffee to go?" and before she could respond, he ran off to the bakery's bathroom to, likely, destroy it.

She had no hard evidence that he was doing anything except taking a whiz; he just struck her as the type to use a private establishment's restroom without paying for anything and then making it unusable for the next half hour. And all without feeling properly ashamed of himself.

She fixed his coffee, put it in the to-go cup, and didn't secure the lid completely.

And she felt zero remorse for it. "See you tomorrow," she said as he took the cup and hurried out.

Only two other patrons besides Sampson and Kumal remained in the cafe, and Jessica was thankful for the break.

For some strange reason, she wasn't sure her customer service skills were firing on all cylinders.

Destinee's hand slid onto her shoulder. "Sure will be nice to have help, won't it, baby?"

Jessica stared though the window, wistfully wishing she could be there to see when Dwayne went for his first sip and the lid came right off.

"Yeah," she said. "It sure is."

Chapter Ten

Jessica toweled off her hair, bone tired but excited. And anxious. The tiredness came from not taking a full day off work in almost three months, which was the same amount of time It is Risen had been open, coincidentally. The excitement came from it being her twenty-second birthday. And the anxiety came from it being her twenty-second birthday.

The day she was born came with all kinds of strings attached, the worst of which was always the Jimmy Dean string. But then there was also the deep-seated fear she carried in a tiny box stashed away somewhere between her stomach and her lung that she would follow in her half-brother's footsteps and not live to see thirty-four. No matter how many people told her it was unfounded, no matter how much she told herself it was unfounded and just a dumb holdover from childhood bullying, she couldn't shake it. And every year, on July 7th, the lid to the tiny box cracked open, and that fear seeped into her bloodstream.

She tousled her hair to let it air dry while she slipped into her outfit for the night, which she'd carefully laid out on her bed. It was the nicest thing she owned (outside of the formal dress she'd bought for attending the NFL draft): boot-cut blue jeans with no holes or grease stains and a charcoal-gray boat-neck T-shirt with a sketched flock of white birds across the front. Maybe she needed to up her wardrobe.

But what would be the point?

From the living room, a commercial blared for medication to help with medication-related constipation.

She would wear makeup tonight. She'd almost forgotten the stuff existed, because who had time for it when you hardly got five hours of sleep each night? If she had ten minutes to spare, it wasn't going toward clogging her pores and drawing more attention to her tired eyes.

The five hours of sleep was her *new* normal, only attainable now that she had Sampson, Kumal, and Dwayne. Sampson saved her long nights of bookkeeping, and Dwayne saved her early mornings of prep. Kumal saved her nothing but the insidious dread that she *should* be building an online presence for It is Risen but wasn't, and that was gift enough.

Of course, it came at a cost exceeding the actual wages she paid them, which, turned out, were even higher than she'd feared. But since Sampson handled all that, she could easily clear it from her mind, shove it aside and pretend it wasn't an issue.

And then there was the sheer frustration of working with the men. She'd almost grown used to it, which was a true testament to the power of routine to normalize even the most insufferable behavior. Like how Dwayne had put chocolate chips in the banana nut muffins twice, and when she called him on it the second time, he outright admitted he'd done it on purpose because the muffins were better that way.

Well, no shit. Everything was better with chocolate. But that wasn't the point.

Then there was the photographer Kumal had brought in to take pictures of the bakery. She was fairly certain it was a close relative—a cousin if not a sibling—but it was never mentioned, and far be it from her to inquire and be branded a racist who thought all Indians looked the same.

In her defense, they also shared a last name.

This wouldn't have been a problem if Aisha had seemed a professional. However, after an hour of setting muffins in odd locations to take drastically angled pictures of them with a cell phone rather than a real camera and harassing customers with her phone in their face, which Jessica was fairly sure would require a release or something to use, it had become quite obvious that Aisha Darinda was not a photographer by trade.

And then there was Sampson ... and all the snippy,

judgmental emails that came with him, always acting put upon when she asked him to do things within his job description and patronizing her whenever she grew tired of his griping and offered to help. Thank whoever that he worked remotely. She thought of the email he'd sent her that afternoon, belittling her for asking if she needed to sign anything for him for the monthly bills that were coming up. She could have sworn she'd done it the first week he was on the job, but he insisted she wasn't necessary and insinuated she was trying to insert herself into the process to feel important.

She shuddered, thinking about how much she wanted to wring his neck and how unfortunate such a thing would be to the functioning of her business.

She needed to put it out of her head. Tonight was a special night, and she deserved a few hours out with friends and family.

And she deserved a drink. Now.

Going out with more than one friend at a time was a muscle she had let atrophy. Sure, she was around *people* all day, but that wasn't the same.

"Want a beer?" she asked as she emerged from the bedroom and into the kitchen.

Chris turned where he relaxed on the couch to cast a glance at her. "Yeah, I'll have another." Jessica squinted at the one he had in his hand, which he rested on the back of the couch. It was almost completely full. She didn't know why that agitated her so much, but it did.

Or maybe it wasn't that. Maybe it was everything else in her life that left her in a constant state of mild agitation that flared up at random moments.

Chris had been in town for the last two days, staying at her place. He'd requested a few days off so he could be there for her birthday, and it had been mostly nice. She did feel bad that she left him alone all day to go to work, and when he did come to visit her at the bakery, she wasn't able to give him much attention. As far as she could tell, though, it didn't bother him.

She cracked open two beers and went to join him but didn't sit down.

"You just missed it," he said. "Jimmy was on the news."

"God dammit. Of course he was." He knew it was her birthday. "More denials about the accusers?"

"Not so much denial as ..." Chris cringed, and Jessica's throat clenched. "One of the woman who was in his cult or whatever in Elbow, she's sort of, um, dating him now."

"*What?!*"

"Yeah, it's super creepy. But she claims it was nothing more than a bible study and there weren't just a bunch of girls there; there were boys too, and it's just being blown out of proportion."

"But no men have come forward!"

He shrugged. "Jimmy says it's because they're not naturally gold diggers."

"Oh, *he's* one to talk. You know how much he used to hit up my mom for money?"

Chris held up a hand to calm her. "I know. Trust me, I do. And I don't buy a word of Jimmy's nonsense."

She scowled at the TV, which had moved onto commercials. A male bodybuilder popped a handful of supplements before dragging a small aircraft down a landing strip by a long chain tied around his waist. "Why would she lie about it for him?"

Chris shrugged. "No telling. People do strange things."

"He probably paid her."

"Maybe," Chris said apprehensively, "but I don't know if he'd have to. I've seen some weird stuff since moving to Philadelphia, Jess. The way women throw themselves at my teammates is creepy. Even the ugly dudes, the ones that look better with their helmet on, women are chasing after them with this crazed look in their eyes. Some folks want fame no matter what."

Jessica stared at him, blinking dumbly. She knew what he'd said made sense, but it was what he *hadn't* said that hooked her attention. There was no way women threw themselves at all of Chris's teammates, even the fugly ones, and skipped over the pretty quarterback. That wasn't how this batshit crazy universe worked.

"What do you do when they throw themselves at you?" she asked, struggling to keep the jealousy out of her voice.

"Huh?" Not the question he was expecting, clearly.

"What do you do," she repeated slowly, "when they throw themselves at you?"

He shook his head gently. "I tell them no thanks. What do you *think* I do?"

The image of Chris holding a hand palm-out and politely saying "No thanks" to an oncoming stampede of women would have struck Jessica as humorous if she weren't already so damn agitated.

Fucking Jimmy. (And Sampson. And Kumal. And Dwayne.)

"That asswipe *planned* on announcing his new relationship on my birthday," Jessica said. She wagged a finger at Chris. "Make no mistake, he knows full well what day it is. He's trying to ruin my birthday, and it's not going to work!" She took a hard swig from the bottle and stomped back into the bathroom to dry her hair and paint her face.

She managed to knock back most of her beer as she aimed the hairdryer in the general direction of her head and scowled at herself in the mirror. Why couldn't people just do the right thing? Men were ruining her life. And here she was putting on make-up to look pretty for them. Why? What was the point?

It was not the ideal state for putting on eye liner. Each dab of foundation and brush of blush, each attempt at a straight line on her eyelid and around her lips felt like an expectation that she, with her minimal application skills, was unable to fulfill. She was attempting to be beautiful, and she was failing miserably. Once she finished with the mascara and paused to examine herself, she felt a strong sense of self-loathing well up in her.

Makeup was supposed to be a trick she had in her back pocket in case she needed to look pretty for something. But now she'd played that ace up her sleeve, and it hadn't been as helpful as she'd hoped. She still looked like Jessica— tired, plain, plain tired.

By the time she left the bathroom after a half hour of primping, she wanted nothing more than for nobody to look at her.

Chris turned and looked at her. "Whoa! You look amazing, Jess."

Liar.

"Eh," she grumbled.

But he kept gaping lasciviously and sauntered over to her while she gathered up her strewn belongings to throw them into her purse.

He wrapped his arms around her from behind, pressing up against her.

She was annoyed by how nice it felt to be wanted, despite her unfortunate appearance. She didn't deserve Chris, stupid, ugly thing that she was. Why did he bother pushing away the women throwing themselves at him? He should have taken them up on the offer. Instead, he was stuck with her, and what good was she? They couldn't even have sex! Chris was probably the only guy in the league that was still a virgin, and it was all her fault.

He nuzzled the top of her head, inhaling her deeply and groaning, "Mmm ... you smell like fresh bread."

She stepped away quickly. "God *dammit!*" Bread? How in the nine circles of fuck did she still smell like bread? She'd shampooed her hair twice!

"Whoa, what is it?" Chris said, stumbling back quickly.

She rounded on him. "I smell like bread all the time! I can't get rid of it, no matter how many times I shower. It's like it's in my freaking blood! When I sweat, I smell like yeast. That's not what a woman wants to smell like, Chris! A woman doesn't want to smell like yeast!"

Chris raised his hands defensively. "I don't think you smell like yeast. I wouldn't want you to smell like that either. I just said bread, which is a good thing. I love bread, Jess. You know I do. You've seen how many rolls I eat at restaurants. I love bread more than any other food. I pretend to enjoy the entree, but I'm always just thinking about bread."

"Bread is so plain! It gets old!" she snapped. "And quite frankly, *I'm* fucking sick of bread!" She stomped her foot, understanding how ridiculous the gesture was even as she did it. "You only think you love bread because you're not around it every waking moment of your life! You ran off to Philadelphia so you don't have to be around bread full-time."

A crease formed between Chris's eyebrows. "They have bread in Philly," he said, hardly above a whisper.

"Oh, I know they do. I bet they have all kinds of bread you want to gorge yourself on. And how do I know you don't? I just have to stay here, smelling like the same old bread day in and day out, and trust that you're not stuffing your face with Philly cheesesteak buns! But you know what? Maybe you should!"

Chris put his hands on his head, weaving his fingers together like he was trying to catch his breath after a suicide sprint. "What in the hell are you talking about Jess? I'm so— Ohh ..." He rolled his eyes and dropped his hands to his side. "I thought we were done with this. I said your hair smelled like bread, and you twist that into me cheating on you? Good lord. It's your birthday! Can we not do this right now?"

"When are we going to do it, then, Chris? You're never around long enough for us to have a proper fight."

"I've been in town for days!" he exclaimed. "Isn't that plenty of time to accuse me of eating the wrong bread? I've literally been sitting on this couch"—he gestured to the evidence—"waiting for you to take a break from work and come spend time with me—hell, even to come yell at me! Anything."

"And how come it's just a few days?" That intense twenty-four hours of learning chess back in high school felt like it might finally be paying off. "You're in the off season and this is the first time I've even seen you since you moved. If you wanted to see me, you could have made time. It's not like you don't have the money." *Checkmate.*

Chris's jaw tightened and his nostrils flared. He stared at her with an expression she hadn't seen on him before, at least not while he looked at her. It seemed more the type of glare he'd reserve for Jimmy Dean or Greg Burns, not his girlfriend.

She'd crossed a line. That much was obvious, though she wasn't sure exactly when it'd happened. And she wasn't going to apologize for it.

Chris grabbed his wallet and phone off the coffee table,

crammed them in his pants pockets, and made for the door. "You're going to be late to your own party if we don't leave now."

He didn't wait for her to grab her purse and follow as he let the door close behind him.

Chapter Eleven

There had been only one buffet restaurant within fifty miles of Mooretown when Jessica was a growing up. It was called Buckingham Palace for reasons no one, including the owners, could put a finger on. Perhaps it was an attempt at sounding posh and regal and up-to-health-code.

Despite the copious sneeze guards, the buffet was always referred to as Botulism Palace, and people ate there despite the nickname, understanding the risks.

Because of that early childhood experience, when Jessica had started at college, she'd hesitated to visit the buffet-style dining halls on campus, worried that, having avoided botulism in her youth, it would finally catch up with her, because you can't outrun the past forever. But those buffets never proved to be harmful, either, despite the dearth of sneeze guards over certain spreads.

She was long overdue for food poisoning by the time she moved to Austin, and she'd half expected to give it to herself, considering she only had a shadow of an idea how to bake and prepare food in a safe way.

So, when Quentin had first suggested they grab food at the dinner buffet at Mauricio Forticello's downtown for one of their friend dates two months before, she'd responded with a firm no thanks. It took three more mentions of it from Jeremy and Jesus, Cash Monet, and finally, Destinee, whose blunt culinary opinion Jessica trusted above all others, before she was willing to give it a shot and check it out with Quentin. And she was glad once she finally did.

It was the perfect place for a birthday dinner, as guests could come and go as worked with their schedule and help themselves to the best buffet Jessica had ever seen. And Chris had generously offered to pick up the evening's tab.

The two of them didn't speak on the walk from her condo to the restaurant. Chris had stayed a half-step ahead of her the whole way. As they entered in the front door and spotted Destinee and Rex already waiting at the table, Jessica forced a smile and was relieved when Chris donned his trademark confident grin.

"Oh, baby, you look gorgeous," Destinee said as they approached the long table.

"Thanks," Jessica said, letting her mother hug her like they hadn't seen each other in weeks, when it'd only been a matter of hours.

Rex beamed as he took in Chris, the pride of Mooretown Mexicans' football. The men shook hands, did the back slap thing Jessica didn't really understand, exchanged a few words, then Rex turned to Jessica. He nodded and said, "Your beauty is so much more than your looks, but I appreciate that you put thought into your appearance to commemorate this special occasion, and I think you did a fine job, not that you need the validation of a man for it to be true."

"Thanks, Rex." As she leaned in for the hug, she caught sight of Destinee who cringed and mouthed, "Sorry."

Jessica didn't mind. It was her own damn fault for introducing Rex to feminism in the first place. They decided to wait until a few more guests arrived before getting started on the buffet line. Rex appeared entirely enraptured by every detail Chris could provide regarding training camp and the other summer workouts. It seemed Rex's disappointment at his golden boy being an Eagle had dissipated, at least for the time being.

"You catch the news?" Jessica asked her mom.

If anyone could fully commiserate with her about Jimmy's nonsense, it was Destinee.

"Jess, you know I don't have the energy for big-city news. Midland was almost too much for me. In Austin, if it ain't one thing, it's another."

If it ain't one thing, it's another. That was some wisdom she could relate to.

"Well, look who it is!" Rex exclaimed, his eyes locking onto someone just past Chris's shoulder.

Quentin gasped dramatically when Chris turned

toward him. "Is that ... is that *the* Christopher Riley?" Quentin fanned himself.

"You're an idiot," Chris said, grinning as he stood, and the two men hugged unabashedly. No back slap thing required.

There was little chance of the conversation at the table to be about anything other than football at that point. Quentin and Chris were too loud. So Jessica let it wash over her. There would be intense conversational expectations of her later, once more guests turned up.

The next to arrive, though, would be just fine carrying on a conversation amongst themselves.

Jeremy Archer and Jesus Christ snuck up to the table without anyone noticing until they were hovering behind two empty chairs. "Mind if we have a seat?" Jeremy asked. He seemed genuinely curious if anyone would mind, his brows knitted together tightly as he pointed at the chair without making contact. Jessica nodded and motioned for him to go for it.

Once Chris noticed who had arrived, he said hello reverentially, which earned him a side-eye from Destinee, who was understandably confused what made Joshua worthy of that tone. Jess knew she should probably tell her mother, but she wasn't sure how that would go, and if outing angels was a faux pas, surely outing messiahs was as well.

Jeremy's casual fashion sense had officially worn off on Jessica's half-brother, and each of the men rocked black band T-shirts and jean shorts, meaning it would naturally seem a bit off to the casual observer why Chris, a millionaire, would speak with such deference to someone in flip-flops, cut-offs, and a Lynyrd Skynyrd shirt.

"I think you met everyone at the It is Risen party," Jessica said, stepping into host duties, "but everyone, this is Jeremy Archer, my neighbor across the hall, and ... Joshua."

"Great choice of venue," Jeremy said politely. "Sure, it's owned by the mob, but it's one of the nicer factions. Their intimidation tactics are more subliminal marketing-based than physical."

Joshua chuckled, jabbing a thumb at his bestie. "This guy. Isn't he wonderful? He knows so many things, and he's not even a priest or other holy keeper of texts!"

Catching her mother's eyes, Jessica shook her head minutely and mouthed, "Don't ask."

"How many more are we waiting on?" Chris asked. "I'm starving."

"Just a few more," Jessica replied. "But no one's going to be mad if you get food now, Chris. They'll understand."

"He's a growing boy," Quentin said, standing along with Chris. "I'll chaperone him to make sure he leaves some for others."

As they made a beeline for the buffet line, a cluster of familiar faces arrived at once. Jessica waved them over.

Kate's rich auburn hair was easy to pick out, even with her face obscured behind a curtain of it. By her side was Natalie, who was secretly Jessica's favorite Nu Alpha Omega, though she would never tell Kate or Judith that. The woman won the honor simply by being the most blunt and ornery of the bunch, saying things Jessica wished she could say but never had the words for or the courage to actually pull off. Kate was honest and direct but would never say anything that could later come back to bite her in the ass. Judith was honest through sarcasm, but it was often difficult to tell if she was mocking someone or supporting them. Meanwhile, Natalie said whatever the hell she wanted whenever she wanted, and she spoke it plainly, even though that often wasn't in her best interest.

What would it feel like to be that reckless? Jessica wondered.

Chatting along with Natalie and Kate were Brian Foster and his live-in girlfriend, Judith. As much as Jessica regretted knowing that her former junior high science teacher was sleeping with one of her sorority sisters, she couldn't complain. For one thing, she'd thought they would make a great couple within a few minutes of meeting Judith, and it turned out they *did* make a pretty good couple, in a codependent sort of way. Both felt constantly misunderstood, and in that regard, they understood each other.

But also, Brian had become a bridge between two of Jessica's worlds: Mooretown and San Marcos. And now, in many ways, Austin. Having him around would hopefully keep the party's conversation from breaking off into its usual groups.

The chorus of hellos rang out as the quartet approached the table, and Jessica was relieved when Judith made the effort to walk all the way around the table to give

Jesus a hug, despite their short-lived romance that had ended the moment Jesus came clean about his true identity.

She whispered something in his ear, and his eyes grew wide, and when they pulled away, he grinned and thanked her like she'd just given him the most amazing gift.

Conversation became more subdued once each guest had a plate stacked with pasta.

Jessica had specifically asked for a table for eleven when she put in the reservation, but they'd provided an extra, which sat open at the head of the table. Jessica had taken a spot at the center to better jump in and out of the various micro-conversations taking place, but the empty seat at the end kept catching her eye. The restaurant was running at a wait by the time Jessica went back for her second plate, and as she sat down, one of the waiters who'd been busy refilling everyone's drinks approached the seat, asking, "Do you mind if I take this one?"

Jessica smiled and nodded, but Destinee, who sat closest to the empty seat, grabbed the back of the chair, holding it in place and barking, "No. We need it."

What was this nonsense?

Jessica tried to catch Destinee's eyes, but her mother wasn't having it and returned to her conversation with Brian and Judith.

A few minutes later, though, the pieces fell into place.

Jessica almost couldn't believe it. The white-blonde hair caught her attention initially, and for a split second, Miranda's appearance seemed natural. Of course she would be at Jessica's birthday dinner. Then the mudslide of messiness between them hit the scene, and Jessica remembered she was supposed to be embarrassed and ashamed, not happy.

Miranda forced a smile and waved timidly as she approached from the host stand, so Jessica did, too.

"Happy birthday," she said, opening up her arms.

Was this forgiveness? Maybe. At least partial. "Thanks." Jessica left plenty of space between them as she went in for the hug, and Miranda didn't bother pulling her any closer.

It was weird hugging Miranda. They'd always been so close that hugs had seemed extraneous. Growing up, when they'd seen each other almost every day, each conversation felt like a continuation of the previous one. The fact that they needed to hug now felt like a sign of distance rather than intimacy.

"Have a seat," Destinee said, gesturing to the empty chair.

"Thanks. We'll need one more."

Only then did Jessica realize that Miranda had brought someone with her. He'd hung back so many feet that Jessica had assumed he was with some other party.

"Of course," Destinee said, jumping up to seek out another one. "I didn't know you were bringing someone. That's my fault, honey."

"Jessica, this is Desmond. Desmond, Jessica."

Jessica struggled not to let her annoyance show as she shook Desmond's hand. But how could Miranda show up and bring a new man with her, parading him around in front of Quentin?

Desmond had an easy foot on Jessica, and his hand enveloped hers as he shook firmly. "Jessica, it is so nice to finally meet you."

Oh shit. The moment he spoke, she realized this was even more of a blow than she'd thought. Desmond was African. Not African American, but straight up *African.*

She'd had enough honest conversations with Quentin about the black community to suspect this wouldn't play well. "Nice to meet you, Desmond."

Destinee returned with a seat just in time and squeezed it at the end of the table next to Miranda's. Jessica used it as an excuse to sneak back to her seat at the center of the table and let Miranda and Brian Foster say hello.

Quentin sat on the other side of Chris from Jessica, and she leaned back in her chair and tapped him on the shoulder. He broke from a conversation with Jesus and leaned back to see what she wanted. "I didn't know," she whispered. His eyes flickered to Miranda and he shrugged.

No. There was no way he was okay with this. He was in love with Miranda. He'd bought her a ring. They'd only been broken up four months, and she'd already taken up with some new guy? And a new guy who was ...

"Bathrooms," she whispered. "Now."

Quentin rolled his eyes but casually excused himself, and Jessica waited as long as she could before she did the same.

Once they were sheltered in the long L-shaped hallway leading to the restrooms, where gold-framed prints of the Italian country side lined the walls, she confronted him to get the real scoop. "I didn't even know she was coming, let alone bringing some ..."

"Other black dude?" Quentin suppressed a grin as he crossed his arms and leaned against the wall, knocking one of the pictures slightly to the left.

"No, not that. Well, yes, that. But also, I assume they're dating."

"Yeah, I think that's a safe assumption." He sighed. "What do you want from me?"

"Are you okay?"

"Surprisingly, yes. I mean, it hurts, but I knew she would move on, and honestly, I'm glad she is, even if it *is* glaringly obvious to anyone with one functioning eye that she's trying to find a replacement for me."

Jessica leaned forward, placing a comforting hand on Quentin's shoulder and saying, "You'll always be my favorite black guy Miranda's ever dated."

Quentin bit back a grin and nodded, placing a hand over Jessica's. "And you'll always be my favorite white messiah Chris dates."

"Thanks. Although the specificity is worrisome." She let her hand drop and sighed. "If you decide you want to head out, I won't be offended."

"Nah. I'm good."

"Whatever you say."

As they walked back to the table, Jessica still had her

doubts. Four months, and Quentin was already at peace with the breakup? Miranda and Quentin had seemed even more sure about marriage than Jessica was when it came to Chris.

The thought crept in before she could force it out.

I could be okay without him.

No, no, that couldn't be right. Stupid thought. She didn't even remember life without Chris.

All eyes were on Jesus as Jessica found her seat.

"I tried to tell them to treat the homeless like they would Jesus, and the test group was even *worse* to those in need!" He shook his head in disbelief as the rest of the group listened intently. "It's like the name of Christ means nothing around here."

"I tried to tell you," Jessica said, whipping her napkin onto her lap again.

"Anyway," Jesus continued, "that idea was clearly not a winner, so I'm going back to the drawing board and will need to host another focus group and contained test soon. If anyone here has particularly malicious feelings toward the homeless, I invite you to join Jessica in the next experiment."

"I don't hate the homeless," she said quickly. "I don't know why he thinks that."

"It's because your treatment of them is dismissive and sometimes combative."

She opened her mouth to respond before realizing he wasn't far off. She settled with, "They call me names." It was a weak defense, and she knew it.

Chris jumped in. "Y'all see the news today?" As an afterthought he turned to Jess and mumbled, "You mind if I talk about this?"

"Nope." She might have minded a group discussion of Jimmy Dean on her birthday two minutes before, but considering it shifted the focus from her lack of rapport with the homeless population of Austin, it was actually an improvement.

"You talking about Jimmy Dean?" Judith said. "I know it's wrong, but I can't get enough of this scandal."

"What are we up to now?" Quentin asked. "Ten accusers?"

Jessica nodded. "Something like that. But now he's dating one of them who's trying to discredit all the others."

"Figures," Natalie added. "There's always that one bitch that goes and does something stupid and sets the rest of womankind back another decade."

Rex bobbed his head up and down adamantly, humming, "Mm-hmm ... Mm-hmm ..."

"From a psychological standpoint," Miranda said from the end of the table, causing the rest of the chatter to fall silent, "there's likely an element of Stockholm Syndrome present in her decisions, so we probably shouldn't vilify her. It's not uncommon for people who experience trauma they can't work through to bend it to a narrative that's less painful to confront." She paused, and Jessica considered all the trauma Jimmy had put her through and how she'd never once let it stir lust inside of her for the horrible man.

She was trying to find the words to express that

without ruining the tenuous truce with Miranda, when Miranda added, "But regardless, fuck Jimmy."

"Amen!" shouted Destinee, slapping the table and causing a few of the nearby glasses of water to slosh over the rim.

"I honestly do not know how you haven't smote him yet, Jessica," said Natalie. "I would've if I were you."

"We know," Kate said.

"God doesn't want me to," said Jessica. "Believe me, I've thought about it."

"Who cares what God wants?" said the least likely person to spout such a thing.

Jessica's head swiveled around to stare at Jesus, who shrank in his seat a little at the sudden attention. "I don't know where that came from," he murmured.

Destinee was the first to speak. "Don't worry, Joshua, a little blasphemy with friends is no biggie. Otherwise that child-support-dodging son of a bitch would have struck me down a long time ago."

"I don't think anyone would blame you," Chris said, "if you did end up smiting him. It's like he does everything just to make you mad."

Like being all over the news on my birthday?

"I'm not smiting him," she reiterated.

"But if you did," Chris persisted, "no one would blame you. That's all I'm saying."

"Maybe you ought to head out to the smiting range to blow off some steam," said Miranda. "Especially when he's

—" Her hand flew up to her mouth, and her eyes went wide.

Jessica groaned and flopped back in her seat, waiting for the onslaught of questions.

Quentin was the first with a simple, straightforward one: "Smiting range?"

"Sorry," Miranda said, staring at Jessica who struggled not to be angry.

"Is that a joke?" Chris said, his attention ping-ponging between Jessica and Miranda. "A smiting range?"

"No," Jessica said. "I was practicing."

Chris shifted in his seat. "That's ... Wow." He didn't seem upset. Quite the opposite.

"I don't go anymore," Jessica said. "We just went a few times. My aim still sucks."

Chris was a bloodhound who'd caught a scent. "But we could go back, right? I could watch you smite?"

"Easy, there," Quentin warned. "Keep that kind of shit in your shared dreams, Riley."

Jesus cradled his face in his hands. "Please don't mention those."

"Oh right!" Quentin shouted, shaking a finger at Jesus. "We *did* meet that one time! You looked totally different, though. Jess and I were in the car and you—" Quentin cut himself off, clearing his throat.

The significance of Jesus's appearance in the shared dreams was lost on those around the table who didn't know Joshua's true identity or the nature of those dreams.

But it wasn't lost on Chris. "The fuck?" he said, shoving Quentin. "When was this?"

"A long time ago," Jessica said. "Don't worry about it." She stood. "I'm gonna go get some dessert."

"Good idea," said Quentin, standing abruptly.

Chris stood, too. "Not without me, you're not."

"Why don't we *all* get some dessert?" Judith suggested dryly, pushing out of her chair.

As they snaked their way through the tables, Chris hung back and grabbed Jessica's arm. "Why didn't you tell me about the smiting range?"

"Can we talk about this later?"

He conceded with a minute nod.

And when dessert plates were cleaned without a single person at the table having suggested going out afterward, Jessica felt a heavy weight lifted from each of her shoulders.

While Chris squared away the check with the waiter, Jessica moved outside into the hot July night to say goodbye to her friends.

Quentin peeled off quickly after telling Jess they'd do another night out on the field soon. While Judith and Brian shared a few last jokes with Natalie and Kate, and Jesus, Destinee, and Rex listened closely while Jeremy explained the role of Big Soda in a recent rise of gang-related drownings, Miranda and Desmond approached her, smiling.

"Thanks for coming," Jessica said.

Another awkward hug.

"Yeah, I'm glad your mom invited us. Hey, I wanted to say"—Miranda stared at the ground for a moment before meeting Jessica's eye in what appeared to a Herculean effort—"I understand why you covered for him. And I'm not mad at you anymore. Or Chris. Or even Quentin, for that matter. Everyone becomes comfortable with who they are at their own pace."

While Jessica wanted to ask if that meant Miranda would get back together with Quentin, she suspected the answer already hovered over Miranda's shoulder in human form, smiling in a way that seemed to say, "Oh yeah, she told me all about this. We talk about everything. I know her better than you do."

"I'm really sorry I didn't tell you, Miranda. I didn't know what to do."

"No, you did the right thing."

Jessica decided to take a chance. "Want to get coffee soon? I work all week, but if you come into the bakery, I can hook you up and take a little break."

When Miranda winced, Jessica felt some of her lasagna climb back up her esophagus. "I would, but"—she cast a quick glance behind her, into the face of her new man—"we're leaving for Berkeley in the morning."

"Oh. Well, what time? Maybe you can swing by before."

Miranda shook her head slowly. "Red-eye. Have to be at the airport at four thirty."

"Ah. Okay."

Desmond piped in, "Actually, we had better get going

if we want to get sleep." He wrapped an arm around her shoulder, and with one last halfhearted wave, she left.

"Aw, damn ..." Chris said when he joined her a few minutes later. "Did Miranda already leave?"

"Yep." Jessica said. "She's gone."

Chapter Twelve

"Come on, Jess. Just one. *Please* just let me see you do it once." Chris extended the hand-painted ceramic plate to his side, ready to chuck it into the air toward the high ceiling of the empty ballroom at a moment's notice.

"No. I don't want to."

He threw his head back, groaning. "But it'll be so hot."

She probably should have been suspicious about what Chris was up to the moment she fell asleep and found herself in this grand ballroom, a long banquet table running down the center with startlingly incorrect place settings. She wasn't exactly Miss Manners, but she knew the forks and knives weren't supposed to be wrapped in a napkin and stuck in a juice glass next to each plate.

"I don't find smiting hot, Chris, I'm sorry. And I don't understand how you do, either. I can still see the look on your face when I smote that grackle."

Chris tossed the plate to the side, sending it shattering

on the marble floor. "Jess. That was"—he paused for the math—"seventeen years ago. You think I'm going to let a little childhood trauma stop me from making sweet love to my woman after she smites the shit out of a dinner plate?"

"I would hope so, yes."

He reached past her and grabbed another plate off the table. "Well, I'm not. Ready, set, go!" He chucked the plate into the air, his eyes glued to it, waiting for the moment of explosion.

But Jessica didn't lift a finger, and when the plate remained whole until it collided with the tile floor, he glared at his girlfriend. "Come *on!* It's not a big deal."

"Why are you so set on this?" she demanded. "It's a fucking plate!"

"I just think the smiting could, you know, spice things up a bit," he said. "Not that sex isn't already great, it's just that ... we haven't been having it."

She flopped back onto the king-size four-poster bed placed conspicuously next to the banquet table. Chris had been in charge of the location this time, and it was clear he hadn't put that much thought into it, failing to consider how each piece would complement every other one. "Oh come on, Chris. It's not like we've been trying and you can't get it up. We haven't been trying to begin with. We don't need to worry about spicing things up until we start putting in a little effort again."

He stepped forward eagerly. "Then let's do it! Let's have sex!"

Jessica winced and scratched the back of her neck. "I

don't know ... A girl can only get tackled by a three-hundred pound man so many times before the mood is lost."

Chris crossed his arms. "And a man can only be interrupted mid-orgasm by an oven timer so many times before he develops performance anxiety."

He raised a valid point. Jessica softened. "Don't you see what's going on here? If it takes me smiting something for us to want to have sex, maybe ... the spark is dead."

"No," said Chris precisely. "That's not it. I refuse to accept that."

"You don't have to accept it for it to be the truth."

He reached out and placed his hands on her upper arms. "Sex is what's keeping us together long-distance until one of us can move to where the other lives. I refuse to give up on it."

Did she want to give up on it? Was that what was happening here? She'd fought for it, even when God had done so much to make it impossible. She didn't want to follow the path God laid out for her, and that meant staying with Chris until ... marriage? Death? Was it worth it just to prove a point if the relationship was no longer what she wanted?

She was tired, even in her dream. Tired of fighting her so-called fate. Maybe she could fight it later, in another arena, but when it came to her and Chris, it felt like the war was over. They'd lost.

Tiny hooks that had lived in her heart for all these years, tethering her and Chris together came unstuck all at once. But not without leaving behind deep, stinging, open wounds. "I don't want to live in Philadelphia, Chris. I have a business here. And you're there for at least four years. If sex is the only thing holding us together, and we haven't been having sex ..." She let him fill in the blank.

He swallowed hard, the corners of his mouth sagging as he stared at her. "I don't want this to happen."

"I know," she said. The impulse to hug him was strong, though it wasn't colored with the usual sentiment. "I don't know that I want it either. But I think it's already laid out for us. Like this table." She motioned to it, adding, "Well, probably better than this table."

"Yeah," he said, morosely, "I never took cotillion."

"Neither did I. But just for reference, the forks and knives lie flat next to the plate."

"But which side?" he asked, desperately.

She shook her head slowly, regretfully. "I really don't know, Chris."

His hands fell from her arms. "Can we still call each other, or should this be a clean break?"

"I'm fine with calling."

He bowed his head. "Okay. You can call me anytime you need, Jess. Day or night. I still love you."

"And I still love—"

He disappeared in a puff of white powder before she could even finish.

It was over. She and Chris were broken up. The fact that it had been amicable and logical made it instantly worse. Or at least it would probably feel worse if she could feel anything at all.

How could she not want to hurt him yet want him to beg her not to end it at the same time?

Wait, no, there it was. She *could* feel something. Something big, like the bulge in the ocean surface just before a tidal wave ...

She whirled around just in time to smite every last plate, cup, and spoon along with the entire banquet table.

Chapter Thirteen

Breakfast for dinner had become the new norm for Jessica since she opened the bakery. While she bagged most of the leftover items that could be put in pairs or groups of four to sell at a discount the next day, certain ones like the cream cheese danishes and broccoli and cheese empanadas didn't have that long a shelf life before they became soggy and the dairy became unfit for public consumption. Those along with the odd ones left after the rest of their kind were grouped went home with Destinee, Judith, or herself. The pro was that Jessica hadn't needed to cook dinner in months. The con was that pooping was becoming a real labor. She suspected the same drawback might have been affecting her employees as of late, as they politely refused what Jessica tried to send them with at the end of the day.

Tonight, though, Destinee wasn't refusing, and Jessica was happy to have company at her condo for her carb-y dinner. Her mom and Rex had accepted the invitation gladly, perhaps sensing that Jessica would only make a point of inviting them over if there was a good reason for it.

It was Sunday, July eighth, which meant Jessica had closed early like she always did on Sundays (and because she now had Sampson, bless his awful heart, she could enjoy a little time to herself after work). It also meant it had only been hours since she'd woken up from her break-up dream to find Chris's side of the bed cold and him and all his things gone to the airport. He hadn't even woken her up to say goodbye.

Jessica pulled a quiche from the oven and popped a baking pan with a half-dozen strips of turkey bacon in its place.

"Smells delicious," her mom said as Jessica set it on the island in front of their high stools where Destinee and Rex were perched.

"I appreciate you going to the effort," Rex added, "and while I believe you when you say you don't need my help, I do hope you'll let me know if that changes."

Jessica forced a smile while she sliced up the quiche. Watching her perform any traditionally female role made Rex crawl in his skin, but she supposed he'd also learned the flip side of that, where he was supposed to let women decide what they did and didn't want to do. She almost felt for him. Feminism, like femininity, often existed in a web of unnavigable contradictions. It must be hard to enter into that logical maelstrom in adulthood, not having been primed since childhood for the confusion by being told you were both too fat *and* too skinny, too passive *and* too bitchy, too prudish *and* too slutty.

"Wait," Destinee said, staring at the slice of spinach quiche on her place. "You're not gonna miracle it first?"

Jessica paused, the knife hovering over the surface where she was about to cut her own slice. "Are you kidding me? You see me do that every day at work."

Destinee pursed her lips. "Well, ex-cuse me for not becoming numb to the miracles of my only child. And no, I'm not kidding."

"Fine." She closed her eyes and waved her hand over the remaining portion of quiche like she was swatting at a fly. "There."

"Ooh! That's a good one, baby! Look, Rex, you can even see that little freckle under her left eye. She's had that since she was a baby."

"That's just a piece of bell pepper, mom." Jessica switching out Destinee's piece with a gluten-free one.

After they'd started in on the meal, Destinee began fishing. "That was quite some birthday dinner last night, wasn't it?"

There were a lot of ways Jessica could have played this. She considered going along for a while, recapping the highs and lows, then slowly leading into the dream and what had transpired. Or she could simply stick to the dinner and wait a while before dropping in that Chris took himself to the airport first thing, inviting Destinee to ask why.

But both of those required more emotional energy than she had left after the long and painful day.

"Chris and I broke up."

Destinee inhaled deeply, sitting up straight, which dislodged a burp. She pounded her chest twice to make sure that was the last of it, then said, "I'm sorry, Jess. You doing okay?"

Jessica leaned her elbows against the island, bending at the waist. "Surprisingly, yes. I mean, I'm not great, but it doesn't hurt like I thought it would. Maybe later on it will."

Rex piped up. "He's a good man, that Riley, but if you believe the relationship was stifling your continued growth, then it was the right call, McCloud."

"Thanks, Coach."

"Mind if I ask why?" Destinee said.

Jessica shrugged and made for the fridge, pulling out three beers—two Dos Equis and one of the craft beers she'd grabbed in her emotional haze on the way home because the labels had zebras on them. She put the two imports in front of her guests and popped open the other for herself. "It's kind of what Rex said. There wasn't a future in it. At least not one right now. I really wanted to make it work to prove God wrong and show him I could make up my own mind, but then it turned out that my mind wasn't into it after all. I just want to focus on the bakery for a while and let Chris focus on his football. Is that weird?"

Destinee reached out and placed a hand on Jessica's cheek. "Not at all. You know I was single for years before I started fooling around with this one. There's nothing wrong with being single. What's wrong is staying in a relationship for the sake of *not* being single."

"You mind if I keep in contact with him?" Rex asked timidly. "I just mean, I enjoy keeping up with his career, and I'm not sure who else is gonna remind him to line up his hips before he throws on the scramble ..."

Probably his professional coaches will do that. She swallowed down the sarcasm. "Yeah, of course you can stay in contact with him, Rex. Hell, I might still stay in contact with him. We decided that was okay, that it didn't have to be a clean break."

Destinee and Rex exchanged a quick glance.

"What?" Jessica said. "What's that look for?"

Destinee was the one who explained. "Sometimes a clean break is the only way to keep from torturing someone when you end it. You may have called it quits on good terms, but if you keep up communication, you're likely to end up obsessing over who they're with and so on until you become so jealous you decide to ruin them for everyone else if you can't have them."

"Sounds like you're speaking from personal experience," Jessica remarked.

Destinee nodded and jabbed a finger up toward the ceiling.

Rex stood. "I gotta take a quick piss." He rushed into the bedroom.

Jessica watched him go, almost tripping on his own feet in his hurry. "He still doesn't like you talking about your eternal ex?"

Instead of answering, Destinee leaned forward and whispered, "It's getting out of control, isn't it?"

"Huh? What is?"

"His feminism."

Jessica wrinkled her nose. "I mean, it's a lot, but—"

"I haven't gotten a full night's sleep in *two weeks!* You know why?"

Jessica had her suspicions, so instead of replying, she cringed, hoping her mother would take the hint.

She didn't. "That man is *hellbent* on giving me multiple orgasms before he gets down to the business himself. It's stressing me out. And I feel like his tongue's going to fall right off from overuse. I swear to your father, the man was slurring his speech the other morning! I think he pulled a muscle. I ain't joking! Meanwhile, I just want to bang. I like it! It's fun, and it's about all the cardio my saggy ass gets. But no, he won't even consider it until I get mine, and then I'm so stressed and annoyed, I can't deliver!" Her cheeks were flushed by the time she finished, and Jessica could tell her mother had been bottling up that complaint for a while.

"You're telling me," Jessica replied slowly, "that Rex's feminism is hurting your sex life?"

Destinee slapped the counter. "Yes!"

"Because he wants to give you too many orgasms?" She hoped she wasn't grimacing as intensely on the outside as she was on the inside.

"Exactly. You nailed it, baby."

The toilet flushed and Destinee quickly hissed, "Don't

tell him I said any of this." Then she stuffed her face with food a moment before Rex appeared again.

As he lowered himself onto the stool, he added, "I just thought of this while I was taking a leak. I want to be clear how impressed I am by your desire to be independent, McCloud."

She decided to take the compliment because she needed it, but then followed up with, "You mean because I'm single now?" She'd considered herself independent in a lot of ways even before the break-up.

"Because I know Riley was helping you pay the bills to keep the bakery afloat, and there's nothing wrong with that, but to cut yourself off from that ... Bold. Brave." He applauded her, an audience of one.

Meanwhile, her heart dropped into her stomach. "Oh ... shit." She set her fork down slowly so that if she passed out, she wouldn't accidentally impale herself with it. "I hadn't ... it hadn't even occurred to me."

"Baby," Destinee said, jumping up. "Are you hyperventilating?"

Jessica couldn't answer the question, though, because she was hyperventilating.

"Breathe, McCloud!" Rex shouted, which didn't help. "Hands over your head. Open the lungs! Tap into the strength of the divine feminine!"

"Knock it off!" Destinee spat. "She *is* the divine feminine, for christ's sake!" She shoved him to the side as she rounded the island to rub Jessica's back.

So caught up in trying to control in the angst and

emotion that came with the split, she hadn't even examined the practical fall out. Chris's money was an integral part of her operational budget until she found a way to generate more profit each month. Sampson had even snidely commented that if she didn't have a man helping her out, her business would be shuttered in a matter of months.

Man, she hated Sampson.

Could she still ask Chris for money now that they'd broken up?

Of course she *could* and he wouldn't turn her down.

But she wouldn't. That wasn't how this worked. She was on her own now. The bakery had to be completely self-sufficient. No more room for low sales days, no more room for setbacks.

"I'm fine," she said, catching her breath. "I'm fine. Everything will be just fine."

But she knew that those words had never been uttered by someone who actually believed them.

Chapter Fourteen

Jessica was not fine.

She stared up at the living room ceiling on a weekend afternoon when she should have been at work.

Of course the first vacation I take is one I can't enjoy.

Destinee hadn't left her much of a choice, though. She'd practically run her out of her own bakery on a Friday and said don't come back until Monday. Jessica might have been the boss, but Destinee was still the boss.

It had taken two weeks and one skin-tight billing cycle before the reality of the break-up hit like an oncoming bus. Sampson had all but lost his mind when she'd explained one of their main streams of income had dried up. His snide and subtle comments she'd grown accustomed to gave way to unfiltered wrath on the next phone call. And she'd simply leaned against the wall behind the display case in the bakery, phone to her ear, and accepted the verbal abuse from her employee like it was a doctor-prescribed bloodletting. *This is fine,* she'd assured herself.

And not unsurprisingly, it was shortly after that when the minor breakdown began to unfurl.

She'd forced herself out of bed that morning since the mattress reminded her too much of Chris, and found herself spread out on the couch a minute later. Had she been there for an hour? Five hours? Eight hours?

IT'S BEEN TWENTY MINUTES.

Not you.

HEAVENLY CHILD, THIS IS NOT A GOOD LOOK ON YOU.

I don't care.

THOU SHALT PULL THYSELF TOGETHER.

She knew what happened when she refused his thou shalts. It was never good. But she hadn't been kidding when she'd said she didn't care.

No.

There was a moment's pause before: *I'LL LET THAT GO, BUT ONLY BECAUSE I KNOW HOW MISERABLE YOU ARE EVERY TIME YOU BREAK UP WITH ANGEL BOY.*

You truly are the most merciful of gods.

(THERE IS NO GOD BUT ME.) FOR THE HOLY RECORD, THE LORD SENSES YOUR SARCASM.

Great. That was the hope. This is all your fault anyway.

ALMIGHTY SHOCKER RIGHT THERE, MAKING ME THE SCAPEGOAT FOR YOUR PROBLEMS.

It's your goddamn path I got back onto! You wanted Chris and me to break up a while ago. No matter how hard I try, it looks like I don't have a choice after all.

DID I EVER TELL YOU ABOUT THE NIGHT I MET YOUR MOTHER?

What? Ew. No.

Considering her birth was a result of a one-night stand, she didn't want to know the details.

OBVIOUSLY YOU WERE CONCEIVED THAT NIGHT, BUT THAT WASN'T UNTIL WE WERE IN THE BACK SEAT OF HER CAR. PREVIOUS TO THAT, SHE SAT NEXT TO ME AT THE BAR AND I OFFERED TO BUY HER A DRINK AND ASKED IF SHE WOULD BE INTERESTED IN GOING HOME WITH ME. SHE TURNED ME DOWN.

Is there a point to this story other than admitting you're a predator? Wait, is this confession for you?

HUSH. THIS IS IMPORTANT.

She thought her concerns were pretty important, too, but she listened anyway.

YOUR MOTHER WAS NOT THE FIRST TO REJECT AN OFFERING FROM THE LORD. IT WAS WHAT SHE DID NEXT THAT IMPRESSED ME. SHE CALLED ME A CREEP—

You were.

—AND MOVED TO THE OTHER SIDE OF THE BAR. THIS WAS NOT PART OF THE LORD'S PLAN. I HAD NOT FORESEEN HER REACTION, AND IT

WAS THE FIRST TIME IN MANY, MANY YEARS THAT I WAS SURPRISED.

Sounds like you got a little too cocksure about your game. Good for her.

I APPROACHED HER AGAIN, APOLOGIZED FOR BEING SO FORWARD. SHE GRABBED HER DRINK AND RETURNED TO HER PREVIOUS SPOT AT THE BAR, BUT NOT BEFORE TELLING ME TO LEAVE HER BE.

BUT I COULD NOT! NOT WHEN I WAS SO SHOCKED BY HER BEHAVIOR.

You're such a stalker.

I DO NOT DENY IT. I RETURNED TO SIT NEXT TO HER AND EXPLAINED THAT I WAS GOD. AND YOU KNOW WHAT SHE DID NEXT?

Not a clue.

SHE SLAPPED ME ACROSS THE FACE.

Of course she did. Why would she believe you were God?

YOU MISUNDERSTAND. SHE DID BELIEVE ME. SHE TOLD ME SO. AND THEN SHE SLAPPED ME ANYWAY. AND SO IT WAS THAT SHE HAD THRICE DENIED THE LORD.

I assume you didn't see the smack coming, either. Jessica hadn't expected this story to cheer her up, but by god, it did.

THE LORD DID NOT.

You deserved it.

INDEED. SHE LAID OUT THE HARDSHIPS OF

HER LIFE AND, YES, EACH ONE WAS MY FAULT. IT WAS ONLY AFTER SHE HAD DELIVERED HER VERBAL LASHING THAT SHE CALMED DOWN AND WE BEGAN TO TALK. AND THEN ONE THING LED TO ANOTHER—THAT WAS PART OF MY PLAN—AND A MIRACLE WAS CONCEIVED.

Okay, so glossing over that last bit, why are you telling me this?

THERE IS NO SET PATH. THERE IS AN EASY PATH, AND THAT IS THE ONE MOST PEOPLE TRAVEL. BUT NOT YOUR MOTHER. YOU MCCLOUD WOMEN ARE FULL OF SURPRISES.

But I ended up on your path after all. I broke up with Chris.

YOU DID. BUT YOU DIDN'T HAVE TO. LOTS OF PEOPLE WOULDN'T HAVE. THE RESULT WAS THE SAME OVER TIME, BUT YOU TOOK ANOTHER PATH TO GET THERE, AND THE CHOICE WAS YOURS.

The phone rang from her bedside table. It was so far away ...

That's what voicemail was for.

Perhaps if she'd had this conversation with her Father at a different point in time, it would have proved helpful. But as it was, God's words brought her little comfort because they brought her no money.

Who do I know who's rich?

God didn't speak. For once, he let the rhetorical

question sit without answering it. He must really feel sorry for her.

Jeremy Archer was rich. He owned an entire media empire, for shit's sake. He could have afforded to buy Jesus his own mansion to live in.

Which begged the question of why he didn't, why he insisted the messiah share his two-bedroom condo ...

Jeremy was also batshit insane from years of denying to himself and others that he was an angel. And that meant he would likely give her the money if she asked (the angelic part) but it would come with so many strings attached, she'd end up just another one of his marionettes that he could jerk around when his next insane conspiracy coursed through his bloodstream.

The only other rich person she knew was Jameson Fractal, and hell no.

Chris was the only person she felt comfortable taking money from without needing to repay it, and she'd cast him off.

The phone rang again.

Should I get that?

THOU SHALT.

She decided not to push her luck and did as He commanded this time.

Swinging her legs around, she pushed herself off the couch with a moan. By the time she'd reached her phone, it'd stopped ringing again. She unlocked the screen, and before she could see who the missed calls were from, it started ringing again.

The contact was Mom.

"What's up?"

Destinee's voice sounded like someone had lassoed her vocal cords as they struggled against the ropes. "Don't freak out, baby, but, well, I don't know how else to say it other than we have a little disaster over here, and it might be best if the boss showed up."

Jessica gripped the phone tightly as if she could intimidate it into delivering better news. "I'm gonna need more details."

"Best if I don't give those to you before you get on the road. Just come over here. And like I said, don't freak out. But, gahdamn, what a disaster."

Jessica ended the call and scrambled to find her flip-flops and bag, then she was out the front door.

It was only when she nearly walked right into Jeremy Archer on her doorstep, and he said, "I dig your style today, Jessica," that she realized she was not dressed for public consumption. But it didn't matter. She reached in her canvas tote, grabbed her invisibility sunglasses and cap, and marched toward the parking garage.

By the time she arrived at It is Risen, she was expecting to find a pile of rubble and ashes in place of the structure. Her worst fear would have been confirmed, that whoever had set fire to her food truck had come back to finish the job.

But instead, the building was still there, not even the least bit charred, and the only sign of something being awry was that the Open sign was flipped to Closed.

She pulled around the back and parked, then rushed inside.

Destinee was waiting by the phone, leaning against the paperwork shelf.

Jessica shivered. The kitchen was freezing. Was her mother having hot flashes already? "Okay, I'm here. What the hell is going on?"

"Follow me." She nodded around the corner toward the cold storage, and Jessica hurried after her.

Destinee pulled open the freezer door, and when no frost swirled out, the problem became obvious.

Dwayne hadn't properly shut the freezer door. "That dumb son of a bitch! Was it open all night?"

"Yep," Destinee said.

"I told him to make sure to shut the damn thing," Jessica growled. How much inventory had been wasted? And just when they were running so tight.

"It wasn't just a little bit open, Jess. I think more of the food would have made it if it was just a little bit open."

"He left it wide open?"

Destinee nodded.

"But that's ... that just sounds malicious."

"I don't know what to tell you. I'm not saying you're wrong, but I just don't get why he'd do it on purpose. I hardly ever interacted with the guy—he always had his earbuds in—but he seemed fine enough, coming in early. I guess you just don't know about some people."

If only that were the case, but Jessica had never had a great feeling about Dwayne. They'd gotten off to a rocky start, and things had never improved. Sure, he got the job done, but each time she spoke with him was an exercise in holding her tongue.

She put her hands on her head, staring at the dough that was probably crawling with bacteria now. And never mind the expense of leaving a freezer like this open all night to cool the entire place. Could she cook away the bacteria? Maybe she had some sort of sanitation miracle up her sleeve.

NOPE.

"It's fine," she said. "It's fine. We can make it work."

IT IS NOT. THE LORD THOUGHT HE MADE HIMSELF CLEAR ABOUT SANITATION IN THE OLD TESTAMENT.

Destinee cleared her throat awkwardly. "There's one other thing."

Jessica whirled away from the crime scene to stare wide-eyed at her mother. "What other thing?"

"Breathe," Destinee said.

"No, no, no ..." She pointed accusingly at her mother. "You're being too calm. Oh no, it's really bad isn't it?" Destinee cringed. "It is. It's terrible. What is it? Just tell me. Did Judith quit? Are there naked pictures of me floating around? Oh God! Did someone accuse Sir David Attenborough of improper behavior?!" She covered her mouth to hold back the scream.

"Knock it off," Destinee snapped. "You're talking foolish! It's none of those things." She reached in her back pocket and pulled out a folded up letter, which she flattened and handed to Jessica.

Before Jessica's mind could make sense of the red lettering at the top, Destinee provided a rundown. "They're claiming the mortgage is two months overdue."

Jessica screwed up her face. "What? No, it's not."

"They say it is."

"But Sampson said he paid it."

"Well, he didn't."

It didn't compute. "But, does that mean we have two months' of mortgage sitting in the account?"

Destinee grimaced, gazing sympathetically at her daughter. "Oh, I doubt that's how this went."

"There's only one way to get to the bottom of this." She reached in her bag and pulled out her phone.

"I don't know that he's gonna answer, but okay."

Jessica called him anyway.

She got his voicemail. "Hey, Sampson. It's Jessica McCloud. Just got a letter from the mortgage company saying we've missed two payments. Maybe you sent it to the wrong address or something? Just let me know and I'm sure we can figure it out."

As soon as she hung up, she realized what a fool she'd been. She narrowed her eyes at her phone screen. "He stole it, didn't he?"

Destinee nodded. "That'd be my guess. And, um, it wasn't just the mortgage." She led Jessica over to the stacks of bills on the shelf. "I opened a few of these. I hope you don't mind."

Jessica pinched the bridge of her nose. "Balls." She inhaled and let it out slowly. There was no getting around this nightmare. "I assumed those were just invoices, so I kept passing them along to him. I didn't even open them. I just wanted them off my plate."

Destinee put her arm around Jessica's shoulder. "You didn't do anything wrong, baby. I know how overwhelmed you were."

Jessica looked up at her mother. "You're awfully calm about this."

"If I didn't already believe Sampson's ass was on a beach in Mexico, I'd have tracked him down and put some lead in him. But he's beyond my reach now, so I gotta let it go. Can't shoot 'em all." She sighed mournfully.

"The timing is just so ... ugh! It's almost like they planned it! Next thing I know, Kumal is going to hand over all my passwords to Eugene Thornton or something." She gasped. "Wait. You don't think he ..."

Destinee shrugged. "It's been that kind of day, hasn't it?"

Jessica ran to the laptop on the shelf and powered it up, immediately typing in her web address. "Oh, for shit's sake!"

Destinee hovered over her shoulder. "Oh, Jess." Her hand flew up to her mouth. "That's *really* offensive."

She'd never thought she'd hear her mother utter those words, but there were none other that would have fit the bright, GIF-heavy page that jumped out at her. "This doesn't even make sense," Jessica whimpered. "Why is Jesus in a bikini?"

"And why are there so many upside down crosses everywhere?" Destinee added. "Where's the menu button?"

Jessica found it, hidden in the top right corner. The button was a pentacle-shaped loaf of rye bread.

When the menu loaded, Jessica yelped and covered the screen. *"What the fuck, Kumal?!"* She turned to see if her mom had caught a glimpse of it before she'd managed to hide it.

Judging by Destinee's open mouth and wide eyes, she had. She placed a hand on her collarbone to steady herself as she said, "I cannot imagine a scenario in which an animated graphic of you deep-throating a baguette is called for."

Jessica couldn't imagine that scenario, either. And she also couldn't remember a time when Destinee had been so far in the red that her accent went into hiding to allow more proper handling of the English language to take over. It was like where the flame was so hot it burned blue. "Please don't kill him, Mom. He's brown. It'll be called a hate crime and you'll be in prison for a long, long time."

Destinee's chest heaved. "Well, I'm gonna need to kill *somebody*, baby. And I'm caring less and less who it is."

"I don't know how to take this down." Jessica scrolled to the bottom, searching fruitlessly for a "take this page down" button that she knew wouldn't be there. "How long has this been live?" she wailed, scrolling frantically.

Finally, she exed out of the window and tried to breathe. It didn't work.

She slapped the laptop closed. "I don't understand," she moaned, squishing her face in her hands.

"I do," Destinee said. "I told you not to let Dolores do the hiring. I told you!"

Jessica parted her fingers to sneak a peek at her mother. "Are you serious? You're bringing this up now?"

"What? I'm just sayin', baby. Why trust the judgment of a woman who sent you off alone at a zoo with a pedophile?"

Jessica's head shot up fully now. "Mom, that was fourteen years ago! You're really gonna act like I should have known this would happen because over a decade ago she made a mistake?"

Destinee braced her fists on her hips, her right leg kicked out to the side. "Yeah, that's how I'm gonna act. I ain't never sent you off with a pedophile, and I had all kinds of opportunities to."

Jessica narrowed her eyes at her mother. "You sent me off alone with Jimmy Dean. Multiple times."

As she swallowed, Destinee's power pose softened. "Well, that's different. He never tried to, you know, touch you." But it was clear even she thought that a weak defense, considering the reverend had found other ways to traumatize Jessica in her early years. And her later years.

Groaning and putting her face back into her hands, Jessica whined, "I don't even know where to start."

Destinee rubbed her daughter's back and crooned, "I

think the best place to start is calling the most tech savvy person you know and getting her to help you take down that awful website."

It was as good a plan as any, and Jessica grabbed her phone and dialed Quentin's number.

She'd expected him to come no sooner than lunchtime, and had planned on spending each excruciating minute growing angrier and angrier at her obvious scapegoat: Mrs. Thomas. But Quentin was over in twenty minutes, coming straight from his work that was fifteen minutes away.

"Whoa!" he shouted, leaning away from the screen as it loaded the bakery's homepage. He snuck a glance at her. "This isn't a joke?"

"No," she said miserably.

"Now *that* makes a lot more sense." He nodded at Destinee who, in her futile attempt to salvage the remaining ingredients, pounded a hunk of dough into a spongy, useless brick.

"Can you fix it?" Jessica asked.

"Yeah, but I'll need a login. Do you have that info?" He pulled up a login page with the host and waited.

"No, I don't know what Kumal used."

USERNAME KUMALLABALLA. PASSWORD DJKUMAL69.

She passed along the message.

You knew that was his password and username and you didn't warn me he was a lunatic?

JUDGE NOT LEST YE BE JUDGED, MEXICANKICKER7. BESIDES, EXACTLY EIGHTY-

SEVEN PERCENT OF PASSWORDS IN EXISTENCE
HAVE THE NUMBER SIXTY-NINE IN THEM.

You keep track of everyone's passwords?

ONLY THE SEXY ONES. THEY BRING THE
LORD MIGHTY GIGGLES.

"Okay, the page is disabled," said Quentin.

"No one else can see it?"

"Nope. But it also means your business is without a website."

Jessica sighed. "A step in the right direction."

"If you want," Quentin said, "I can build you one. Nothing fancy, but also nothing objectively offensive."

Jessica threw her arms around him, nestling her face into the crook of his neck. "I love you."

He patted her on the back twice. "Yeah, yeah." Then he pushed her away. "You know I'm always down to be your fake boyfriend, but never your real rebound. Keep it in your pants, McCloud."

Temporarily ignoring the fact that he knew about the breakup and she hadn't been the one to tell him, which meant he and Chris has talked about it, she asked, "Why do you always help me?"

"I'm an angel. I can't not. Or, I can not, but it would suck."

"Right, that's what I mean. What happens when you don't help me?"

He pressed his lips together and narrowed his eyes in thought, leaning back in his chair with this hands clasped behind his head. Finally he said, "You remember when we had art class together in high school?" She nodded. "There was this one day when you asked if anyone had a pencil sharpener you could borrow for your colored pencils. I did. I had one in my backpack. But I didn't want to let you use it because you were unbelievably bad at sharpening pencils and you always made the tip break off, and then I'd have to dig it out before I could use it."

"That's not true."

"It is. It was a running joke with Chris and me. So, as soon as you asked if anyone had one, I felt this sort of energy in my spine, right between my shoulder blades, and when I decided not to say anything, that energy immediately fell into my stomach and I had to run to the bathroom and because I wasn't sure if I was going to throw up or shit my pants."

Jessica's mouth had fallen open. "God was going to make you shit your pants because you didn't give me a pencil sharpener?"

"Yes, I think your Heavenly Father was the cause of the sudden digestive issues. Even today when you called, I considered not coming, and then I got the rumbles and knew I'd better head over."

She plopped down into the empty chair across from his. "Oh boy. This ... this raises some questions."

"Like how Chris was able to leave?"

"I was thinking more along the lines of ethics and morals, but that too."

"Did you ever ask him to stay?"

She shook her head. "No. Never."

There was a silence, then Quentin added, "For what it's worth, I think he's always helped because he loves you, not because he doesn't want to shit his pants."

"And you?"

He beamed warmly. "I also love you and want to help. But mostly it's the poop thing."

Quentin left to return to his real job, promising to have a new site up by the end of the day. With that small bit of good news, the dense fog in her brain began to lift.

What did she do now?

She supposed she just kept going.

Chapter Fifteen

In the weeks that followed, there was good news and there was bad news.

The good news was that Jessica managed to keep the mortgage company from foreclosing on her bakery. That process involved a long, in-person meeting with a severe woman who didn't want to hear a word out of Jessica's mouth and the severe woman's supervisor, who ultimately granted them leniency under the given circumstances ... and who Jessica highly suspected was an angel.

The bad news was that Jessica hadn't gotten more than four hours of sleep a night, had been unsuccessful in reaching any of her nefarious employees to officially fire them, was experiencing record-low sales, and was fairly sure Judith was searching for another job to escape the miserable work environment for which Jessica herself was solely responsible. Part of Jessica's crankiness could have been due to her decision not to take a paycheck beyond what she needed to fill her gas tank, meaning she ate nothing but leftovers from work (only slightly more extreme than usual) and hadn't had a drink—or a vegetable—in weeks.

The early August heat let itself in through the front door every time a new guest arrived, and as luck would have it, the register was right in the line of the blast, leaving Jessica a sweaty mess as she copped a squat on a tall stool, staring daggers at the lone customer who'd been camping all day, had bought only a small coffee, and had helped himself to a free refill every half hour.

It only made it worse that it was her regular, Darius ... or maybe Donny—god, what was his name? He mentioned it in every interaction, she saw it on his credit card every time he paid, but it just wouldn't stick. Which make it completely different from his gaze, which stuck to her and followed her almost everywhere she went as she served customers, emptied the dish bins by the trash cans, refilled the ice machine, and even sat on her ass like she was now, trying not to melt from the heat mingled with her exhaustion.

She narrowed all her negative thoughts on his weak chin and penis-like nose.

"Damn you, Dante," she mumbled.

His eyes shot open and a hand flew up to his chest. He stared down at his coffee cup like it was the culprit for the sudden heart palpitations. While Jessica felt slightly guilty for letting her anger get the best of her, she also knew it wasn't life threatening.

I should just kick him out and close early.

DO NOT LOSE HOPE, CHILD.

That's not me losing hope. That's me hoping to get in bed before two in the morning.

She glanced at the clock above the door. Only a quarter past five. Would closing two hours early be bad? Probably no one would notice. And who cared anyway? A haze of doom hung over the entire enterprise. With sales what they were, she was simply biding her time until she had to close her doors forever.

YOU SHOULD REJOICE. YOU WANTED FINANCIAL INDEPENDENCE, CORRECT?

Jessica grunted.

YOU ARE ALMOST THERE! JUST SIXTY-ONE THOUSAND MORE TO BE CAUGHT UP, AND THEN THE REST OF THE MORTGAGE.

It feels like you're mocking me.

IGNORE YOUR FEELINGS. I AM THE LORD. I SEE MANY WAYS OUT OF THIS HOLE FOR YOU, AND SOME OF THEM DO NOT INVOLVE BREAKING MY COMMANDMENTS.

But some of them do? Wait, is one of them becoming a contract killer? Because I'm at the point where I would consider it. Maybe two more nights without enough sleep.

THOU SHALT NOT BECOME A CONTRACT KILLER.

That's bullshit. Don't you have the power to forgive me for sins if you want to?

YES.

Then couldn't you just give me a freebie? A get-out-of-jail-free card?

I COULD. WOULD YOU LIKE THAT, DAUGHTER?

Would I— Yes, I would like that very much! "For shit's sake," she mumbled. *Yes, mighty and all that lord, I would very much like a fucking get-out-of-jail-free card.*

THEN IT IS DONE. YOU HAVE ONE. MIGHT THE LORD DISCOURAGE YOU FROM USING IT IMMEDIATELY?

Depends on why.

YOU'LL NEED IT LATER.

You're telling me things are going to get worse than this?

God laughed, rumbling in her skull and making her eyes cross. *OH, YES. SO MUCH WORSE. OOH MANKIND! WHEN I THINK ABOUT THE WORSENESS HEADING YOUR WAY, IT'S LIKE CHANG CHAO PHAT ALL OVER AGAIN.*

Chang Chao who?

YOU'VE NEVER MET HIM. HE'S SUPER DEAD.

Isn't there something you can do to, I dunno, prevent all the misery heading my way?

SURE, BUT IT WOULDN'T HELP YOU IN THE LONG RUN. BESIDES, YOUR STORY IS TURNING OUT WAY MORE INTERESTING THAN I THOUGHT IT WOULD. A MUCH WIDER DEMOGRAPHICAL APPEAL, TOO. THE LORD EXPECTED MORE OF A WOMAN EIGHTEEN TO THIRTY-FIVE THING, BUT THERE IS A

UNIVERSAL INTEREST TO IT. I COULD SEE IT DOING WELL WITH MEN AND THE THIRTY-FIVE TO SIXTY GROUP.

I'm glad you're so pleased with it, but if you don't mind, I have some sleep-deprived misery to get back to.

TRUE ENOUGH.

Jessica rubbed at her temples, the buzzing from God's laughter still aggravating the low-grade headache she'd enjoyed all week. She reached below the register and grabbed a bottle of acetaminophen, shaking herself a couple and throwing them back with a long gulp of cold coffee. When was the last time she'd eaten? It was stupid how she forgot to eat while surrounded by food.

She grabbed a strawberry kolache out of the case and threw it in the microwave. As she took her first bite a minute later, the front door opened, blasting her with hot air and making her eyes roll back in her head.

When she saw who it was that had entered on the heatwave, she gripped the kolache too tightly, sending hot jam dripping down her hand. "Ow, shit!" She quickly licked the scalding substance from her skin, which only meant she now had it on her tongue.

As she sucked air in and out, knowing any chance of actually tasting her on-the-go dinner had just been burned away, Mrs. Thomas made her way over, beaming like she wasn't a major player in Jessica's current miserable predicament.

"Oh good, I don't have to wait in line!" she said brightly.

Didn't she know that wasn't a good indicator for the longevity of a business?

Jessica was unsure how to proceed. Mrs. Thomas had been a perfect scapegoat for all of her frustration in the days since Sampson, Kumal, and Dwayne had screwed her royally.

Of course, she hadn't let Mrs. Thomas know about any of that.

In fact, she hadn't even mentioned the debacle or the firings to the woman. How could she? She had no clue how to confront the one person who'd always had her back.

It was strange seeing her long-time hero in this new light. Features of the woman's face that had always seemed a familiar comfort to Jessica now left her feeling slightly repulsed. The woman's plumpness, which had presented as matronly and congenial before, seemed a bit too lumpy and careless. The smile lines at the corners of her eyes could now be referred to only as crow's feet. And as the woman grinned at her, Jessica noticed for the first time that Mrs. Thomas could have benefitted greatly from some orthodontic work.

The unforgiving filter of Jessica's bitterness left her feeling sodden and ashamed. This wasn't how good people thought about others. Mrs. Thomas had been Jessica's safety net more times than she could count on both hands, and the woman made one mistake and now she was ready to toss her to the wayside?

Wow, I'm really awful.

The self-loathing was a small comfort, and she vowed to push ahead without becoming petulant.

"What's wrong?" Mrs. Thomas said, stopping short and tilting her head to the side.

"Nothing," Jessica lied.

"No, something's definitely wrong. If nothing else, you look more stressed than ever. Are you delegating enough to the new hires?"

Unsure what else to say, Jessica said, "I haven't been sleeping well."

Mrs. Thomas nodded. "I see that." She glanced around the cafe area and then said, "Since you're not busy, why don't you grab us two coffees and we can sit and catch up?"

More coffee sounded good. Catching up did not. "Yeah, sure."

Despite her resolution to avoid coming off as petulant, by the time Jessica had grabbed the coffees and sat across from Mrs. Thomas, who had, oddly enough, picked a table right next to Danny (Drey?), she was fuming and ready to launch an attack.

But she couldn't. Not with his eyes glued to her. Ugh. Could she kick him out on the grounds that she couldn't stand his meek, squirrelly demeanor and penis nose? This was Texas, after all. She was pretty sure she could kick out anyone for anything she liked. The way he stared at her, all watery eyes and moist lips, gave the impression he was always only seconds away from saying something incredibly disgusting about her physical appearance.

Mrs. Thomas thanked her for the coffee then said,

"You know, the whole point of hiring people is to allow you to either work less or work the same but use the time more meaningfully."

"I fired them," Jessica blurted.

"Who?"

"All of them."

Mrs. Thomas sat up straight. "Oh!" She paused, and Jessica allowed her a moment to soak it in. "I imagine it took quite a lot of courage to fire your own mother, but it was probably for the best to let her—"

"What? No! I didn't fire my mom. I fired all the ones *you* sent me. Or at least I've tried to. None of them have returned my calls, but, judging by the fact that I haven't seen or heard from them in weeks, I think they got the message."

"What happened?" Mrs. Thomas asked. "Was their work subpar?"

Jessica's mouth fell open as she tried to think where to start. "Let's see ... They were each rude to me in their own way—which I could have dealt with. But then Sampson stole thousands of dollars from me and left me in deep shit, Dwayne decided not to close the freezer one night and ruined all the stockpile of food I'd miracled so I could take a few days off to recover from a breakup, and Kumal launched the worst website of all time without running it by me first, even though I told him multiple times to let me sign off on it."

Mrs. Thomas nodded sympathetically. "I'm sorry to hear about your breakup, Jessica. Are you okay?"

"I'm fine," she ground out. "I'm sure you're happy. You never liked him anyway."

Gasping, Mrs. Thomas leaned back in her seat. "Jessica, I'm not sure where you got that impression. I love Christopher like one of my own. And obviously I feel that way and more about you." Her posture and voice softened as she continued. "Do you really think I'd be *happy* to hear you broke up with your childhood sweetheart?" She shook her head slowly. "Of course not, Jessica. Of course not. I'm sure you're going through a lot right now. Oh gosh, I can only imagine."

Genuine sadness knocked on the door, and Jessica's temptation to answer it hadn't been stronger in days. Maybe that was all this was. Maybe this whole thing wasn't a big deal and she was blowing it out of proportion to avoid thinking about Chris. After all, Mrs. Thomas didn't seem concerned.

No, that was weird. Why wasn't Mrs. Thomas concerned? "And did you hear the other stuff I just said? The guys you sent me almost brought down my business. No offense, Mrs. Thomas, but what the hell?"

Jessica had expected the question to rattle her teacher, to put her on the defensive, but the woman's expression gave no indication of remorse or self-doubt. She brought her coffee cup to her mouth and blew on the steaming contents. "I'm curious, how did they manage to cause so much damage for so long without you, their supervisor, knowing?"

The answer came to Jessica in a flash and stung her

like only an accusation one knows to be true can. "I trusted them to do their jobs."

"And did you check in on them along the way?" Mrs. Thomas asked. "Or did you hire new people, train them, and then hope they did everything correctly right off?"

"You said they were good. I trusted your opinion."

"They *are* good, Jessica. But they're not perfect. And sometimes people who are good for a long time stop being good. Or sometimes they think they're doing things correctly, but they're not. That's why it's the job of the boss to have regular check-ins and oversee the work. Dwayne left the freezer open. It's unfortunate, of course, but I'm sure you've made mistakes equal to that. I know I have. And Kumal exercised poor taste in his website design. How much guidance did you give him on what you were looking for? If he didn't have much to go on, or you only explained it to him once, it's not his fault he missed the mark. You know men are traditionally poor communicators."

Jessica felt like a thick rubber band was stretched around her chest. "And Sampson just mixed up the credit union's account number with his personal bank account number?" she said, petulantly.

Mrs. Thomas frowned. "Of course not. The man stole from you! I don't deny it. He was always honest when he worked for my husband, but people can change at any time. Who knows what could have been going on in his personal life to make him justify such a thing? And if you weren't checking in with him, building a rapport, you can't even begin to guess. There could have been warning signs you missed. Perhaps his child needed a kidney transplant he couldn't afford."

"Or maybe he's just a crook," Jessica said.

"Oh, I doubt it's that simple. It almost never is. And like I said, he never stole from my husband, and he worked for him for years." She ventured a small sip then took a longer one. "Being a boss isn't simple, Jessica. Trust me, I know. It's tempting to hand off responsibility to others and never check in, but that's not how to become a *successful* boss. You must stay involved, if for no other reason than to avoid things like this happening. Sure, checking in might not have prevented Sampson from stealing or Kumal from building an inappropriate website, but it would have stemmed the damage much sooner, and your business might not have taken quite the hit it has."

Jessica's insides felt like lead. "You're saying it's my fault?"

"If you want to put it in such unpleasant and oversimplified terms, yes, you do bear a large portion of the responsibility for the situation in which you now find yourself. And trust me, it's not easy for me to be this honest with you. I would rather tell you what you want to hear and comfort you, and if you were younger, I might do just that. But you're an adult now and a business owner, and I'm a major investor in that business. My responsibility to you has changed.

"You've said you want to be financially independent, and I want that too. Not that I don't enjoy investing in a business that I believe in, but I have other things I could spend my money on as retirement fast approaches. However, I don't see any other way around it." She sighed and grabbed her purse where it hung on the back of the chair, and pulled out her wallet. "How much do you need to get out of this fresh hell?"

"What?"

Mrs. Thomas pulled out her checkbook and placed it flat on the table, licking a fingertip before flipping to the next blank check. "How much do I need to make this out for?"

"What? No! I don't want to take more money from you."

"I don't think you have a choice, Jessica. Not unless you want to downgrade to a food truck again."

Were those her only two options? Take more money from Mrs. Thomas or downgrade to another food truck? That couldn't be right.

Find a third path.

"I have another opportunity I'm looking into right now," she lied. "So thanks, but no."

The expression flashed across Mrs. Thomas's face in a blink, and no sooner had Jessica glimpsed the contempt than she doubted she'd seen anything at all. "Good, good," said Mrs. Thomas, tucking her checkbook and wallet back into her purse. "Like I said, I have other things I could spend my money on. But the offer still stands if that opportunity falls through." She smiled and stood. "Could I get a to-go cup?"

"Yeah, of course." Jessica jumped up and did as Mrs. Thomas asked, and once the woman had left with little more than a forced smile, Jessica felt the rubber band around her chest snap. She inhaled deeply and had to brace herself on a nearby chair as her head spun and her vision blurred.

What had just happened? She replayed the conversation in her head from the start, or as much of it as she could remember. Was Mrs. Thomas angry with her now? Was it really her fault that everything had gone so poorly with the new hires? That part made more sense than she liked to admit. Maybe it was her fault. Things usually were.

Naiveté strikes again, you idiot. Why couldn't she just instinctively know how to do things? She should have read a freaking book about managing people. Instead, she'd just assumed she knew the basics. Why would she know the basics?

It's not like you had any extra time to read while you were getting the business started.

No, stop making excuses. I could have taken the bus to work and read on the way. I could have spent five minutes less in the shower every day and used that time to read a book. I was just lazy and stupid, that's all.

The refill camper finally stood from his table, and the movement caught her eye. He mumbled something in a weak, airy voice that could have just as easily been "I'll see you" as "I'll eat you" and almost crashed into the glass door when his watery eyes stayed on Jessica a moment too long.

The second the door shut behind him, Jessica hurried after, turned the deadbolt, and flipped the sign.

She'd screwed up everything. This was her fault. All of it.

But that didn't fix the problem at hand, which was that she needed money, and fast, and if she wouldn't take a loan from Mrs. Thomas or a financial gift from anyone else, the only way she could do that was by generating more business.

YOU KNOW HOW TO DO THAT.

For fuck's sake. You're right. I do.

IT WON'T BE EASY, BUT IT COULD BE FUN.

So says you. You're not the one that has to do it.

THAT'S WHAT I MEANT. FUN FOR ME. TO WATCH.

Is there another way?

WE HAVE ALREADY COVERED THIS. THERE ARE ALWAYS OTHER WAYS.

Let me rephrase. Are there any other legal ways?

OH, NO. THERE IS NO OTHER LEGAL WAY THAT WILL DELIVER THE OUTCOME YOU DESIRE.

Do I still have that get-out-of-jail-free card?

YES, BUT YOU DON'T WANT TO USE IT YET.

Jessica leaned against the door, staring at the landscape of her labor. "Okay," she said, "I guess it's time to go full-on celebrity."

Chapter Sixteen

While Jessica hadn't held incredibly high hopes for the focus group, she *had* expected it to be slightly less mind-numbing. The nature of the event lent itself to boredom, but it was mostly the company that put Jessica on the verge of standing from her chair, walking out the door, across the hall, and into her condo, where she would proceed to scream into a pillow until she fell asleep.

The main issue was that Jesus's idea of who society's most heartless were needed some serious updating.

"Thanks so much, Gretchen," Jesus said, waving to the last of the bank tellers as they filed out of Jeremy Archer's condo, which was decorated exactly how one might expect it to be: not at all. The furniture they'd sat on during the feedback session was a well-worn hodgepodge that left Jessica wondering if Jeremy had simply robbed a Goodwill. The walls were bare except a few black cords sticking out from behind his mounted 60" flatscreen—the only sign in the entire place indicating that Jeremy had some money and wasn't simply an illegal squatter.

Jessica followed behind the last of the money changers, and Jesus caught her arm, stopping her from leaving just yet.

"What do you think?" he asked, grinning.

"You already know what I think. You've been asking me about it for the last hour and a half."

"True. You think the slogan will work?"

Jessica hesitated for a moment, then said, "No. I don't think 'Keep Austin Friendly to the Homeless' is going to catch on."

He sighed. "I won't rub it in your face when you're wrong."

"Oh thanks, *Jesus.*"

He beamed warmly. "You're welcome, sister."

"Why are you working so hard at this anyway? Is it just boredom? I know you're *you* and all, but you already gave this a shot two-thousand years ago, and it clearly didn't work. And now you're trying it in an age when the world finds Hobo Wars videos too *dull* for their taste? Not to discourage you, but why in the hell do you bother?" She was hoping his reason might apply to relevant things in her own life.

Jesus nodded along. "I'm here to help you accomplish your mission, so that's what I'm going to do."

"While helping the homeless is admirable, I don't see how it helps me with the bakery."

Jesus wrinkled his nose uncomfortably. "You still think

your mission is the bakery." He sucked in air sharply as if he'd pricked his finger on a thorn. "Wow. That's ... We've talked about this *multiple* times. Your mission is to bring peace to the United States."

"Hard pass on that."

"Not an option."

"Of course it's an option. I can do whatever I want. It's called free will. Maybe Dad fucked up when he gave us that, but add that to the list of things he fucked up. Has he ever told you about Australia?"

Jesus nodded. "Many times. And of course you have the option to ignore your destiny. Everyone has that option. I don't mean it's not an option *literally*. You seem to think you aren't part of the country you live in, which I could understand if you lived in, say, the Middle East where it's common for people to disagree on what country they're presently in. But there's no doubt you're in the United States. You also seem to be under the impression that if something terrible happens in this country, you'll be exempt from it and can therefore ignore it. We can all only hope to be so privileged as to ignore the unpleasantness happening around us, but that is only possible until the unpleasantness knocks on your door. Then it will be *you* looking around at the unaffected, wondering when they'll come to your aid.

"To answer your question, I'm here to help you, but, as usual, I've been provided very little useful information on how I'm supposed to do that, and without any formative years spent in this strange new world to shape my understanding of how things work, you could say I'm floundering a bit. So, I'm focusing on what I could tell was a blind spot of yours. And it happened to coincide with the little bit of experience I've had in the modern age. I've been on the inside reaching out for help. Now, but for the grace of Dad, I've made it out, and I don't plan on forgetting what it was like before. I'm covering for you where your empathy fails, and I have faith that it will bear fruit when the time comes for you to make your stand."

"Make my stand?"

"Yes."

That seemed like a bold assertion, especially considering Jessica was anti-stands, with the exception of her firm position against taking a stand. "How do you even know that day will come? Can you see the future?"

"No, but *everyone* must take a stand sometime, and I've learned enough about you to know that day will come. And, assuming no one tries to crucify me before then—that's not still a thing, right?" Jessica shook her head. "Good. Assuming no one tries to crucify me, I'll be standing behind you."

"Just you and your Salvation Army of hobos. How comforting."

"You must remember why you're here, Jessica. If the bakery brings you joy, then you should continue it, but instead of using it as a means to gain wealth, use it as a platform to spread your message."

"First off, I don't have a message. Also, and I don't think this has changed much in the last couple millennia, wealth is a platform to spread whatever you want—charity, propaganda, small pox—so don't knock it."

Jesus sighed and glared up at the ceiling. "I *am* trying to explain it in simple terms!"

Jessica's eyes darted upward, and once she was sure there wasn't a security camera there, which was not out of the realm of possibility, she glared accusingly at her half-brother. "Is our father feeding you these lines?"

"No," Jesus said guiltily.

"But he is speaking with you privately."

Jesus mumbled, "More like speaking *at* me."

"God, I know you aren't busy in Asia and can hear me," she announced. "If you want me to bring peace to the US or whatever, you're welcome to drop me a hint at *any* time as to how in the hell to start."

She waited, hoping for a response, but none came.

Not to her, at least.

Jesus said, "He says he'll give you a hint."

"Really?"

"Yeah, he says ... that doesn't make sense, Father. Fine, fine." He cringed apologetically as he said, "He says the hint is: your mother."

"Ooh ..." She clenched her fists and tapped into her shallow well of restraint to keep from punching the messenger. "I finally ask for his help and he responds with a poorly executed yo mama joke? For shit's sake!"

"Yeah," Jesus said. "Sorry. He says he's feeling sassy today."

"That's never a good sign."

Jesus's eyes went wide and he shook his head stiffly, like a hostage trying to convey an intricate message without detection from his captor.

A few minutes later, once Jessica was back in her condo, had tossed her key and bag onto the coffee table and poured herself a glass of water from the refrigerator filter, wishing she could afford beer, she thought back to what Jesus had said. She should probably listen to him. After all, he was Jesus, right? He ... had done some stuff.

Man, I should probably read up on it.

Chris had once derided Jesus for losing his swagger, which implied, of course, that Jesus once had real swagger. What had happened to him?

Scratch that. She knew what had happened to him. He'd been betrayed, whipped, nailed to a cross, and dried in the sun. Then the poor guy wasn't even allowed to stay dead. Yeah, that would take the swagger out of anyone, she supposed.

Did she share the same fate as her brother? Dr. Bell had done a good job of snapping her out of it when it came to her fear of an early death, so the anxious thoughts regarding that were infrequent at most, but all this talk of "taking a stand" was dredging it back up. Putting herself out there seemed like asking to be crucified if such an indirect request existed. Sure, the odds of anyone seriously doing it were slim, but figuratively, it was incredibly possible. She saw modern crucifixions on a daily basis and had been subjected to mild forms of it herself, thanks to Eugene Thornton. Nowadays, the torture could drag out for much longer than three days and the perpetrators were much crueler *because* they didn't kill the victim. All the shame, none of the relief.

Would she be risking the same outcome when she stepped into the spotlight, playing on her celebrity to increase the revenue for the bakery?

The fear crept in, but for once, with the bakery and so much more on the line, the risk of hiding was greater than that of stepping forward.

Chapter Seventeen

Jessica knew the night out was intended as an opportunity for her to relax, stop thinking about work, and enjoy a meal that wasn't ninety percent carbohydrates.

But just because the opportunity was dangling in front of her didn't mean she had the first clue how to seize it.

The carbohydrate part was easy; she was the heaviest she'd ever been from constant stress-eating before, during, and after work—she'd even caught herself sleep-eating a stale oatmeal raisin cookie in her kitchen a few nights back, and she couldn't even remember the last time she brought one of those home. Although she'd be the first to admit the new weight left her well shy of what anyone would consider overweight. The problem, of course, was that the weight didn't go where she wanted it to. It went to her middle and her upper arms, not her butt and boobs, and accentuated her high waist, leaving her resembling her mother much more than she felt comfortable with.

When the waiter came by their table on the terrace, Jessica ordered a large club salad and a beer with lime, and Judith seemed to approve of the healthy choice. After all, Jessica was here because Judith wanted her to start making healthier choices. You know, like an intervention. (But because it was Judith, it was a low-key one.) The woman had said as much at work the other day when she caught Jessica stuffing a scalding hot snickerdoodle into her mouth and chewing through the tears.

"Judith's been telling me about how much you've been doing lately," Brian Foster said, sipping his apple cider vinegar cocktail and doing a fine job of pretending to enjoy it. "I'm glad you could take some time to unwind with us."

Jessica smiled at the odd couple, thinking about all the ways she would prefer to unwind besides being a third wheel. Except she hadn't done any of those other ways, and she likely wouldn't. She needed someone else to force her to take a breath and pause while she dug herself out of the ditch Mrs. Thomas had left her in.

"Yeah, it's been a long month."

Brian leaned back, tossing an arm over the back of his wooden chair and reaching around Judith's to rub lazy circles on her back. "I should have—" He paused, bit his lips as if to reconsider, then bulled ahead. "I should have done more to warn you against working with Dolores."

Jessica squeezed the last few drops of lime into her beer, wondering if that was close to enough vitamin C for the day. "Trust me, you haven't exactly hidden your dislike. I was just stupid to ask her to do me a favor like hiring all my staff. I should have done it myself. At the very least, I should have checked in with them more. That way I could have stemmed the damage. I'm an idiot."

"Not an idiot. Trust me. Now that I work with her again, I'm treated to a front-row seat of highly educated adults trusting her implicitly. You know she actually does the hiring for our district?"

"Shit, really?"

"Yeah. And she's done a really good job of it … so far."

Jessica inspected him. "What do you mean, 'so far'?"

"I just mean people who are reliably unreliable never let anyone down, do they? It's the ones that are unreliably unreliable that leave our heads spinning."

"I guess?" God love the man, but he needed to lay off the Kierkegaard, a name Jessica was only familiar with due to the quote from him Judith had tattooed on her inner thigh.

The fact that Mrs. Thomas did in fact seem to be good at hiring, and now did it as part of her job, only fueled Jessica's festering suspicion that she was, as the woman had said, the main reason why things didn't work out with Kumal, Sampson, and Dwayne.

"It's unfortunate you still have to maintain a business relationship with her," Brian continued.

"It's not that bad," Jessica said quickly. "I mean, yeah, maybe she didn't hire the best guys for the job, but she still did me a favor, and I wouldn't have the bakery at all without her. I'm not sure I'm ready to write her off entirely for one mistake. We all know I've made bigger ones."

Brian gave a be-that-as-it-may shrug, and changed the subject. "Judith said you had a plan for getting back on your feet."

"I have a plan, sure, but I don't know how to get started on it."

Judith groaned. "Yes, you do. Wendy already gave you the full scoop on how to go about it. Cash is *dying* for you to give them the photo ops they need. All you have to do is *do*."

"Okay," Jessica said, opening her eyes wide and finishing off her first beer. "Looks like someone doesn't have any more patience for my bullshit."

"I'm surprised *you* still do," Judith said. "No offense, but you've spent the last month looking and acting like a fucking zombie. Unless your plan is Lazarus performance art to draw crowds, I suggest you take the *much* easier route that Wendy suggested."

Brian asked, "And the much easier route is ...?"

"Play up my notoriety," Jessica said. Even saying the words drained her. Sure, she'd determined it was the best course of action when Mrs. Thomas had offered her more money, and, yes, Wendy had practically begged her to do this for years, but when it came time to actually step into that role, Jessica couldn't find her footing. Maybe the first step was the hardest, but she suspected the second, third and fourth would be awkward and unpleasant as well. It simply wasn't in her McCloud DNA to own a specialness she had done nothing to earn.

Brian nodded slowly, staring at their wrought iron

table illuminated by the string lights overhead. "I can see why you would resist that, Jessica."

"See?" Jessica said. "He gets it. I tell you, Brian, it sure is nice to have someone who was around for the Jameson Fractal debacle."

"You mean the assassination? Please," said Judith, "I remember that. It was all anyone at my school talked about."

"Yeah, but you weren't *there*," Jessica snipped. "And even though Brian wasn't at the rally, he was lucky enough to have me unload on him the next week."

Brian leaned forward again, clasping his hands together on the table. "That was five years ago, Jessica. I know it's traumatic, but look how far you've come in that time. You can risk it again. The odds of Jameson Fractal, or anyone, being assassinated as a result are ... not incredibly high."

Judith smacked his arm. "'Not incredibly high'?" she hissed. "Wow, I can't imagine why you were only a college counselor for one year."

"Excuse me." The deep, honey-smooth voice just behind Jessica's shoulder made her whirl around, preparing for an assault.

Instead, she found herself staring up into soft, dark eyes that were locked onto hers. "Yes?" she said.

This stranger's gaze was a laser. "You're Jessica McCloud, right?"

She ignored her impulse to tell him no, that there was a mistake, and she was definitely not the person he'd been sent to murder. Instead, as she observed his long lashes, his full lips and inhaled a gentle whiff of tastefully applied cologne, she said, "Yeah."

A beautiful smile bloomed on his caramel face. "Hi. Anthony Aguilar." He moved around to the side and dropped down to squat by their round table, inserting himself between her and Brian.

The name didn't ring a bell in the slightest, but she continued to stare at him in a not entirely hostile manner.

"It's, um, it's so great to meet you," he said. "I'm a big fan."

"Of what?" she said dumbly.

He blinked a few times, his eyebrows pinching together. "Of you."

"Me?" She struggled to follow along. "Cool."

She was vaguely aware of Judith's eyes on her, but she couldn't decipher the woman's expression in her peripherals.

"Yeah," he said. "Sorry to interrupt your dinner. I just thought it was you, and I couldn't believe my eyes, and I jumped up and ran over here before I realized how rude it must be."

"It's okay," Jessica said. "It's nice meeting you, Nathan."

"Anthony."

"Right, sorry. Anthony."

His eyes finally left Jessica for the first time to dart over to the empty seat. "I, um—"

Judith cut in. "Would you like to—"

"Come by the bakery if you get a chance," Jessica said. "I'll give you a free coffee."

Anthony's attention returned to Jessica. "Oh, uh, yeah. For sure."

"'Kay," Jessica said, giving him her best customer service grin.

But he didn't leave. Why wasn't he getting the hint?

He cringed slightly as he added, "Do you mind if I get a picture with you?"

Judith answered for her. "Sure! I'll take it." She jumped up and extended her arm toward Anthony, who handed over his phone eagerly.

Jessica immediately wished she'd put more effort into her appearance.

"Jessica," Judith barked. "Stand up."

"Oh, right." She scooted her chair out and stood just as Anthony was beginning to crouch. She swallowed hard and apologized as he straightened up.

Judith took her sweet time on the framing. "Scoot in a little closer."

They did, their arms brushing against each other's. Goosebumps sprang up on Jessica's. When was the last time she'd been this close to someone like Anthony? Sure, she'd taken all kinds of pictures with people in It is Risen, but context was everything. Out here in the night air, under the string lights, the sound of drunken decisions wafting in on the breeze, was a completely different experience.

"You can put your arm around her, Anthony. It's fine. She doesn't mind," Judith said.

Brian reached behind Anthony, grabbed Jessica's wrist, and moved her arm around the fan's waist.

"Smile!" and Jessica knew it was directed specifically at her.

Jessica let out the breath she'd been holding while being so close to the handsome stranger and nodded dumbly as he thanked her and said he'd stop by the bakery before he left town. When he finally returned to his table, Jessica was relieved she'd made it through the awkward part. And she hadn't done too poorly, if she did say so herself.

But when she turned back to her dinner companions, she found Brian with his head in his hands and Judith staring at her openmouthed, shaking her head slowly from side to side.

Clearly, they didn't agree with Jessica's assessment. "What?"

Brian groaned into his hands.

"That," Judith began, "was a train wreck."

"What? Why? Was the picture not good?"

Judith rolled her head over toward her boyfriend, and the two exchanged a look. "Was the picture not good?" Judith mumbled. "Jessica, you holy disaster, the picture was fine. It was everything else that was a nightmare. How has Wendy not quit?"

"Be nice," Brian warned.

"Yeah," Jessica said. "Be nice. It wasn't that bad."

Judith leaned over the table. "You know he wanted to sit down, right? He was looking for an invite."

"Yeah, so?"

"Were we looking at the same guy just now? Because Anthony might have been a male model, and not the gay kind. The rare, one-in-a-million straight kind." She turned to Brian. "Sorry."

"No, no. He was hot. I would have gone for it."

Before Jessica could inquire, Judith asked her, "You know what would have happened if he'd sat down?"

Jessica shrugged. "More awkward conversation?"

"Exactly," Judith said, "which would have eventually led to awkward sex, and let me tell you, Jess, with as stressed out as you've been, even awkward sex is a step up."

"Except," Jessica said quietly, "you know I can't have sex."

Judith deflated. "Ugh ... right. Because God cockblocks you."

"What's this?" Brian asked.

Never in a million years would the high schooler she used to be have imagined filling in Mr. Foster on her sexual woes. "I can't have sex with anyone. When they try, God sort of, um ..."

"Melts their stick of butter," Judith finished.

Brian's head tilted to the left as his eyes widened. "That ... is ... the most horrible thing I've ever heard. You and Chris never did then?"

Jessica explained the big picture of dream sex, and when she was done, Judith added, "Even still, that's not a reason to avoid dating other people. There are plenty of fun things you can do in a relationship that don't involve vaginal sex."

"Like oral sex," Brian offered. "Sometimes it's better."

"Please stop there," Jessica said, avoiding looking at him.

The waiter dropped off their food at the best and worst moment. Best because it stopped the conversation, but worst because Jessica had mostly lost her appetite.

As she started on a fresh beer, Judith said, "If you're not ready to move on from Chris, fine, but I swear to your Father, Jessica, I can't bear to see another awkward encounter like the one that just happened. If you don't get better with fans, I will straight up quit working for you."

"Fine, fine," Jessica said. "I'll see what I can do on that front." She sighed. Hiring someone new was out of the question, and Judith was her second-best employee.

It was clear this proposed solution would only work if she put some conscious effort into learning the ins and outs of human interaction with strangers who worshipped her.

Would have been nice if you'd given me that gift along with the curse.

But God wasn't listening. Big shocker.

Chapter Eighteen

Local Female Business Owner Victimized by Male Scammers.

It was the headline Wendy and Maria had developed together to breathe life into It is Risen, and it worked like a charm. Jessica's initial unwillingness to sign off on it, hesitant to assume the role of victim rather than crappy boss, was washed away after the first few days of increased sales made their way down the tributaries of commerce, straight into her aquifer of debt.

Whatever stain Kumal's nightmare circus of a website might have left on her reputation was promptly scrubbed clean. Quentin explained that the damage was probably minimal if anything, because Kumal, along with having no understanding of basic decency or Photoshop, also didn't know anything about SEO. Neither did Jessica, and Quentin refrained from explaining it to her, for which she was grateful.

While she got a thrill of publicly shaming Kumal, Sampson, and Dwayne for their part in her unfortunate financial predicament, she'd drawn a hard line when it came to Mrs. Thomas. The woman wasn't to be named or even hinted at in the article. After all, she was still an investor. And besides, Jessica was only inches away from forgiving her.

Of course, with increased business came more things to do to keep the place running smoothly, and Jess knew that it wouldn't be long before she needed to hire a third barista to free up more of her time for managerial tasks.

And all the while, more and more customers were asking for a picture with her. Maybe that was because she'd stopped charging for it, finally accepting Cash's argument that the publicity was more valuable than the ten dollars. But she suspected it was also due to an openness and acceptance of the situation. She'd stopped fighting it. She'd made up her mind: she was going to accept being a local celebrity. Now, when people asked her if she was really the daughter of God, she answered in the affirmative and pretended she didn't hate the fact. She didn't go on about it, obviously, but provided them with a simple, "Yes, I am." That was enough for most.

And for those who inquired further, she'd learned to simply pretend they hadn't said anything, pose for the picture until they got the hint and shut up, and then she'd thank them and give them a gentle push on the small of their back to send them off.

After weeks of it, though, the increased work load and

the higher demand for her to be personable pulled her in two directions, stretching her like a piece of dough, and she was starting to feel a bit thin in places.

When Jameson Fractal sauntered into It is Risen that sunny day in late September, just as Jessica was organizing the cups and lids at the drink station, she wasn't sure if she wanted to hug him or dive behind the counter and hope Destinee would get the hint and take over until he was gone.

Ultimately, indecision won out, and the latter option evaporated as soon as he pulled off his sunglasses and spotted her. And as he did, the customers spotted him. She watched as their eyes tracked his path toward her.

"Hey there," he said, with a warm intimacy that hinted they were former lovers who'd left on unrealistically good terms.

"Hi," she said abruptly, like they were strangers who'd never inhabited the same planet.

He pulled her into a hug, and who was she to refuse?

Once she was in his arms, she made a fatal mistake: she inhaled his scent. Somehow, he'd managed to smell the same since the first time she'd met him on that platform in the hospital parking lot in Midland, Texas. Emotionally speaking, there was a lot for her to unpack with every whiff of him, too much at present, especially while he was whispering instructions into her ear.

"Relax and smile. Everyone's watching. I'll take the lead." He pulled back, leaving his hands on her shoulders as he stared into her eyes.

She mustered a shit-eating grin and hoped it would suffice.

"I'm starving," he said. "Anything new I need to try?" He led her toward the counter, and she felt much more in her element once she was on one side and he was on the other.

"We have a pistachio danish," she said, walking the length of the display case to where she'd set them out that morning. When she looked up, though, he wasn't facing her on the opposite side. Instead, he'd stopped in his tracks at the start of the display.

He hunched over, his face so close to the case it made Jessica's fingers itchy for a bottle of glass cleaner and a rag.

"You've gotten so much better at this," he said. "You can even see some of your freckles now." He pointed toward the cookies. "Or maybe those are chocolate chips." He straightened. "Still not as beautiful as you, but what can you expect from a pastry?"

Jessica swallowed hard, and she was glad for once that someone was filming them. (In fact, it was half a dozen someones with their phones held out shamelessly.) She'd have to search for the clips later to verify that Jameson Fractal had, in fact, just called her beautiful.

She slid open the case. "So, did you want the pistachio danish, or ...?"

"Yeah, that sounds great," he replied casually, taking in his surroundings and nodding politely at a few oglers.

Jessica plated it for him and faced a conundrum when she brought it to the counter: Did she charge him?

On the one hand, she was living in his condo for free, so obviously she shouldn't.

But on the other hand, no one here knew that context, and if she didn't require him to pay, it might look like there was some sort of favoritism, like celebrities eat free, and ...

And what? A bunch of celebrities will start coming in? Boo hoo, you idiot.

She said, "Oh the house," when he reached for his wallet, and he nodded. "Thanks. You didn't have to. I'm not exactly hard pressed."

A woman in her mid-twenties at the table closest to them giggled maniacally.

"I know. But old friends eat free."

He winked at her, and she wasn't sure if that was a "nice one, they're going to love it" or if he was flirting again.

Was there a difference with Jameson?

He took a seat at the long counter against the window, staring out onto the street as he enjoyed his snack. She watched him eat, vaguely aware of how creepy she was being, while she served two more customers. In her defense, she was not the only one watching him enjoy that danish. Not by a long shot. Every female in the place, and two of the men by Jessica's count, keep a close watch on him, even while pretending to go about their business.

She could almost hear Sir David Attenborough's voice narrating the scene as it unfolded.

Patiently, from a distance, the hungry predators observed their prey, careful not to alert him to their watchful eyes. Perhaps the predators believed he'd settle into a relaxed state on his chair, but Jessica knew better. He was still alert, totally aware of his surroundings, ready to grin sexily as a defensive maneuver if someone came up on him too quickly.

It would happen as a coordinated attack, but of course that could change in an instant; any of these predators would turn on the others if they thought they could get the prey without having to share. But for now, these women needed each other.

Two of them chatted closely across their table, their eyes darting to Jameson's back, and Jessica guessed they'd be the first to approach him.

She guessed wrong, though.

Instead, it was the giggly woman in her mid-twenties who was the first to get to her feet with a clear degree of intention and strut across the cafe to sink her teeth into the defenseless movie star.

Jessica ignored the next customers in line, two men in slacks, pressed shirts, and watches more valuable than Jessica's car, to observe the scene unfolding.

The woman gently rested her hand on Jameson's shoulder, which seemed a downright brazen thing to do to a stranger. He twisted in his seat to stare up at her, and a smile bloomed on his face like they were old high school friends. It was so convincing that Jessica wondered if they *were* old high school friends. He was the first to offer his hand, and he stared fearlessly into her eyes as they shook.

Though Jessica couldn't hear his words across the

room, she could tell he was the one leading the conversation. But how? What in the hell could he be asking when he didn't know the first thing about her? How did he find a conversational fingerhold?

The woman was, remarkably, the first to exhibit body language that it was time for the conversation to come to a close (did he know mind control?), and she bowed, bending slightly at the waist before making one last request.

And then came the phone, sliding easily from her back pocket. Jameson did the honors, holding it at arm's length for the selfie. Then it was done. The woman left, beaming like she'd just won a prize.

"How did he do that?" Jessica whispered.

"Ma'am? You work here, right?" said one of the two businessmen.

She whipped her head around. Where was Destinee? She must be taking a bathroom break or shoving down a kosher pig in a blanket in the back. "Yeah. One second."

She stuck her head into the kitchen to yell, "Mom! Customers!" then she poured a fresh cup of coffee, breezed past the waiting customers, hoping her mom hurried up, and delivered the cup to Jameson, just as the two watchful women were about to make their move. "Sorry," she mumbled as she pushed by.

Setting the cup next to him, she cut him off midway through his thank-you with a quiet, "Tell me how you do that."

A playful smirk turned the corners of his mouth. "How I do what?"

She narrowed her eyes. "You know what. Interact with fans."

He chuckled. "It's just the same as interacting with anyone."

"Right! That!" She pointed at him. "How do you do that?"

She checked over her shoulder and saw that Destinee had arrived on scene and was fussing at the two customers, undoubtedly for what she construed to be a rude tone. When she caught sight of Jessica and then Jameson, she gave them a hearty wave and a thumbs up.

Jessica put her back to her mother quickly.

"I'm not gonna tell you my tricks," Jameson said. "But I'll show you."

"You will?" Jessica said too eagerly.

He nodded and took a spunky bite of the danish.

"One last question: how much prodding did Wendy have to do to get you to come in here and prove to me I could use a little help?"

Jameson's finely crafted composure cracked down the center. "Huh? Wendy? Wendy Peterman?"

"Yeah, she put you up to this, right?"

"Put me up to what?"

If Jessica didn't know better, she'd swear Jameson truly had no clue what she was talking about. "So, you just came by because ... you wanted to see the bakery?"

"Yeah, I was in town, and I wanted to see how things were going. And how you were doing."

"Oh. And that bit of coaching before?"

He held up his hands defensively. "I shouldn't have assumed you needed coaching."

"No, you should have. You were right, clearly."

He laughed. "Good. Glad you weren't offended. Anyway, how does seven work?"

"How do you mean? In multiplication? I don't ..."

He cocked his head to the side, inspecting her like he might have missed a joke. "No, seven o'clock. Tonight. I pick you up and show you how to be famous in Austin."

She sucked in air. "I dunno. That's short notice, and we don't close until seven, then I'll be here for another few hours cleaning and prepping for tomorrow, counting money, logging ..." When she noticed that nothing she said had any effect on his eager grin, she ran out of steam. "Let me see if my mom minds covering for me tonight."

"Cool."

"Oh, and ..." She wasn't sure if she should ask, but her insecurity gave her a little push. "It's really nice of you to do this, but I have to ask"—she leaned close—"are you an angel?"

His attentive expression lit up as he broke into a wide grin. "People ask me that a lot."

That wasn't an acceptable answer. "No, I mean it. Are you?" She stared at him unblinkingly until his grin wilted.

"Um ..." His eyes darted around as though he suspected she might be playing a prank and filming it. Then, finally, he said, "No. I'm not an angel."

She pointed at him. "Are you sure? You can't see auras or anything?"

"Auras?"

The confusion in his voice was genuine enough, and she decided to take his word. "Right. Sorry. I believe you. I just had to be sure."

"Are angels a thing?" he whispered.

"Yeah, but don't worry about it. I— I probably shouldn't have told you that." She waved for him to turn back toward the window. "I'll check on tonight."

The business men had taken their food to-go and were heading out the door when Jessica rounded the corner of the counter and snuck up next to her mother. She waited for Destinee to finish a transaction for a hassled woman in yoga pants with a baby on her hip.

"Got a question," Jessica said quietly. "Jameson wants to take me out on the town tonight and show me how to not be a complete mess when people approach me in public. Think you could cover for just one night?"

Destinee, ignored the request, acting like she hadn't heard a word of it while grinning and flapping her hand at the baby when the mother left to claim the last open table.

Then Destinee rounded on Jessica, putting her back to the rest of the cafe so the customers couldn't see her eyes grow large as she said, "Baby, I will run a goddamn marathon naked in Antarctica if that's what it takes for you to spend a rowdy night breaking that wild stallion."

Jessica shut her eyes. "Holy hell, Mom. That's not gonna happen. It's totally not like that between us."

"I love you, but that's horse shit. I saw the way he was looking at you just now."

Jessica tilted her head back, shutting her eyes for patience and inhaling through her nose as she braced her fists on her hips. "He's an *actor*, Mom. He's been professionally trained to look at everyone like he wants to bang them. That's how he makes his money."

Destinee conceded with a minute nod. "And it wouldn't hurt if you learned some of that. I get it. And, yes, baby, the offer still stands, even if you don't get laid. You deserve a real night out. You're twenty-two, for crying out loud! Twenty-two-year-olds should have fun. Granted, when I was that age, I had a five-year-old."

"Thanks, Mom."

"Sure thing. Let me call Rex and tell him to get his ass over here after work."

"He won't mind?"

She shrugged, pulling her phone from her pocket and poking around on it. "He might. But I'll let him go down on me for an hour later and he'll forget all about it."

Jessica allowed herself a staunch grimace before helping the next guest.

When she was finally able to catch Jameson's eye, she nodded, and he held up seven fingers while grinning and waggling his eyebrows.

That was definitely flirting.

Wasn't it?

Before leaving, he approached the counter, waiting patiently for the line to move through, managing fan attention effortlessly as he did. She thought he'd completed three selfies in the time it took her to box up a baker's dozen assorted cookies for a frazzled man around Jessica's age whose name badge around his neck identified him as Fallon Jakovic, Production Assistant. Maybe it was only two selfies, though.

Jameson placed his hands flat on the top of the counter and leaned over it. "Wear something you wouldn't mind being seen in. Meet you at your place." He flashed her a dorky a half grin that reminded her of Chris and therefore functioned like a cup of cold water to her face.

"Yeah, see you at my place."

It *was* a date, wasn't it? She was going on a date with Jameson Fractal.

Chapter Nineteen

When she and Jameson arrived at their first destination for the evening, she felt like this whole thing might be an elaborate setup.

A setup for what, she didn't know, but she would be the butt of the joke. That much she *was* sure about.

"Why are we here?" Jessica asked, staring at the gaudy sign on the roof of Bat-Ass Brew.

"I thought you loved this place," said Jameson. "This place certainly loves you."

She hadn't been back since the unfortunate incident when she was required under exigent circumstances to cave on her no-resurrection policy and save a barista riddled with bullets.

"You're confused," she said. "The *internet* loves this place. Specifically, it loves the cellphone footage of a man being shot multiple times because he slept with another man's wife." Her eyes wandered to the gun-free zone poster with a picture of a crossed out gun and the city ordinance in fine print underneath. They were still sticking with that, huh?

"Come on," Jameson said, taking off his sunglasses. "We're here, and if we're going to be chipper and friendly to fans, we need more caffeine."

More caffeine? Poor guy had no clue that in her veins pumped more coffee than blood. She relented, though. After all, Jameson was doing her a huge favor by training her to be a social human being.

"Yeah, all right."

But as soon as she stepped through the door and her eyes adjusted to the dim lighting, she felt like fleeing.

The barista's eyes locked onto her immediately from where he leaned against the counter, staring at something on his phone. Then his eyes crossed *just* a little. "Holy shit ... I'm higher than I thought."

Jameson put a hand on the small of her back and gently steered her forward.

"Hi, Rebel," she said, approaching the counter. She really should have checked up on him after he was shot in the face, but, you know, things came up.

He blinked slowly, lines appearing at the corners of his eyes as he squeezed them shut two times. "It's really you? Jessica fucking McCloud!"

At least he got my name right. Or, close enough.

Considering what she'd done for him, she'd half expected the surname of Christ to be tagged on.

Rebel tossed his phone onto the counter before

stomping over to her and throwing his arms around her. Her ear pressed against his chest as he squeezed her tightly, and she tried not to focus on his heartbeat that was all her fault. Jameson bit back a smile as she flapped a hand, motioning for assistance. He mimed hugging, and she got the picture, briefly clasping her hands behind Rebel's back.

When one of the barista's hands started to slide farther down her back, she pushed it away, but forced a smile like she knew Jameson would want.

"I didn't know when I'd get a chance to thank you," Rebel said, finally letting go. "I can't even count how many times I watched the leaked footage of the shooting and then you bringing me back."

"You watched yourself get murdered again and again?" Jessica asked, unable to maintain the smile.

He chuckled. "Yeah. Hey, what can I get you to drink or eat? Anything. On the house."

As he hurried back to his place behind the counter, Jessica said, "You don't have to— ow!"

Jameson had given her a subtle but firm thumb to the ribs to cut her off. "Thanks, man," he said on her behalf. "Really cool of you."

Rebel noticed Jessica's friend for the first time, and he seemed to approve, if the flick of his chin in Jameson's direction was any indicator, which it might not have been, once Jessica considered it. "Least I can do," said Rebel. "Hey, haven't I seen you in stuff?"

"Yep." He turned to Jessica. "What's good here?"

"I like the Nosferabrew and the Mocha Guano."

"Yeah, the Nos— ... thing sounds good."

Once they were seated with their drinks a moment later (Jessica had never seen Rebel move as quickly as he had when preparing their order), Jameson leaned over the two-person table, his coffee cradled between his hands, and said, "Objectively speaking, how was that interaction?"

She thought about it. "Not terrible. There was that bit where he tried to grab my ass ..."

Jameson nodded emphatically. "Oh, that's always going to be a thing. Just get used to it. Your fans love you, but yes, they think your body is a commodity for them to consume."

"That doesn't just go for actors?"

Jameson laughed. "No. It goes for actors, sports stars, singers, and especially for messiahs. When someone worships something, they want to consume it and make it part of themselves. It's like spiritual cannibalism. Or, in your half-brother's case, literal cannibalism."

Jessica choked on her spit. "People ate Jesus?" She really needed to read the New Testament at the very least.

"No, no. Not exactly. But they eat his body in church every Sunday."

"Oh, right right. Eat him and drink him." She shrugged. "I guess I should just be grateful no one's tried to bite me."

Jameson laughed. "Yet. It'll happen."

"What?"

"Don't worry. It's not as painful as it sounds, assuming it's not on the face or … below the belt."

"That's comforting."

"The trick is, the sooner you stop caring about where people put their hands on your body, the more you'll enjoy the ride. They're just hands."

Jessica tested her Cherry Oldman and found it cool enough to sip. "I like the *idea* of that. It sounds very Zen or whatever. But at the same time, you just told me to accept sexual assault."

Jameson nodded. "Yeah. I didn't say there wasn't a price to pay for being famous. But do you have another option here?"

"Not that I can see."

"Then let's make the best of it!" He straightened in his seat. "Outside of the molestation, what's it like to be in a place where people are smiling at you and buying your food and drink?"

"Ignoring my ever-present suspicion that I don't deserve any of it? Pretty great."

"Yes!" He pointed at her excitedly. "It feels pretty great. You have to tap into the pretty great part. There's always a downside you can find if you look. But why bother? Why not focus on the awesome parts?"

"You have a point," she said, "but the reason I feel okay with it here is because, despite how much I didn't want to do it at the time, I actually *helped* someone. I saved Rebel's life, or, you know, returned it to him. And assuming it doesn't come back to haunt me like my acts of kindness usually do, I don't mind being thanked for helping someone. The attention from people who I *haven't* helped, though, is just weird."

"I take it you don't think I deserve the attention I get?" He issued the challenge with an arched brow.

"What? No. I mean, you've been acting since you were a child. You've been in all kinds of movies and TV shows. And, shit, Jameson, just look at you." Were it not for the fact that his attractiveness was so profound that it really wasn't a matter of opinion so much as a statement of Truth, she wouldn't have been able to point it out so blatantly. But as it was, telling Jameson he was mega fine was as much of a compliment as someone telling her that her hair was straight.

Jameson sighed. "You still don't see it, do you? The money from my movies isn't going to feed starving children. My TV shows aren't extended calls to action for animal rescue. And yet, I'm helping people. I'm helping them feel less resentful toward their husbands while they fold clothes and watch my movies. I'm playing characters they can relate to so they don't feel so alone. I'm not a messiah, I know that, I'm just saying that help looks a lot of different ways, and you're dismissing all the ways you help others just by existing. Those people who want to take pictures with you, who adore you, you've given them something to believe in. And you're not even a false idol, like me or every other celebrity! You're, like, the person people are *supposed* to worship."

She leaned back, giving herself a moment to consider

how to respond. As she looked around the coffee shop, she was incredibly annoyed to realize Jameson might have a point. Two high school girls were staring right at her and when she smiled and waved, they gasped and giggled, then waved back. It was a vastly different response than she would have received from high school girls when *she* was in high school.

She returned her attention to Jameson. "I would prefer for people to like me for what I do, not who I am."

He laughed, and when she didn't, he said, "Wait, are you being serious?"

She nodded.

"But then you have to keep *doing* to be loved. Isn't the whole Jesus thing about being worthy of love just by being you?"

"I don't know. That sounds more like Mister Rogers to me. And I'm not Jesus or Mister Rogers. I'm Jessica."

"I see that. And for what it's worth, I think you're amazing for who you are, and, as someone who's been resurrected by you, I also appreciate what you do." Then, to her complete bewilderment, he reached across the table, placed a hand on hers, and gazed into her eyes.

No cameras caught the moment to her knowledge, and she wasn't sure if she was relieved by that or annoyed.

"I didn't have much of a choice," she babbled. "It was my fault you got killed in the first place."

"Just hush. You didn't pull the trigger. And if it'd never happened, you and I wouldn't be here right now, in this weird bat-themed coffee shop, enjoying our time together."

Enjoying our time together? Is that what we're doing?

She supposed it was, or rather, it *would* be if she could just loosen up. She inhaled deeply, letting the air out slowly. "That's true. As long as you're not upset about it."

"I'm not," he said, squeezing her hand. "If you haven't caught on yet, I think you're pretty great, whether you're a messiah or just the owner of a gluten-free bakery. I'm glad I finally get to spend some time with you."

That smile. She'd seen that smile on him before, but in other contexts, with other women. If she wasn't careful, she'd have to have the "I physically cannot have vaginal sex because God forbids me to outside of marriage" talk a lot sooner than she'd hoped for, which was never.

"I don't understand that, but I'll believe you."

He laughed and straightened in his seat, letting his fingers slip off her hand. "Hey, it's a start. Let's talk about something else."

"Like what?"

I mean, seriously. What could Jameson Fractal and I have to talk about outside of—

"What's your favorite animal?"

"Giraffe!" She didn't mean to yell, but she couldn't take it back now.

"Nice! Giraffes are one of my favorites, too. I also love lions."

While it wasn't polite, she did feel like she could clear the air. "Are you a pedophile?"

Jameson's jaw dropped. "What? No!"

"Are you a demon?"

"What are you talking about?" he whimpered. "Did I say something wrong?"

Jessica blinked. What *was* she talking about? She shook her head to clear it. "Sorry. Just old trauma. Had to cover my bases. Also, I haven't been on a first date in a while." When she realized what she'd just said, she felt her whole ass clench. "No, not like, I mean, I said 'first date' but I just mean I haven't hung out with someone I don't know that well, a man, just one-on-one, since college."

Jameson sipped his Nosferatbrew silently as she spun her wheels, and when she was finished, he waited a moment before saying, "It's okay. This can be a first date."

She waved him off, avoiding eye contact at all cost. "No, no. It really doesn't have to be like that."

"Well, *could* it be like that?"

She risked a glance at him to see if he was being serious. "Um, I guess so."

"Great. Just so you know," he added, "I don't put out on the first date."

She laughed, and as she did, the tension evaporated from her chest.

"We can just be friends going on a date, Jess. I don't care what we call it, so long as I finally get to hang out with you a little. I think you're interesting, and I know I'll only be in town a couple months, but it's nice to have someone to spend quality time with while I'm here."

"I doubt you have trouble finding people to spend time with."

"Quality time. I can't very well get on a dating app,

and when I get done on set, the last people I want to be around are other actors and people in show business. You're authentically you, and I find that an attractive quality in a person."

While she knew he was speaking generally, and that sometimes adults were honest with each other and handed out compliments without needing it to be a big thing, *Jameson Fractal thought she had attractive qualities!*

If she'd ever kept up a journal like she knew she should've, this shit would be going straight in it later that night.

"You feel properly caffeinated?" he asked.

"Yep. Where to next?"

"Another surprise. But I think you're going to love it."

"I bet I will."

She was terrified.

* * *

For a moment, Jessica thought her nightmares might be coming true as they approached the thumping bass and long line leading into a windowless club downtown. She would rather be buried alive than have to go in there, which would undoubtedly feel a little like she was being buried alive. Was he bringing her here to give her a molestation crash course?

But just before they reached the front of the line, he grabbed her hand and pulled her after him through a narrow door leading to a narrower set of stairs. At the top was a pink neon sign that said *S8 Su4.*

"Hope you like sushi," said Jameson from in front as they climbed the stairs, single file because that was the only way they fit.

"Oh, is that what this place is?"

"Yep. Strictly speaking, it's Japanese-American fusion."

"And what's the name?" she asked, wondering if she'd ever heard of it and expecting that she hadn't.

"Sate Sushi."

She glanced up at the neon sign again, slightly less puzzled but still pretty damn confused.

"You usually have to get a reservation months in advance for this place, but I know the owner, so I gave him a ring this afternoon and he said he'd get us the best seat in the house," he added.

"Oh great." Was she dressed for a place like this? Bat-Ass Brew, sure. You could show up to that place in a see-through nightgown and no one would judge you. Rebel might not stop staring, but that was no aberration.

She needn't have worried, though, because as soon as she stepped out of the dim, claustrophobic staircase and into the brightly lit restaurant, she knew nothing in her limited wardrobe could look too casual for the neon tackiness of this place.

The walls were bright yellow under fluorescent lights, and the floor was covered in what looked like astroturf. Each low table was painted a different shocking color. The chairs, which looked like they were built for wide-assed toddlers, were a mishmash of colorful polkadots and splatter paint.

She'd heard about drug flashbacks before. Was this one? Had some sudden movement or jerk of her head dislodged chemical remnants of those magic mushrooms from her spinal cord?

Something brushed against her leg and she yelped.

Jameson grabbed her to hold her steady, laughing as he did so. "I hope you're a cat person."

Jessica had always found cats tolerable, but if being a cat person meant wishing to spend an extended period of time in this acid trip of a setting, surrounded by no fewer than three dozen felines (two of which were engaged in a standoff in the corner, their backs arched, tails skyward), she might not be a cat person after all.

Perhaps the strangest thing about it all was the fact that no one, not a single person enjoying their raw fish and white rice, seemed to mind the visual assault or the animals circling underneath the legs of their tiny chairs.

A black cat jumped onto a table to Jessica's left and, without pausing a beat in the conversation, the customer grabbed the feline and set it on the ground. The cat wasn't deterred, though, and jumped right back on, and the human repeated the process, grabbing the cat and tossing it a little farther away this time without a second thought.

The host, a lanky teenage boy with a bright red nose that made Jessica want to suggest he look into allergy testing, led them to their table in the corner. Jameson stooped over to pull her chair out for her, and she thanked him absentmindedly before lowering herself onto it. Lower ... lower ...

Where the hell was she supposed to put her legs? She tried to take a cue from the nearby tables. Some people opted to put their feet flat on the ground in front of them, simply ignoring that their knees were even with their necks, while others opted for sticking their legs out straight to straddle the table, and one shameless couple even kicked their legs straight under the table, leaving their feet in each other's lap. Jessica noticed the young woman's right calf flexing and relaxing over and over again, and it wasn't until she saw the man's face that she realized what was happening.

She looked away quickly, but Jameson had already caught her looking. "They must have ordered the oysters," he said, and she felt her face redden.

She opted for knees-in-the-face position, and Jameson, clearly being more limber than she was, sat on the very edge of his chair and crossed his legs like he were meditating, resting his knees on the floor.

"Pretty cool, huh?"

Unsure whether he meant the restaurant or his flexibility, and wanting to remain congenial, she said, "Oh yeah."

A fluffy gray cat stalked over to her and rubbed against her shin. Its coat was feather soft, and who was she to turn down a little affection. Maybe adding cats to the mix wasn't so strange after all. She reached down and scratched the cat on the head, which she assumed was what it wanted, considering it was doing nothing *but* rubbing its head on her. The cat purred gratefully, and she felt vibrations of the soft drone rumble up her fingers.

Then the cat whirled its head around, bit her hard on the soft skin between her thumb and pointer, leapt a foot straight up into the air, and took off like someone had lit a rocket in its ass.

"Ah, god *dammit!*" She shook out her hand, noticed the pinprick puncture wounds, then brought them to her mouth to suck on them. Then she realized a cat mouth had just been on them, and she quickly spat out her hand and rubbed it on the rolled chopsticks she hadn't yet taken out of the napkin.

Jameson laughed. "Cats are so ridiculous." He grinned at the lunatic that had just sprinted off and was already calmly licking its crotch by a table of young professionals clinking glasses.

For all the discontinuity of this restaurant, the tiny blonde waitress who greeted their table seemed the most out of place with her extraordinary ordinariness. She could have been a Nu Alpha Omega with her hair pulled back into a thoughtless circle bun and that look of vague disinterest resting on her face like a misplaced sock that had simply become accepted as a part of the decor.

But when she glanced up from her order pad and saw who was at the table, her tired eyes widened. "Oh, hi," she said, staring at Jameson like he was an ex she hadn't stopped thinking about.

"Hi, how's it going?" he asked, grinning.

"Good."

"No, I mean, really. Is Travis treating you okay? Not being too much of a hard ass?"

Jessica made a mental note of the name drop and how instantaneously it broke through the waitress's shock.

I should've brought a notepad and pen.

She suspected this date night would only continue to be a master class.

The waitress laughed. "Yeah, he's all right."

"I didn't catch your name," Jameson said quickly, staring up at her with rapt attention.

"Jessica."

Her eyes flickered to Jess when she said it, indicating she knew she wasn't unique in this quality, and before either of the women could say another word, Jameson gasped excitedly. "Hey! She's Jessica, too!"

The waitress giggled. "Yeah, I know."

Oh shit. They're looking at me. "Uh, nice to meet you." Did she offer a hand to shake? This felt way more intimate than a normal introduction with a server.

"Two waters and two lotus Buddha sakes, please," Jameson said, politely dismissing the girl. Once she was gone, he turned back to his date. "How do you think that went?"

Jessica shrugged. "Horribly? I mean, you were great."

"You wanted to shake her hand, didn't you?"

"What? No. That would be so weird."

"I saw your arm twitch. It was a good instinct. Simple

touches are a quick way to neutralize the fan's anxiety and force an instant connection. A person can go from someone who recognizes you to a fan for life with one simple touch."

"Are you saying I *should* have shook her hand?"

He cringed. "Oh no. That would have been *incredibly* awkward, don't you think? Never do just a handshake. A handshake is touching, but have you ever felt more relaxed around someone after a firm handshake?"

She thought about it. "No, I guess not."

"Right. Because it's more of a challenge than anything else. Who will squeeze the firmest? Who lets go first? Did the other person look you in the eyes? For how long? Sure, there's an art to it, but it's not the art of intimacy. It's an art of sizing up."

"You some sort of intimacy guru now?" she asked.

He chuckled. "I'm thirty years old and have never had a serious relationship. You decide."

An image of Jameson smashing that incredibly lucky actress against a wall in *Cutthroat Times* flashed on Jessica's mental projector, and she quickly turned her attention downward to the faux bamboo menu. "I don't know what any of this is."

Jameson gazed down at his, though he didn't seem to be hoping the secrets would reveal themselves if he just squinted hard enough, an approach Jessica had taken without meaning to. "Got any food allergies?" he asked.

An orange tabby jumped onto the table, stepping over his forearms and rubbing its back against his chin until its tail brushed against the underside of his nose and he finally seemed to notice its presence. He blinked rapidly, scrunched up his nose on the verge of a sneeze, then gently grabbed it and set it on the ground.

"No," she said. "No food allergies. I don't know that I've ever eaten mass amounts of cat hair, though."

The tabby jumped right back up onto the table, aiming its butthole at Jessica like a threat.

Jameson set the menu down and grabbed the tabby, once again moving it onto the turf. "I can order a few different rolls and some sashimi, and you can do a taste test. Also, don't worry about the cats. Travis assures me that they clean them every morning before they open."

She considered all the morning prep she already had to do before the bakery opened each day and wondered what sort of a masochist would willingly add "bathing three dozen cats" to the list.

When blonde Jessica returned with the drinks, Jameson ordered a series of plates that seemed to go on forever and finished by ordering another round of the sake. "Give it a taste and you'll understand."

She gave it a taste, and she understood.

"Don't drink it too quickly," he said once the waitress left them alone. "You want to relax, but whatever you do, don't get sloppy in public. And only do it in private if someone has confiscated your phone." He sighed heavily. "I learned that the hard way. I thought Cash was going to put a hit out on me the next day."

"They can be a little bit scary," Jessica added.

"And we can be pretty stupid."

She raised her nearly empty drink. "I hear that." They clinked glasses.

By the time the second drink was gone, Jessica was feeling rather sloppy, and Jameson was more talkative than she'd ever seen him.

"Yes, you can *absolutely* have a selfie with us!" he said to two women twice Jessica's age. He picked up one of the sushi pieces in his chopsticks and acted like he was about to eat it in the photo. "Now one with Jessica," he said, waving for her to lean in. That was clearly not why they were there, but they tolerated Jessica's photobomb at Jameson's request.

"This is not at all the night I imagined," she said once the women hustled out of the restaurant, jabbering excitedly.

"It's not?"

"No. Or rather, if I'd imagined it to be this way, I wouldn't have imagined myself enjoying it."

"You're telling me you're enjoying yourself?" He feigned astonishment. "We should probably leave right away, huh? I would hate to see you enjoy yourself."

"Oh, hush, you." She swiped away his jibe with a flick of her chopsticks. "I just mean, this is nice. I'm trying new things and it's not horrible and I'm not worried about it leading to my crucifixion."

Jameson's head twitched to the side, and he stared at her from an angle, his eyebrows cinched together. "That something you worry about a lot?"

"Oh yeah. I mean, sure, there are other things for me to worry about in the day-to-day, but it's always kind of there, you know?"

"I do not."

"Right, right. You wouldn't. No one would, really. I guess it's just—"

"Your cross to bear?" He grinned playfully and waved his arm until their waitress spotted him, at which point he jabbed a finger at each of their empty glasses.

"To be clear," he said, addressing Jessica again, "I'm totally willing to hear all about your crucifixion phobia—cruciphobia? Is that a thing?—I'm willing to hear all about it on the first date, but we'll for sure need another drink."

"Whatever happened to not getting sloppy in public?" Jessica asked.

"I think we already established that we're both pretty stupid."

"Ooh! You know what we should do?" she said.

Jameson leaned forward, elbows on the table.

"We should send a selfie of us to Cash."

Jameson shut his eyes slowly, biting his lip in a sensual way that pulled back the bedroom curtain just a little too far for her comfort, and he moaned. "Yes." He opened his eyes. "Yes, we should do that. They will die. Here, scoot this way so we can get a good one."

Jessica did, moving her chair next to Jameson's. He put his arm around her shoulder, pulling her close against him. His body was a warm comfort she'd missed these last couple months, and she had no impulse to move away. As he held out his phone in front of them, still fiddling with the settings, she caught the blink of other camera flashes. Someone was taking a picture of the two of them taking a picture.

Jameson snapped a half dozen selfies of them grinning up at the angled lens until they got a good one. Jameson didn't bother adding a filter before he sent it on its way.

"Great," he said, tucking his phone back in his pocket. "We have a few more dishes on their way out, but we should probably start thinking about dessert."

"What is there to think about?" she asked. "I'm in."

He flashed her a sly half-grin that made her mind jump to Chris, and as his arm bushed against hers, she realized she was still sitting right next to him. She quickly scooted her chair back to its original spot at the table and stuffed a large piece of salmon sashimi into her mouth.

Her phone buzzed in her back pocket, and for some strange reason, she was sure who it would be before she answered. That was how things had always worked with her and Chris. It was like they were on the same emotional timer. Maybe it was because he was an angel and she was the daughter of God, but she thought there was something more magical to it than that. Had his face flashed in her mind a moment ago because he was thinking of her, or had the cause and effect gone the other direction? What if, as she'd considered only a handful of times before, she and Chris were destined to be together, and this was just a bump in the road? Was she betraying that destiny by enjoying herself with Jameson?

She unlocked her screen.

The message was from Cash, not Chris.

I will murder you two if you do not make babies
TONIGHT.

Her stomach tightened and she felt the blood drain from her face. When she looked up at her dinner companion, he was already looking back at her, the screen of his phone still lit up in his hand. "Sorry," he said, "I don't procreate on the first date, either."

She laughed because she couldn't think of what else to do. "And I don't procreate before marriage."

He laughed at her presumed joke. Good.

The other Jessica dropped off the next round, and Jameson raised his glass. "I'm glad you came out with me. It's been fun."

"Yeah," she said, nodding. "It has."

"Do it again sometime?"

She hesitated, then said, "Yeah, that sounds great." And she meant it.

Chapter Twenty

"It feels a little like we're in detention," Jameson said, slinging an arm over the back of his leather sofa. Although, technically, it wasn't his sofa; it belonged to whoever owned the short-term rental he was living in during his months off work. The space looked like it'd been designed by a serial killer who'd been very good about limiting his evil impulses to non-human animals. A mounted deer head above the electric fireplace stared glassy-eyed at Jessica, while the stretched leather lampshade on the coffee table made her doubt her original assumption that the serial killer *had* managed to limit his impulses before. She half expected to see a dried nipple on the thing.

Wendy Peterman stood on a bearskin rug facing the couch, her fists on her hips, her fuchsia heels digging into the rug in a way Jessica appreciated greatly. Maybe it would ruin the morbid decoration.

For anyone else, Wendy's posture would have been

considered a power pose, the kind one does to psych up for a big opportunity but then ceases the second she's in the company of others. For Wendy, though, it looked meditative, almost restrained. "Maybe it feels like you're in detention because you two are easily my worst clients and my patience has worn thin."

Jameson held up a hand to stop her. "Okay, I know that's an exaggeration. You represent *Jeremy Divorak.*"

"Who?" Jessica asked.

Wendy's eyes remained locked onto Jameson. "Not anymore. I fired him."

He furrowed his brow. "You believed the allegations then?"

Wendy rolled her eyes and blew a half-hearted raspberry. "Even if I only believed one out of every ten allegations, that's still a lot of women to grope."

Jessica felt the need to contribute: "One is definitely too many women to grope."

Wendy pointed at her. "Correct, but you're not off the hook."

Jessica sank back into the couch.

"Speaking of which," Wendy said, narrowing her eyes at Jameson. "You haven't groped anyone who didn't want it, right?"

"No!" He glared at her.

"Not even a little bit?"

"What does that even mean?"

"No nipple tweaks?"

Jameson rolled his eyes. "No."

"And no dick pics?"

"Nope."

She sighed. "Good. I swear, I'm never taking on another male client again."

Cash, who'd been sitting on an ottoman to the right of the couch and hadn't looked up from their phone once since entering Jameson's death shack, said, "Women aren't exactly angels, either."

"Nuh-uh," Wendy snapped, pulling their attention away from the screen. "Just because you don't play for either team doesn't make you the referee."

The social media consultant rolled their eyes and returned to scrolling on their phone.

"Can we get on with this?" Jessica said. "I promised my mom the meeting would only take an hour, and it was fifteen minutes just to drive here from work."

Wendy nodded. "Fair enough. I'm happy that you've taken my advice, Jessica, and connected with someone who can help you navigate these waters, but a freaking heads up would have been wonderful. Cash has been playing clean-up on paparazzi stories all day. You know how many photos you two took with randoms last night?"

Jessica did not, but she ventured a guess. "Twenty?"

"Try forty-seven and counting," said Cash. "Those are just the ones I've found on public accounts."

Judging by his bored expression, Jameson had been through this kind of thing before. "You wanted me to get out more on my time off. And you wanted Jessica to amp up her social interest. I don't understand why you're so pissed."

"Oh, this isn't me pissed," Wendy said.

"It's really not," Jessica said. "I've seen her pissed. You throw Jimmy Dean in the mix, and *then* she's pissed. But who isn't, really?"

"Jessica's right," Wendy said. "And, truthfully, I'm not that upset with her."

"Sexist," said Cash.

Wendy ignored it. "There's no way for her to know that these kinds of relationships need to be arranged in advance with the help of publicists who carefully orchestrate the outing, including fan interactions, or lack thereof. You, on the other hand"—she jabbed a manicured finger at Jameson, and Jessica thought the bloodred nail polish seemed appropriate—"know how things are done, and you did whatever you wanted anyway."

Jameson tossed his arms into the air. "Maybe I'm tired of those rules. Maybe that's part of the reason I went to It is Risen to ask her out in the first place! I wanted to be around someone who didn't have all these rules rattling around in her skull."

Jessica would have corrected him on that last bit, explaining that she had more rules orbiting her than possibly any other living being, but she was too preoccupied with the revelation that Jameson Fractal had visited It is Risen the day before with the *intent* to ask her out. He wasn't just looking for a gluten-free bite to eat and to say hello to an old friend. She'd thought she had been the one to initiate the outing, but no. She'd played right into his hands.

And she'd loved every second of it.

Wendy grabbed her laptop bag off the oak coffee table and rifled through it. "I'm glad you're taking this journey to find yourself, Jameson, I really am." By her tone, she was not. "But in finding your bliss, you left Jessica open to be blindsided." She pulled out a small stack of papers and tossed them on the couch cushion between her two clients.

Jessica grabbed the print-out off the top. She read it aloud, hoping for some insight from the others. "The Temptation of Jameson?" Below the headline was a photo to presumably illustrate the point. An over-the-shoulder shot had her in plain view and only the side of Jameson's face visible. She was giving him the most obvious bedroom eyes she'd ever seen. Or maybe she was just about to blink. Her lips were slightly parted like she was preparing for a kiss at any moment. Or maybe she was just chewing rice. The caption read, *Jessica McCloud sloppily seduces Hollywood nice-guy Jameson Fractal.*

She looked up at him. He was grimacing. She looked at Wendy. The publicist's smirk was one of vindication.

Jessica grabbed the next print-out. Across the top was the logo for Thornton News. This wouldn't be pleasant. "Self-Proclaimed Messiah Rebounds with the Anti-Chris." She read it again silently. "What in the hell is this nonsense?" She glanced down at the photo and when it sank in what she was seeing, she felt like tearing the paper in half. Maybe burning it. Possibly even salting the ashes.

Below a picture of Jessica making the most grotesque face she'd made in her life while Jameson walked next to her on the sidewalk, beaming, looking generally care-free as he guided her forward with an arm around her shoulders, was the caption of, *Is Jessica McCloud spiritually manipulating men to get back at beloved ex and pro football sensation Christopher Riley?*

"No!" she shouted at the page. "I'm not! And I'm sneezing in that picture! Doesn't a girl get to sneeze in public?"

Wendy shook her head. "Not anymore."

Jessica rounded on Jameson. "You took me to a cat bar! You knew I would sneeze!"

"I couldn't have known. Not everyone is allergic to cats," he said.

"No," said Wendy, "I'm pretty sure *everyone* is allergic to cats. It doesn't matter, though. The point is that your life has changed, Jessica. Don't take this the wrong way, but I've read shampoo bottles more interesting than your life over the last year. Whatever attention you had before is nothing compared to what will result from you dating a well-known actor."

Jessica held up a hand to stop her. "First of all, if you're talking about Dr. Bronner's shampoo, I'm not offended. Also, we're not dating. We went on one date as friends." She looked to Jameson for corroboration, and he nodded.

"It's true. We were just hanging out. I walked her home after dinner and we hugged on her doorstep. I didn't even go in the building because I didn't want any rumors starting."

Wendy sighed. "Small victories, I guess. But regardless, you know better, Jameson. There's no 'one date' in Hollywood. No being friends with single women, either."

"Couldn't we just tell someone in the press we're just friends?" Jessica asked. "I mean, that's your *job*. To release information about us."

Wendy wrinkled her nose. "Oh yeah, I could do that. But I'm not going to." When she paused, the hint of a grin appearing, Jessica assumed it was for dramatic effect and didn't jump in with the obvious question. She was correct. "The notion of you two dating is the best thing that has happened to me in years. It might also be the best thing that's happened to you."

Jameson jumped in this time. "Like Jessica said, maybe it was a date, but we're not dating."

"Oh yes, you are," said Wendy firmly. "Everyone thinks you're dating, so you're dating. I honestly don't care what you call it, but next time you two go hang out as totally platonic friends, do yourselves a favor and flirt just a little more." She brought a hand to her chin and nibbled her bottom lip at she stared pensively at the ceiling now. "And then you walk her home again, and ... the two of you need to have a moment on the doorstep, but it doesn't happen. Yes!" She wagged a finger at them for the grand finale: "And then Jessica, you grab him by the shirt collar and pull him inside and up the stairs!"

When she returned her gaze to her clients, Jessica wasn't sure if she would have to be the one to burst Wendy's bubble, or if Jameson would resurrect chivalry and do it himself.

To his credit, he took the lead. "I'm not going to make Jessica invite me up after we hang out. That's creepy."

Wendy waved him off dismissively. "Oh please. I'm not saying you have to go upstairs and sleep together. Hell, you could go upstairs and watch reruns of *The Office* and then go home. In fact, that would probably be a better time, considering the complete lack of chemistry between you two."

Jameson's head snapped back. "What do you mean, lack of chemistry?" and Jessica nodded along, offended even while she understood the odds of an Adonis like him and someone as bland as her lacking genuine sizzle were high.

Wendy rolled her eyes. "Don't take it personally. Jameson, everyone thinks they have chemistry with you, and Jessica's need for a rebound is about as clear on her face as her need for a good night's sleep. And Jessica, you play right into Jameson's need to chase after women who make him feel inferior. Two suitable pathologies does not chemistry make."

When Jameson opened his mouth then quickly shut it, Jessica couldn't have agreed more.

"The point," Wendy said, "is just to make everyone else *guess* what's going on between you two."

"What if I don't want people guessing?" Jessica said.

Wendy groaned and rolled her eyes. "Just call him and tell him the truth then."

Jessica's mouth fell open. "Call who?"

"Chris," said Wendy. "You said you don't want people guessing and what you really meant was you don't want Chris thinking you're sleeping with Jameson. That's the only thing it could be, because *everyone* wants the world to think they're sleeping with Jameson."

When Jessica looked at Jameson, he shrugged; clearly he didn't disagree with the assessment.

Oh, to have that level of confidence.

"You want me to talk to him?" Jameson offered. "I don't mind. I like Chris. I can just tell him we're friends and this is just for PR."

It was tempting, like most things about Jameson. But she said, "No, I can talk to him myself."

"Outside of Chris," Wendy continued, "you're fine with people thinking you're hooking up with Jameson Fractal?"

Why was she making a big deal out of this? Of course she was fine with that! She might even email links to the more favorable articles about it to a few select frenemies from Mooretown.

She shrugged as casually as she could. "Yeah, I guess that's okay."

"Great." Wendy finally sat down on the leather armchair behind her. "Now we should talk about what to expect. Those pieces"—she pointed at the papers on the couch—"are just the beginning. If the angle of you seducing him doesn't work, tabloids will find some other unflattering way to paint you. I assume they'll go for the money angle first, like you're only with him because your business is failing and you're desperate for cash."

"But my business *is* failing, and I *am* desperate for cash."

"Right," she conceded. "But you're not asking for handouts from him."

Jessica cringed. "I mean, I live in a condo he owns, rent-free."

The publicist had forgotten about that, if her slow nod was any indication. "Yes, but people don't know that yet."

"They will," said Cash. "They'll dig into all her financial records once they suspect she's hurting for money."

"Fine," snapped Wendy. "We'll deal with that."

Jessica looked down at the print-outs again. She flipped past the first two and found a second one from Thornton News. The photo was grainy, and she couldn't figure out what was happening in—

"Oh sweet hell!" She flipped the page facedown on the couch so she didn't have to look at it for another second, but more importantly, so Jameson didn't glimpse it.

"Yeah," Wendy said remorsefully. "Pulling no punches."

The actor looked back and forth between the women. "What? What is it?" He reached for the paper but Jessica snatched it away. The secrecy only drove his interest. "Oh come on!" He leaned forward, reaching for it again, but

Jessica extended it as far over her head as she could, leaning back against the arm of the couch. It didn't deter him as he crawled over her, pressing her into the leather cushions. She got a face full of his toned chest a moment before he grabbed the top half of the page, tearing the thing in two and escaping with his piece.

Jameson only needed the top half to see the problem. As she attempted to right herself again, he inspected the picture quickly and said, "Oh, it's just this one?" He tossed the torn half onto the coffee table, the gruesome photo of his assassination landing face-up. "Sort of a stretch. Stupid headline. 'Savior Complex'? Not even original."

Wendy said, "Yeah, well, this is Eugene Thornton we're talking about. Or at least his publication. More likely than not, some unpaid intern was forced to write that after days of workplace harassment."

"How are you okay with that picture?" Jessica demanded. "Isn't it weird to see yourself with your jaw ..."

"Nearly shot off?" he said. "Yeah, it's weird. And the look on Monica's face is upsetting, too. But trust me when I say I've been through a *lot* of therapy since that event. Like, so much. So, so much."

"Yeah, all right. I'll trust you on that."

"You should try it!" he said. "It's fantastic!"

She thought back to her one attempt in college, when the therapist had diagnosed her with Daddy Issues and convinced her she wasn't God's daughter. What a nice fantasy, but ultimately an unhelpful one. "I think I'm good." Just before she threw her half of the torn page onto the table, she caught sight of the second headline. "Wait, what's this?"

"Hold it up?" Wendy requested, and Jessica did. "Oh, yeah ... *that*." She shook her head disapprovingly. "One of Jimmy's accusers. Eugene is running an expose on each as they come forward. Never mind that Jimmy has enough accusers to run a hit-piece a day for the next week and a half, let's dig up every piece of dirt, every man she's ever slept with, every church she's ever attended, and every Tweet she's ever drunkenly hit send on."

The headline read *Misandrist No. 10: Rachel Forrester*. And below it was a picture of a woman, presumably in her late thirties who looked to be in her early fifties. She was slightly overweight with short, frizzy orange hair and was in the middle of eating a donut. "That's awful. Wait, what's a misandrist?"

Cash answered. "Someone who hates men."

"Why are they saying she hates men?"

Wendy answered. "Because she's one of the women accusing Jimmy of brainwashing her when she was a teen. Ergo ..."

"Hold up. Hating Jimmy suddenly means you hate men? Psh. I guess I hate men, then." She turned to Jameson. "Not you. Sorry."

His arm was over the back of the couch again, and he raised a hand to assure her it was just fine.

"How can Eugene do this? Do people actually read this stuff?"

"Oh yes," Wendy said tersely, "people read this stuff.

They suck it down like it's their morning Mountain Dew. And to answer your question, Thornton can do it because none of these women are more powerful than him or Jimmy. And he can keep doing it until someone more powerful than them decides to step up, fill her own damn shoes, and set the record straight once and for all about Jimmy Dean."

Jessica tilted her head back, staring down her nose at Wendy. "I feel like that was pointed at me."

"Mm-hmm." Wendy forced a smile as she stood. "Glad you're catching on. Whenever that time comes, you just let me know, and I'll happily help you exonerate all those innocent women whose lives are being ruined. Until then, I better see you two in the papers. The best thing you can do for those women outside of, you know, womaning up and embracing your literally God-given role, is to knock them clean off the front page. And I believe we've already covered how to do that." She winked at Jameson, and that concluded the meeting.

Chapter Twenty-One

Jessica surveyed the array of outfits draped over her comforter. She almost never made her bed anymore, but she had today, because this was important. She needed a canvas to help her make this impossible decision, and her cheap, lumpy white comforter would do the trick.

What did one wear to a music festival? There would be pictures galore taken of her, she was sure, but did that mean she should wear something nice? Maybe put on some makeup and try to curl her hair without burning the back of her neck like she always did?

She'd be outside all day, and while it was early October, that meant little in Texas. It was short-sleeve weather by a mile. Maybe a dress would allow for nice airflow. Except, her only dress was formal.

Shorts then.

She looked down at her legs where they stuck out from her cotton underwear. The leg hair she'd neglected shaving was noticeably lighter than the ash brown hair hair on her head. Maybe no one would notice.

No, surely the sunlight would make it more obvious.

Then again, this was Austin. Plenty of women didn't shave.

But this wasn't "I don't shave" growth, though. That was the problem. This was "I can't accept my own body hair, so I shave, but I've also let myself go," growth. Her leg hair was a cosmetic cry for help if she ever saw one.

There was no wearing jeans, though. Much too hot for that. She'd have to shave. Unfortunately, she'd already showered, which meant it was dry shave time. And if she was going to wear shorts, her legs weren't the only things she'd need to clean up.

Beauty is pain.

That still didn't solve her wardrobe problems. She discarded the no-gos into a pile in the corner.

"Okay, jean shorts and ..." She looked at her shirts. When did she buy so much green? Sure, It is Risen's color was green, and she had purchased a few shirts in that color for work, but holy hell, this was all green. She would blend into the grass and trees at an outdoor music festival.

Actually, that didn't sound so bad. Maybe she could slip off into the wilderness and make friends with the wildlife and leave everything behind ...

A knock on her front door sent panic through her veins. She looked at the clock on her phone and cursed.

Sliding into a sage green tank-top and wiggling into jean shorts she hadn't worn in two years (and realizing she'd gained a few pounds in the meantime), Jessica scrambled to the front door.

As soon as she saw what Jameson had on, she knew she'd picked wrong. And if his clothing didn't tell her, his expression did.

"Come on in. Just need to shave my legs."

"And change into your clothes, right?"

She paused. "Right. And that. Um ... I'm not sure what I should wear."

He shut the door behind himself and nodded. "Okay. This is fine. There's no reason you should know how to dress for this."

He pulled his phone from the back pocket of his bleached jeans, which he'd cut off just above the knee, and began poking at the screen. He wore a Texas flag muscle tank, a red bandana around his head, and his sunglasses rested just above the bandana, the temples tucked underneath. All Jessica could think of when she looked at him was a gay rodeo and she definitely didn't have the clothes for that.

He held up his phone, and she squinted at the image. "That's how women dress for festivals."

"Oh. I don't have a headdress, and even if I did—"

"No, no, forget the head dress. It's super racist anyway. The girl next to her."

Jessica zoomed in on the picture more. "Yeah, I don't have any of that stuff, either."

Jameson worried his lip for a moment then nodded. "Let me just call some people, and we'll get you set up."

He was already dialing by the time she asked, "Which people?"

* * *

While she felt bad about their late start leaving for the festival, she felt even worse about what she was wearing.

The emergency stylists Jameson called arrived like a hurricane and left her bedroom looking the part.

She adjusted her posture in the backseat of the ride share, fidgeting with her shirt. Only an hour before, it had been a standard black T-shirt, a size too small for her, with the It is Risen logo on the front. It was one among a couple dozen she'd ordered months before, with the intent to sell them, when she was feeling a little flush on money— Chris's money. But she'd never gotten around to displaying them for sale, and the box of various sizes and colors had sat in her closet untouched, until Hailey, one of Jameson's cavalry, had cautiously and curiously opened it like it was a newly discovered sarcophagus deep under a pyramid. And Jessica had been the recipient of the obligatory curse.

Hailey had proceeded to take scissors to the extra small until Jessica was left with a shamble of a sleeveless razorback top that exposed her midriff in a way that was unholy at best. Hailey and Amber had also done Jessica the solid of bringing two clear silicone blobs that were specially made for unpadded bras, to give a little lift. Then the two proceeded to dig out Jessica's most padded bra, put the blobs in that, and strap it on her underneath the shredded shirt. The jean shorts, she got to stick with, but only after an inch and a half was cut off from the bottom so that the tip of the pockets showed no matter what. They reminded her of little white flags, which was appropriate considering how she felt in the presence of her bullish stylists.

A borrowed pair of cowboy boots and a bedazzled elastic headband later, and Jessica was officially festival chic.

"You look amazing," Jameson said from the backseat next to her.

She worried the skin underneath her boobs might tear. "Thanks."

"Hailey and Amber for the win." To his credit, he addressed her eyes and not her shelf-like and tender breasts.

She adjusted the headband, trying not to visualize her skull being squished like a stress ball but failing quite profoundly.

"So you're aware," said the driver, a man in his early twenties who Jessica assumed introduced himself to woman as "an entrepreneur," "I can't charge you for the traffic, but it's, like, sort of expected that you'll account for it in your tip."

Jameson leaned forward, clapping the driver on the shoulder. "Yeah, man. Of course. We got you."

I wonder if he only reminds passengers he knows are loaded, or if he's a douchebag all the time.

ALL THE TIME. HE SHOULD HAVE FAILED THE BACKGROUND CHECK.

She found herself more eager than ever to get to the festival and out of this Kia.

A year ago this week, she realized. She'd been stuck in the same traffic, but on her way to a loan meeting, not the music festival that caused all the congestion, and she'd been riding in an F-150 instead. How much things could change in a single year. Some for the best, some not.

But one thing remained the same: this traffic could suck a sack of shit.

"Oh, screw it," she said, and she closed her eyes.

Please don't let this result in an accident.

She inhaled, summoning the power, and then pushed outward with her hands on the exhale.

Rubber screeched around them as cars slid sideways in both directions. There was a moment of eerie silence before the honking began.

"Holy shit," breathed the driver.

"Yes, it is," said Jessica. "Now you'd better get going."

She relaxed back into her seat, leaning her head against the headrest and shutting her eyes.

That was probably a mistake.

WHY WOULD YOU THINK SO?

Because it's unnecessary. And it draws unnecessary attention to me.

THAT SHIP HATH SAILED, DAUGHTER. DID YOU SEE WHAT YOU'RE WEARING?

In contrast to the warmth of the sun on her exposed

skin, Jameson's hand felt cool as it slipped onto her knee. Her eyes popped open, and she rolled her head toward him to see what was the matter.

Oh. Ohh ...

It seemed Chris wasn't the only one positively affected by her miracles.

"You just ..." He licked his lips instead of finishing.

"Parted the traffic. Yeah." She flashed an apologetic half-smile. "Sort of a useless skill."

From the front seat, the driver added, "Useless my ass! You know what kind of tips you would get if you had my job? Part traffic, get people across town in half the time. You could make a killing."

"Huh." Maybe that was the answer to her money woes. Maybe she could start driving for ...

But when her eyes landed on Jameson again, the most minute shake of his head knocked some sense into her. Yeah. That was stupid. If she didn't care how she made her money, she would have already been rich by now.

She let her gaze dance to his hand on her thigh, and a strange idea washed over her. She acted upon it before she could think better, and placed a hand on top of his. He didn't pull away.

And when they pulled up to the festival drop-off ten minutes later, Jameson hurried around to her door, opening it before she could, and offered his hand to help her out. She took it, but once she was on her feet, she didn't let go, and neither did he.

* * *

"I have a couple friends who flew in for this," Jameson said as they crossed the crowded field. "I didn't want to tell you because I didn't want you to freak out."

"Why would I freak out?"

He shrugged. "They're kind of famous, too."

Maybe it was the energy of the festival or the shots of vodka they'd snuck in the backseat just before they arrived, but she was starting to feel like this might not be a terrible day. What's more, the fact that she was thinking that didn't strike her as a giant omen of impending doom like it usually did. "So what? I'm famous too."

Jameson laughed. "That you are. And they're excited to meet you."

"They don't think I'm the antichrist or ... whoever?" As they walked, her gaze locked onto a man equipped in nothing but a loin cloth and shield made of soldered beer cans.

"Not at all. Two of them think you might actually be who you say you are, and the other is a scientologist, so I think believing in you might be too ... *obvious*?"

They passed two women on the ground, one crushing the other into the soft earth with forceful pelvic thrusts, both giggling while a male counterpart aimed a cell phone their way.

"Two *might* think I am who I say I am?" Jessica said, struggling to keep hold on the thread of the conversation.

"Trust me, that's big for Hollywood types. Our default

is to assume nobody is anything like what they say they are."

Her confidence bottomed out the moment immediately following when Jameson let go of her hand to shout and wave and Jessica saw who, specifically, they were meeting.

Not one for keeping up with pop culture, Jessica had assumed she would recognize maybe one of Jameson's celebrity friends, not all three, and definitely not as immediately as she did.

He wrapped an arm around her waist and steered her toward a giant Mexican blanket spread out below a large flag. The flag bore the image of a squirrel shotgunning a beer, and Jessica wanted to know and didn't want to know all at once.

More than a few nearby concert-goers had their backs to the crew, snapping supposedly incognito selfies with the celebs in the background that would undoubtedly be captioned with "OMG look who I found!" and "Just hanging with my bffs. Nbd."

Before hugs could commence, though, Jameson positioned Jessica a half-step ahead of him and shouted over the music from the two distant stages, "Jessica McCloud." He pointed at her eagerly, and Bolt Stevens, star of the Dark & Dirty action franchise was the first to wrap her in his bulky, exposed arms. "Bolt," he said as he let her go. "So glad to meet you Jessica!" Was he the scientologist? And what *was* a scientologist? Jameson had said it like it should mean something to her. Maybe it was a fancy name for "atheist."

She supposed it didn't matter. He gave one hell of a hug, and that wiped away any minor strikes against him like holding completely wrong spiritual beliefs or none at all.

Valerie Villarreal was the next to offer a hug after sharing a long one with Jameson. She, too, had starred in every Dark & Dirty movie that had come out in the past ten years.

While Jessica had personally boycotted the Dark & Dirty movies when the first three came out, due to her intense desire at the time to avoid anything with Jameson Fractal in it, post-assassination, they were the kind of iconic franchise one knew all about by cultural osmosis. Each time a new one was released, and she was pretty sure there were five or six now, the commercials were everywhere. Jessica must have watched the one-second clip of Jameson tearing off Valerie's shirt in the back of an eighteen-wheeler a thousand times on the dorm TV during her freshman year of college.

The memory caused the age gap to sting acutely. She felt small and insignificant in the presence of *real* adults she'd seen on screen since she was child.

Lastly came Jon Damien. She'd seen him in more movies than the rest of them, and he always reminded her of her old teammate Romeo—short but built like a cinderblock, always ready with a joke. Or at least the characters he played were.

Not now, though. He nodded at her with an overly serious expression and she quickly thought, *I bet he's the scientologist*, before realizing she was judging him unfairly for not living up to her unrealistic expectation. She knew him as a funny guy because he read funny lines, but he had every right to be serious outside of work.

Rather than a hug, he offered a hand and they got on a first-name basis as they shook.

Jameson leaned close and spoke in her ear. "Jon is incredibly high right now. Don't take it personally." She laughed, and immediately felt better.

Valerie patted the blanket next to her, and Jessica complied, trying to make sure she didn't flash vag as she maneuvered down on the ground in her short shorts.

NEVER BEEN TO A MUSIC FESTIVAL BEFORE.

With all the noise around her, Jessica wasn't sure if the voice was in her head or not. Surely God didn't just say he'd never been to a music festival.

God?

YES.

How have you never been to a music festival? I know you can't be everywhere at once, but come on.

LOOK AROUND YOU. DOES THIS SEEM LIKE A PLACE WHERE I'M WELCOME?

Since when has that stopped you? You haven't been welcome in my head for twenty-two years.

Jessica scanned the crowd. An older couple, the man in short khaki shorts and white socks pulled up his calves and the woman wearing a sundress with tiny floral print and clunky leather sandals, watched a semi-nude woman manage five hula hoops at once.

Besides, this seems like a place where everyone is welcome. Sure, you may not be hot stuff here, but does everything have to be about you all the time for you to feel welcome?

FIGURES YOU DON'T UNDERSTAND.

For the love of yourself, please stop sulking.

I'M NOT SULKING. YOU'RE SULKING.

What about Christian music festivals? They're all about you.

... HAVE YOU LISTENED TO CHRISTIAN MUSIC?

Remember Mason White? Sure, the lyrics were a little strange and nonsensical at times, but his music was great. Nice, complex melodies. Interesting beats.

God didn't respond immediately, but she could still feel his presence in her head.

Oh right. I almost forgot he only did ... what were those, parodies? Covers? Does most Christian music not sound like that?

NO. IT DOES NOT. THOU SHALT LISTEN TO CHRISTIAN MUSIC AND THEN YOU'LL UNDERSTAND WHY I WOULD RATHER BE SUPERVISING THE CLEANUP OF OIL SPILLS.

His unsaid words hit her like a flick to the forehead. *Shut. Up. Do you cause an oil spill every time there's a Christian music festival just so you can get out of going?*

When God's presence evaporated, she thought she had her answer.

"Are you already high?" Valerie asked, leaning close to Jessica.

"Huh?"

"Did you and Jameson already smoke before you got here?"

"No. Why?" Did Valerie have some goods she wanted to share? It'd been a long time since Jessica had been high, and she was ready to jump right back on that horse.

"You were just spacing out, is all. I was curious."

Damn. "No, no. I was just ..." She wasn't sure what exactly inspired her to say what she did next. Perhaps pushing past her social anxiety had given her a bit of momentum to try new things. Or perhaps there was something about Valerie that engendered trust. Or perhaps it was the vodka from the back of the Kia. "I was talking to God."

Valerie's mouth popped open into a little o, and her eyes turned to slits, but to her credit, she didn't laugh, and a moment later, she nodded her head. "Right. You can do that, huh?"

Jessica let out the breath she was holding. "Yeah, although, when you say it like that, it sounds like I have a choice in the matter."

Now Valerie laughed, and Jessica was reminded not for the first time how important timing and context were when it came to people laughing at her. "You're the real deal, huh?"

"Yeah," said Jessica. "Yes, I'm the real deal."

Valerie nodded toward Jameson and said, "He told us that, but I wanted to meet you for myself before I believed it. Basically no one I ever meet anymore is the real deal. Drawback to being in show business. I hope you don't mind that I had to see for myself."

"Of course not."

"I like you, Jessica McCloud." Valerie slung an arm around her shoulder and pulled her close, and when she did, Jessica wondered how in the hell she hadn't smelled the deliciously overpowering scent of marijuana on the woman sooner and how generous of a person Valerie might be ...

Chapter Twenty-Two

Jessica snaked through the crowds, tacos in hand, trying to relocate Jameson and the others.

As it'd turned out, Valerie *did* have some weed to offer, leading Jessica to vape for the first time in her life. And now it was motherfucking taco time.

She tried to wrangle a bite of one before all the ingredients fell out of the other end. It was clearly too much to manage while she was on the go, and she got all tortilla before the majority of fajita, onions, and peppers fell out the other end and into the paper boat. "Shitballs." She should have grabbed a fork.

When she turned around to head back to the taco stand and pick one up, her eyes were locked onto the mess she was creating rather than where she was going, and she stepped right into the path of an oncoming concertgoer.

When he knocked right into her, she was only just able to keep from dumping out both tacos.

"Oh, my bad. Wait, Jessica?"

She looked up and decided she'd smoked way too much. "Quentin?"

"Hey!" She held out the tacos away from her body just in time as he threw his arms around her. "You didn't tell me you had tickets," he said.

"You didn't tell me you had tickets either," she replied.

He pointed at her. "Fair point. In my defense, I didn't know I had tickets until Callie told me."

Only then did Jessica notice that there was someone standing next to Quentin observing the conversation with a pleasant smile. "Oh, hi." Jessica wiped her greasy hand on her shorts before offering it for a shake.

"So nice to meet you, Jessica! Quentin's told me all about you."

Jessica scrunched up her face. "Really?" She turned her gaze to Quentin, who shook his head almost imperceptibly.

Right. Callie was just being nice. "And he's, um, told me all about you," Jessica lied halfheartedly.

Callie turned a skeptical eye on Quentin as she said, "Yeah, I bet."

The skepticism looked good on this Callie chick, and it was only then that Jessica realized she generally thought skepticism looked good on women. It might even be her favorite look, and Callie wore it especially well. She had latte skin that could have been mistaken for a dark tan, were it not for the way she wore her hair, natural and free in an afro held back by a purple and orange bandana.

"Who are you here with?" Quentin asked, changing the subject abruptly.

Jessica hesitated, but why? Only later would she realize it was because mentioning who she was spending the day with might sound like a brag. "Jameson, Valerie, Bolt, and Jon."

Quentin grinned. "You're really going for it with Jameson, aren't you?"

"Ooh!" said Callie, taking the opportunity to grab Quentin's arm. "New boyfriend?"

Jessica leaned forward. "Between us, no. But we're trying to make it look that way."

Callie's excitement died. "Oh."

"Jameson Fractal," Quentin supplied, filling in the blanks.

Callie dropped his arm. "Wait, what?" Blinking, she looked at Jessica as her mouth fell open into a giant grin. "Jameson Fractal is *here*?"

Quentin threw his head back and groaned, and Jessica immediately felt bad for bringing it up. But not that bad. "Yeah, you want to meet him?"

Callie nodded emphatically and grabbed onto Jessica's arm. "Lead the way!"

Jessica laughed and glanced over her shoulder at Quentin, casting him a look that she hoped clearly said, "You're in trouble for not telling me about her." And he gave her one back that she thought said, "Your boy better not steal my girl."

* * *

Callie fit in with the group better than Jessica did, but Jessica didn't begrudge her for that. She was one of those people who couldn't help but be magnetic, who was apparently born without crippling self-doubt and an inner voice that repeatedly told her no one gave a shit what she had to say. Weird.

Quentin chatted congenially with Jameson, but Jessica knew her old friend well enough to know he was only half listening. Something else was on his mind, and she was just high enough to want to get *right* in the middle of it.

She stood, grabbed him and told Jameson, "I'm going to steal him for a minute." No explanation provided, but none was needed.

Quentin put up no resistance as she hauled him off into the shade of a giant oak twenty yards off, high stepping around blankets and over sprawled-out festival goers.

"You looked like you could use a break," she said.

He cringed. "Was it that obvious?"

"Oh yeah. You've used that glazed smile on me a bunch of times when I start talking about the bakery. Hey, how come you didn't tell me about Callie?"

He shrugged. "I didn't know about it until like two days ago. I'm still not sure where it's going, but hell yeah, I'm going to take her up on a free AMF ticket."

"She seems really cool," Jessica said, fishing.

Quentin scrubbed a flat palm over his close-shaved

hair. "Yeah, she is. I could actually see this going somewhere."

Jessica had expected that answer just from the way he and Callie had related to each other, sneaking conspiratorial glances even when they were involved in different conversations. What she *hadn't* expected, though, was how devastated she was by the idea of Quentin being in a new relationship. It blindsided her. "Going somewhere like marriage?" she asked.

He jerked his head back. "I wasn't talking about that exactly. I was talking about being exclusive. Jesus, Jess, are you caught up in that fever, too?"

"What fever?"

"The one people get into where they're obsessed with everyone getting married so they don't have to focus on their own failed romance."

She puffed out her lips and arched a brow at him. "That's not a thing. And no, I'm not there."

"All right. Just asking. Is that what you wanted to talk about?"

She considered it. "Yeah, mostly."

"Great. But before we pop back over there, and I pry my date free so I can get a little one-on-one time, how in the hell are you not gonna give a guy a heads up about who was waiting for us over there? I almost made a complete ass of myself when I realized 'Bolt' was Bolt Stevens."

"Sorry," she said. "Calling them by their full names seemed like too much of a name drop."

Quinten shook his head disappointedly. "Sometimes

you gotta drop the names, Jess. If you're living it, don't be shy."

"Noted. Hey, you know things about the world, so maybe you can tell me this. What's scientology?"

"A religion," he said.

"Right, but what ... is it?" She couldn't find the right words. She was pretty sure it didn't fall under Christianity or Judaism, which meant she had a zero percent chance of knowledge through cultural osmosis.

"Um." A deep crease appeared in his forehead and he put fists on his hips. "Basically, this science fiction writer got bored of mass producing books, so he wrote out some scripture."

"About?"

"Aliens, mostly."

"And then people ... just believe it's real?"

He nodded. "Yep."

She wrinkled her nose. "I dunno, Quentin. Aliens, a sci-fi writer ... So, this guy just comes out of nowhere and makes up a bunch of nonsense and people believe it ... why?"

Quentin shrugged. "Because it takes their mind off their problems?"

"That sounds more like a fandom than a religion."

"I'm not sure there's a difference."

Jessica was just high enough to consider it but too high to come to any intelligent assessment. "Shit."

They began their journey back to the blanket.

Weaving through the crowd made it impossible to chat

further, which was fine. Jessica became lost in her own head. Not about Scientology, though. That seemed pretty straightforward; if Sir David wrote scripture about the elegant gazelles or prankster ring-tailed lemurs—which, she supposed in a lot of ways he had—she would follow it— which, she supposed in a lot of ways she did.

Her mind was on something else entirely, though. While she was happy that Quentin was happy, something about his new potential relationship left her panicked. She could feel it in his words that his energy had officially shifted away from Miranda and attached itself to Callie.

The twinge in her sternum alerted her that she might have just hit on something.

Miranda and Quentin. Jessica had presumed Miranda dating someone new was just a phase. It would end, and she'd be free to go back to Quentin, who had been carrying the torch. But if Quentin and Callie ended up together, he was as good as tossing the torch into the lake. There would be no one left to fight for that relationship, and she *really* wanted someone to.

But more than that, she realized she'd been relying on Chris to carry the torch while she went out and had her fun. What if he interpreted her staged relationship with Jameson as a hint to move on. *And then he did!*

Could it really be *over* over between her and Chris? A relationship that had seemed like an inevitability in her life for so long now seemed an impossibility.

"I hope you don't mind if I steal my girl from you," Quentin said to Bolt as they returned to the blanket.

Bolt laughed generously and held up his hands. "All yours."

Callie crawled to her feet. "Actually, I'm all mine." She addressed Quentin. "You're just lucky enough to take me for a test spin."

"How do you know it's just a test spin?" he said coolly.

OH, THAT WAS GOOD.

Yeah. Yeah it was.

She wouldn't have expected any less game from her favorite fake ex-boyfriend.

Chapter Twenty-Three

Jessica thanked Jameson for picking up the cost of the ride share and crawled out of the BMW. Her ears were ringing from the prolonged musical assault from multiple stages, and the only thing she wanted in the entire world after a day full of greasy trailer food and sucking in her stomach for candid photos was to crawl upstairs and spend the next half hour taking the world's most gratifying poop while playing mindless games on her phone.

But as she shut the car door behind her, she heard a similar sound from the other side of the vehicle and saw Jameson walking around the back toward her.

Exhaustion washed over her as she remembered she wasn't done yet.

It was a Friday night, which usually meant downtown was a bit of a mess, but with it being a festival weekend, bringing in tens of thousands of tourists from around the world, the energy in the air felt like could explode at any moment into a group brawl, an orgy, or chain-reaction vomiting. Or all of the above. She tried to ignore the phones pointed at her and flashing through the dark when passersby realized who had just slipped out of a ride share together.

Jameson wrapped a protective arm around her shoulder. "You still okay with this?"

"Yeah, of course. I know what I'm getting myself into."

He chuckled. "No, you don't."

They paused at the entrance to her building and he leaned in. "Any ideas for giving Cash a heart attack tomorrow morning?"

She laughed, surprised. "What? What are you talking about?"

He shrugged, and as the streetlight caught the side of his face, she experienced a jolt when she remembered this was Jameson Fractal in front of her. "Sometimes when I'm trying to figure out the best way to get a little extra publicity, I ask myself 'What could I do right now that would give Cash Monet a heart attack in the morning when they see the paparazzi photos?' It almost always works."

She giggled. "Any ideas?"

He leaned in, whispering in her ear, "Making you giggle on your doorstep is a pretty good start, but whispering in your ear really amps it up."

She made an exasperated noise and shoved him away playfully. "You're too good at this. You coming up?"

He grinned and opened the door, holding it for her. "After you."

Jessica found it remarkable how the moment the door shut behind them and they lost her audience, the prospect of inviting Jameson up to her condo—his condo—became an incredibly intimidating one.

This was all just a show, right? Wendy had told them to do this. They were just flirty friends who were trying to advance their clout.

But there was that moment in the sushi bar ... and when they were listening to the headlining act only an hour before, reclining on their elbows, there was a moment when she looked at Jameson, and he was already looking at her. And then, like freaking sociopaths, they just kept looking at each other and grinning.

She was embarrassed even thinking about it. Because it was quite clear that Jameson could take or leave a real romance with her. And she could take or leave a real romance with him. Three out of four of those combinations meant nothing would happen, but if they *both* decided to take it ...

No, it was irrelevant. She couldn't have sex with him anyway.

She shushed him when he tried to speak in the hallway, worried that it would alert Jeremy or Jesus to their presence, and she didn't want to have to explain the complications of this arrangement to her half-brother. Or explain the complications of her neighbors' living arrangements to Jameson.

As she shut the door quietly behind them, she breathed a sigh of relief to be back in her own space.

She brought two glasses of water over to the couch and sat on the opposite end from Jameson, both of them spreading their legs longways across the cushions. "I would ask you to rub my feet, but I haven't had a pedicure in weeks," he said jokingly, and she suspected the humor lay in the idea of her giving him a foot rub rather than the fact that he would consider two weeks without a pedicure a long time.

Flexing her feet to minimize the angle by which he could view her toenails, she chuckled.

"I had a lot of fun today," he said.

"Yeah, me too."

He grinned, and she almost rolled her eyes at how good it looked on him. "I'm glad. That was the point of this, right? To go have a little fun after working nonstop?"

"I think the point was for us to be seen together in public so everyone thinks I'm dating a movie star and you're dating a good-girl."

He shook his head. "No, that was the excuse, but not the point."

After a heavy moment of silence, he said, "Do it again soon?"

"How about tomorrow?"

He laughed at her stupid joke, and somehow that only made her think it was even stupider.

Her bloated stomach gurgled like a volcano, issuing polite notice to every inhabitant of the island to get the hell off and quick, and she cleared her throat to try to drown it out. "Your friends are nice."

He nodded. "Did you guess who the scientologist was?"

"Nope."

"Guess."

She thought about it. "Jon?"

"Nuh-uh. Bolt."

She pushed herself up further on the armrest. "No way."

"Yep."

He hadn't struck her as the fanboy type.

She finished her water and used it as an excuse to flip her legs around and push herself to standing. "If we're going to do this all over again tomorrow, we should probably get some sleep."

He sat up quickly, his hands on the couch cushion next to him. "Right, so should I just ..."

"Yeah, you're welcome to crash. I mean, we're leaving together bright and early tomorrow anyway."

Staring at her sideways, he said, "Right. I can swing by my place for fresh clothes tomorrow, but, um, just the couch or—"

"Yes," she said firmly. "The couch. I'll get you a blanket."

Slowly, he settled against the armrest again, looking slightly relieved. "Yeah, yeah. Perfect. Thanks."

She held her breath until she was in the closet, looking

around for the extra set of sheets, where she finally exhaled, feeling the heat rise in her face.

When she returned with the sheet and a pillow, she said, "You're welcome to use the bathroom if you need, even if I'm asleep. Just let yourself through."

He smiled at her but said nothing, and she refilled her water and hurried into the bedroom.

Her head had hardly hit the pillow when her phone buzzed on the nightstand next to her. Who was texting her this late at night? Had Cash already seen the photos?

She unlocked her screen and felt a rush of guilt wash over her when she saw the sender's name. Despite her intentions to do so, she hadn't given him a heads up about her new staged relationship.

Chris: Saw the pictures of the festival on Twitter. Glad to see you're enjoying yourself.

Was that bitterness or was he being genuine? And which one did she hope it was?

She wrote a rambling message then quickly deleted it. She did that two more times.

The she settled on something simpler.

Jessica: Thanks. Jameson's just a friend.

His response was immediate.

Chris: It looks like he's more than that. That's fine. You don't have to worry about me.

What the hell? Why *wouldn't* she worry about him and his feelings? Why didn't this bother him like it should? Was he being generous or had he already found someone new?

After five minutes of googling "Christopher Riley, Philadelphia Eagles, girlfriend" and only turning up images of herself and three or four of a pig in a green jersey, she had to admit that the results were inconclusive. If he had someone else, he wasn't making it public like she was.

Jessica: I miss talking to you. How's work?

Chris: I miss talking with you too. It's busy. How's yours?

Jessica: Same.

Her glowing screen burned into her eyeballs as she waited for his response. But it never came and she fell asleep.

Chapter Twenty-Four

Jessica showered and dressed in the day-two outfit Amber and Hailey had picked out for her. It was while she was blowdrying her hair that she first smelled the bacon.

"Whoa," she said when she finally set eyes on the pile of food on the kitchen island. "Thanks."

He grinned at her. "Least I can do for you hosting me. There's coffee in the pot, too."

She narrowed her eyes on him. Was there any way she could set it up so that Jameson did this for her every morning and she didn't have to put out or pay him?

CONGRATULATIONS. YOU'VE JUST INVENTED SLAVERY.

Not what I was getting at.

BUT IT KINDA WAS.

"Figure you should start the day on a full stomach," he said as she shoveled eggs into her mouth. "Big plans in store."

"Really?" she said, secretly reveling about the massive dump she'd taken right before bed the night before. If this breakfast was any indication of the day's eating habits, she'd be due for another one later that night.

"Yep. Breakfast, then festival for a while, and then I heard about this super cool event happening tonight that I want to take you to."

"Super cool, huh? How did you know I liked super cool things?" She crammed two pieces of bacon in her gullet before he could tell how much she was lying.

Nothing in her history or her personality made her a fan of things that people like Jameson, with their supreme likability and natural social skills, would call a "super cool event."

But wait, wasn't the festival "super cool"? And their dinner at S8 Su4, albeit strange as hell and possibly the reason she'd been forced to treat herself for a tapeworm the week before, that had been enjoyable enough.

Jameson was able to repurpose Jessica's day-two backup outfit for his own use, saving them a stop by his place to grab more clothes. As they descended the stairs to the front door of her building, after a quick pep talk about the paparazzi who'd been camping out all night to snap photos of them leaving together, Jameson pushed open the door, shooting sunlight straight into her eyes and reminding her to move her shades from the top of her head onto the bridge of her nose.

"Jessica!" cried a frantic voice as soon as she stepped across the threshold.

She turned to her left and saw Jesus hobbling at her along the sidewalk. "What in the ..." She motioned for Jameson to step back and allowed Jesus to go inside. She followed him, dragging Jameson right back in with her, and shut the fogged-glass front door for a bit of privacy.

Though Jesus didn't have a black eye, there was distinct bruising and a cut on his cheek that indicated he might have one the next day. The Ratt T-shirt Jeremy had lent him was torn at the shoulder—which was probably for the best if it meant getting the thing out of circulation—and one of Jesus's shoes was missing. And that didn't even begin to account for the strange wet spots and dirt on him. "What in the hell happened to you?" Jessica asked.

"Joshua?" Jameson said, one of his eyes squinting to half the size of the other. The two of them had hit it off at Jessica's bakery launch party a half-year before, but she was surprised that with everyone Jameson met, he remembered her half-brother's name. Or rather, his fake name.

Jesus took a moment to catch his breath. "I believe I did something wrong, but I'm not sure what it was."

"It looks like you were beat up."

His head swayed back and forth rhythmically, and she wasn't sure he was agreeing with her or about to pass out. "Yes, I was beaten. To be clear, I don't think the intent was to murder me."

"That's good, but it also sounds like you're defending whoever did this to you. Why would you— Oh." She rolled her eyes as it dawned on her. "You were beat up by a bunch of homeless people, weren't you?"

He steepled his fingers in front of his mouth, bowing his head solemnly. "Yes. But I believe it was just a misunderstanding. I was trying to help them, you see."

She exchanged a glance with Jameson, whose wide eyes indicated he was even more out of his depth than she was.

"It looks like they didn't want your help."

THEY DID NOT.

"You stay out of this, Dad!" Jesus said. He looked to Jess for sympathy. "Always with the judgment."

What did he do?

"Nope." Jesus snapped his fingers in front of her face. "You cut that out. I can tell you're talking to Him. I see your eyes glaze over. No gossiping behind my back. All I did was try to provide for them, and they turned on me like a pack of meanies. It's like I'm being tested. I— I can't explain it."

I CAN. HE TURNED A CRACK ROCK INTO A BUNCH OF FISH.

"Oh, for shit's sake, Jesus," Jessica moaned, dragging a hand over her face.

"Daaad," Jesus whined. "I asked You to stay out of it."

Jameson looked back and forth between them. "Did you just call him Jesus?"

"Yeah. His name's not Joshua. He's Jesus." She saw the question in his eyes. "Yes, *the* Jesus." She grabbed Jameson under the armpits to pull him up as he attempted to kneel to her half-brother. "Seriously not necessary."

Jessica turned to Jesus. "Go get yourself cleaned up. And in the future, don't steal people's drugs, okay?"

"Their signs said they were hungry," he protested.

"Yeah, for McDonalds. Not a bunch of dead fish."

Jesus opened his mouth to respond, then snapped it shut.

She let out a long, exhausted exhale and pinched the bridge of her nose where a headache was starting to bud. "They weren't dead, were they?" she asked.

Pressing his lips together tightly, he shook his head. "And now I'm starting to see where the misunderstanding might have started."

With lessons learned, Jessica nodded for Jameson to follow her back onto the street again to greet the paparazzi for real this time.

Chapter Twenty-Five

"Are you going to tell me what the surprise is, or do I have to guess?" Jessica asked as they parked on the street in a warehouse district and Jameson led the way down a poorly lit sidewalk. "Oh, is it my murder?"

"Of course not. If I'd wanted to murder you, I've had way better opportunities before now."

"Not thrilled that you've already thought about it."

Day two of the festival was much like day one, except she didn't run into Quentin and Callie. Perhaps they weren't there or she simply didn't see them in the massive crowd. Or maybe they were avoiding her.

She and Jameson had left before the headliner to return to her condo and shower (separately) and prepare for the evening's surprise plans, which her limited imagination had kept her from making an educated guess about. Her only clue was that she could wear whatever she wanted.

She'd taken that to mean whatever she was wearing would likely be destroyed by the end.

Paintball?

No. No one played paintball at night.

"How about I just give you a hint?" he said.

"I'll take it."

"It's a blind date."

She stopped walking and stared at the back of his head until he realized she was no longer beside him and also stopped. "That's not— You just plain told me what it was. Are you setting me up on a blind date?"

She'd thought this was a date already. Or close enough.

"No, no. That's the hint. *Blind* date."

Shit, was he blind? Had he been blind this whole time and she was too unobservant to notice the signs? Or was he introducing her to some blind friends? That last one would be fine, and it would explain why he didn't care what she wore.

He reached back and grabbed her hand, pulling her forward. "Never mind. You'll figure it out in a second."

It was much more time than that before she wrapped her head around the situation. In fact, it wasn't until she was seated at the table across from Jameson, she presumed, surrounded by total darkness that the hint landed. "Ohh," she said. "Blind because we can't see."

"Right."

The reception area for this event *was* lit by fluorescent lights, which meant that when she first entered, the light streamed in through the door, illuminating some of the surroundings. The tiny glimpse of them left her wondering if this place would pass inspection for tenement housing in the 1800s, let alone a place that served food in modern days.

"How does this work?" she asked, feeling around the table carefully for her napkin.

"The same way it does at any old restaurant, only now you're blind."

"I got that bit. I'm more wondering *why* we're blind."

Jameson laughed. "When you eliminate one of the senses, the others are heightened. You can try it yourself. Close your eyes next time you're eating a chocolate bar. It makes the sensation much more pleasurable. It also works for other things, but, well, not everyone's into that."

She knew he was talking about sex, so she changed the subject. "I guess the food must be really good here, huh?"

"I assume so. This is more of an exhibition, meaning it's only in town a limited time."

That made sense of the location and lack of decor, at least.

She could hear Jameson lean toward her by the change of volume as he spoke. "But mostly, I wanted you bring you here to celebrate."

"Celebrate what?" Hadn't they been celebrating all weekend? Granted, she lacked quite of bit of life experience in the celebrations department, but she imagined it looked a lot like getting high at a music festival two days in a row.

"The progress you're making. I know it was hard for

you to embrace this role as a major celebrity"—she wanted to correct that to "minor celebrity" but she refrained—"but you've done a tremendous job of it. And as a reward, I thought it might be nice to take you out to dinner somewhere no one can recognize you and you can let your hair down a bit."

"That's incredibly sweet and thoughtful of you, Jameson. Thanks."

"Don't act so surprised." He laughed. "I'm more than good looks."

"That you are."

Jameson explained further about the blind dinner, saying it was to raise awareness and (more importantly) funds to help the visually impaired around Central Texas. He also said he'd heard that the waitstaff was entirely blind.

As the waiters handed out the dishes, she heard an awful lot of clatter as they ran into objects here and there. Either these people weren't blind and were struggling to navigate the darkness the same way she had upon first entering, or these people were not great at being blind. Either way, when one of them set her plate down in front of her, she pretended that not only was she blind, but she was totally into it.

What would a blind person do? She thought.

The blind person would use her sense of touch, smell, and taste to enjoy the meal, obviously. She held her palms over the chicken-fried steak she'd ordered, excited to use the heat to warm her chilly hands.

Huh. Maybe her other senses were still adjusting, because she felt no warmth coming off of her plate.

Or perhaps they got the orders mixed up. Maybe it was a salad they'd brought her instead of a chicken fried steak.

She reached down to touch the food, and her fingertip hit cold gravy followed by soggy breading.

Her sense of touch was not impressed.

It was still entirely possible that the thing *tasted* good. So she cut off a bit and threw it back.

Oh god. Holy hell.

There was no doubt in her mind that the deprivation of her sight led to other senses becoming heightened. It was just that she wish they weren't.

The beef was like trying to chew a rubber band ball. The breading was incredibly generous with the pepper, causing her to search the air carefully but urgently for her glass of water.

"Damn," Jameson muttered.

Jessica leaned forward, whispering, "Does yours taste like shit, too?"

When he burst into laughter, so did she. "I didn't think you could screw up mac and cheese," he said.

"'I'll take the check and my eyesight back."

"No kidding." She heard him set his fork clumsily back onto the table, clattering it against his plate in the attempt. "Sorry, I thought this would be fun."

She reached forward on the table, knocking an unidentified but extraneous utensil to the ground, until she found his hand. "It is fun. If I'm hungry later, I can eat.

This is a sweet gesture, and it *is* nice to not have to worry about being photographed."

He squeezed her hand back. "As long as you're enjoying yourself, so am I."

One of the waiters bumped into her chair, and she instinctively said, "Oh, sorry," which was of course short for "Sorry for existing and occupying space," even if her conscious mind wasn't aware of that.

Then a hand landed on her shoulder, gripping confidently, and the squeak of a chair across the linoleum floor followed, turning the table for two into a table for three.

"Jessica," said an all-too-familiar voice. "Fancy seeing you here. Get it? *Seeing*?"

How in the ...? "Go away, Jimmy."

"Jimmy?" said Jameson. "As in Jimmy Dean?"

Jimmy chuckled charmingly. "Actually, it's Reverend Jimmy Dean, but I won't hold it against you. There's someone I'd like you to meet, Jessica."

She remained silent, not wanting to give him the slightest morsel of anything, except maybe a forceful mouthful of her chicken fried blob. How dare he interrupt their meal to barge in and introduce random people. "Jessica, this is Emily. Emily, Jessica."

The back of a hand clumsily whapped Jessica's face before she was able to snatch it for a microsecond of a shake. Judging by the angle, Emily was standing next to Jimmy's chair. "So nice to finally meet you, Jessica. I've heard so much about you."

"I bet you have."

"Emily is my fiancée," Jimmy explained, "in case you don't watch the news."

"Congrats," Jessica replied sarcastically. "And I watch enough news to know that. It's cute that you introduce her as your fiancée rather than your favorite victim."

Emily sighed like a patient mother. "I was so wrong, and I feel terrible. I'd misconstrued his love for us as a need to control, and in my mistake I poisoned the minds of so many others. It's all my fault Jimmy's being tried in the court of public opinion."

Jessica's sense of empathy had not been heightened by the visual deprivation. "Doesn't that work out well, considering it's all *Jimmy's* fault that I'm tried in the court of public opinion on a quarterly basis."

"Don't be dramatic, Jessica," Jimmy said. "Your social clout is higher than it's ever been. Due in part, I presumed, to the tireless efforts of Mr. Fractal and the rest of your PR team."

"What do you want, Jimmy?" It was always best to get to that question sooner than later.

"What do I want? All I truly want is for you to give me the benefit of the doubt every now and then. You treat me as your whipping boy, your sacrificial scapegoat, and it's like there's no path for redemption for me in your eyes, nothing I can say or do to snap you out of this false and negative opinion of me."

"You're right," she said. "There's nothing you can do or say to make me stop thinking you're a sleaze. And I'm not withdrawing the lawsuit, if that's where this is going."

He leaned forward, the heat of his breath far warmer than her meal. "Look, I know I've made mistakes, but I'm only human. Sumus omnes porcos, you know? That doesn't exclude me. If you want to harden your heart to the point where people who care about you are punished forever for making simple mistakes, well, I hope you're ready for the disastrous results of that over the long term. It can truly calcify the soul."

"Are you kidding me? You're trying to play off your malicious attacks as mistakes?"

"Have you never made a mistake that wounded someone? And take Emily here. She was just where you were not so long ago. She had made up her mind that I was some sort of charlatan who rounded up a bunch of teenaged girls with an improper motive. Nothing I could say or do would change her view on that. And then ... well, tell them what happened, Emily."

"God spoke to me."

NOT TRUE.

"And He told me to start softening my heart, that the bitterness was what was causing my nightmares and depression and that if I just let go of it, He would guide me to healing. So that's what I did. I released the bitterness and called Jimmy to apologize for the part I was playing in his persecution."

"Prosecution," Jessica corrected. "Or maybe that's just wishful thinking."

"You know," Jimmy said, "it pains me to think that you'd even entertain the possibility that what I've done was intended in any sort of malicious way. I mean it. It genuinely *pains* me to think of that. And I just can't stand the idea that you might be going around perpetuating that false belief without giving me a chance to properly explain my actions to you."

"I'm sorry you can't stand that idea, Jimmy." She wasn't sorry. She was only sorry she hadn't talked shit about him publicly more often. "And I'm sorry I wrote a mostly false book about my life and included a fraudulent foreword by you. Oh wait. That wasn't *me* who did that. That was ..."

Jimmy clucked exasperatedly. "Oh, come on, Jessica. We both know the judge will throw out the suit as soon as he lays eyes on it. Your claim is so entirely unbelievable! How are you going to write such a lovely introduction to my memoirs and then deny you ever wrote it?"

"Deny I—" She couldn't finish. Or rather, she could, but it would be extra loud and assault the heightened senses at the tables around her. Instead, she hissed, "You're so full of shit, Jimmy. One day, everyone will know it."

Emily laid a hand on Jessica's shoulder, and she swatted it off. Undeterred, Emily said, "I am so sad for you. Holding so much hate in your heart is a heavy burden. Just know that whenever you come around, I'll be waiting here with open arms to receive you."

"Didn't I tell you, Em?" said Jimmy. "I told you she was just like how you used to be. Yes, I'm upset that you would dismiss me, Jessica. But mostly, like Emily, I'm just sad. Sad for you." His voice shook. "You must feel so alone, thinking the man who helped bring you into this world would, what, exploit you? That's what you think, isn't it? That I exploited you? Deus Aper! You must feel so terribly, terribly alone."

The word "alone" was the last one Jessica heard, but she was sure there were more. However, she'd grabbed Jameson's hand and whispered for him to follow her out as soon as the Jimmilogue began, and Jameson was more than happy to do so.

They gave themselves away the moment they opened the door out of the dining area and light streamed in. But that was fine. They had a head start and could disappear before he followed.

On the drive back to her condo, Jameson asked, "Do you think it's possible Jimmy is just misunderstood?"

"No."

"Not at all?"

"Not even a little bit." And yet, that conversation nagged at her. Even as she knew he was trying to manipulate her, the manipulation seeped in.

"Gah! I hate him!" She smacked the dashboard of her car.

The idea that Emily would go from patient zero of his scandal to his fiancée seemed so unbelievable that she must be missing some key bit of information. Was Jimmy blackmailing the woman? Obviously he wasn't above that. But no, she didn't get that feeling at all from Emily. The poor woman genuinely seemed to have had an impossible change of heart that convinced her that not only should she forgive Jimmy for taking advantage of her, but she should stop believing that he had taken advantage at all.

Could that be the case with Jessica? She *did* tend to assume the worst about everything Jimmy did. Benefit of the doubt was something she'd afforded Ice Cream Jimmy as a child, and Church Jimmy had cashed in on it when he'd invited her and Destinee to White Light. Since then, she'd assumed the worst. But maybe that was a mistake. Maybe if she'd given him more of a chance …

Then she remembered his fake resurrection in front of his congregation. And his memoirs. And how he got his followers to antagonize her at college. And, and, and.

"How does that happen?" she asked.

"What?"

"How does someone like Emily *used* to be turn into someone like Emily is now?"

Jameson sighed as they pulled into the parking garage for her condo. "You're asking me to understand more about women than you do, Jessica, and it's just not going to happen."

"Fair enough." She looked around. "Oh, are you coming up?" Usually he would drop her off at the curb, unless he planned to stay.

"If you want me to. I also thought you might like to be able to get inside without people seeing you."

"Yeah, it's been a nice change of pace being invisible again."

"Oh, no. That's not why." Jameson put the car into park and grimaced as his eyes locked onto her chest. "You have a huge gravy stain all down your front."

She looked down at her black blouse and saw the white gravy. A large chunk of it still clung, but the rest had dried and begun to crust. "Ah. Yeah. Probably don't want to be seen with this."

He shook his head. "Especially not getting out of the car with me."

She grabbed her purse, then thought, Oh what the hell? "Come on up and we'll order a pizza."

Jameson grinned. "You better stop talking dirty to me if you're not going to put out."

"Ha!" She hurriedly opened the car door and jumped out, unsure what else to do in the face of a fantastic come-on that could never amount to anything.

Chapter Twenty-Six

There was a price to pay for everything. Jessica knew this. Even as she'd enjoyed her weekend and the late-night chat and drinks with Jameson that had felt remarkably comfortable and familiar and hardly awkward at all, she'd been aware that on the other side of it would be extra work and extra problems for her.

What she *didn't* expect, however, was the envelope taped on the back door of It is Risen that she discovered upon arriving the following Monday morning. Probably a heads up from Destinee, Judith, or Rex, she figured, still floating on a high from the weekend. Maybe they were running low on flour and they weren't sure she'd notice it on the inventory form before it became an issue. Something like that. The three of them had graciously taken full charge of the bakery while she was out on her adventures in celebrity, and in exchange for their overtime, she'd given everyone Monday off. It was all Jessica now.

Could she do it by herself without any help for an entire day?

The answer was simple: she had to. So she would.

The first thing that struck her as off about the envelope was that she didn't recognize the handwriting. She knew her mother's handwriting, and she was fairly certain this wasn't Judith's, though she couldn't precisely visualize what Judith's looked like. She was sure she'd seen Rex's handwriting before outside of just Xs and Os, though, again, she couldn't visualize it. No, this scrawl was unfamiliar, and the fact that her name was in the center of a large heart was further evidence that it wasn't from Rex or Judith.

She pulled it off the door where it was taped at eye level and tore open the seal, pulling out a stiff, folded sheet of cream-colored card stock. Something tumbled free when she separated the letter from the envelope, and she stooped over to grab it from the ground.

It was a photo. She rotated it one-hundred and eighty degrees before she realized what it was.

"Motherfuck!"

She spun around, sure whoever had snapped this invasive picture was standing right behind her.

But no one was, at least no one she could see through the pre-dawn darkness or in the small area covered by the security light over the back door.

Whatever was in this letter would still be there when she was securely indoors.

Fumbling with her keys, she cursed and missed the

lock multiple times as she took her eyes off of it to glance back over her shoulder.

She slammed the door shut behind her and locked the deadbolt in the same motion as she flipped on the lights of the kitchen. Remaining absolutely still for a moment, she didn't need a blind dinner to heighten her senses now. She listened for any sound of movement until her heartbeat slowed minutes later. She was too panicked to even go for her phone. The moment she looked down at her screen would be the moment someone attacked—that was just her luck.

She wasn't sure why it rattled her so bad. There was simply a shapeless jitter running through her, like when she'd spotted a spider on the shower curtain the other day while she was washing her hair. Yes, it felt strikingly similar: caught by surprise, naked, on unsteady ground.

She glanced at the clock above the entrance to the cafe and realized she'd been standing against the back door, hardly breathing, for almost ten minutes.

Shit. The bakery wasn't going to prep itself.

Only then did she remember that she still hadn't read the letter.

The photo had been alarming enough, taken from the street looking up at her condo window. It featured her and Jameson Fractal entering into the living room after day one of the festival. Whoever had taken this had likely been one of those on the street only feet from her when she'd left the ride share before he (she had a firm gender bias on this one) had waited for her to go inside.

She'd sworn her blinds were shut, but she must have had the slats the wrong direction, allowing for slices of the interior to be visible from the low angle.

Whatever was in the letter was unlikely to make this eerie situation any less so. The best-case scenario was something like, *"Hey, just a friendly reminder to rotate the blinds the other direction. Here's what people can see from the street. I'm a totally normal person, but you might someday let a creep spy on you, so I thought I'd give a heads up."* But even *that* explanation would feel a little disingenuous.

She slid onto a stool next to the stainless steal prep table and unfolded the letter.

Dearest Jessica.

You deserve so much better than that pretty-boy scum. He is a rat and you are an ancient force, mightier than God himself. I see who you truly are, and I embrace it. Your power must be tamed and shaped, your wild passions broken, and I am the one who can do that. If you accept this gift I offer you, tilt your open sign to the right and I'll see it and know. I eagerly await your answer.

Hard pass on that, she thought. She checked the bottom of the letter for a signature and only saw "Your Loyal Master," which she assumed was not the sender's legal name.

She inhaled deeply, granting her heart permission to slow the hell down.

This was creepy, yes, but it was only low-grade creepy. After seeing the picture, she'd half expected to open the card and find it written in blood or semen. It looked to be blue ink, though. Almost a let down. At least with the other substances she would have clear DNA evidence if it came to that.

Should she call the cops? This seemed like something someone might call the cops about, but then again, what were *they* going to do? Just show up, say, "Yep, that's creepy as hell," maybe tell her to have someone accompany her to and from work for a while? She could do that without wasting their time and possibly raising questions about why cops were seen at It is Risen in the early morning hours. Eugene Thornton could have a real field day with that.

It was probably nothing to worry about. After all, the sender seemed to like her. It wasn't a "go die in a ditch, u antichrist cunt" like she occasionally saw in her filtered messages on Facebook.

Yet comparing the two was apples to oranges. Cyberstalking was perfectly normal; in-person stalking was not.

While everyone complained that the internet made the world a less safe place, she'd long suspected it was the opposite, that the internet had conditioned everyone to be too lazy to leave the house to properly stalk. Instead, they just stole people's identities as a result of their obsessive need to control the target, and she'd happily give up her identity and assume a new one. It was the closest thing to an erotic fantasy she had the energy for nowadays.

Another ten minutes had slipped by while she considered the letter, and now she was super screwed on time. She'd have to drop a couple of the sweeter items from the menu today, but that was no big deal. Sales on sweets were always down on Mondays as everyone repented from their weekend diets and decided to turn over a new leaf for a few days. Meanwhile, things like oatmeal raisin cookies and the spinach empanadas were hot sellers.

After double-checking that the open sign wasn't tilting even one degree to the right, she did her best to put the letter out of her mind.

She prepped the food and got the first trays in the ovens before heading over to the shelf by the telephone where she kept all her paperwork. This was not the first time she'd considered having a beer before six am, and it wouldn't be the last. At least not until she could catch up on the bills and taxes. She'd had to prioritize what expenses were paid on time, and she'd opted for paychecks. But now, staring at all the unopened envelopes, she wondered if she'd made the right choice.

It wasn't like she didn't have the money flowing in. In fact, in the days since she and Jameson had first been spotted frolicking about with each other, the bakery had seen record sales numbers. The money was there, she simply didn't have the time now to move it to where it needed to be.

And there was the crux of the problem. More time with Jameson meant more money, but it also meant less time to be a proper business owner. Was there a balance where she could have enough time and money to keep this business open, or was she doomed to teeter-totter from one deficit to the other?

She tossed the stalker's letter and photo in with the rest of the litter and went to check the empanadas.

* * *

The imbalance of her work and personal life was highlighted the moment she finished setting out the pastries in the glass display case and looked up toward the front windows of the bakery.

No, surely all those people weren't lining up for this place.

The line extended beyond the view of the windows, and she hoped they weren't wrapping around to the back of the building, because she'd spent zero time making *that* a friendly place.

After a glance at the clock, which showed that she still had ten minutes before her official opening time of six a.m., she considered her options. Open now and try to hurry some of the line through, or give herself ten minutes to mentally prepare for the shitshow that was to come?

Of all the days to be working without help.

It should have been good news that the demand for her gluten-free goods had risen to this. The whole point of running around with Jameson all weekend was to drum up gossip, interest, personal brand value, and therefore, sales, wasn't it?

And to have fun.

It'd worked like a charm on all fronts, and now she wished it hadn't.

Typical.

She split the difference, deciding to give herself five minutes alone in the back to suck down another cup of coffee, which was just a little too watered down from the amount of ice she had to mix into it to keep it from scalding her mouth.

ASK FOR HELP.

Fine. Please help.

OH. UM. THIS IS AWKWARD. NOT FROM ME.

What, you can't help me?

I CAN. IT'S NOT THAT.

What is it?

I ALREADY PROMISED A LITTLE ERITREAN BOY I WOULD KEEP HIS ENTIRE FAMILY FROM BEING SLAUGHTERED TODAY.

There it was. The Almighty Guilt Trip.

Whether God had actually made that promise with any intent to keep it would never be known. Jessica *hoped* He would, obviously.

Then maybe you ought to be in Eritrea, not breathing down my neck.

*I WAS JUST ABOUT TO GO, **MOM**. JUST ASK FOR HELP, OKAY?*

Who do I ask? I already gave all my help the day off.

But God had left the building. And if He was doing His job, He'd also left the continent.

The immediate face that leapt into her mind when she tried to think of who to call seemed equal parts ridiculous and brilliant. Ridiculous because there was just no way he'd ever worked a job like this in his child-star life. But brilliant because probably no one would care if he knew what he was doing and he was the reason the line was stretching down the block anyway.

She called Jameson, who she'd obviously woken, and he agreed to come immediately.

"Wait," she said before he hung up. "Better to come a few minutes later and look your best."

His voice was deathly serious. "Of course. What should I wear?"

The dress code at It is Risen was incredibly loose, and she was willing to make it even less restrictive for him. "Jeans that cost more than my car and a designer tee you don't mind getting dirty."

Before heading back into the cafe, she paused at a mirror by the door and smiled. Nope. Too forced. Whenever she forced a smile, only half of her face was on board. She needed full facial compliance to pull this off. She focused on the fact that she was about to have Jameson Fractal working for her, and that did it.

She made for the front door to unlock it but paused when her eyes caught sight of the small dry-erase sign she'd stashed underneath the register.

Photos with Jessica McCloud: $10

She grabbed it, pulled the marker from the drawer and replaced the ten with a fifteen. Then she added "Photos with Jessica and Jameson: $20" and set it back up on the countertop.

With this kind of traffic, she might be able to pay the month's mortgage in a single day of photos.

Granted, she still had to find the time to sit down and do finances ...

By the time Jameson arrived nearly forty-five minutes later, every table was full, waiting for his arrival, which she'd announced in advance as the line filed in. Word spread quickly and organically through the waiting customers.

Jessica had instructed Jameson to come in through the back, and when he stepped out of the kitchen, high-pitched cheers echoed painfully off the walls.

Being the genius at this that he was, he waved at the crowd but made straight for Jessica. She couldn't help but grin at the way he radiated warmth and gratitude and—

He grabbed her, pulled her close and asked quietly, "Ready to make headlines?"

"Huh?"

"I'll take that as a yes." Then he wrapped a strong arm around her, leaning her back and kissing her straight on the mouth.

She wondered if her hearing would ever recover from

the sonic blast of squeals. Or if her stomach would ever lower from her throat.

Too absorbed in her own shock, she couldn't have said how the kiss was, even seconds afterward. Her mind went blank, trying to catch up to the fact that Jameson had just kissed her in public.

You're welcome, fourteen-year-old me.

However, Wendy was right: they had little to no chemistry, but chemistry be damned! A smoking hot movie star had just kissed her in a crowded room like he meant it. There didn't need to be genuine fireworks for her to get high off that rush of social power.

It was imperative that she came up for air grinning. Otherwise, they'd make headlines all right, but it would be more about sexual assault than a new out-in-the-open romance.

However, she found that it wasn't all that difficult to smile afterward. She even suspected both sides of her face were on board. She locked onto Jameson's eyes, as he stared back into hers and she thought this was quite a fun game they were playing. It was reminiscent of the one she'd played with Quentin in high school to get back at Greg Burns, only this time it was with a movie star and there was no revenge motive.

She knew by his sly grin that this was a game for him, too, and one he'd been playing most of his life.

He turned to the predominantly female crowd and said, "Sorry, I shouldn't hog her all to myself." He grabbed a cookie from the display case with his bare hands, causing

Jessica to cringe, though she managed to refrain from saying anything about health code, then he held it up, showing her image to the crowd. "Who else wants a piece of her?"

Judging by the roaring laughter, you'd have thought he'd said something genuinely clever.

He split the cookie in half, took a large bite out of it and nodded his approval animatedly before handing her the other half.

It was then that she understood without a doubt: she might be the boss, but Jameson had been in charge the second he'd stepped out of the kitchen and onto his stage. All she could do was laugh along with the crowd and take a bite of the damn cookie.

Jameson at his most magnetic was dangerous.

She was glad he was on her team.

The morning went by in a flash, and, while she knew it could never be, she wished she could hire Jameson full-time.

Not because he was good at the job. In fact, he was remarkably terrible at it. He couldn't remember a single order long enough to fetch it from the case, and as a result, kept bringing back the wrong items.

But he knew how to play it off while also convincing the customer that it was what she wanted all along, and after two hours of it, Jessica noticed a trend. He kept bringing back more expensive items. Not every time. But when there was a price difference, the item they received was always the more expensive of the two. And when there wasn't a price difference, say a chocolate chunk cookie instead of an oatmeal raisin, the item he replaced the original with always had more sugar.

He was an evil genius, giving people what they wanted rather than what they claimed they wanted, indulging them in a small way each time to ensure their experience was as epicurean as possible. By mid-morning, she'd had to rush through batches of the sugary items after all, Monday resolutions be damned.

The line moved slowly with so few people passing up the chance for a picture with the celebrities. Not singular. Plural. In the pit of her stomach, Jessica had feared that a special request would be made for a picture with Jameson only, that having her in it would somehow ruin the viral potential of the image. But no one asked for that. No one even so much as hinted at it by looking unhappy when she squeezed in on one side of them or by handing the camera to Jessica to take the picture.

After all these years of a hit-or-miss celebrity status, where she never knew if people would recognize her, and when they did, if they would want to, say, crucify her, there was no ambiguity. This was her bakery, the House of Jessica, and she was apparently dating Jameson Fractal, and everyone she had encountered all day had been thrilled with her. Some even said they wished they could be friends with her.

Granted, most of those folks had been staring dreamily at Jameson as they said it, and she suspected they were scheming up some usurping scenario.

Once the lunch crowd died down, Jessica set out a fresh plate of cookies that she miracled for the crowd (those watching were freshly impressed) and told the remaining customers to help themselves to it. Then she put up a sign that the cafe was closed for the next fifteen minutes. She caught Jameson's eye where he leaned over a table, chatting with a young couple, smartly giving most of his attention to the boyfriend so as not to spark jealousy. She nodded for him to follow her into the back, and he did.

"Hungry?" she asked.

"Famished."

She sat at the small table in the corner and gestured at the other chair. She already had a half dozen kosher pigs-in-a-blanket on a plate in the middle, and he dove right in. "You are really something else," she said.

He grinned. "Hope you didn't mind the entrance."

"You kidding? It's like you belong in Hollywood or something."

He shrugged, feigning modesty. "You can tell?" He dropped the cute act. "I just mean I didn't plan it. I walked out there, felt what the crowd was wondering about us, and decided to give them a little something to wake them up first thing in the morning. It wasn't until after that it occurred to me I'd basically assaulted you."

Jessica laughed. "I'm fine. As far as assaults go, that was among my favorite."

He wagged a roll at her. "You know, I forget that you're from this completely different life. Yeah, you were awkward and terrible with fans at first, but I guess I've always seen you as a celebrity from the moment I heard about you and just knew what people said was true."

"Which people?"

"Not Jimmy Dean."

"Great. Go on."

"I forget that you had a normal upbringing in a small town—"

"Not normal."

He conceded the point with a nod. "You're not from Hollywood, is what I mean. I guess what I'm trying to say is that if I ever do anything that makes you feel uncomfortable, will you let me know?"

"Yeah, of course."

"I mean, the kiss ... I can't tell you how many fake girlfriends I've had to pull a stunt like that with before. But you've gotten to live this real, genuine life where you don't have to put on a show all the time."

She laughed. "First of all, I wish someone had taught me to put on a show as well as you do. I might not have been bested by Jimmy fucking Dean over and over again that way. But also, who says you're my first fake boyfriend?" She raised her chin as a challenge and Jameson cackled.

"What?" he shouted. Then his grin wilted. "Wait, was Chris just a—"

"No, no," she said, her stomach clenching at the mention of him. "But my friend Quentin who you met this weekend?" She let the sentence hang and Jameson picked up on it immediately.

"Oh, I have to hear this story. And why was he just a fake boyfriend? You should have gone for it. Quentin's a catch."

She paused to consider it. "Yeah, I suppose so. I guess I was too focused on revenge to notice it. And then I noticed Chris."

As she launched into her high school plot to make Greg Burns seethe with jealousy, she watched Jameson's reactions closely and noticed a new depth to them. There was some sort of glisten, an unselfconsciousness about him that told her this wasn't a show for anyone's benefit; he was delighting in this simple and stupid tale of high school drama.

"How long have you been acting?" she said.

"Started in commercials when I was eight. Was in a show on the Kiddo Network from ten to fifteen, at which point I aged out. Took a couple years off to knock out four years of high school in two through distance learning. No one wanted to hire me until they saw how puberty turned out for me, then at seventeen I started landing roles in movies again, and it's pretty much been nonstop since.

"But go back to your story. When did you decide to end it with Quentin?"

By the time she finished, all she could think about was Chris—their first kiss against his truck, the way he'd kept her safe from the worst of the bullying, those days spent riding to and from football practice together, and last but certainly not least, how he'd decked Greg Burns in the face on prom night.

"Shoot! We'd better get back there," she said, stuffing the last pig-in-a-blanket into her mouth as she jumped out of the chair.

"Right!" Jameson seemed almost dreamy after the story, and she wondered if he was finally fading after a crazy morning. But if he was, he rebounded instantly as he stepped through the swinging doors into the cafe, grabbed a freshly brewed carafe and said, "Who needs more coffee?"

Chapter Twenty-Seven

The following day started with a similarly long line down the block, but once it was clear Jameson wouldn't be making another appearance, that issue took care of itself.

Judith was on duty, meaning there was no shortage of snide comments about whether Jessica expected them to make out on the counter to drum up business.

"I already told you," Jessica said after the third joke in under an hour.

"Yeah, yeah," Judith said. "Say what you want." She leaned close as she passed Jessica behind the counter. "I saw the pictures, and I can't blame you for loving it."

"It was a show," Jessica hissed back.

Judith scoffed and opened the case, reaching for a blueberry muffin. "No, Jessica. It wasn't. You're a shitty actor. You couldn't have pulled that off."

When closing time approached, Jessica's lack of acting skills became apparent again when she told Judith to go home early, hoping it sounded like a treat from the boss and not a desperate measure to end the teasing.

Judith rolled her eyes. "I'm just going to pick up where I left off tomorrow."

"You don't work tomorrow."

"Right, but I have big plans to come in on my day off."

When Jessica groaned, Judith added, "Don't worry. Both Brian and I agreed that the videos were super hot. I genuinely hope you guys have fake sex and we get to watch that, too."

Jessica pushed her toward the kitchen.

The main perk of Judith over Jameson was that the woman actually knew what she was doing and the cafe didn't look like Hurricane Fangirl had passed through. Closing wouldn't be so hard by herself, and she really could use a quiet moment after the last four days of being around people nonstop.

As she bagged up some of the remaining food to sell in bulk for half price the next day, the last customer packed up the book she was reading. The woman had been a regular in the evenings for months, and it was only recently that Jessica had stopped feeling uneasy around her, wondering when the other shoe would drop and the woman would hand Jessica a pamphlet about sin. But it'd never happened.

"Night, Pastor Adisa," said Jessica as the woman grabbed her bag from the back of the chair.

Pastor Adisa smiled brightly. "Night, Jessica." Then, as

usual, she waved at the stuffed giraffe Jessica kept on the countertop and said, "Night, Asha."

Jessica ushered the woman out and locked the front door behind her, then returned to the counter to continue bagging what would keep well—bagels, scones, cookies. As she carried an armful of the bagged goods over to the display cart, she paused as something white caught her eye against the dark backdrop of the night.

Something was taped to glass of the front door. Was that there before? Had Pastor Adisa left her something? She had, hadn't she? Oh, here it was. The woman had played the long game and now she was finally ready to pull the trigger on some religious propaganda. It always happened this way. Always. Trust a religious leader and you eventually get burned.

Having worked herself up into quite a self-righteous fever, Jessica flipped the lock and flung open the door, ripping the paper off and unfolding it as she held the door open with her foot.

Dearest Jessica,

Don't let him put his filthy mouth on you again. If he does, he'll be sorry and so will you. Real love tastes like blood and brimstone, and I offer mine to you. Do not allow yourself to be tainted by the false lust. My craving for you is eternal, as is my commitment. I will be your right hand and ride with you to the fires of Hell.

She looked up quickly, leaving the next three paragraphs unread. There was no doubt in her mind this was another correspondence from Her Loyal Master, and she didn't need to read all of it to know this had just become a genuine safety issue.

The night was quiet in this part of town. Two cars drove past, and she used their headlights to search for the sender. He must be watching, right? At least, he *had* been watching for quite some time, waiting until the last customer left before making his move.

She slipped back into the bakery and turned the bolt swiftly.

Her guilt for having jumped to conclusions about Pastor Adisa, who was still a wonderful person, apparently, was drastically overshadowed by the paranoia she felt and her inability to decide which direction was safest for her to put her back to.

She checked quickly over her shoulder, and when there wasn't anyone creeping up on her, she faced the giant windows again and inched backward toward the kitchen, the note still clutched in her hand.

Would this have happened if she hadn't sent Judith home early? Why was she here all by herself? This was stupid. She was an idiot. She deserved to be murdered, being this careless, thinking she had a right to safe alone time.

Pull it together. He didn't even threaten you.

Yet.

While she now regretted the multiple refusals to allow

Destinee to hide a shotgun under the counter, she wasn't completely defenseless. She had knives. Lots of them.

But they were all back in the kitchen, one flapping door away.

The next best weapon was under the counter, though, and she snatched up her cell phone before sliding down to sit against the shelves, hidden from view of the front windows. No one could sneak up on her here. She unlocked the screen and, in a daze, scrolled through her contacts for who to call. The first name that caught her eye and gave her a spark of hope was: *Chris Riley DO NOT CALL*.

What could he do anyway from all the way up in Philadelphia? Calling would just worry him and show him that she didn't have anyone else in town she could rely on. And it seemed a cruel thing to do the day after videos of her kissing another man began circulating. Chris, unlike her, didn't avoid social media like the plague. Why would he? Social media usually thought so highly of him.

She had plenty of people around to call. Most of them were women, sure, and dragging another woman into this didn't seem like the kind of sisterhood she strove for. Dragging a man, though, would be just fine.

Jameson?

Of course not. Jameson was there for the easy part, and sure, he'd enjoyed hearing a bit of realness from her teenage years, but no one actually *wanted* to live the realness. Not when it was like this. Jameson was available for the good times, not the messy and terrifying ones.

As soon as she scrolled to the Qs, she saw who she needed.

He answered with, "Now, Jess, you know I can't have my fake exes calling me up when I'm with my new girl."

His voice lowered her heart rate by ten beats per minute immediately.

"Quentin. Are you super busy?"

"Hanging with Callie. What's up?

"Shit. Are y'all about to bang? I can call someone else if you're about to bang."

"You sound like you're hyperventilating. What's going on?"

"Can you come to the bakery? And, like, bring a weapon or something?"

A scuffle on the line told her he was shifting the phone to a better position, and she heard Callie's concerned voice in the background, though she couldn't make out the words. "Jessica, what's going on?"

"Someone's left me a creepy letter, and I'm hiding behind the counter."

"Aw hell, Jess. Call the cops."

"Maybe, but can you come by first?"

"Yeah, sure. But then don't call the cops until I'm already there. Last thing I need is them catching wind of a stalker and then finding a black man lurking on your place with a weapon."

Jessica was finally able to breathe now that Quentin had agreed. "Right, right. Thanks."

She remained behind the counter for the next twenty

minutes, scared to move and scared to enter the kitchen, where all kinds of hiding places existed. Had she locked the back door? Could her stalker pick a lock?

When Quentin finally knocked on the front door, Jessica peed just a little.

She hurried over and waved Quentin inside quickly. He had left Callie behind, and she was especially grateful for that. Not only did it mean another woman wasn't in danger, it showed that Quentin believed her when she said shit was dangerous.

"You didn't bring a weapon," she said.

"Yeah, I did." He reached in his pocket and pulled out a small pink object. "Pepper spray."

She shook her head in disbelief. "You're the worst defender ever. I should have called Rex."

As she waved for him to follow her toward the back, he laughed. "You know that would have been a terrible idea."

She paused at the kitchen door. "At least he would be armed with my mom."

"Who would be armed with a shotgun and complete indiscretion. We know."

Jessica nodded for Quentin to go first through the door, and he nodded casually, but she didn't fail to see his hand slip into the pocket with the pepper spray.

It only took a minute for him to clear the kitchen, then they took a seat at the tiny fold-out table as she tried to slow her racing heart.

"You gonna show me the letter?" he asked.

She pulled it out of her jeans pocket and flung it at him.

When he was finished, he nodded, folded it neatly and said, "Yeah, that's fucking weird, all right." Then he shrugged. "What do you want me to do about it?"

She hadn't thought about that. All her focus was on getting someone else here, not what they would do once they arrived. "I guess just agree that it's fucked up."

"You could have snapped a photo of this and sent it to literally anyone to get that opinion back."

"Fine. Would you just hang around while I close, then maybe walk me to my car?"

He nodded. "Of course. So long as the stalker stays downwind of us, I got you covered." He held up the pink sprayer and sighed when she remained sitting, not yet ready to get to work. "So, I see I've been replaced by Jameson."

She laughed. "I hope you can find the strength to move on."

"I think I'll make it." He checked his phone subtly, then said, "How's all this going?" He motioned broadly to the surroundings.

"Great."

Quentin said nothing.

"Okay, I'm so fucking stressed and, like, ninety percent sure I'm behind on a handful of major payments, but I haven't had a chance to sit down and go through the bills and update my ledgers, but first I have a bunch of transfers to make, because the money is coming in, but I've been so behind that I didn't even bother checking on late fees, because what was I going to do about that anyway?"

Quentin held up a hand to stop her. "Bring me a laptop and the bills. Write down all your login information on a notepad, then finish closing this place down."

Jessica stomped her foot petulantly and her shoulders sagged. "You sure I can't just hire you to do everything for me?"

"I dunno. Let me see how much money you're making, then I'll tell you if you can afford me."

She already knew that wasn't a possibility, but she dumped all her unopened bills on the table next to him, wrote down the logins for every bank account and supplier she could think of, then set out to work cleaning the kitchen.

Hours later, she brought him another cup of coffee from the cheap coffee maker she kept in the back for long nights such as this.

Quentin took it gladly.

"How's it looking?" she asked.

He dug the butt of his hand into one of his eye sockets, yawning. "You want the good news or the bad news first?"

"Good news."

He squinted at her. "Who the hell picks the good news first?"

She blinked. "Me, I guess."

"No, that's dumb. Never pick the good news first. Leave it for last. You know, sometimes, Jess, I think you might actually be a masochist." He clicked the touchpad, mumbling, "Bad news for last. Jesus..." Then he flipped the screen around. "Okay, bad news is that you still owe this much for mortgage and suppliers." He pointed to the amount on the spreadsheet.

"Ew."

"That's one word for it."

"But I've made so much money since I started hanging around with Jameson. Are you sure I'm still that far behind? I figured I'd be all caught up."

"Listen, I get it. And you did double your sales in the last couple days, so things are looking up for you to be in good standing in a month. You ready for the good news?"

"Hell yeah, I am." She was ready to punch something, so good news was welcome.

"I told you." He pointed a finger at her. "Can you imagine if I saved that bit for last?"

"Just get on with it."

"The good news is that you were four months behind on a couple accounts, and most of these 'bills' were actually threats to take you to collection. But I paid all those off, and now your business won't be destroyed."

"Yay?" she said, feeling weariness grab hold of her internal organs.

"Major yay." He paused. "I hate to lecture, Jess, but you can't let it get to this again. Your business is finally making money, and, you know, stalkers aside, you seem to be enjoying it. You have to hire someone else to take care of this on a regular basis. It's not that difficult. Hell, I've never done it before, but I figured it out in"—he glanced at the clock above the door—"oh hell. Nine hours? Wow."

She cringed. "Yeah. Sorry. You were so into it, I figured I'd get started on prep for tomorrow since I was already caffeinated and way too spacey to drive home safely. And the last thing I need is to call a ride share at this hour and have it turn out to be whoever left that note on my door."

Quentin nodded sympathetically. "That's actually not a bad idea for a stalker. Just hang around, waiting for someone to call for a car."

"Right?"

He took two more long gulps from his mug then stood. "You know I'd love to stay longer, but unfortunately, I have to be at work in a couple hours." He adjusted his shirt and stretched his neck. "I guess you don't need me to walk you to your car, then?"

"No. I'm just gonna stay here."

He tilted his head. "You okay being here by yourself?"

Maybe it was that all the adrenaline had left her limbs and if someone decided to break in to attack her, she was prepared to simply give in and accept her fate, but the threat of the stalker seemed far away now, almost an impossibility. Maybe someone was just playing stalker. No one really *did* that sort of thing, right?

"Yeah, I'm fine. I'm just gonna keep working. I open in a couple hours anyway."

"Okay, well, if you need anything ..."

"Call someone else. I got it."

He winked and shot her a finger gun. "That's my girl."

After a quick hug, he let himself out through the front, as Jessica began preheating the ovens. She held onto the mental note to lock the door behind him just as soon as she was done with a few things here. Realistically, a couple minutes didn't matter.

As she'd poured the last banana nut muffin batter into the tin, there was a hard, quick knock at the front, and she heard the door open and shut.

She searched the surfaces nearby for what Quentin might have forgotten and returned for. Nothing caught her eye.

When the normal time frame for him to appear again in the kitchen came and went, she was pleasantly surprised to discover that her body *did* still have some adrenaline left, and she quickly grabbed her phone and a large bread knife from the counter, wondering absently if the serrated edges would necessitate a sawing motion for effective self-defense, and crept out of the kitchen and into the cafe. As she'd suspected, Quentin wasn't there. He would have announced himself, anyway.

A powerful chill ran down her spine when she saw that there was yet another note taped to the front door.

Only, this time, it was on the inside.

She retreated quickly into the kitchen, put her back against a wall with the bread knife in front of her and did just as Quentin had instructed. She called someone else.

Chapter Twenty-Eight

The red and blue lights washed over the interior of Jessica's bakery from the curb out front. Deciding it was best not to pop up from her hiding place and scare a couple armed officers, she put herself in plain view and set down the bread knife before they got out of their vehicles.

The first officer she saw looked better built for running an ultra marathon than taking down thugs on the streets. The caps on his short sleeves flowed loosely around his scrawny, pale arms, and even with the vest on, the circumference of his chest left much to be desired.

This? This was who the department had sent over to help her deal with a deranged stalker?

The officer introduced himself with a deep, robust tone. "Officer Downey."

Jessica nodded and shook his hand. His grip was more like his body than his voice.

When the other officer stepped out of her vehicle,

Jessica had a jolt of recognition. It wasn't until she'd opened the door and greeted the officer that she noticed the name tag and could complete the mental connection.

"Ms. McCloud. So we meet again," said the female officer.

"Hi, Officer McBride." Jessica's first encounter with McBride had been brief, taking place in the parking lot outside Bat-Ass Brew after an unfortunate resurrection of Rebel the barista. She wished she could meet the woman under better circumstances for once, but that wasn't the nature of calling the cops, she supposed. "Come on inside."

"This the note?" she pointed at it on the door where Jessica had left it, being afraid to touch it for a multitude of unreasonable reasons.

"Yeah."

While Officer Downey took a look around, Officer McBride opened the letter and read it through. When she was done, she folded it back gently, her eyebrows raised as she whistled. "That is one hell of a Shakespeare you got pining after you." She held the letter out toward Jessica. "You should read it."

"No thanks."

McBride shrugged and held onto it. "You're quite the shit magnet, Ms. McCloud."

"McBride!" Downey warned.

"*Sorry,*" she replied mockingly. She turned to Jessica again. "A poop magnet."

"It's fine," Jessica said, "and you're right."

"First you gotta clean up the mess down at Bat-Ass

Brew and now this? I'm guessing that's not even the extent of it, either. That's just what *I've* responded to."

Jessica nodded. "Yeah. That's only the tip of the shitberg."

McBride held up the evidence. "You got more of these?"

"But of course." Jessica paused at the door, letting McBride enter the kitchen ahead of her.

Once Jessica had handed over the other two and McBride was done reading them, she said, "You're just now calling us?"

"I didn't want to overreact."

McBride frowned then said, "Yeah, I get it. This one wouldn't"—she jabbed a thumb at Downey who was busy searching the walk-in freezer—"for obvious reasons. Look, I'd put money on this being a man who stuck you with these."

Jessica blinked. "I hadn't even considered the possibility that it wasn't."

"Why would you? Women don't even feel this sense of entitlement over their own bodies, let alone other people's. We got better things to think about, like trying not to be controlled by men."

"For god's sake, McBride," groaned Downey.

"Focus on what you're doing. I think you mighta missed a drawer back there." She returned her attention to Jessica. "Any idea who might be behind this?"

"None."

"I noticed you have a camera set up out there. Is it just for show?"

Jessica felt a blush come over her face. "That hadn't occurred to me. No, it records."

"Does it erase every so often?"

"I don't think so. It's backed up to the cloud."

McBride nodded. "Not sure what that means, but let's have a look at it."

While she was glad all the money she'd put into her security system wasn't for naught, it was obviously a mixed blessing, like having flood insurance pay out. She'd never needed to access the footage before, and the process required an embarrassingly long call with a customer service rep before she could log in and begin sorting through all the files to find the right time code. Eventually, she let McBride take over.

"That him?" the officer pointed to the screen. Jessica leaned in close and could feel Downey hovering over her shoulder. "No. That's Quentin. He came over right after I found the second note."

McBride side-eyed her. "Any reason to believe he might be the one leaving the notes?"

Jessica chuckled. "No. He's not afraid to say what's on his mind to a person's face. But it should be right after he leaves that the person comes. Just a few minutes. I thought Quentin had left something and that was who came back in."

As it turned out, it was actually a full ten minutes

between when Quentin left and when another figure appeared on the screen. "There," she said. McBride moved forward frame by frame to get a clear angle on the face obscured beneath the Houston Texan's baseball cap. "Looks like maybe white or light skinned Hispanic," she relayed to the others. She pressed the arrow keys to move back and forth between a span of five frames. "Yeah, one of these will be the clearest, but it still doesn't give us much. He was aware of the camera and avoided the angle. What about the other two letters? Maybe we caught something then."

It took a while of sorting through old footage to locate the others, and by the time they'd reviewed all three, they had only grabbed a slightly better angle to identify him. In all three, he had the Houston Texan's hat, but other than his presumed sports fandom, they didn't know much about him right off the bat other than he stood about five-foot-ten.

While Downey didn't strike Jessica as a rookie, McBride seemed to have seniority, and she stuck him with the report. Before Jess knew it, two hours had passed. "Sorry to keep you so long," she said.

McBride waved her off. "This is nothing. Before I got here, I spent four hours on a noise disturbance call. Guy wouldn't turn down the radio. Insisted it was his God-given right as an American to blast country music in his own house whenever he wanted. I told him the law didn't agree. He eventually asked for a male officer instead, and I was happy to comply, and now here I am." She grinned.

The backdoor of the kitchen burst open like a gunshot, and McBride's right hand dropped down toward her belt.

"She ain't done nothing wrong! You'll have to arrest me too!"

"Mom!" Jessica lunged forward, intentionally putting herself between Destinee and McBride until she could be sure the shotgun had stayed in the car. "It's fine. They're not arresting me."

Destinee pulled up short, her pupils large, her head jerking around like an agitated horse. "What the hell's happening, then? Someone get murdered?"

"Everything's fine, Mrs. McCloud," said Officer McBride.

Jessica stepped to the side as Destinee narrowed her eyes at the female cop. "Miss. Not missus. Or just Destinee."

Jessica hastily hissed, "She's cool, Mom. Be nice," as Destinee approached and shook hands with McBride.

"Nice to meet you, Destinee. If you want, you can call me Misty."

Destinee continued inspecting the female officer closely before she cracked a wide grin and said, "Damn, you got a cheap stripper name, too, don't ya?"

McBride laughed. "Ain't it the truth!" Where had that Texan accent come from? She hadn't had it just a minute ago.

But Jessica wasn't going to complain, because Destinee and Officer McBride had gone from potential enemies to friends in six seconds flat, and that meant Jessica wouldn't have to be the one to fill her mother in on the situation. Considering the severity of it, it was probably best someone with handcuffs and a Taser be the one to break the news.

At half past five, Jessica figured she could use a little fresh air to wake her up before another long shift. With the cop lights still flashing out front, there was little chance of anyone creeping around. She could risk it.

She stepped out the back door, wishing not for the first time that she'd taken up smoking, and stuffed her hands into her pockets, leaning back against the building, letting the cool October air bat at her hair and shirt.

A car door shut, forcing her eyes open, and she saw Rex pacing over.

"Morning," Jessica said, surprised to see him.

He crossed his arms over his chest and bounced on his toes anxiously once he reached her, shooting glances at the back entrance. "They arrested her, didn't they?"

Jessica shook her head. "Surprisingly, no. She's just made a new best friend."

"What's going on?"

Exhausted, Jessica shrugged. "Some dude is stalking me, leaving gross notes."

Rex's jaw dropped along with his crossed arms. He set his hands firmly on Jessica's shoulders, and she wondered briefly if he was about to give her a pep talk before the state championship. But instead, he said, "On behalf of my entire hemisphere of the broad gender wheel, I am truly sorry. It's just not fair that so many men feel a deeply ingrained sense of entitlement over the bodies and choices of women. He has no right to control you through fear, and

I truly hope I get a chance to meet him so I can rip his balls off before your mother shoots him and ends up in prison."

"Um. Thanks, Rex. I appreciate the sentiment."

"I mean it," he said, shaking her gently. "If I find him, I'm gonna castrate him. And not because I don't believe women are capable of that, but because society has put the burden of cleaning up messes men make on women for time out of mind, and I want to do my part as a cis male to help clean up what I've unintentionally contributed to all these years."

"Yeah, that's ..." Her words caught in her throat when Rex sucked in air through his nose, staring up briefly at the pre-dawn sky before meeting her eyes again. His were now red.

"This is something I've been meaning to say to you for a while, McCloud."

Oh no. This can't be good.

"It's been weighing on my conscience. What I was just talking about, with women cleaning up the messes of men?"

"Yuh-huh?"

"I did that to you for years when you were on the team. I didn't even know that's what I was doing, but it was. I and the rest of the team, we failed to get the job done. We half-assed it so many times. And guess who we had to fall back on to finish the job and win us the game? The sole woman. I am guilty of perpetuating the unhealthy cycle of expecting women to get the job done while men get all the glory, and I can't change that—"

"You don't have to, it's—"

"But I need you to know I acknowledge my mistake, my ignorance, and I see you." He set a fat hand on Jessica's cheek. "I see you. And I promise not to let it happen again."

She nodded then said, "Did you hear that?"

"Huh?"

"I think they were calling for you in there."

Rex straightened. "Oh, I'd better go help. Can't leave it up to your mother."

He took one step and Jessica quickly said, "Rex?"

"Yeah?"

"One of the cops, she's a woman. Maybe don't say much around her."

His eyebrows pinched together, but he nodded. "Whatever you say. I trust your opinion over my own on this."

"Great."

Once he was gone, she inhaled deeply and made up her mind that it was *definitely* time to take up smoking.

Chapter Twenty-Nine

Getting the cops out of the way before she flipped the open sign felt like a victory in and of itself. There was no doubt someone had seen them outside and she'd have to answer inquiries about it (or rather, direct them to Wendy), but she had enough now problems on her hands to forget about the later ones.

Without being asked, Rex had already called his assistant coaches and asked them to run practice for him, allowing him a couple hours to help out with setup before he had to go teach world geography and art. After explaining in detail how he'd come to realize the ridiculousness of viewing the kitchen as a woman's domain when the creation of sustenance should be a genderless pursuit, Jessica assigned him to watch the ovens, plate what was ready, and, once Jessica could miracle it, bring it out to Destinee, who was managing the front of house on her own temporarily.

Would she shout at a customer or two for complaining something wasn't cooked enough or that what she gave them wasn't what they'd ordered? No doubt. But Jessica had felt compelled to make an important phone call since Quentin first mentioned hiring new employees, and now that the stalker situation had settled, she could finally make it.

Granted, it was months overdue, but if she'd called before ... No, she'd been too ashamed.

"I thought I'd hear from you soon," said Dr. Bell airily as she answered the call. "Actually, I thought I'd hear from you much sooner, given the circumstances."

"Yep. That's what I'm calling about."

"Of course it is. I'm terrible conversation for other topics. Why did you wait so long, Jessica?"

She sighed, leaning on her elbow on the shelf by the phone. "I wanted to fix things first."

"And have you?"

"Kinda."

"I'm impressed you can even say that. You got royally fleeced by those three men."

Jessica sighed. It had been almost three months since Kumal, Dwayne, and Sampson had disappeared, and time had done little to lessen her desire to see each get hit by a particularly smelly garbage truck. "You're not lying. Wait. How did you know about that?"

"You're not the only one with my phone number, you know."

Spies. Someone close to her had been reporting back to her former professor. "Who was it?"

"Doesn't matter. What matters is that you're finally calling for my advice, right?" Static hit the phone line and Jessica guessed Dr. Bell was outside, probably walking across the Texas State campus to her office.

"Yeah."

"Have you hired new people?"

"No."

"Hire new people."

Jessica rolled her eyes. She'd had a feeling this was what would happen. As if it were that simple. "I'm still behind on the bills. How can I add more people to the payroll?"

"That's a complicated question, but to start, I'd say cut costs and increase profits."

"I've increased profits. I don't know where to cut costs."

Dr. Bell spoke away from the phone and the words were muddled, but Jessica knew they weren't for her anyway. "Then start looking for places to cut costs. And if you need help with that, I'm happy to go over it with you."

"Okay, but how do I make sure the people I hire next aren't going to be awful like the ones before?"

"I'd say you start by vetting them yourself. Your mother said that— I mean, um, I heard— oh screw it. I've been keeping contact with your mother. I might as well tell you because what are you going to do about it? She said you let Dolores Thomas do the hiring for you, is that right?"

"Yeah, but—"

"Mind me asking why in your Father's name you would allow—yes, Jerry, thank you"—the wind cut out but now her voice was drowned out by a chorus of other echoing voices—"why in your Father's name would you allow someone else to make that decision for you?"

"She's an investor," Jessica said, "and I've always trusted her. I figured it was in her best interest to help me hire the best possible people to run the business she had put so much of her own money into."

"Mm-hmm."

"What?"

"I'm not a fan of 'figuring' when it comes to business practice." A door shut, and the background noise stopped. "It sounds like she hired the *worst* people for the job, why do you *figure* that is?"

Jessica sighed. "I figure it seems that way because I have no clue how to be a boss. I just gave them the tasks and expected them to know how to do them the way I wanted." The words began tumbling out. "I was just so relieved to have help after being so overwhelmed that I wanted to be able to hand off the tasks and forget about them so I could focus on doing a few things well instead of everything terribly. I should have known better, and I probably did deep down, but I was stupid about it and it's my fault things turned out the way they did."

She waited for Dr. Bell to jump in immediately, to congratulate Jessica on taking responsibility. Maybe she even hoped Dr. Bell would agree with her assessment that everything was her fault, but that didn't happen.

Instead, the angel said, "Who told you it was your fault?"

"What?"

"I'm just curious who suggested it was your fault. That doesn't seem like the immediate place a person's mind would go after being scammed by con men if not actual demons. It wasn't your mother who suggested it, obviously. She'd break the jaw of anyone who tried to blame you for what those men did. So, who was it?"

"No one. I just realized—"

"It was Dolores, wasn't it?"

"No," Jessica snapped. "Well, she did suggest that I should have kept a better eye on them."

"And she was right," Dr. Bell added. "A boss ought to check in with her employees frequently. But that doesn't make their gross errors in judgment and blatant crimes your fault. You know, I believe that if you'd hired them yourself, you would have felt more in charge and empowered to check in with them regularly, telling them what to do, and how to do it. I understand Dolores has been a boss for years; she should understand that basic rule of ownership."

"Oh, Dr. Bell. They were *awful*. They wouldn't even let me train them! They said they already knew everything I told them."

"Then they're assholes. Might I suggest something for this time around?"

"Yeah, of course."

"Do the hiring yourself. And only hire angels."

Jessica opened her mouth to speak, but she wasn't sure what to say. How would she make sure of that? The logistics began spinning in her mind, then another pressing question surfaced. "Isn't that discrimination?"

"Oh, it would absolutely be discrimination if the laws knew to address that specific distinction, but lucky for us, lawmakers are rarely aware of angels, so few being them and so few of those understanding what they are. Regardless, there's no way to be prosecuted for it, so you might as well do it. You already know angels will naturally feel inclined to serve you and your interests. Think about it."

She did. "Yeah, I guess Quentin did spend all night over here helping me pay bills and update my spreadsheets."

"There you go," said the professor. "Now, that doesn't mean every angel is necessarily going to do exactly what you say, how you say it. We're not mind readers, and, as you've found out, Dolores is an angel but clearly puts her own interests above yours."

The assertion didn't sit right. Mrs. Thomas had made a mistake, shown a lapse in judgment, but to say she'd put her own interests above Jessica's? That didn't add up. "That's the thing, though," Jessica said. "It can't be that because we're working toward the same goal with the bakery, and that's to keep it open. It must be that she just messed up. Or maybe they were great workers for her husband's campaign, and they suddenly stopped being honest."

"Jessica," Dr. Bell said softly. "Listen to yourself. You think all three men went through an identity crisis at the same time as soon as they worked for you? Why are you trying so hard to exonerate them?"

"Because the alternative doesn't make any sense either. I made Mrs. Thomas my scapegoat right after it happened, blamed her for everything, even ... I'm embarrassed to even admit it."

"You thought she might have done it on purpose?"

"Yes! And that's ridiculous! She's an angel, and she's always done everything in her power to help me. And then she messes up once and suddenly my mind goes to the worst possible scenario? How horrible does that make me? And then I spoke with her and it all made more sense. I was really just upset with myself for being such an easy dupe. Nothing new there. Jimmy's known that about me for years. Instead of admitting that hadn't changed, I'd imagined Mrs. Thomas in the most horrible light just to keep from admitting the unpleasant truth that I am horrible at being a boss, and that's a real problem if I want to run a business."

There was silence on the other end, and Jessica wondered if Dr. Bell had hung up. But then the angel said, "You're not a fool, Jessica. You're a twenty-two-year-old. Jimmy has years of practice and a lack of conscience that allow him to pull the nonsense he does. And being a boss takes practice. Lots of it. So don't beat yourself up. If Dolores was expecting you to be the world's best one without any guidance on how to go about doing that, she was setting you up for failure, plain and simple."

"But why on earth would she do that? She must be working toward the same goal as me, right? So, the only conclusion is that she made an honest mistake."

"Maybe," conceded Dr. Bell, but it sounded more like a no. "You know, I would still like to see the contract the two of you signed. I know I've asked for it quite a few times, but somehow I still haven't seen it in my inbox. You have it though, right?"

"Yeah," Jessica said. Because of course she did. She'd asked Mrs. Thomas for it nearly half a dozen times. "It's probably in my inbox or texts."

"Great. Will you send it to me now?"

Agitation prickled at Jessica's neck. "I'll do it once I'm off the phone."

"I'd prefer you do it now. I'd like a chance to look it over before my first class today."

The relief Jessica had felt at the start of the conversation was overcome by a petulance she was all too familiar with but was normally directed toward her Father. "Fine. Let me grab the laptop." She flopped over to the laptop and brought it back to her seat. First, her internet was running slow. "Just one second. This stupid cable company charges me for high speed and doesn't believe me when I say they're underdelivering." Then, she opened her business email and searched for Mrs. Thomas's address in her inbox. "Nothing in this one. I'll have to open up my personal one, and I don't even remember the password for that."

"Ah, yes. I know the struggle all too well," said Dr. Bell patiently.

Really? She was going to sit and wait for this? Ugh. It was *not* what Jessica wanted to be doing right now.

She went to the login page of her personal account and clicked the recover password option. "Shit."

"What?"

She stared down at the confirmation message. "The recover password was sent to my *old* personal account. I'm not even sure that one still exists, so I'll have to see if I can even recover it."

"Sounds frustrating. Why don't you just call Dolores and ask her for it again?"

"Fine. But not right now. It's been a long night, I didn't get any sleep, and I have to get going on work before my mom runs off too many customers."

"Okay, okay," Dr. Bell said. "What time should I text you later to remind you to send it?"

Was she for real? "I dunno. I'm going to be here until close, then I'll have to clean and prep, then I'll probably want to go straight home and crash out."

"Okay, so like, nine? Ten?"

Her stomach was knotting, but that could have been

from too much coffee and not enough food. "Ten. Sure. Thanks."

"Of course, Jessica. I'll text you tonight and then I can look over the contract before bed."

They said their goodbyes, and Jessica set her phone down onto the table just a little too hard.

What was the point of that call? She'd hoped to feel better after it, but she'd just felt more annoyed. Something was nagging at her that she hadn't yet figured out.

YOU DON'T HAVE THE CONTRACT.

What?

SHE NEVER SENT IT TO YOU.

For fuck's sake! Stop going through my emails!

NEVER.

So I have to call her and ask her to send it again? I'm going to look like such an asshole.

INDEED.

And did you go through my texts as well?

YES.

Stop it! Shit. Don't I get some privacy?

YES, YOU DO. IN THE BATHROOM. THE LORD DARE NOT TREAD THERE.

Guess I know where I'm leaving my phone from here on out.

HA! YOUR HARDWARE MAY BE SAFE THERE, BUT THE LORD CAN ACCESS THE CLOUD.

Of course He could. She really needed to figure out what that even meant.

NO DATA IS SAFE FROM THE PIERCING JUDGMENT OF THE LORD.

Okay, great. Now could you get lost? I need to sell my image for some people to worship at fifteen dollars a pop.

She shook her head to clear it and went to join her mother in the cafe.

Chapter Thirty

The reminder text from Dr. Bell sat ignored on Jessica's phone as she trudged up the stairs of her building, passing the coke machine and slogging down the long hallway toward her front door. She wondered briefly what Jameson was up to, then realized she was too tired to care.

As usual, her keys had hidden themselves beneath a bunch of other inexplicably sharp objects in her purse. And as she twiddled her fingers through the clutter, the telltale jingle teasing her, the door behind her opened and she looked back to find Jesus and Jeremy ready for a night on the town, meaning neither of their heavy metal T-shirts had obvious holes in them.

"Evening, Jessica," said Jesus. "On your way in or out?"

"In." She tried not to gawk at Jesus's black eye that was already starting to yellow around the edges.

"I noticed you didn't come home last night," said Jeremy matter of factly.

She paused in her digging and turned to face him head on. "And you know that how?"

He nodded back at his door. "That blue speck at the corner of the door frame? It's a motion sensor camera." He shrugged a single shoulder coolly. "Don't tell anyone because the technology isn't available to the public or legal. Anyway, I review footage over coffee each morning, and I didn't see you."

Her left eye twitched as her mind rewound through everything she'd ever done outside her front door when she thought no one was watching. At the very least, he'd seen her pick a few wedgies. At most ...

"Great."

"You out with that handsome actor of yours?" Jeremy asked casually. She knew he wouldn't judge her if she stayed the night with someone, but Jesus might.

"No. For the record, I was stuck at work due to a stalker. And then I decided I might as well get some paperwork done that I was way behind on."

"Business, eh?" said Jeremy. "I know a little something about that." He chuckled at his modest understatement.

Jesus leaned forward. "Seriously. This guy." He jabbed a thumb Jeremy's way. "Things have gotten so complicated in the last two thousand years."

"The first thing you should know," Jeremy said, "is that very few businesses make it into the black in the first three years. And in food services, that's even lower. The fact that you've managed to stay open as long as you have is very impressive."

Her neighbor was the last person she'd expected to make her feel better today, but he *was* a stupid-rich media mogul, so maybe he knew what he was talking about. "That's great to hear," she said.

"I should've told you sooner," he added. "If you make a profit this year, or even next year, you would be well ahead of the game."

Perspective. That's all she needed. It was truly remarkable how much zooming out on a tough situation could make it all the more tolerable. It was so easy so lose sight of the bigger picture when she was constantly down in the trenches.

"Of course," Jeremy continued, "your success probably already means you've been put on the registry."

She blinked, thinking she'd misheard. "The what?"

"The registry. You know, the one the IRS keeps. Audits are never random as they'd have you believe. What happens is they put businesses with any real earning potential on the registry, and every year, they check back to see if that business is worth auditing. The more growth in the year, the more likely the audit. Obviously, they do this with the goal of killing as many small businesses as possible. That leaves more people dependent on the government for money, more need for another large-scale bailout as markets crash, and therefore justification for printing more money and creating the hyperinflation we've been working toward for years. Once that's accomplished, the nation will be economically destroyed and the shadow government can finally step forward to take public control.

Personally, I don't know why they don't just go straight to the hyperinflation. Nothing you or I could do to stop it, and it would take down all the small businesses, and even some of the big ones, at once, accomplishing their end game in less time. Doesn't make sense."

"No," she said. "It doesn't. Not even a little bit."

"See, Joshua?" Jeremy said, "I told you she had a clear mind on her."

Jesus nodded once. "By the way, sister, I thought you might like to know that since becoming more acquainted with the vernacular of the times, and having learned from"—he cleared his throat—"*recent* mistakes, I've landed on a slogan that I believe might actually change the hearts and minds about the homeless population."

She had to give it to Jesus, he was nothing if not perseverant. Even while his jaw was visibly swollen from the fish incident, he insisted on helping. It also wasn't hard to see how that'd had gotten him killed the first time around. "Yes?"

He adjusted his feet to shoulder-width apart and inhaled to steady himself. "Now, don't naysay it till you let it simmer."

When would she be able to go to bed? "Okay."

"Here it is. 'They're transients, not trans-*ain'ts*.'"

"Wha—"

"Upp-upp-upp!" Jesus held a finger to her lips. "Let it simmer."

She glanced at Jeremy. Surely someone with his marketing knowledge would know that good slogans shouldn't have to *simmer* to make any goddamn sense. Even *she* knew that. Hell, Kumal probably knew it, too.

But Jeremy wasn't the backup she was looking for. He stared at her expectantly, his brows raised excitedly, his mouth slightly open. "Let it simmer," he whispered, nodding slowly.

Then he threw his arm around his roommate's shoulders, steering him toward the exit. He rustled Jesus's blond hair, murmuring, "That really is a winner, Joshua. Don't let her or anyone else convince you otherwise."

Chapter Thirty-One

Quentin sat on a stool by the counter of It is Risen, wolfing down a BLT while Jessica counted the cash in the register, waiting for the next customer to come in. "Of course you're right," she said. "I've told you this. But it's been a week, and I still don't have the time to even begin the hiring process."

"I get that it freaks you out," Quentin said. "But ... get the hell over it?"

She snapped her head around, and he stared at her with zero remorse.

"He's right," said Judith, moseying up and leaning against the back counter to face the other two. "Get over it."

She lowered her voice to keep from being overheard. "I just don't know how I'm supposed to create a job post that attracts angels."

"You're overthinking it," said Judith. "Did you advertise for angels for NAO?"

Jessica jotted down the total and closed the register drawer. "No."

"And yet somehow the founding members were all angels. Well, except for me." She jabbed a thumb toward the floor and blew a raspberry.

Jessica held up her hands. "See? You're the only member I personally recruited. Kate rounded up all the rest. Clearly I'm the worst possible person to find more angels."

Two business women approached the counter and Judith moved in to handle it.

Jessica moved closer to Quentin to continue the conversation. "Maybe I just need to get you to do it."

He paused with the sandwich shoved halfway into his mouth and narrowed his eyes at her before biting off a chunk and shaking his head firmly.

She pouted her lips. "Please? Just one more little bit of help?" She knew asking it of him was wrong, but it felt so right.

"No."

She grunted. "I thought you were supposed to be unable to resist helping me."

"I am. But this wouldn't help you. It would be considered enabling you. Besides, just because I'm an angel doesn't mean I'm your slave."

They both cringed uncomfortably, and Quentin added, "I didn't mean it like that. But now that we're on the topic, I'm gonna pile that on top. I'm not going to hire people for you because keeping you from learning this process doesn't help *and* because, in general, and I'm not talking about you, so don't get all defensive, white folks tend to expect black folks to help them for free and get none of the glory. I'm done contributing to that."

"For what it's worth, I'd exploit any angel's help right now, regardless of race."

He leaned forward and set a hand on her shoulder, looking her in the eyes. "I know you would. And I know that if Chris were here, we wouldn't even be having this conversation because he'd already have done everything for you."

She glared at him and let him sit with it.

When he went back to eating, she said, "Hey, can I ask you something?"

He nodded, sucking coke through his straw.

"Does it bother you that I'm white?" It was such a silly question. She couldn't help being white just like she couldn't help being the daughter of God or a woman or really into wildlife. But still, there were probably people who *were* bothered by the fact that a white person was claiming to be God's daughter. Sure, there was a long history of white people claiming a direct line to God, but they were all crazy, and she was the real deal.

She figured Quentin wouldn't care, since their relationship transcended race, but now that the ludicrous idea had popped into her head, she just had to be sure.

Quentin said, "Yeah, it does."

"Huh?"

"Was that not the answer you wanted?"

"I just thought that since you knew me ..."

He shrugged. "Oh, yeah, sure. I mean I'm not mad at you for it. I think it's a little shitty of God to feed into the stereotype that white is right and so on."

"But I can't help it," she said, feeling around for where this miscommunication had taken place. He had to have misunderstood the question.

"Neither can I," he said. "Hey, don't get worked up. I get it. I mean, it's disappointing, but I'm used to that. God hasn't exactly been the go-to guy for black Americans. Or really, black anyone."

"You believe in him though, right?"

He shrugged a shoulder. "I mean I believe He exists, obviously. I'm an angel. But do I believe in Him in the way I believe that if I needed bail money I could rely on Chris to send it? Nope."

"Wow," she said, feeling her hackles lower. "That makes me pretty sad."

He grabbed his sandwich again. "Then you're starting to get it."

"Maybe next time around," she added. "Maybe God's next child will be black."

Quentin nodded. "I remember you telling me that God gave you miracles the world is ready for. Obviously He knows a thing or two about what people want, listening to prayers all the time—"

"He doesn't really listen," she said, before quickly adding, "don't tell anyone."

He nodded succinctly. "That makes sense. Either way, He could probably tell that there wasn't a chance in heaven, hell, or earth that this country was ready to listen to a black messiah."

"If it makes you feel any better, which it probably won't, I don't think this country's ready to listen to a female messiah, either."

"It might be if you ever said anything worth listening to."

She groaned and rolled her eyes. "You're lucky I like you."

Judith inserted herself back into the conversation, picking up where she'd left off. "Why don't you just hire a bunch of NAOs? You already know most of them are angels, and those women would do anything for you. Seriously, it's sad. They would probably leave jobs that paid a living wage to move across the country and live with four other roommates in a two-bedroom apartment just to work here if you asked."

"Can I quote you on that for the advertisement?" Jessica said. But Judith did raise a good point. And it would be nice to have people she trusted around her all the time. Would people notice if she only hired females? Probably, but in this town, it might be a plus. The titty bars got away with it. She'd just have to find a way to make the case that only females could do the jobs she had in mind. Was there anything especially hazardous to penises she could include in the job description?

Having to work with her mother might qualify.

"Do I have anything in my teeth?" Quentin asked, baring them for her.

"A little lettuce right there." She pointed on herself.

"Perfect." He didn't bother to dig it out. "They just hired a new manager who tries too hard to be down with all the black employees. If I have something in my teeth and grin at him all day, he might just have a nervous breakdown trying to decide if he should mention it or not."

"That's petty as hell," Judith said, then she held up her hand and Quentin high-fived her.

"Gotta get my kicks where I can." He winked at Judith, grabbed his bag, and left.

Chapter Thirty-Two

Jessica had cleaned her condo—thoroughly cleaned it, including dusting, wiping down the microwave, and scrubbing off the invisible scum from the shower—for the first time since moving in. It only required one night of not sleeping at all to fit it into her schedule.

It seemed important, though. She wanted to exude as much togetherness as she could for the new hires, even though it wouldn't be long before they stepped into the trenches and discovered the messy truth of her life. And even though they'd already seen her living space in the NAO house and knew the deal.

Judith and Destinee were already there, downing their second round of beers at Jessica's kitchen island when the others arrived in close succession.

When Jessica had first conceived this welcome dinner for her new hires, it had seemed fitting that the food should be from It is Risen, almost as part of the initiation. But within minutes of welcoming Tamara, Pippa, Maddy, and Jade into her home, she decided the menu was actually sort of creepy.

"Welcome to my home! I'd love to have me for dinner!"

She regretted miracling the food, but then she remembered that she didn't know how to cook regular gluten-free foods, and Tamara and Maddy were two of her legitimately gluten-free NAO sisters.

"This place is so nice, Jessica!" Maddy said after hugging Judith hello and reminding Destinee of her name.

"Thanks," Jessica said, feeling genuinely happy to see her old friends.

"It's not hers," Judith said. "It's Jameson Fractal's. He just lets her live in it."

"Judith!" Jessica snapped.

"What? You seriously want them thinking you can afford a place like this off your revenue from the bakery while they're being paid next to nothing?"

Jessica sighed. "I guess not." She turned to the guests who had spread out around the island and were helping themselves at her invitation. "It's true, I couldn't afford this place. But don't tell anyone it's Jameson's. Actually, we were supposed to have him sign it over a while ago, but we still haven't gotten around to it. It would just look bad if it got out to the press that I was living for free."

"I think it's romantic," said Jade, and Tamara nodded along. "No guy I've ever dated has put me up in a place like this indefinitely."

"We're not really dating," Jessica clarified. "He's a friend, and we spend a lot of time together, and—"

"Y'all made out," said Tamara.

"Yes," Jess conceded. "We did do that, but we're not actually romantically involved."

"Ohhh, right," said Pippa. "Because you can't have—ouch!"

Judith had kicked her right in the shin to silence her before nodding subtly toward Destinee, who wasn't yet privy to that unfortunate aspect of Jessica's existence.

Jade picked up the conversation again, "I have to say, I think the all-female bakery thing is a great idea. Strong personal branding."

Jessica wanted to take the compliment as it was, but accepting compliments wasn't one of her God-given strengths. "It wasn't intentional. I tried to hire some men, and it didn't work out well, so I just hired people I already knew I could trust. And you all happened to be women."

"Big coincidence," mumbled Judith before taking a sip.

"Right, right," said Maddy. "You hired three guys who stole from you. I think I read about that online."

"Technically only one stole from me. The accountant, the one you're replacing."

Maddy smiled and nodded, appearing satisfied. "I like the bar to be low when I show up to a new job."

"And what about me?" said Tamara. "Who am I replacing?"

Jessica chuckled. "You're replacing this big, hairy Croatian guy who left the walk-in open all night."

"And me?" said Jade.

"If you have a single ounce of common decency in you, you'll outdo your predecessor who thought it would be a good idea to include an image of me deep throating a baguette on the homepage."

Destinee added, "Don't forget the one where you had a black leather saddle on Jesus and were riding him."

"I can *never* forget that," Jessica said, remembering the horribly inaccurate depiction of her half-brother's appearance, "no matter how hard I try."

Jade cringed. "Please tell me it wasn't a GIF."

Jessica nodded solemnly. "It was. It was a GIF of me riding vaguely BDSM Jesus."

"That's going to be hard to top," said Jade, still grimacing.

"Was that a pun?" Judith asked.

Pippa chimed in. "And what about me? Who am I replacing?"

"No one," said Jessica.

"Me," said Judith. "So I can take more days off to sit at home, be poor, and read obfuscated books like my English degree intended."

Jessica arched a brow at her. "You done?"

Judith shrugged.

"We just need a third person to switch off with Destinee and Judith so they don't have to work as much."

Destinee added, "And you, baby. You could use a break sometimes. If you have Tamara on prep and three of us who can help run the place, you can finally stop working seven days a week."

"Right," said Jessica. "That too. Theoretically."

"No offense," Judith said, which Jessica knew was more sarcasm than earnestness, "but you are not exactly miss sunshine after forty days of work and forty nights with no sleep. I know you can't afford to give us real benefits, but having you out of my hair for an entire weekend while you were partying with Jameson was a lot like a paid time off."

"Drinks?" asked Destinee as she stood to get herself another.

Once another round of beers was distributed (with two ciders in the mix), they migrated over to the living room, where there were more places to sit.

Destinee led the toast. "Cheers to my new coworkers, even the ones I'll probably never see." She nodded toward Jade and Maddy, who sat next to each other on the couch.

The day before, Jessica had googled "how to lead a team" over her fifteen-minute lunch break and come up with a whole list of structured discussions to conduct to "build team cohesion" and "engender trust between colleagues."

But none of them seemed appropriate now as Jade launched into a story of a website she'd created for a business called Baby's First Gun.

The conversation veered drastically, when, seemingly out of nowhere, Pippa said, "You know, if you decide to hire someone else, to do what I'm doing, I think Courtney would be great for the job."

Jessica felt her eye twitch. "Courtney ... Wurst?" She struggled not to laugh through the question. While she'd reached a tenuous truce with her former bully for the sake of harmony in NAO, and because the girl did seem genuinely remorseful for the way she'd treated Jessica for so many years, the thought of hiring her was one that had never crossed her mind.

"Holy fuckeroni," Destinee yelled, the beer in her mouth dribbling down her front. She rubbed it into the fabric of her It is Risen T-shirt absentmindedly. Her astonished eyes turned to Jessica. "Did she just say Wurst? You wouldn't hire a Wurst, right?"

"No, Mom. Don't worry," she replied quickly before Destinee, who was four beers in, could decide it was fightin' time and take to the streets. She decided it necessary to address the rest of the room who wasn't aware of her mother's deep history with the family. "My mom and her mom go way back."

"Now," Destinee said, hardly able to sit still in the armchair, "that almost sounds like we were friends. And let me tell you, that ain't the case. I beat Ruth's ass twice, and I've been dreaming about a hat trick."

"Courtney has changed, Mom. Even *she* doesn't like her mother anymore."

That gave Destinee something savory to chew on, and she fell silent long enough for Jessica to ask, "What's she doing now?"

"She's down in San Antonio," said Pippa. "She works for a local news station. She hates it, though. That's why I thought she might like to come work for you."

"Eh," said Jessica reluctantly, "it's one thing for me to forgive her, it's another thing for me to want to spend time with her. And my mom has a point. The rest of her family is still White Light, drinking straight from Jimmy's silver troughs. That's a whole lot of crazy I don't care to invite into my life."

"Oh right, they worship pigs, huh?" said Pippa.

Before Jessica could explain, Judith said, "Yep, except I think the word you're looking for is 'fuck.' They fuck pigs."

Even Destinee cringed at that.

"No," Jessica said, upon seeing Maddy's especially horrified face, "they don't *actually* do that."

Judith shrugged remorselessly. "Listen, I wasn't the one who started calling them pigfuckers. It had to start *somewhere* right?"

While Destinee continued to cringe, she also nodded a concession. "She's got a point."

Jessica couldn't believe what she was about to do. "Listen, White Light had a lot of faults. In fact, it's entirely faults. But ... *that* isn't one of them, okay?"

"That almost sounds like you're defending them," Judith replied.

"I'm not. Trust me. I just don't think we have to make up stuff about them to prove they're terrible. And if we do make up stuff, all it does is discredit all our other arguments against them."

Judith let the issue drop.

Destinee jumped in. "That's wise of you, Jess."

And Judith was right back in it. "Yeah, are you, like, a prophet or something?"

Jessica sighed. "It'll be so nice to give you time off, Judith."

"Preaching to the choir, God girl. Preaching to the choir."

Chapter Thirty-Three

After a busy week of training her new recruits (none of whom insisted they already knew everything she was trying to show them), dust and clutter had reclaimed her condo like when nature springs up through the cracks of an ancient city with intrusions of grass and moss and vines, shouting, "You thought you got rid of us, motherfucker, but we always win in the end."

However, despite the mess, Wendy Peterman was relaxed enough to sit during this team meeting. She made herself comfortable on a chair across from her clients while Jameson leaned back on the couch, his arm comfortably around Jessica's shoulders. They didn't need to put on a show, even while the reporter Maria Flores was present and sat attentively but patiently on one of the barstools Jessica had brought in from the kitchen. But after weeks spent pretending to date Jameson, including his occasional visits to It is Risen to stoke sales and nights out at expensive restaurants he was happy to pay for, she felt a pleasant level of platonic intimacy with him that allowed her certain perks, like casual human contact.

And perhaps their firm alliance deserved some of the credit for Wendy's almost serene expression and the fact that Cash Monet hadn't been required to attend this time around.

"How does it work, exactly?" Maria asked. "Break down the logistics for me."

Jessica was happy to do so, but she decided to give the floor over to Joshua, who had also been called across the hall for this preliminary interview.

He'd opted to sit crosslegged on the overly furry living room rug, like a contented little buddha in his loose Judas Priest T-shirt and tattered jean shorts. "Every evening, an hour after It is Risen closes, I arrive with the truck and collect the remaining food that she won't be able to sell the following day. Then I bring the food to the trailer I've set up by the homeless shelter and distribute it for free."

Wendy swooned gently.

"I must say," Jesus continued, "the homeless greatly prefer muffins to fish, and they haven't been meanies to me at all. In fact, they've been quite kind. Haven't been kicked or punched in the face a single time!"

After a few more questions about the logistics, Maria appeared satisfied. "I'll type this up and get some eyes on it, and then I'll call Gabrielle, and we'll come by with the camera for in-person interviews sometime next week." She tucked her pen and pad away and grinned. "I think it's going to do wonders, Jessica. And for what it's worth, I'm proud of you."

Jessica allowed herself to take the compliment without exposing that the setup hadn't been her idea but Jameson's. She would have passed the credit along to him in a heartbeat, had Wendy not coached her against it prior to Maria's arrival.

"It's very nice to meet you, Joshua," Maria said, reaching down to shake his hand.

"Peace be with you," he replied.

"And also with you."

And when Wendy escorted her to the door, Jessica swore she heard the reporter say, "His aura is remarkable. What aren't you telling me?"

Chapter Thirty-Four

"Just one more," the frat bro begged.

"Yeah, all right," said Jessica.

She leaned toward him again, a few hairs that had pulled loose from her ponytail over the course of a long workday catching on his stiff, gelled helmet of spiky hair. The smell of his cologne managed to overpower the scent of the donuts she'd just pulled from the oven that were cooling on a rack, glazed and miracled, only feet away.

She smiled, using her reflected appearance in his phone screen to make sure both sides of her face were in on the cheery expression.

He snapped the selfie, looked at it, and nodded his approval. "Sweet."

Another fifteen bucks in the bank. It was hard *not* to smile for that kind of cash from ten seconds of work, or in the frat bro's case, twenty seconds spanning eight pictures where he looked exactly the same yet was somehow only happy with the last one. If there was any variance in her expression over the array, it was that she appeared much less enthusiastic by the last one. But maybe that was how he preferred women to look.

She hadn't had a week so good in … ever. At least she couldn't remember one.

Maria's piece about feeding the homeless had only aired on the Midland station, but from what Cash Monet reported, it was making the rounds online, being tweeted, shared, even pinned, which made the social media specialist endlessly happy, citing something about reaching the target demographic. They'd told Jessica that a story like this was exactly what the world wanted. Sheesh. Who knew? She'd thought people wanted to read about things like Jimmy's brainwashing scandal, which had turned up sixteen women claiming to have been part of his cult at last count.

That number was laughably low. She'd been to White Light Church, which had since undergone massive renovations after buying up the land around it and growing larger than many towns in the surrounding area. The number of people in Jimmy's cult ranged closer to ten thousand. What else could White Light be called? And now that it'd expanded, opening branches in Katy, Beaumont, Lubbock, and Brownsville, that number might even be higher. She couldn't be sure. She'd never looked into how big those satellite locations were, and she had no plans to check on them. Unwelcome news like that usually did a pretty good job of finding her, no assistance needed.

Like when White Light celebrated its tenth anniversary. It had just celebrated its twentieth this past February. She shuddered, thinking about all the much better things than White Light Church that hadn't lasted that long—TV shows, marriages, koalas.

"Don't you have somewhere to be tonight?" Judith asked as she passed Jessica on the way to delivering a warmed-up blueberry muffin. "Shouldn't you already be on the road?"

"I still have an hour. It doesn't take that long to drive to San Marcos."

"True, but I figure you've already jumped the gun on this entire scholarship thing, so you might as well jump the gun on leaving work for it."

Jessica groaned and helped the next customer in line.

Judith may not understand Jessica's reasoning for starting the scholarship now, and that was fine. But she was on a roll, and she needed to keep it going if she hoped to drag out, for as long as possible, the heady high of being in the public's good graces.

It would come to an end eventually. It always did. And that didn't so much worry her anymore. Jessica was a pro at disappointment. She slipped right into it like it was her favorite pair of pj pants.

It was good fortune that she could really use more practice with.

WE'VE BEEN OVER THIS. I NEVER ESTABLISHED KARMA. IT IS NOT A THING.

She thanked the young mother with her toddler on her

hip and directed her to the glass display where Judith would plate her items for her.

Then maybe Original Mistake did it. Because it's a thing.

NO, IT IS NOT. ORIGINAL MISTAKE DOESN'T CARE ABOUT BALANCING THE UNIVERSE. THAT'S MY JOB.

And you're doing a fantastic job of it, let me say.

THE LORD DELIGHTS NOT IN YOUR SARCASM.

It didn't matter what God said about Karma. He'd been wrong before ... hadn't he?

Regardless, she was playing the odds here and putting as much good into the universe as she could in hopes of receiving the same back. And establishing a scholarship fund for NAO was just step one of her master plan.

Had she paid up on all her debts? Not by a long shot. But could she stash away a few bucks of her own paycheck here and there to establish the fund?

She wasn't entirely sure about that, either, but she was going to try. If it meant she only ate things from the bakery for the next year, well, that wouldn't be too different from the last year, and she'd learned just the right coffee-to-carb ratio to avoid becoming constipated to the point of a medical emergency.

Again, life was all about balance.

When Judith passed by again, Jessica hissed, "I'm not jumping the gun. I'm being proactive."

"Don't know if your creditors see it that way."

Jessica ground her teeth briefly before helping the next in line.

Thanks to Pippa's smart accounting work and suggestion to transfer existing credit card debt to a few more business cards with no-interest offers, Jessica was only one-month behind on mortgage. Pippa had even accompanied Jessica to the credit union to touch base again about the agreement, and, after speaking with the same two people, Pippa confirmed that the boss was in fact an angel. So that, at least, didn't weigh as heavily on her mind.

The other main source of debt was, of course, Mrs. Thomas. Jessica had fallen a few months behind again on those payments. At Pippa's urging, Jessica had called Mrs. Thomas and explained the full situation, and as she'd expected, her story was received with full understanding.

But she didn't think her good fortune could afford to wait until she was paid up before adding to Karma's coffer. Feeding the homeless cost her nothing, and brought her good will, and with that, increased sales. But she knew the main bolster to the bakery's sales was her continued relationship with Jameson. And he wouldn't be in town forever ...

If she wanted money Karma, she needed to give money. And who better to receive it than her old sorority? Not everyone could pay for college with scratch-off lotto tickets.

"Let me worry about the finances," Jessica said as Judith passed behind her again.

"Oh, I do. Listen, don't think I'm ungrateful for the fact that you always pay on time even when you're tens of thousands of dollars behind on payments. I'm just saying, setting up a scholarship fund might be a little ambitious when you got that crazy investor of yours breathing down your neck. If I were you, I'd want to pay her off and be done with that as soon as I could."

"She's not crazy. She's actually being incredibly understanding. And you think I don't want to finally be out of debt? Of course I do! But I'm not going to wait until everything's perfect before I start giving back. Besides, if there's anything Mrs. Thomas would understand, it's the importance of helping people get a quality education. She's even praised me on becoming a philanthropist."

Judith cocked a skeptical eyebrow at her. "Is that what you need? Praise?"

Jessica glared back at her. "No. But it doesn't hurt every now and then."

When Judith raised her arms into the air and bent at the waist, bowing down, Jessica slapped her hands away. "Go take a smoke break."

Chapter Thirty-Five

Jessica hadn't been back to San Marcos once since moving to Austin, and the sight of the campus buildings on the skyline wasn't unlike a bad drug trip. The feelings in her gut had no words for them. There was a sense of pull, like she'd swallowed magnets and the town was made entirely of steel. There was a tingling nausea associated with it, but not in her stomach. Rather, it was in her chest and a little in her forearms as she clutched the steering wheel.

The NAO house was on the other side of town from the highway, forcing her to drive through campus to get there. As she passed the Christian Student Center, her gaze wandered restlessly to the giant, blocky structure.

She slammed on the brakes in the middle of the road. Cars behind her honked, but she didn't care.

On the building's tan siding had long been a dark brown cross: her half-brother's torture device. Now, next to it, in much fresher paint was a symbol she didn't recognize that looked strangely similar to the cross, but with a circle on top and what appeared to be a halo above that. She had a bad feeling about it.

By the time she'd pulled onto the gravel leading up to the sorority house, her limbs had stopped shaking. She took a deep breath after parking and looked onto the passenger's seat where she'd buckled in the stacked boxes of It is Risen goods.

What was she even doing here? Her sisters kept insisting she speak to the new NAO members, but what did she have to say? All she had to offer was some danishes and muffins with her face seared onto them.

This is gonna be so uncomfortable.

YOU HAVE NO IDEA.

Care to fill me in?

THE MIGHTY-AND-ALL-THAT LORD LACKS THE PROPER WORDS TO DESCRIBE IT.

Couldn't you make up some?

INDEED. YOU CAN EXPECT A HOMMERNOMINY OF DRANBLOOTLES AWAITING YOU INSIDE.

She groaned (more at herself for having thrown Him such a slow pitch to hit a Dad joke right out of the park) and unbuckled the boxes.

As promised, Kate was waiting to play liaison. She sat on the porch swing Jessica had enjoyed on so many stressful nights. Her auburn hair was magnificent in the first hint of twilight.

She jumped up and ran over, taking the top half of the

boxes from Jessica's stack. "They're *so* excited to finally meet you."

"Oh great," Jessica lied.

She hadn't prepared a speech or anything for this visit, and she was wondering now if she should have.

Of course I should have. Never prepared.

"And the scholarship fund should be ready to start distributing next fall to incoming freshman and existing students. I just have a few more documents to get notarized and then the attorney will type up the official statement and so on."

Jessica inhaled deeply, letting it out in a whoosh. "Thanks. I really appreciate you taking this over. I know I should be more involved in the behind-the-scenes part, so if you want me to—"

"I'm not going to screw you, Jessica. Have I ever done anything to help you that went awry?"

While standing on the front lawn of the sorority house, the memory of Kate's excessive hazing in this same spot, where she'd shouted "pigfucker" at Courtney Wurst until Jessica had been forced to intercede, came readily to mind. But she decided not to bring it up. "You're right. I trust you."

"Judith told me about what happened with the bakery, so I know you're a little gun shy when it comes to trusting others to simply take care of business without your constant oversight. Which is why I'm taking so long on this. I want to make sure everything is done properly so none of it comes back to bite you. You have so much on your plate, Jessica. It means a lot to me that you let me help. Really."

"I guess this is what you do now, huh?" She wasn't sure if setting up a scholarship and working as a contract grant writer for non-profits was the same, but it seemed closely related through a similar need to read fine print, play by cumbersome government rules, and spend hours concentrating on something so boring it made Jessica want to weep.

"Sort of," said Kate, shrugging a shoulder, which told Jessica the two things probably had less in common than she'd guessed. "But my uncle works in estate law, and he's been helpful. Now can you loosen up? You're about to be filmed by no fewer than thirty of your sisters."

"That's supposed to help me loosen up?"

Kate nodded, missing the contradiction. "Yes. You have to loosen up or you're going to be all over Twitter, Instagram, Snapchat, and Facebook looking like a robot, or worse, an unrelatable human."

Balancing the boxes in her hand, Kate held open the door for Jessica, who cleared her throat, worked out her jaw in preparation for the plastered grin, and then sauntered into the house as casually as she could.

Her feet had hardly left the welcome mat when she planted them again, and any hope of appearing relatable vanished. The jaw stretches, however, proved extremely useful as her mouth hung open.

Opposite the front door, on the living room wall stretching up toward the vaulted ceilings, was Jessica, staring right back at Jessica or whoever else was foolish enough to enter this veritable shrine.

"Kate," she hissed, ignoring the girls lounging around the main room and the long dining table who had begun squealing as soon as they spotted her.

Kate let the door close behind her and stepped forward to admire the work. "Isn't it incredible? Caitlyn did that. She joined right after you left. She's an art major, if you couldn't guess."

"The artist's name and major weren't among my main questions," Jessica grunted, staring at the giant image of her face in ecstasy.

She knew the moment the mural had recreated. She remembered it well, and yes, it was a defining one for her career, but there was something about her expression in it that seemed profane. If *only* casting miracles felt that orgasmic.

While the focus of the art was Jessica's face, there was quite a bit more happening in it. It depicted the moment in the Nu Alpha Omega kitchen when Jessica had first discovered her ability to make things gluten-free. Except Caitlyn had taken a few liberties for the purpose of artistic balance, no doubt. In the center of the wall was a ten-foot tall version of Jess, her eyes shut, her chin raised ever so slightly as she extended her hands out over a fresh spread of crescent rolls. Jessica knew for a fact that light did *not* radiate from her hands or any part of her when she miracled, but in this depiction, it did. The rest of the founding NAOs were pictured as well. There was Kate peeking out from behind Jessica to stare at the holy mystery with wide-eyed awe, her auburn hair a shade brighter than reality, though that was hardly the exaggeration Jessica needed to fixate on. On her left stood Judith, arms crossed, staring skeptically with a single eyebrow raised. And on her right, Natalie shared a similarly subdued interest.

And smaller were Tamara and Maddy and Jade and the rest, each in a pose that captured her personality so well, it made Jessica a little less upset about this entire display of insanity.

Were she not herself, she would have appreciated the thought put into the mural. But as it was, she was entirely put off.

Before she could snap at Kate for not giving her a heads up, the NAOs descended on her, and she only just handed off the rest of the boxes to Kate before she was surrounded in a group hug.

The size of the sorority had almost tripled, and when Kate suggested Jessica take a seat on the couch and let the others gather around, that meant girls were sitting cross legged on the floor and standing around the perimeter of the living room just to squeeze in and catch whatever words Jessica happened to utter, which she desperately hoped made sense and didn't come back to bite her in the ass.

As Kate had warned, most of the sisters had their phones aimed at Jessica, but she could spot a handful who were actually posing for selfies with the front-facing camera on.

"It's so great to meet everyone," Jessica said, tossing a pleasantry into the air to see if anyone grabbed it.

It played well. The girls gabbed their own replies, and Jessica wondered at how big the age gap felt between her and some of these women who were only a year or two younger than her. Had she had this much energy and enthusiasm when she was only twenty? She didn't suspect so, but there was no denying running a business had taken a lot from her.

She would have paid good money for Jameson to be on the couch next to her instead of the twitchy blonde who smelled like a caramel corn. He would know *exactly* how to work a crowd like this. In fact, this was his ideal audience. She chuckled, thinking about how he would react when she told him about this. He would be so excited, so supportive, so ...

Well, she should just send him a picture now. "Can y'all scoot in?" she asked, motioning with one hand while she leaned over and pulled her phone from her back pocket. "I want to get a group selfie to send to Jameson."

Those were the magic words, and the girls practically clawed each other to make sure they were in the frame as Jessica lined it up. Only when she inspected the photo before sending it away to him did she notice something fascinating about it.

She almost missed it, and she easily could have, because there was no single thing that tipped her off. More a general *mis en scene* that alerted her to the reality: she was in total control.

Her arms tingled as the truth of it settled into her body. She controlled the room.

For shit's sake! There was a ten-foot picture of her on the wall to her right! Not only did she know the beloved Jameson Fractal, she had his personal cell number and was supposedly dating him.

Oh, and she was the daughter of God.

And all of them believed it.

Holy shit. These were her people. These were her goddamn people!

"Kate," she said, letting the rush of power do its thing, "can you collect everyone's cell phones?"

The looks of shock and horror dissipated slowly as Kate went around, shaking down each person and not taking "I don't have it on me" for an answer.

Once she was finished, she nodded to Jess.

"Great. Now we can have a real discussion." What came next? Did she ask each of them to introduce herself?

No, no point. Jessica wouldn't remember anyone's name, and if they said it, she would be expected to. Better to just jump into it.

"I'm guessing you have some questions for me." Heads bobbed. "Shoot."

"Is God okay with premarital sex?" blurted a bronze-skinned girl with large blue eyes and full, dark eyebrows. Jessica forced herself not to laugh at it. Of course the first question was "do we get to bang?"

"Yeah, he doesn't care. As long as it's consensual, respectful, and doesn't include non-human animals."

Another girl raised her finger into the air then followed up. "When you say consensual, that means both parties have to say 'I want to have sex' prior to penetration?"

Jessica's eyes searched for Kate, who winced apologetically.

"Uh, I don't know if there's a specific set of words that have to be said. I think both parties just have to be up for it."

A sister with a pacific islander face and dark hair that seemed to generate its own glow said, "Does that mean there's no take-backsies in the middle?"

"Nooo," Jessica said, suddenly feeling vastly under qualified to lead this discussion. "I think there can still be take-backsies ... assuming I know what that means."

The girl clarified. "Like, if he's already inside you and then you start thinking about how he's actually a horrible person, like, he drives on the shoulder to cut bad traffic and tells the Starbucks barista his name is 'harder, daddy' and brags about the time he ran over his neighbor's dog and got away with it. And then you also remember he was the one pushing drinks on you the whole night and maybe he was just trying to get you drunk so you'd bang him. If you are like, 'this was a mistake and I'm not into it anymore,' and you tell him to stop and he doesn't, is that still consensual?"

"No!" Jessica blurted. A flop sweat came over her, and she paused, cleared her throat and said more calmly, "No, it for sure stops being consensual the moment anyone involved says no. Also, you should probably report him for the dog thing."

The questioner appeared skeptical, then the doubt slowly faded as her expression drooped. "Oh. Damn."

"Yeah," Jessica said, cringing. "I think you were raped. At least a little."

Another girl scoffed, drawing Jess's attention across the room. "If that's rape, then I've *definitely* been raped."

"It's ... entirely possible," Jessica said, trying to read the girl's sharp features. "And to be clear, God's *not* cool with rape."

"What about threesomes?" asked a bulky brunette, sitting on the ground with her knees pulled up to her chest. "He cool with that?"

Jessica hadn't truly considered it before. Sure, she might have briefly fantasized about a sexy compromise between Team Chris and Team Jameson, but she'd never worried about whether her Father would approve. "Well, he's never said anything *against* it."

"Assuming they're consensual, respectful, and don't include non-human animals," the brunette added.

"Right. Um."

THE LORD CONSIDERED INFINITE POSSIBILITIES BEFORE ESTABLISHING THE LAWS ON THIS.

You considered threesomes.

EXTENSIVELY.

And He hadn't ruled them out. Okay then.

"Yeah, he's fine with it. Maybe too much so."

The bulky brunette turned to her sister next to her and they high-fived.

"Anything not about sex you want to—"

"Going back to the rape thing ..."

Jessica searched the back of the room for the source of the voice and only found it when the girl spoke again.

"Is it consensual if, like, he's your friend, and you respect and trust him, but you'd never thought about him like that, and then one night you're out at a bar and he's there, and you're a little torn up about a recent break-up so you confide that in your friend and he buys you a handful of drinks and shots to help you forget, and then he offers to give you a ride home, but instead he takes you to his place and makes you a few more drinks, and the two of you are just talking in his room and then you sorta black out but eventually you realize the two of you are going at it, and you decide it's probably easier just to finish up and not piss him off than to stop in the middle, because even though you aren't attracted to him, he's your friend, and he's already going to think you're a slut since—"

"You're not a slut!" Jessica shouted.

The room went so silent, she could have heard a mouse queef. Her desire to smooth over her sudden outburst was in direct conflict with her horror at the story.

"He knew what he was doing," Jessica said. "You trusted him to be your friend. You're not responsible just because you trusted the wrong person and they took advantage of you. And you're not a slut because, well, all kinds of reasons! You're a victim."

"But I don't want to be a victim. And he's my friend," said the girl meekly. "And we're still cool. Like, it never happened again."

This time, it wasn't Jameson's easy charm and command of a room she channeled, but Judith's deep, morbid sarcasm. "What a gentleman to only sexually assault you that one time."

"I'm sure he just misread the signals," said the girl. "I mean, I was letting him buy me all those drinks. And I asked him for a ride home."

"To *your* house," Jessica cut in. The girl looked so young sitting there, and every defense that came out of her mouth churned Jessica's insides. "You know, I was ..." Should she go there? Did it even count? She hadn't thought about it for years. Would mentioning it here around these legitimate victims seem melodramatic? Would it seem like she was just trying to get some of the attention back to her? It wasn't like it ruined her life.

But on the other hand, she was the daughter of God. And she could feel more than see the heaviness that these stories brought to the surface of the girls that told them. Maybe if they could see that victimization wasn't a sign of failure ...

The taste of the words on her tongue made her sick and lightheaded. "I was sexually assaulted once." She'd never said it before, never wanted to admit that's what it was. She'd wanted the memory to go away, not claim more attention.

"It makes you feel like a fool," she said. "Like a

goddamn fool. So much so that you'd rather make excuses and call it a million other things than admit you were tricked, outsmarted, or overpowered, and that someone stole something from you. That's what it feels like, doesn't it? Like they're stealing your ability to trust, and not just them and other men, but yourself." Her hands began to tingle in time with a stirring in her chest like a storm cloud gathering.

Without any target watermelons in sight, she was forced to steady herself.

"I was assaulted," blurted the girl on the couch next to her. "By my boyfriend. Does that count?"

"Yes."

"What if it was a girl who did it?" said another.

"Still counts."

"What if you can't remember it?" asked another, "but you were told about it later?"

The tingling increased, and she flexed her fingers to try to work it through. "Definitely counts."

"My manager," said another one. "I can't quit my job, though. My tips are the only way I can afford to buy food and books each semester. No one would believe me anyway. I've ... I've slept with a few of the other servers, so ..."

Jessica stood suddenly. "Will you excuse me for a moment?" Weaving between the girls on the ground, she stumbled through the crowd until she reached the front door, where she promptly let herself out, slamming it behind her without meaning to and clearing the stairs down from the porch in a single leap as she hurried across the lawn, looking for just the right tree at the perimeter. A large juniper made a perfect target. It was an invasive species, a plague upon the native vegetation that did nothing but cause seasonal misery when it blew its load of pollen indiscriminately each year.

She could hear the door open and close behind her, but it was too late to stop. If she took her eyes off the tree, she'd end up smiting something else by accident.

She focused on the space where the trunk met the earth, determined to root out every last bit of it, and then she let the heat rush through her and tug free.

The lowest yard of the trunk exploded, and she shut her eyes against the splinters that flew her way. In her fury, she hadn't considered what would become of the rest of the tree, and as it started to fall toward the gravel where the NAOs' cars were parked, Jessica had to think quick. Luckily, she had more than one smite in her, and two more bursts made sawdust of the rest.

Her heart raced but her blood pressure dropped quickly along with her adrenaline. She copped a squat on the manicured lawn, staring at the hole in the ground where the tree had been.

"Let's hope that wasn't a heritage tree," Kate said from behind her. "The city of San Marcos might give us a citation if they ever checked on that sort of thing."

"I didn't know it was so common," Jessica said.

"Yeah, they stick those dumb little tags on any tree with a diameter of—"

"No, not the heritage trees."

Kate squatted next to her and placed her hand on Jessica's knee. "I know."

"Those girls look up to me, and I should have something useful to say to them. But I don't know what to say to anyone."

"'I'm sorry that happened to you,' is a start. 'Do you want me to smite him?' would also go over well, I bet."

Jessica turned toward her so Kate could see the eye roll. "Women could really use a better rite of passage, couldn't we?"

"Yeah," said Kate simply. "We really could."

"Have you ever—?"

She shook her head. "No. I feel a little left out, honestly. My trust issues with men are all on me, I guess." She stood. "Why don't you go back in there and answer some more inane questions. And if assault gets brought up again, which it most likely will, you can practice what you're gonna say to people from now on."

She agreed, and when she turned and glanced at the front window, openmouthed faces were staring back. "I'm going to be expected to smite a tree every time I visit a chapter, aren't I?"

"Oh yeah," said Kate, and she opened the door for Jess.

The girls were silent as Jessica crossed back to her place on the couch. "How about we pass out some of those cookies?" she asked, and Kate jumped to while the rest of the sisters gathered round again.

"Did you just smite a tree?" one of them asked.

"Yep. I did."

"Are you mad at us?"

She didn't mean to gasp; it just came out. Or, rather, in. "No! Why would I be mad at you?"

"Because we're sluts," said another.

A strange authoritative impulse welled up in her.

DO IT.

No.

JUST SAY IT. IT FEELS INCREDIBLE.

No way.

I'LL START IT OFF FOR YOU. "THOU SHALT NOT..."

If she were going to start issuing commandments, though, there was no way she would sound like her Dad.

"Don't say that word," she said. Then, to be clear. "Don't say the word slut. Not about you, not about anyone. It's a dead word now."

"A— a dead word?" said one of the reasonably confused girls.

She knew they would do whatever she told them, so rather than admitting dead words were just something she'd made up, she doubled down. "Yeah, it's a dead word. Imagine it dying out from your vocabulary. From here on out, you don't even know what that word means. And if you hear someone else say it, *you* tell *them* it's a dead word." She was spouting gibberish now, but she couldn't stop.

"Why?" said a muscular girl from the back with her toned armed folded over her chest.

"Because it's only ever been used to shame people."

"Women are reclaiming it, though," said the same sister. "We're taking it back and taking the power away."

"Oh bullshit," Jessica snapped. "You can't reclaim what was never yours. It's nothing but a word men use to punish women. And one women use to punish other women. You don't take on the language of abuse. You stomp it out!"

"What if I'm proud to be a slut?" asked the same standoffish girl.

"For fuck's sake," Jessica said, losing her patience. "You're not proud to be a slut, you're just proud to own your body. You lose the word slut, and nothing changes except you're not acknowledging the abuse of people who hate you by using their word."

A freckly girl next to the muscular questioner jabbed her with her elbow. "Just do as she says, Beth. Jesus."

"Any other questions?" Jessica said, feeling like she could get the hang of this being-right-no-matter-what thing.

Kate handed out cookies as the next one was asked. "Do we have to worry about God getting us pregnant?"

"No," Jessica said. "Just don't have sex with him."

"You're saying abstinence is the only way to ensure we don't get pregnant by God?"

Jessica put her head in her hands. If this was what being a female messiah meant, she was entirely underqualified for the job.

* * *

Jessica's head was still spinning as she laboriously climbed the stairs inside her building. The unearthed stories from the NAOs had swirled and melted together on her drive from San Marcos, forming a messy lump of fear and anger in her bowels. So many stories, all different but with one upsetting thread tying them together. Not all the girls had something to confess, but far too many did. One was too many, really, but one could be called an anomaly, an unlucky encounter with a demon, if nothing else. The sheer number she'd just heard, though ... that went beyond bad luck to a deeper, more omnipresent threat.

As her foot found the top step, she spotted a six-pack of Dos Equis on her doorstep, and her first thought was, *It's a miracle.* She could really use a drink.

Not far on the heels of that, though was the much more rational thought: *Who is leaving me alcohol when I'm not home?*

When she noticed the letter propped up next to it, she froze, still ten feet away from the thing.

No way. It'd been a month since the stalker had last paid her a visit, and she'd begun to suspect she was in the clear, that the police presence at the bakery had been enough to make him find a new hobby, or at least a new target. But maybe he'd simply been waiting for her to become complacent.

How could he have made it through the keypad entry at the front door of the condo to swing by her unit and drop off this delivery? And if he'd made it this far, who was to say he hadn't also found his way into her home?

She gnawed at her bottom lip as her eyes traveled to the small speck on Jeremy Archer's door: the motion sensor camera.

Yes! Her spiritually insane neighbor might actually have quality footage of the stalker's face!

"Fucking men," she grumbled as she stomped over to her male neighbor's door to ask for his assistance. It was really the least he could do, after being genitally complicit in so much unacceptible behavior.

But before she knocked, she cast one last spiteful glare across the hall at the beers, and that's when she noticed it.

Her name on the envelope was written in her mother's handwriting. She paused, her fist poised in midair, then let her hand drop to her side.

"Oh. Balls."

She should have known. Dos Equis should have been a dead giveaway. A stalker would leave something like Keystone or Boone's Farm. Or maybe she was thinking of pedophiles. Didn't matter.

She pulled the card from its envelope. It was a single slip of card stock with Destinee's bubbly handwriting giving it a cheery feeling despite the message.

Jess,

Thought you might need this today. Let me know if you're too hungover to come in to work tomorrow and I'll cover for you.

Love,

Mom

How did Destinee know about the downer of a homecoming in San Marcos already? Had Kate felt it necessary to give her a heads up as soon as Jessica pulled down the gravel driveway of the NAO house?

But then she saw the P. S.

P. S. For what it's worth, I sent a large box of cock and balls confetti to his office at White Light. Anonymous, of course. Won't change anything, but it felt good to do. Maybe you can think of something like that too. Not cock and balls confetti since it's already been done. Maybe cock and balls gummies? Or it doesn't have to include cock and balls at all. That's just the first thing that keeps popping into my head. I'm sure you can come up with a better idea. The drinking should help with that.

As she read through the P. S., the nature of the gift clicked and her stomach sank like a mammoth in a Texas tar pit.

Amid her anxiety about public speaking and the collective trauma she'd taken on just an hour before, Jessica had forgotten what day it was because today was the most forgettable of all crucially important days: it was the midterm elections.

Despite the efforts of sixteen women who'd come

forward with the same disturbing story about Jimmy's past, he must have been elected to the Texas Railroad Commission.

Sure, he hadn't abused those women physically, but the implications of a grown man luring a bunch of young girls into a doomsday cult shouldn't need to cross *that* line to throw his mental health into serious question.

But it hadn't. The story, the women—none of it mattered to the majority. And she suspected that even if he had taken that small step across the line into abuse, that wouldn't have mattered either.

She grabbed the six-pack and unlocked her front door. But before she stepped through, she whirled on her heels and pointed at Jeremy's tiny illegal camera. "Men are the *worst!*" she shouted, simply needing to go on the record as having said it.

She didn't expect a response. But a muffled voice from the other side of her neighbor's door supplied one: *"You're right."*

Chapter Thirty-Six

Jessica couldn't wait for pumpkin spice season to wrap up.

There were no official start and end dates for it. She supposed it began as soon as the first cold front hit in September and lasted until everyone was sick of smelling the stuff. She'd been sick of it for weeks now, having catered to the public demand and added a few new items to her menu. She promised herself Thanksgiving weekend would mark the end of it for her, but that was still two weeks away. She probably wouldn't even be able to enjoy pumpkin pie by then, which was nothing short of a tragedy; it was one of the few things Destinee ever baked herself rather than buying ready-made.

She watched as a girl chatted away on her cell phone over by the condiments shelf and attempted to shake out the last of the pumpkin spice from the large shaker onto the top of her coffee cup.

I'm gonna strangle the next person who comes in here and orders a pumpkin anything.

IS THAT A PROMISE?

Obviously not. I have a business to run.

YOU COULD PULL IT OFF, YOU KNOW. YOU'VE MADE LARGER MISSTEPS AND MANAGED TO KEEP THE LIGHTS ON.

Thanks?

THOU ART WELCOME. AND MIGHT THE LORD REMIND YOU OF YOUR GET-OUT-OF-JAIL-FREE CARD YOU HAVE YET TO USE.

Did you grant me that specifically for today? You've been planning on me murdering someone over pumpkin spice?

NO. THAT'S NOT TO SAY LITTLE MISS FREE WILL CAN'T CHOOSE TO MURDER AS SHE PLEASES, THOUGH. AND IF YOU DO, THE LORD SHALL FIND A WAY TO BAIL THINE ASS OUT OF JAIL.

Small blessings.

The door opened and Jessica beamed at the new customer—a woman in her mid-fifties with silky gray and silver hair that flowed loosely past her lightly tanned and makeup-free face, down to her waist. Wearing a loose and richly colorful long-sleeve blouse that looked noncommittally Indian and had only the slightest hint of a tapered waist, elaborately embroidered harem pants, and rope-woven slippers, this woman was far and away Jessica's favorite kind of Austinite.

Jessica referred to the type as a *galru*, but only to herself. She'd said it aloud once to test it out but decided to keep the term her little secret after realizing it sounded like a dog vomiting.

Galrus were necessarily women—if a man strolled up in this sort of fashion, Jessica prepared herself for an interaction full of condescension and references to Osho, whoever the hell that was.

These women had transcended to some higher level of not giving a fuck that Jessica hoped to one day attain herself. But in doing so, they remained friendly, gracious, humble, and present. They asked her how her day was going and then stared silently until she actually told them. And then they listened and responded accordingly. And then, the biggest blessing of all, they would say something encouraging, maybe reach across the counter and place a gentle hand on her wrist, and drop cash into the tip jar. And finally, they would glide away to wait patiently for their food or drink, doing *nothing*—no phone, no book, no headphones—just observing and offering warm hints of a smile to anyone who made eye contact.

She felt her body relax, readying itself to receive whatever good vibes the woman would bring with her into the bakery.

But then the galru stepped to the side, glancing over her shoulder at the woman entering just behind her.

Mrs. Thomas.

Shit. The sight poured a bucket of water on her nervous system, which snapped into action.

Were the two women together?

"Hi, Mrs. Thomas."

"Just the woman we were looking for!" said the teacher as they approached the counter together. "Jessica, this is Caren Powers. Caren, Jessica McCloud."

Caren made gentle but persistent eye contact with Jessica as she offered her hand. Wendy Peterman had once drilled her on the art of the handshake, impressing upon her the importance of going in strong and firm. But knowing what type of woman she was dealing with in this present situation, she held back. It would be no good to crush Caren's hand and send signals that she was a bully and closed off to receiving all the good vibes a galru had to offer.

She went with a gentler grip.

And Caren crushed her hand like a trash compactor.

Jessica tried to adjust, but it was too late. The bones in her hand were in no position to recover their grip, and by the time she attempted, the shake was over.

"So wonderful to finally meet you, Jessica. Dolores has been telling me about you for years. Truly. I remember her mentioning this 'bright young girl' who entered her kindergarten class."

Jessica was too embarrassed to look at Mrs. Thomas, so instead she nodded and looked down at the countertop.

"Caren is just in town for the day, and I told her she absolutely had to come here and see this remarkable place."

Now Jessica did look at Mrs. Thomas, but only to read

her expression. Those words seemed ... off. It was just a bakery. Sure, it had a vivid tree of life mural on one of the walls, and Jessica had secretly been adding more potted plants around over the last few months, hoping no one would notice the gradual transformation until the entire place was so jungly that there was no going back, no matter *what* Wendy said.

Did Mrs. Thomas really think it was remarkable?

"I tell you," said Caren, "she brags about you like you're her own daughter."

Mrs. Thomas chuckled. "Wishful thinking." She looked at Jessica. "You know I would have adopted you in a heartbeat if I could have. But now"—she held up her hands and rotated at the waist, looking around at the bakery like she'd never been in it before—"I see you can do things all on your own, and my opportunity to adopt you has passed." She grinned. "Alas, I'll just have to keep mooching free coffee from you instead."

"Two coffees then?" Jessica said, unsure how else to respond, and feeling buried under a mudslide of shame for every negative thought or suspicion she'd had about Mrs. Thomas in the time since the three shitheads had almost ruined her business.

Caren nodded. "Coffee sounds lovely."

"Anything to eat?"

Caren inspected the long display case at her leisure. When she returned, she said, "Yes, the bran muffins look amazing. Would you recommend them or something else my first time?"

She knew Caren was genuinely wondering. "If you want a muffin, I'd recommend the apple strudel or lemon poppy seed for your first visit. Both are a little more moist than the bran, just by nature."

Caren nodded. "Lemon poppy seed sounds divine."

She said it so earnestly, Jessica wasn't sure if it was meant to be clever wordplay or not.

"And I *must* try the pumpkin spice empanada," said Mrs. Thomas. "Actually, I'll take two."

As a self-imposed penance for the weak handshake, Jessica comped the food along with the coffee, and Caren thanked Jessica softly, resting a hand on her forearm as she slipped a fiver into the tip jar when Mrs. Thomas wasn't looking.

Judith returned from her smoke break just as the empanadas and muffin finished in the microwave, and Jessica was able to hand off the register as she carried the order out to the two women.

"Come sit," said Caren, pulling out a chair next to hers at the table.

Jessica looked around briefly. It was only two in the afternoon, which meant those not working a nine to five were dropping in to fight the afternoon lull, though for the most part they only ordered a coffee and a cookie and didn't require maintenance beyond that.

"Yeah, okay."

"I was just telling Caren about the time when you were, what, a junior in high school? And two girls—oh, I can't even remember their names—they accused you of cheating on your algebra test, and you kept denying it until the matter ended up in my office. You remember that, Jessica?"

Of course she did. Just because the traumatic events of her school career in Mooretown were numerous didn't mean they did her the service of all blending together. If only she could be so lucky as to forget any of it. "I do."

What she also remembered were the names of the two girls who'd challenged her. One was Stephanie Lee. The other was Sandra Thomas.

"And I believed that your perfect score plus full points for the extra credit *wasn't* definitive evidence of cheating. After all, I had you in my math class and the subject always came naturally to you." She turned to Caren. "So, I told her bullies exactly that—that she was an exceptionally talented mathematician and cheating wasn't her style. Then I assigned them in-school suspension for making false accusations and ended up firing the teacher who allowed that sort of a witch hunt to not only continue in his class, but escalate to a matter the principal was forced to handle."

Jessica's heart sank. *That* was the reason behind Mr. Deja's mid-year disappearance? He'd been fired for allowing Stephanie and Sandra to bully her? No, she must have misheard. That seemed so extreme.

She jumped when Mrs. Thomas laid a hand on her upper arm. "You really did withstand so much bullying growing up. Made me sick. That's what happens to the brightest lights. Darkness flocks to them. Sad but true reality of the world. The fact that you've managed to keep your light from going out and built yourself this flourishing business is just—" She pressed her lips together and for a moment it looked like she was about to cry. Had Jessica ever seen Mrs. Thomas cry?

"Well, I couldn't have done it," she said stiffly, "any of it, without your help."

She couldn't believe how quickly she'd forgotten the many well-timed interventions on her behalf Mrs. Thomas had made over the years. She'd let it all be washed clear out of her memory when the woman had hired a few bad apples in an attempt to *help*.

Jessica decided to set aside fifteen minutes later that night to feel properly ashamed.

Mr. Deja, though? She'd liked him well enough. He was one of only a few math teachers over the years who had never been short with her when she was the only one raising her hand to answer a question. There was probably more to his story that the woman was just leaving out. Maybe he groped a couple students or something and this was the last straw. She remembered his thick blond mustache and the way he regularly licked his lips mid-sentence. Yeah, that was probably it—he was probably a molester.

"You two bring me so much hope," said Caren. "Unfortunately, it's still such a rarity to see women helping each other out like this, boosting each other up rather than tearing one another down. And Dolores also tells me you employ an all-female staff, as well."

"Oh, well, not on purpose. If the right man came along, I'd hire him."

The unsaid things about former male employees hung heavy in the air, but the Caren didn't seem to notice it.

"I see a lot of potential in you," she said. "Already you've done so much, but you have unlimited potential. And I should know." Her soft chuckle sounded like a sigh.

"Caren hosts leadership retreats for women. She's done it for, oh, twenty years now?"

Caren nodded. "Yes. It will be twenty-one in February."

"Really?" asked Jessica. "What kind of leadership retreats?"

"How to tap into your full store of moon energy in a world overexposed to the sun."

Jessica continued to wait for a clearer answer but none came. Wait, was she supposed to understand ...?

"You know," Mrs. Thomas said, "I think you might be a perfect candidate for one of her retreats, Jessica. What do you think, Caren?"

The gray woman pulled open her muffin, letting the steam rise up from the crack in a swirling burst. "I believe it would be a perfect fit indeed. I could feel it the moment we shook hands."

"Don't you have one coming up?" Mrs. Thomas continued, and Caren nodded.

"Where is it?" Jessica added, trying to gauge the price without asking directly. If it were in a Houston or Dallas suburb, she would know instantly that it was out of her price range.

But the answer didn't educate her guess.

"Just outside of Carlsbad on a little ranch I own."

"Carlsbad?" Jessica asked. "Is that in Arizona?"

"New Mexico."

"Oh. That's quite a drive."

Mrs. Thomas cut in. "It's really not that bad. Seven, eight hours. And you get to cut through the mountains. Parts of it are really quite beautiful. Lots of time for introspection, as well." She chuckled. "I do love a good road trip."

Caren reached in a loose pants pocket and pulled out a business card, setting it on the table in front of Jessica. "If you're interested, the website is on there. We would love to have you."

"And when did you say the next one was?"

"Thanksgiving weekend."

Jessica cringed. "Ooh, I don't think my mom would be happy about me missing Thanksgiving."

Caren's and Mrs. Thomas's eyes met and Caren gave a tiny nod of recognition. "Maybe not at first, but she'll understand once she sees the incredible transformation in her daughter. Besides, what better time to learn how to be the best boss to her and your friends than a weekend reserved for giving thanks? A faithful leader is a humble servant."

"Maybe you're right. I just ..." It would be best not to mention money in front of Caren and when she still owed

Mrs. Thomas so much, but it was a solid excuse not to go. The retreat itself sounded interesting, but maybe at another time. Maybe in a year or two when she could easily afford it.

What she knew most people would do was lie, agree to look into it, act excited and then totally flake later on. But she couldn't bring herself to do that. Not to a galru.

"It's the money," Mrs. Thomas said, "isn't it? Listen, I know better than anyone how tight it is for you, but you're thinking of this in the wrong way. A retreat like this, a weekend in the care of someone like Caren is not an expense, it's an *investment* in your future. It will benefit you for years to come, perhaps the rest of your life. You can't put a price tag on that."

But Jessica bet Caren *could* put a price tag on it. And she bet that price tag was enough to make her teeth itch. A moment later, she confirmed she was right on both accounts.

"It's fifty-eight hundred dollars," said Caren, "but that covers lodging, the classes, and food. Quite cheap for this type of thing."

Jessica didn't much care what it covered. Fifty-eight hundred covered a lot of things in her business already, things she couldn't afford to not pay.

"It sounds great," she said. "I just don't have the wiggle room. Maybe next year."

Mrs. Thomas cut in. "Not to doubt your abilities, but without the leadership skills Caren can provide you, I wonder if you'll have a bakery to run in a year." She cringed apologetically. "Anyway, it's not that much money. I tell you what. I'll loan It is Risen the money, as an *investment*, then you can use that to pay for this conference. That way, it's a tax deductible expense at the end of the year."

"I can't keep asking you to loan me money, Mrs. Thomas, not when I'm behind on payments to you."

Mrs. Thomas chuckled sweetly and shook her head. "You didn't ask. I offered." She turned to Caren. "See? How many others in her position would simply expect a handout, and here she is trying to turn them down left and right. I told you I had to force her to take my help in the first place."

Caren nodded approvingly. "You'll be a great fit at the retreat. Lots of women like you will be there. It's so important to create connections with people who have experienced what you're going through."

Jessica thought about Jesus and how she could kinda take it or leave it with him, despite their similar positions. "I'll take your word on that."

"You'll consider coming?" Caren said, tilting her head to the side.

"Definitely. I mean, it sounds great. It's just a matter of looking at finances and making sure—"

"You're overthinking it," Mrs. Thomas said. "I just told you I'd give you the money. I don't see what there is to look over. I give you fifty-eight hundred dollars, you tack it onto the amount you currently owe, and you make that money back twice as quickly using the skills Caren and her wonderful cabal of teachers give you."

"I don't know that I'm overthinking it," Jessica said. "If I keep getting further in debt—"

Holding her palms flat toward Jessica, Caren cut in with, "I'm sensing a lot of resistance."

No shit.

"I imagine that's your natural reaction to new things, yeah? You hear about an opportunity and your first response is always no."

"I don't know about that," Jessica said defensively.

"Mm-hm." Caren had her eyes closed now, her hands still up, reading who-knew-what coming off Jessica in waves. "Yes, that resistance can affect all sorts of things— the energy you attract, your liver health." She opened her eyes. "It's the sort of thing that builds up over a lifetime of broken trust and disappointment."

Okay, she might be onto something.

"It can be removed, and quite easily," Caren continued. "And a single weekend with us is plenty to completely shift your energy, release the resistance, and begin attracting only the best things into your life."

Resisting the impulse to resist, Jessica said, "That sounds pretty good."

"It *is*." Caren rubbed a hand gently up and down Jessica's arm, staring into her eyes. "It's quite a burden to have lifted."

Jessica sighed and held up the business card. "Okay, I'll check it out after work tonight. I'd better get back to it."

She stood, and while she was feeling emboldened, she added, "Oh, hey. Mrs. Thomas, I still can't find the contract in any of my inboxes. I hate to keep asking you over and over again to resend it, but could you?"

Mrs. Thomas chuckled and pulled her cell phone out of her purse. "Of course, Jessica. I know you're a little overwhelmed with the paperwork. I'll send it right away."

Jessica pushed in her chair and was already behind the counter when Mrs. Thomas caught her attention with a wave and said, "Just sent it. Mexicankicker7, right?"

Jessica sucked in air, her eyes darting around quickly to see who all might've heard that. "No. I had to delete that one." When would that ill-advised address stop haunting her? She hadn't used it for years. Mrs. Thomas had her new one, right? Yeah, she'd sent her emails from it and gotten responses. Did *everyone* age out of technology, even someone as savvy as Mrs. Thomas? "The other address."

"I only have that one saved for you."

Jessica's eyes caught sight of a man waiting impatiently for service while Judith helped the customer ahead of him. Not in a hurry to scream her personal email across the restaurant where anyone could jot it down for later cyberstalking, Jessica said, "I'll send you an email from it after we close tonight and you can just hit reply."

Mrs. Thomas nodded, returned to her conversation, and Jessica went on to help the customer, who was, unfortunately, Doug—David?

"Hi," he breathed, his weak chin quivering.

She swallowed down the acidic taste in her mouth and took his order and swiped his card.

"Do you need a name for the order?" he asked.

"No."

"It's Donald."

"Great."

"Do you like TV?"

Now she looked up from the register. "TV?"

"Yeah. Do you like watching it? I thought maybe sometime we—"

"Not big on TV. Any of it." It was the "we" that tipped her off to where his question was leading, and she had so little desire to spend alone time with whatever-his-name-was that the lack of it might fold in on itself and create a black hole that swallowed up her desire for other things like money or sleep or nature shows.

She grabbed a thermal to-go cup from the stack by the register, hoping he'd take the hint and not camp all day, and shoved it at him. When he missed his cue to walk away, she took the responsibility upon herself and left the register to clean out the microwave.

She never saw Caren and Mrs. Thomas leave. She simply looked up a minute later, and they were no longer there.

Chapter Thirty-Seven

Sometimes Jessica wondered if Jameson spent all of his free time looking up new places to eat. Just in the time since the two of them had started seeing each other, a handful of the restaurants where they'd grabbed dinner had opened and shut down. She suspected the one they were in now would meet the same fate before long. (Somewhat inexplicably, though, S8 Su4 was really taking off.)

Instead of music, tonight's new restaurant played the synthesized sounds of a heavy downpour. The walls were covered in fake, backlit windows where a never-ending cycle of water washed down. While it did make the place feel cozy, So Wet's menu was a strange hodgepodge of hot dishes. Soups, mostly, but plenty of simple carbs, too. And the drink menu was mostly varieties of spiked hot chocolate and hot apple cider.

She wasn't complaining about that. After all, it was the

middle of November, and the temperatures were getting all the way into the low sixties at night.

A plasma TV on the wall behind Jameson showed a fire burning on loop. She was sure she'd seen that pattern of flames only a minute before. She set out to determine exactly how long the loop was. She'd thought she'd had it when the waiter had interrupted her concentration to drop off a giant basket of warm, fluffy buttermilk rolls. *Chris would love this place,* she thought before catching herself and insisting she pay better attention to Jameson.

"Table reads start Tuesday," he continued. "So I need to spend tomorrow packing, then I leave Saturday morning for Vancouver."

"And you'll be there ...?"

"Probably six months. I'll have a handful of mini vacations mixed in there, stretches of days when they're not shooting any of my scenes. I'd like to come down to Austin to visit during some of those."

He was asking for her blessing, she could tell. "That would be fun."

"Wendy already told me I don't get to be seen with any other women while I'm up there until we call it quits."

"That sucks. Should we call it quits now?"

He shrugged a single shoulder as he stuck a pad of butter on the top of his bread. "Nah. No need. I'll let you know if I meet anyone, but I've met most of the principal actresses already, and none of them are my type. Besides, this is about the speed of dating I prefer."

"The kind where you don't get laid?"

"Well, okay. Admittedly this is the first setup like this where there weren't fringe benefits, but—"

"I know. Don't want to bang God's daughter. I totally get it." She failed to mention that he couldn't even if he tried. She had yet to bring up that catch and had no plans to.

Later, as she dipped her buttermilk roll into her broccoli cheese soup, her discussion with Mrs. Thomas from the day before popped up in her mind. "Have you ever been to a leadership retreat?"

He looked up from his chicken noodle soup, his spoon hovering above the surface, and his expression brightened. "Not a leadership one, but I *love* retreats!"

"Really? Just ... any old retreat?"

"Yes. It's like pressing pause on life. You get to escape into a completely different universe and be whoever you want to be for a few days. It's kind of like taking on a new role in a film. You get to try being that person for a while, and if it feels good, you can incorporate it into your personality. For instance, there was this time I played Al Capone's muscle in this weird sci-fi indie film—it was terrible, and I'm pretty sure they canned it right after the premiere—but during the shoot I got to go around pretending to murder robots all day and be this tough guy who took no shit off anyone. Afterward, I chain-smoked for like two years."

Jessica narrowed her eyes. "The character smoked, I take it?"

"Yeah. They offered me fake cigarettes, but I was really

into method acting at the time, so I insisted on smoking real ones. Sometimes I would go through two packs in a day because of all the takes. Anyway, that character taught me I really liked smoking, so I was able to incorporate it into my real life."

"Jameson, I think you're talking about addiction."

"Well, same thing."

"Not ... quite." And just like that, her lasting desire to take up smoking was temporarily abated.

"Right, not quite, but basically. My point is retreats allow you to try new things without any long-term consequences. You get to experiment and be free."

Jessica made a note not to try any new addictive substances if she did decide to attend. "You think I should go to a leadership retreat then?"

His eyes widened. "Yes! That would be perfect for you! Oh, I'm so jealous. I wish I could go. When is it?"

"In two weeks. Out near Carlsbad."

"Ooh! I bet there will be a sweat lodge!" He spooned soup into his mouth excitedly while Jessica puzzled over why anyone would seek out sweating.

"I didn't see that mentioned on the website, but maybe." What she *had* seen mentioned was an on-site masseuse, a Michelin-rated chef, private suites, meditation sessions, ovarian acupuncture, transformational play, and something called "spirit animal visioning." She assumed the leadership training was a given and that's why they failed to mention it on the list of activities.

"You're going, though?" he asked.

"Not sure. It's more time away from the bakery, which usually turns out poorly, if for no other reason than the emails I have to go through when I come back."

He waved that off, "Oh, but you'll have all these great leadership skills!"

"It's also pretty expensive," she added, acknowledging the resistance in herself. She wasn't completely sold that it was a bad thing to say no as a default. Maybe the retreat, if she went, would change her mind on that. Or maybe not.

"Yeah, they can get pretty pricy," he said, and she appreciated him acknowledging her concern. "What are we talking about here, like, seventy thousand? We talking six figures?"

"Holy shit, no. Are there retreats that expensive?"

He bit off a chunk of saturated roll. "Are there *not*?"

"This one is only fifty-eight hundred."

He stopped chewing, and set down his bread. "That doesn't sound safe, Jess. Is it just ... camping? Wait, is this one of those survivalist retreats where they drop you off in the desert?"

"That sounds more like a mob kidnapping, and no."

He nodded. "True. That was one of the scenes from *Al Capone*, actually."

"It looks pretty luxurious on the website. They have an on-site masseuse."

The corners of Jameson's lips remained firmly downward. "At a fifty-eight hundred dollar retreat? Have they done a proper background check on him?"

"I didn't see that in the FAQs."

"You should probably ask."

"Will do." She had no plans of it. She wasn't letting a strange person touch her, past felony convictions or not.

"Do you need the money for this? I'm happy to shell out, assuming, you know, it checks out and I won't be paying for you to be murdered in the New Mexican desert. I don't want that on my conscience."

"I also don't want that," she said. "And no, Mrs. Thomas already said she'd lend me the money for it."

"She's the one who invested in the business right away, right? Your teacher?"

Jessica nodded. "She's friends with the woman who runs the retreat."

"Hm." He nodded slowly and sipped his bourbon hot chocolate. "Maybe it's safe, then. Or maybe I've been paying too much for retreats. Either way, you're pretty lucky to have someone like her in your life. A lot of people don't have that kind of support. Did you have to sign an amendment with her for the loan adjustment?"

"No. Shit. I forgot to email her from my new address." She waved it off. "I'll do it later."

"She must really believe in you if she doesn't make you sign anything. You could take the money and just claim she gave it to you as a gift and never pay her back for it. I have plenty of friends who would do that kind of thing."

She didn't want to tell him how to live his life, but it seemed like he shouldn't hang out with those kinds of people. "I honestly don't know why she trusts me. I'm already months behind on my payments to her. She just sort of allows it, doesn't hound me or anything. I know she has a little money because she's married to a congressman and they're not spending anything on her kids' college, but ... yeah, I don't think I'd be so generous without anything in writing."

He sighed and extended his hand across the tabletop. "I guess it's just one more person who believes in you, Jessica."

She chuckled at the sappy compliment and put her hand in his. "Seems a bit misplaced."

"Hasn't been for me."

She smiled at him, cheating her head to the side when she noticed the phone recording them at the table over.

"You're learning," he said, squeezing her hand before letting it go. "I'll sleep well in Vancouver knowing my lessons didn't fall on deaf ears."

"I'll miss hanging out with you, Jameson. I don't know how I'll have the time to sniff out all the newest niche restaurants in the three months they stay open. Plus, I won't have anyone to go with."

He blew a raspberry at that and returned to his food. "You have all kinds of people to eat with. Just be less picky."

"What can I say? You've set the bar so high," she teased.

"You sound like none of my exes."

"That's because I'm not one. Yet."

He smiled but his tone was serious when he said, "I'll be sad when that day comes."

"Yeah," she said. "Me too."

He laughed. "No, you won't."

"Huh? Why not?"

"You'll be in a real relationship again."

"You don't know that."

He rolled his eyes. "I'd bet you money, but I know you don't have any to spare." Then he flagged down the server and ordered another round of hot drinks.

Chapter Thirty-Eight

Jessica bit into one of the So Wet-inspired broccoli and cheese croissants she'd been experimenting with after-hours over the last few days. It was perfect, and since she was alone in the kitchen of It is Risen, she allowed herself to moan loudly and obscenely.

She jotted down a few last details about preparation and baking, plated two more for herself, and moved to her laptop to type up the official recipe.

On impulse, she pulled up her internet browser, auto piloting instead of pulling up the text document. The headline on the homepage caught her eye, and she knew she shouldn't click it.

But it was eleven at night, she had eaten nothing but bakery food all day, and her paper-thin self-control tore down the middle. How often was the news something she wanted to read, anyway?

And damn, Chris looked fine in his warm-up gear,

gripping the football effortlessly by the laces, left arm pointing downfield while the right extended behind him, ready to launch a pass. Someone ought to paint him like that.

She clicked the headline of *Rookie QB Brings Super Bowl Hopes to Philadelphia*.

The article was more of a profile, and she enjoyed reading about someone she knew, outside of herself and Jimmy, to see just how much the writer got wrong. There was plenty. For instance, he said Chris had been starting quarterback at Mooremont High for four years, but that was impossible, since high school in her hometown only lasted three years, with ninth graders having a separate transitional campus they attended between junior high and high school.

Chris's stats looked pretty good, too. Since the Cowboys, Redskins, and Giants had done piss-poor in conference play, with the Redskins and Giants both losing to the Eagles twice this season and the Cowboys losing by a point in their week two match-up, the Eagles were positioned for play-offs despite a 7 – 5 record on the season so far. Their next game could clinch it for them, and it took place on none other than Thanksgiving. Against the Cowboys. She quickly made up her mind to call Chris and chat about the conflicting feelings he must be having, but she changed her mind just as quickly when she scrolled to his name in her phone and saw *Chris Riley DO NOT CALL*.

Right.

Even still, there was no way she could go off into the desert over Thanksgiving and miss that matchup. Then again, Rex might literally have a brain aneurysm trying to decide if he should root for the Cowboys or his boy Riley. She didn't need to be there for that stress.

She did a search on the page for her name and came up with no results. Leaning back in her chair, she stared at the search bar for a moment. Chris had done it. He'd finally made an independent name for himself. She was happy for him.

Wasn't she?

Yes. Of course. This is what he's always wanted.

Before she could think too hard about it, she browsed the rest of the article to the last sentence: *"If he pulls it off, his rookie season could be one for the books."*

Goddamn, that was lame. Chris deserved a better closing line.

A related article on the sidebar caught her attention. Or rather, the picture on it did. She shoved a croissant into her mouth to keep from screaming. Her name might not be on the page, but calling this a "related article" meant she still loomed over Chris as a keyword specter. How else would an article about Jimmy Dean's ongoing scandal be related to the Philadelphia Eagles?

She positioned her cursor right between Jimmy Dean's eyes and clicked as hard as she could on the touchpad, hoping that somehow, somewhere, Jimmy felt like he was getting flicked hard on the forehead.

She followed the link to the article headline: *Reverend Dean: Latest Accuser "Looks Extra Sinnery."*

After the latest woman has come forward, alleging that the Reverend Jimmy Dean lured her into a doomsday cult, the founder of the White Light Church network has released a statement. His defense is more of the same we've seen since this scandal first broke. Responding the the victim's claim that the language he used to describe transcending into heaven was sexually charged, the reverend refused to address the issue directly, saying, "I've never seen that woman before in my life. But I've been presented with pictures by my legal counsel, and she just looks extra sinnery, you know? That can happen when you spend your life lying and rolling in the muck. It starts to show. Despite the false claims, I would welcome her into the White Light community along with all the other pigs of the congregation, and together we could work to scrub her soul clean. Sumus omnes porcos, sed Deus est Aper."

Hours after the statement was issued via a screenshot of a handwritten note on Twitter, Reverend Dean's lawyers filed a lawsuit against the female accuser.

Aside from being the founder of the rapidly growing and high profile White Light Church, Jimmy Dean was elected to the Texas Railroad Commission in this recent election.

Dean's rise to notoriety has always been intertwined with that of Jessica McCloud, who he has claimed, at various times, to be the Daughter of God and the embodiment of Original Sin. Knowing where his church stands at any given moment can be difficult, as last month's interview with some of his parishioners unveiled. No two seemed to hold the same understanding. One even went so far as to say that Jessica was whoever Jimmy needed her to be every Sunday, and he was okay with that changing frequently. Those who speak out about White Light point to this dehumanization of a woman as an indicator of a deep-seated misogyny on Dean's part. The same sort of misogyny, they say, that makes the story of his doomsday cult especially believable. Many don't require that level of psychoanalysis and simply hold the belief that identical claims of over a dozen women should be evidence enough to indict him, though on what charges many do not know.

Regardless, it might be in the best interest of the State of Texas to reconsider granting power to someone who once prepared for the end of the world by gathering underage girls to a repurposed barn in a remote part of the state without the smallest shred of parental consent. Such an act might not be illegal, but it's nothing short of morally and ethically questionable. After all, if our behavior when we believe the end of the world is near isn't an indicator of our true character, what is?

Jessica almost couldn't believe it. She scrolled up to the top to find the name of the writer and considered sending this *Linton Davenport* fellow a thank-you email.

Were there more smart, articulate people on her side? Was ole Linny an angel? Well, she supposed just because this man clearly had little love for Jimmy didn't mean he was pro-Jessica all the way. But she realized at once that she didn't need that to appreciate a person like him. So long as he felt the same way about Jimmy as she did, she could respect him, even if he didn't respect her.

Was this an anomaly, or were other news outlets speaking unfavorably about Jimmy Fucking Dean as well?

She did a quick news search for "Jimmy Dean, Scandal" and glowered at the first result that showed up.

The little she understood about SEO told her that either Eugene Thornton had a team dedicated to hitting just the right keywords to get impulse clicks or more people read the Thornton News than she wanted to admit. Or both.

She clicked on the top result, her stomach already turning to a fist at the insulting headline: *New Victim Actor Joins Reverend Dean Money Grab.*

Rebecca Holtz Johann, 41, a resident of Fox Hole, Texas, has joined the team of women hellbent on destroying the squeaky-clean record of the venerated Texas Railroad Commissioner Reverend Jimmy Dean. Known for his generous charitable donations and humility in the light of attempts to praise him, he has recently fallen into the crosshairs of the militant feminist movement. This week, Rebecca Holtz Johann of Cherry Grove Avenue has decided to throw her pointy hat into the ring for her fifteen minutes of fame and a shot at some of the Reverend's hard-earned wealth.

Her story is unoriginal, clearly lifted from those of the dishonest women who've come before her. While women-run publications claim the similarities between the victims' stories is proof that the ludicrous allegations bear truth, every publication worth its weight in ink is saying it's a clear example of copycatting. Maybe even the clearest in recent history. Thornton News agrees with that assessment.

You might be wondering who Mrs. Johann is. We wondered the same thing, which is why we've performed an exhaustive investigation into her, using anonymous sources as needed, and they were needed frequently, as most of her closest friends remained tight-lipped about her. Are they afraid of what she might do to them if they were identified as our source? Would this vengeful charlatan go after them with the same unfounded, forked-tongue vitriol she sprays at the world-renowned Reverend Dean?

Make no mistake, the signs of a victim actor are all there. Her junior year of high school, the same year she claims to have been "lured" into Reverend Dean's "doomsday cult" of "young women," Rebecca was cast in the role of Mrs. Higgins in the Elbow High School production of *My Fair Lady*. An anonymous former classmate of hers described Rebecca's performance as "realistic" and "convincing." When asked if she had all her lines memorized on opening night, the source said, "Yes, Becky was always on top of that. She studied her lines constantly." Was she already planning to use those memorization skills to learn her lines for destroying the reputation of a revered and indisputably trustworthy religious leader? If not, *when* did she set out upon this nefarious mission?

The anonymous interview also raised a big, fat question regarding Rebecca's former alias of "Becky." It's been known for ages that changing one's name can be a sign of dissociation, a mental illness common in women who engage in sexual acts too freely prior to marriage. While we were unable to confirm the exact point when Rebecca began going by Becky, we can conclude it happened prior to her junior year of high school.

Let's entertain, for a moment, that Rebecca's completely false claims are true, that the honorable Reverend Jimmy Dean did assemble a group of willing young women to him for a doomsday cult. Like the other girls publicly hurling these falsities, Rebecca Holtz Johann doesn't claim that there was ever any inappropriate touching. *But even if there were*, we can safely assume, based on the dissociative behavior, that this would not have been her first time to engage in that level of sin—not even close. Would it even matter, then, if he'd crossed a line she'd already crossed dozens of times before?

Furthermore, according to records, she was already seventeen on the sixth of July, the date when she claims the end of the world was supposed to take place. And she had been seventeen since before she claims to have met Jimmy. That means anything that happened between them would have been legal and consensual in the state of Texas, and according to *her own story* and how little resistance she put up in joining his "cult," you can bet she would have been a willing participant in those adult relations.

And so, even if all of her claims were true, this would be little more than yet another case of a morally loose woman luring a man of faith into temptation only to claim much later that she had not "consented."

That is, of course, the *worst case* scenario for the reverend if Rebecca "Becky" Holtz Johann's claims held water, which they clearly do not.

So we at Thornton News ask: When will this stop? When will the growing cabal of feminitpickers simply address the bitter loss of their domestic roles and return to their place of comfort rather than lashing out at those in power, destroying the hard-earned reputations of innocent men who have steadfastly remained in their rightful dominant roles throughout the mass displacement of men from breadwinners to castrated, voiceless caretakers?

While Mrs. Johann is the most recent of the plaintiffs in this scenario, you can bet that she will not be the last.

When Jessica's eyes reached the end of the article, they crossed involuntarily, and she felt like someone had slapped her in the back of the skull.

Was it possible to permanently lose IQ points from reading a few hundred of the most illogical and infuriatingly dumb words she'd ever laid eyes on?

The recommended articles for continued reading were all about Jimmy. The first few looked like more of the same: profiles discrediting the accusers. She'd known about these for a while, thanks to Wendy. Or rather, she'd known about them in theory, that they existed and they were probably pretty horrible, but this was the first time she'd really plumbed the depths of one. And, amazingly, it was even worse than she had imagined.

A particularly scathing headline, *Victim Actor's Dark Sexual History Revealed*, caught her eye, mostly because the thumbnail picture above it was so eye-catching. It showed a woman with a youthful round face, sandy hair and mocha eyes with hellfire Photoshopped all around her. Devil horns had also been added to her head.

"Are you kidding me?"

Jessica's curiosity and late-night moral outrage cravings got the best of her, but the moment she clicked the link, the back door of the bakery shook behind her, creating a brief moment of confusion, as her tired brain assumed the actions were somehow tied together.

She looked back over her shoulder at the door. The knob jiggled again and the deadbolts, which she'd thankfully remembered to lock, withstood the following attempt to open the door by force.

While she desperately hoped the thwarted attempt to enter would be followed by a voice she recognized requesting she unlock the door and providing an explanation as to *why* he or she was showing up at midnight and trying to enter without knocking, she already knew in her gut that wouldn't happen.

Without putting her back to the door again, she reached behind her, grabbing the laptop and pulling up the security camera app to see who was there.

An icy jolt ran through her, starting between her shoulder blades and exploding out like a supernova the moment she saw who was trying to force his was in. It was the Houston Texans cap that gave it away.

Ooo, she could just smite him!

Who *was* this asshole, and why wouldn't he leave her alone?

Shit. Had she locked the front door? As soon as he gave up on the back door, she worried he would try the second best way in.

She sprinted out of the kitchen, saw that the front door was locked, and then hurried back into kitchen, where hiding spots were more plentiful if it came to it. Then she called the cops.

However, she found she wasn't in the mood to hide like last time. She was in the mood to fight. And maybe that was what worried her the most as she spoke with the 911 call taker and explained what was happening.

The call taker asked her to stay on the line, and Jessica did, though she remained at the small table, her back toward the wall, in plain view if anyone were to enter through the back or from the cafe.

I'll be damned if I let this asswipe terrorize me in my own business. I'm sick of this shit!

The same unfortunate bond she shared with the new generation of NAOs began to form between her and Rebecca Holtz Johann and all of Jimmy's other accusers.

Except for Emily, his fiancée.

Or, maybe even Emily.

By the time Officer McBride arrived with a new male officer, Jessica was ready to suit up and hunt down the stalker herself. "I'm gonna kill him if I see him again," she confided in McBride.

"I'm legally supposed to advise you against that, but, well, we can't stop or solve every murder, ya know?"

"I'm so sick and tired of men making women feel like we're losing our goddamn mind. If we're overly emotional, it's their fault!" Her memory conjured up her lousy training sessions with Sampson, Kumal, and Dwayne because she could always use a little more fuel for the fire.

Rather than responding, Officer McBride hollered to

the other on scene, "Hey, Woodley, would you make one more circle around the perimeter?" Once he was gone, she said, "You know what I do for a living, right?"

Was this a trick question? Wait, was police work just a hobby for her? "You're a cop?"

"Correct. I've been doing it for years now, and you want to guess how many times I've seen a man shot by a woman he wasn't abusing?"

"I don't. That's ... not a fun game."

"You're right. I'll just tell you. Once. I've only seen it once."

"And what happened?"

"Her aim was shit. She'd meant to shoot the victim's brother, who *had* been threatening her and her children for quite a while. My point is I understand where you're coming from. So do the men I work with, quite frankly."

With her anger abating, Jessica sighed, inhaling exhaustion, exhaling the desire to murder another living being.

"If you could live in a world without men, would you?" she asked the officer.

McBride didn't hesitate. "No way. Don't let the haircut and career choice fool you; I love me some men. I just wish they'd stop killing everyone. Now, if there were an island that was only women, well, I might use my vacation time each year to visit it, sure. Everyone can use a detox. Hell, there are a lot of decent men who could use a detox from men, you know?"

Jessica didn't, but mostly because she'd stopped

listening closely. An island with nothing but women. She knew of a place like that. Or rather, it was more like an oasis, right in the middle of the dry New Mexican desert.

Later, while McBride wiped down the back doorknob for fingerprints, Jessica went to the website on the business card Caren had handed her, and she registered for the retreat.

Chapter Thirty-Nine

"I hope you don't mind," Jessica said, bagging up some leftover croissants from the display case for Jesus, "but today was kind of crazy, and I haven't gotten around to miracling some of these things. I can take a minute to do it now if you want. Not sure how many of your customers are gluten intolerant."

Jesus held out his hands for the unmiracled bags. "They are intolerant of many things, but I've never heard gluten mentioned. And it's fine if the food lacks your image."

"Well," she shrugged and shot a glanced at Destinee, "it's not ideal for my branding, but I guess it's good to give without getting recognized for it sometimes."

Jesus nodded. "Indeed. Also, I recently caught a man, who I can only assume is a direct descendant of Onan, enjoying the sight of your image just a little too much behind a Dumpster."

Jessica cringed and allowed herself a moment to imagine a world where an image of her face wasn't on anything ever again.

Shutting down the bakery for five straight days while she was staying in a luxury suite seemed like a wholly unwise business decision, but it was too late to go back now; she'd already given Judith and her mother the days off.

"Gonna be weird not having you at home, baby," Destinee said as she pulled a blueberry strudel muffin out of one of the bags Jessica had just closed and took a bite. Before Jessica could say anything else, Destinee held up a hand and added, "I know, it's an important retreat." She dusted off the countertop where the crumbs from her mouth had landed.

"I have a feeling it'll be worth every penny."

Every penny I owe to Mrs. Thomas.

She hadn't mentioned that bit—or any of Mrs. Thomas's involvement—to Destinee. It would only earn her a hard look and a warning from her mother, and there was no point in bringing that on herself if she didn't have to. While Jessica's high opinion of Mrs. Thomas had been resurrected in the last couple weeks, Destinee wasn't so quick to forgive.

"I know, I know," Destinee said. "But you know I already think you're a great boss, right?"

Jess refrained from rolling her eyes. "Yeah, I know."

"I mean it. I don't have a clue how you do half the things you do. If I were running this place, it wouldn't've had a chance to run at a loss because it never would have gotten off the ground in the first place!" She turned to Jesus. "What about you, Joshua? You got plans for Thanksgiving?"

He nodded, pausing from the loading to lean against the bumper of his truck. "For part of the day, yes. Jeremy and I will be serving lunch to the homeless."

"Ah," said Destinee cheerily, sneaking a peek at Jessica. "Jeremy Archer. Right. You know, I don't think I've ever told you how cute of a couple the two of you make."

Jesus bowed his head humbly. "Thank you."

"They're not a couple," Jessica said. "They're just friends."

Destinee blinked at Jesus. "Oh. I though y'all were boyfriends."

"Menfriends," Jesus corrected.

"Nooo," Jessica cut in again. She addressed her mother to clarify. "They live together and Jeremy is—" She caught herself just in time. Considering Jeremy didn't even believe he was an angel, it was probably best not to go around convincing others he was. "Jeremy owns the condo, and Jesus just rents a room. They're friends. Not romantic. Not that it would be wrong if they were romantic, just that it's not the case."

Destinee bit back a smile. "You mean to call him Jesus?" She chuckled when Jessica gulped in air. "Baby, if you wanted a sibling, you coulda just told me. It's a little late for that now," she kidded, "but I could give it a shot."

Jesus stepped forward after glancing at Jessica for

confirmation, which she was too shocked to provide. He set a hand on Destinee's shoulder. "She meant to say it. I'm Jesus."

Destinee narrowed her eyes at him. "Like hell you are. You're way too sexy to be Jesus. Besides, I'm pretty sure I've had that book spoiled for me enough times to know he didn't make it to his happily ever after."

Jesus's hand dropped from her and he took a slight step back, passing off the baton to Jessica, who begrudgingly took it. "No, Mom. It really is him. He's in a different body. I"—where did she even start?—"he kept interrupting my sex dreams, so I told him to ask for a promotion, and God gave him a body."

Destinee only squinted harder as Jesus added on, "Don't worry. The man was already dead and—wait ... Huh. I suppose there was a good chance God just killed him specifically for this purpose. Had not considered that. But, no, that makes sense. He was so freshly dead and I was assured his was a healthy body simply in need of a soul ..." Jesus looked down at his hands. "Oh boy. This is awkward."

HE WAS NOT LIVING A GOOD LIFE.

"Oh, I don't believe that at all," Jessica said.

Jesus shook the dead man's head. "Neither do I. Father, why would you trick me?"

"Is he here right now?" Destinee demanded, but they both ignored her.

NO TRICK. I TOLD YOU HE WAS ALREADY

DEAD, AND HE WAS. I KILLED HIM, JUST LIKE I KILL MANY PEOPLE. NOT ALL, MIND YOU.

"Yeah, yeah," Jessica said, waving Him off. "Original Mistake. We know."

"Hold on," Destinee said, stepping between them so she wouldn't continue to be ignored. "You're really Jesus?"

"Yep."

She looked over her shoulder at her daughter. "Y'all ain't shitting me, right?"

"Nope."

"Goddamn," she breathed, taking in the sight of him. "I have a son?"

Jessica answered, "Nooo ... You didn't birth him."

"But he's your half-brother, right?"

"Yes, but—"

"And I'm your mother. So he's my half-son."

Jesus seemed happy to go along with that, so Jessica kept her mouth shut about the inaccuracy.

"Come here, son." She threw her arms around him, and he nestled against her bosom, clasping his wrists behind her back.

Jessica looked at the clock. She still needed to pack before she left first thing in the morning, and they had more leftovers to load up.

When Destinee finally let go of him, she started gabbing. "You and your manfriend ought to come over to my place after you're done with the homeless and a shower! We'll have all kinds of delicious dishes since Jess won't be there and I don't want to do all the math on making smaller portions of what few dishes I make myself. Y'all can watch the game with Rex! Oh, he'd love that. You watch football? I think you'll like it."

"Oh football!" Jesus exclaimed, clapping his hands together. "I've heard about that! It's what Christopher plays, correct?"

"Yuh-huh!" Destinee replied. "And you'll get to see him play it!"

"How wonderful! Yes! Jeremy and I would love to come over to eat of your food and watch of your television."

Jessica bagged up the rest of the food, setting aside a small stash to take on her road trip, and did the rest of the loading herself while Destinee explained to the son of God the importance of pecans in a Thanksgiving dressing.

Chapter Forty

Mrs. Thomas was right. There was something about a road trip that was simply magical. Jessica had only made it as far as Llano, but already she was feeling incredible. The weight of the bakery that had rested on her shoulders for over a year now was buoyed by the hope that when she returned from the retreat, she would know more and everything would be easier. She wasn't sure how that worked, exactly, but both Mrs. Thomas and Caren had seemed sure it would be the case, and they had much more experience with this sort of thing than she did, considering she had none.

Only after she'd moved away from Mooretown did she realize how depressing the landscape was in comparison to almost everywhere else in Texas. San Marcos was a geographical smorgasbord, being located right along the fault line that separated the lush, green fields on the east from the rolling Hill Country on the west. With a spring-fed river running through the middle of campus, it was like a tropical paradise compared to her hometown. And she'd found Austin no less green and inviting.

It had all served to make her few and far between visits home less desirable than ever, but now that Rex and Destinee were in Austin, she had no reason to go back to Mooretown.

I guess some things do work out for me. She'd be turning off Highway 87 before she reached the exit for it. The drive up familiar roads felt different today, regardless. She had driven this route before plenty, at least this stretch of it, but it never felt like a trek so much as a death march.

Almost three hours later, she passed a sign on her left that she'd seen a hundred times before but never thought much about: *Elbow 2 mi*

Wow, was it really so close to home? Jimmy had spent so much time in Mooretown when she was younger and he hadn't exactly kept a low profile in Midland only a short drive away. It seemed to her that if she had done something iffy like he had, she would lay low until she was a thousand miles away for the obvious reason of not getting called out.

But he hadn't laid low. And he hadn't been called out for years.

Why was this strange scandal happening with him now and not sooner? Some of the women were probably still in Elbow when Jimmy was only a half hour away, making waves. They had to have known about him, to have seen him on TV, on his obnoxious White Light billboards and realized that the man they knew as Jon Sonville was actually Jimmy Dean. What other aliases might he have gone by over the years? If his memoirs were to be believed, it was always a variation of Jimmy or John, but if she knew anything, it was that his memoirs were *not* to be believed.

Maybe the women are lying after all. She flinched, upset with herself for even entertaining the idea. She knew what it was like to be the focus of Eugene Thornton's hit pieces. No one would subject herself to that abuse if she didn't have a good reason to. Thornton News's explanation was likely that the women were paid, but there were so many less unpleasant ways for a supposedly immoral woman to make good money — stripping, prostitution, politics ...

So maybe that was why they'd spoken up now. They had reached a breaking point. They couldn't stand to see Jimmy's insanity granted legitimacy by the government. They were finally ready to do whatever it took to stop him.

Well, it hadn't worked. Sixteen women hadn't been enough. Perhaps Judith was right and twenty-four had been the threshold needed for credibility.

Or perhaps there was no threshold. Perhaps the voters believed the women but simply didn't care.

That prospect was exponentially worse.

Her phone buzzed, and she suspected it was Mrs. Thomas.

She'd texted her former teacher at her pit stop in Llano to tell her she was right about the trip and Jessica was excited to get going. After also thanking Mrs. Thomas for paying her way, she asked her to send over the most up-to-date version of the contract she had. While a major part of Jessica had expected Mrs. Thomas to outright refuse, there was just something about the day that washed away that skepticism and said, "Of course she'll send it over! There's no reason she wouldn't!"

And when Jessica pulled up to the next stop sign just a few miles outside of Andrews, she previewed the text and saw that her optimism was right in the end.

Mrs. T: *So happy to hear you're excited! Of course I'll send the contract. Emailed it to your business address just...*

That was where the preview cut off, but another notification told her the email was there and waiting, attachment included. The preview included a greeting and another congratulations on attending the retreat.

It was only then, once Jessica felt the unmistakeable weight of shame lift from her, that she even realized it was there. Featherlight layer upon layer of "you should have already handled this" had settled on her over the months, a new one sticking to her with each pang in her stomach when she remembered she hadn't yet read the contract or when someone else mentioned it, until the simple act of asking Mrs. Thomas for it was too much heavy lifting.

But in the good mood she was in now, it had felt laughably easy to ask again. After all, it was a simple favor. Jessica wasn't asking too much ...

A car honked behind her. She'd forgotten she was sitting at an intersection. She hurried onward, feeling her burden lift even further, the heavy thoughts of a moment ago fluttering away.

She finally had a copy of the contract. It had been just one thing after another trying to get her hands on it. Now that she had it, though, all the false alarms and miscommunications seemed comical.

I should read it before I start the retreat.

But the thought sent sludge through her veins. No, she was done with work for the week. The contract would still be there when she finished and was Boss 2.0. In the meantime, though, she could send it on to Dr. Bell and cross that task off her list. It sure would be nice to have Dr. Bell off her back about it. See? She was already a more effective leader. When she wasn't overwhelmed, everything seemed much simpler.

An opportunity to forward the contract to Dr. Bell (with the appropriate message that conveyed a little bit of gloating for having finally gotten her hands on the contract and a little bit of nonchalance) didn't present itself until she stopped for gas in Carlsbad, New Mexico hours later. The retreat's website had mentioned in the FAQs that the location didn't have cell service for most of the major carriers. At the time, the idea of being without access to the internet had left her in a panic, but now, as she continued shedding layers of responsibility the farther from Austin she drove, the idea was exhilarating.

No connection with the outside world until Monday morning. What would *that* be like?

Oh shit. She'd forgotten to tell Wendy. She ought to do that before going MIA. After she sent the email to Dr. Bell, she composed the text to her publicist.

Jessica: No reception at the retreat. If anything needs attention, I trust you to take care of it. Do whatever you think is best.

Man. Five days without connection. There was a *lot* she should do before that happened, actually.

The knot in her stomach tightened, begging her to relax and forget about it.

Just a couple more texts, though.

She texted her mother: *I'll miss you on tgiving. Have fun with J&J. Go Cowboys!*

Then, in the same vein, she did something incredibly stupid that she wouldn't have done had she not been about to escape all possibility of a response for the next five days.

She texted Chris: *Good luck this weekend. I have to miss the game for a retreat, but I'll put in a good word for you with you-know-who if you swear never to mention it to Rex. I know you'll do great without any help.*

She hit send before she could second guess herself, except she was already doing that.

She pumped the gas, bought herself a Dr. Pepper inside, and flopped back into the driver's seat. She already had one text response.

Chris: I'll take all the help I can get. Rex never has to know.

She chuckled, took a screen shot of the remaining driving directions in case her GPS failed, then she headed further into the desert.

Chapter Forty-One

The first structure of the ranch to break the horizon was a dome roughly the size of her old elementary school. She recognized it from the website, but it looked much more wiggly through the hot distance. The rest of the domes, sprinkled around behind it, emerged when she was a mile more down the long, straight, stretch of road.

The land was farther outside of Carlsbad than she'd imagined, but she knew how "just outside" in this part of the country could mean anywhere from fifteen minutes to a couple of hours.

As she pulled into the gravel parking area, one thing became immediately clear: she was the poorest person there. Her car had an easy seven years on all the others. Great. She'd probably be the youngest, too, and everyone would call her "sweetie" and think her ideas were "adorable."

Knock it off! You don't know anything yet. You're going

*to make a piss-poor impression on the galrus if you keep that
negative shit up! No resistance!*

She plastered a grin on her face as she parked and
unloaded her bag, and by the time she was lugging her
suitcase at her side over the gravel parking lot, the smile
didn't feel so forced.

A team of women dressed in similarly flowing robes as
those Caren had worn when she'd dropped into the bakery
greeted guests from behind a long table just past an ivy-
covered archway leading up to the main building. A series
of purple and orange cloths were draped over the table,
and Jessica had the distinct suspicion that none of them
were intended solely to be table cloths. They were just
elegant fabric that had been repurposed for this.

The concept blew her mind. You could just use any
fabric you wanted as a table cloth! You didn't have to buy it
at Walmart or a party store!

Already the freedom and write-your-own-rules-ness of
this place was seeping into her bloodstream like a low dose
of drugs.

"Hello there," one of the women said, looking past two
other registrants to zero in on Jessica. Her long, black hair
had only a few glimmers of gray in it, but Jess suspected
that had more to do with good genes than youth. The sides
were pulled back in a braid that ran down the length of her
back, freeing up her face to glow with her smile.

"Hi," Jessica said, pulling up short and plopping her
suitcase on the ground, feeling less graceful than she had in
a long time, and that was saying something. But how could

she not feel awkward when she was staring down a wall of galrus like this?

"I'm Danielle." The women held her hand out over the table, and her vibrant green robes caught a passing breeze.

Jessica went to shake, determined not to go in too soft and make the same mistake she had with Caren.

She grimaced as she crushed Danielle's hand. "Jessica," she said regretfully.

A ripple of recognition ran through Danielle's features before she said, "Right this way. Your domicile is a bit of a walk from here. Can I take your bag?"

"No, no. I got it."

As they veered off the main path toward one of the domes, Jessica struggled to reconcile the clay exterior, with bits of hay poking from the cracked surface, with the luxurious pictures of the lodging on the website.

But when Danielle opened the wooden door for her and Jessica was hit with a powerful gust of air conditioning to combat the unusually warm November temperatures, her worries were cast aside.

Not only did the oak bed and claw-foot tub and cushioned window seat overlooking the vast stretch of desert match up to the pictures, everything far exceeded it.

Not much to look at on the outside, but luxurious on the inside. It was probably a metaphor, but Jessica didn't care so long as she got to spend a portion of the next five days enjoying the interior.

A ceiling fan with three gigantic blades spun silently and lazily, circulating the cool air and causing the leaves on the various indoor plants to dance. The open floor plan, with the toilet only a handful of yards away from the bed, didn't bother her like she'd thought it would. Instead, it only served to show her how little a single living space needed to have for it to be wonderful.

Danielle motioned to a sturdy oak trunk at the end of the bed. "You can open up your suitcase here."

"Thanks," Jessica replied. But when Danielle continued to stare at her, she hesitated then said, "Oh, now?"

"I assume you brought your own clothes."

Jessica laughed. "Yes."

Bowing her head, that serene smile never leaving her lips, Danielle said, "Then I'll take those from you now."

"Huh?"

"We don't put it on the website, but while you're here, we'll provide you with clothes." She glided over to an ornately carved armoire and opened one of the double doors, providing Jessica a glimpse of the clothing inside.

It looked remarkably like what Danielle had on in a variety colors.

"Oh, hell yes," Jessica said, and she couldn't unzip her suitcase and extricate her sloppy, old, unflattering clothes soon enough, tossing them onto a pile on the bed.

"Those too," Danielle said, nodding at the suitcase, but Jessica was stumped.

"There's nothing left."

"I see bras and underwear."

Jessica leaned back slowly, her eyes darting to the

closest exit on animal instinct. "You provide bras and underwear?"

"No. Neither are necessary accouterments, and both stifle the chakras. We request that our visitors take a break from both for the duration of the week. You may find that you have no desire to put them back on once the week is over."

Somehow she doubted that, but she did as Danielle said, and that seemed to please the woman. "Whenever you've changed out of the clothes you have on, you can bring them back up to the table and I'll store them with the rest. Dinner and the opening ceremony start at five thirty in the sanctuary—that's the large dome. Rest up and settle in." Her smile spread around her eyes. "I'm so glad you're here, Jessica. I can tell you're nervous, but don't worry; we'll take great care of you." She reached forward, pressing her palm to Jessica's heart as she spoke the last word.

When the door shut behind Danielle, Jessica didn't immediately change. Instead, she kicked off her shoes and fell back onto the bed to stare up at the tiled ceiling. She knew without a doubt that coming here had been the best choice she'd made in a while.

MOST CULTS ARE VERY ALLURING AT FIRST.

Dammit! Can't you take a vacation?

Not even a lack of cell service could afford her a week without worrying about His surprise appearances.

AND MISS THIS? HEAVENS NO.

It's not a cult.

YOU'RE RIGHT. IT'S JUST BUILT IN ONE OF

THE FEW SPOTS IN THE COUNTRY WHERE THE LAW ENFORCEMENT JURISDICTION IS INCREDIBLY UNCLEAR, TAKES PLACE IN A SERIES OF HUTS, EXPECTS YOU TO PAY TO GET IN, AND MAKES EVERYONE DRESS THE SAME. SOUNDS LIKE NO CULT EVER.

Admittedly, I wasn't aware of the iffy jurisdiction part, but that doesn't mean it's a cult.

THEN WHAT DOES?

I don't know. Maybe they get us to eat or drink something dangerous. Or they make it seem like it's us versus the rest of the world, or they ... Like I said. I don't really know.

AT LEAST YOU'RE APPROACHING IT WITH COMPLETE IGNORANCE. THIS CAN ONLY WORK OUT WELL.

I think you're bitter because it's an all-women's retreat and you weren't invited.

THE LORD NEEDS NOT AN INVITATION TO ENTER WHATEVER PROPERTY HE WISHES. THE LORD IS NOT A VAMPIRE.

What about all that "inviting God into your heart" stuff?

THAT ONLY APPLIES TO YOUR BROTHER. HE REQUIRES AN INVITATION. TOO POLITE FOR HIS OWN GOOD.

Fair enough.

IF YOU WOULD LIKE THE LORD TO

ABANDON YOU IN THIS DESERT FOR THE WEEK, IT SHALL BE DONE.

Great. Do that.

UM.

What?

THAT WAS NOT THE RESPONSE I'D EXPECTED.

But will you do it anyway?

NO, I DON'T THINK SO. I ALREADY CLEARED MY CALENDAR FOR THIS.

She rolled her eyes. *Don't offer if you're not going to follow it up. Now can you disappear for a minute? I need to change clothes.*

She waited until she could feel Him leave then continued to lay right where she was on the bed, reveling in the complete and utter silence.

Chapter Forty-Two

Rows of long tables filled two-thirds of the sanctuary when Jessica entered for dinner. Decorated similarly to the reception table earlier, with soft, vivid cloths of varying colors slung over the wood, the center of these tables held elaborate centerpieces of burning incense, lit candles, and small brass statues of trees and cacti and other natural elements. The whole thing was incredibly flammable. Maybe the iffy jurisdiction was what allowed them to get away with the obvious fire hazard.

Jessica had lost track of time in her suite and arrived when nearly all the spaces along the benches were taken, but she settled in at a space in front of which a brass coiled rattlesnake reflected the dancing flame of a nearby candle. There were perhaps forty women in total, each dressed remarkably like Jessica, though the colors of their robes varied.

Jessica had gone with a matching cerulean blue top

and pants. It hadn't even occurred to her not to match the color of the top and bottom of the outfit, but that idea *had* occurred to many of the other women. Jessica spied a combo of a purple top and brown bottoms and took note to try that one out tomorrow.

"It's a little like fancy hospital scrubs," said the woman on Jessica's left. She turned toward the speaker, a woman in perhaps her mid-forties with dark hair cropped into a structured bob.

The woman wasn't addressing Jessica, though. She was speaking to the woman across the table. That woman had long blonde hair pulled back into a ponytail and didn't look too unlike Miranda—skinny, lanky, and with a smooth, round face, though perhaps a few years older. "I was thinking more like a prison uniform if, you know, the prison was in Sedona or an American commune in Ubud." The blonde caught sight of Jessica eavesdropping, but didn't seem bothered by it. Instead, she made to offer her hand but jerked it back quickly when her eyes landed on her dangling sleeve so close to one of the candles. The woman blew it out then reached toward Jessica again. "Evan."

"Jessica."

"Nice handshake."

"Thanks for not letting me crush your hand."

Evan laughed and nodded across the table at the dark-haired woman. "This is Meghan."

"Meg," the woman said, shaking Jessica's hand. "Wait.

Your last name wouldn't happen to be McCloud, would it?"

Jessica inhaled. "Yes. Yes, it would."

Meg smiled. "I knew it. I *thought* I saw you walking past my dome earlier."

"You swinging loose under there?" Evan nodded to Meg's chest.

Meg rolled her eyes. "Yes. At least my navel's nice and cozy. That rule had to have been instituted by someone under the age of thirty with a B-cup at most."

Evan nodded at Jessica. "Was it you? You can't be over twenty-five."

"Twenty-two, and no, I would never outlaw bras."

Meg's dark eyebrows lifted. "Twenty-two? Wow. You're really getting a jumpstart on this leadership bullshit."

"Don't tell anyone," Evan said, leaning forward conspiratorially and inviting Jessica into the secret with a quick glance, "but I packed some pasties for one of the shirts I brought, and I didn't hand them over." She pointed down at her breasts. "No matter how cold it gets, I'm bringing these nipples to heel."

Meg sniggered.

A line of women entered the sanctuary from a room at the side of the space carrying trays of food. Jessica recognized a few of them from the check-in table. When they made their way around to Jessica and she saw the plate set in front of her, she sighed. The salad looked divine. She loved a good salad to start her meal, but she never spared the time to make one at home, so her encounters with something like this had been mostly limited to dinner dates with Jameson. Pears and strawberries and soft goat cheese crumbles and chopped walnuts were sprinkled over a bed of spinach and kale. The leaves glimmered with a light dressing that she suspected to be vinegar and olive oil, or something healthy like that. When the smell of the cheese hit her nostrils, her mouth began to water. She looked around. Some of the women were already eating, including Meg and Evan, so she dove in, finishing it off in a matter of a few minutes. She sat up straight to avoid indigestion and wondered wistfully what the entree would be.

She was left wondering when Caren Powers climbed a small stage in front of the tables and asked for everyone's attention. A clatter of forks followed, then silence. "I hope you enjoyed the meal. All those ingredients were either grown in the greenhouse out back or bought from local farmers within the New Mexican state lines."

Wait. Had she somehow missed the entree? Surely they weren't expected to make it through the night on just that salad.

Jessica missed the first part of Caren's welcome as she mentally searched her car, trying to remember if she'd eaten the entire bag of Cheetos on the drive over or if she'd stopped halfway through like she'd intended.

"... Sisterhood that bonds us starts in our hearts. It is often our only freedom from patriarchal oppression, and I hope that you can use this week to wrest yourself from toxic masculinity, purge it and all its insidious beliefs from your system so you can discover the shining beauty of your nature within."

Sure, that sounded good. Caren could count Jessica in. But couldn't that still be achieved with a local, grass-fed, free-range steak? Or maybe some biscuits from a local who-gave-a-shit-where? Bakery? Diner? Gas station?

God dammit, she'd finished the last cream cheese danish from her own bakery just as she'd crossed the state line.

"... And if you have any questions for me as you take this journey, you can drop by my domicile just next door to here any hour of the day or night or find me around the land. I'm happy to help guide your quest as needed."

"Is it a journey or a quest?" Evan whispered.

"Is there a difference?" Meg asked.

Evan shrugged. "Quests have a clear sense of purpose, I think."

"Then it's probably a journey," Meg replied.

Caren raised up her arms, lifting her face toward the skylight at the top of the dome and inhaling through her nostrils so loudly Jessica could hear it all the way toward the back of the room. On the exhale, she said, "Danielle will lead a silent walk around the property while we get set up in here for digestive yoga." She beamed. "I'll see you in ten minutes."

* * *

The next morning, as Jessica stared down at her smoothie, a thick wooden straw sticking straight from the middle of the green slush, she wondered if she'd accidentally signed up for fat camp. She couldn't even remember what she'd put in the damn thing as she'd gone down the line at the smoothie bar, pointing at different ingredients for the servers to throw into the glass blending cup. Some of the things she knew the name of—strawberries and pineapple —but most she didn't. Like when she'd pointed to the apples and the woman had repeated something that sounded only vaguely correct before throwing a handful of what looked like juicy red worms into the mix. And that was before they even got to the chakra power ups. She hadn't heard of any of the ingredients, but apparently all of them fought cancer and a few cleansed auras. She couldn't confirm either of those things, seeing as how she couldn't spot cancer or an aura just by looking at a person.

It wasn't the taste of the smoothie that left her feeling forlorn so much as the fact that her cruel brain had been delivering whiffs of fresh-baked croissants via memory at irregular intervals since she'd woken up with the morning gong at five-thirty.

"How's it hanging?"

Meg scooted in on the bench beside Jessica, setting her smoothie down next to her.

"Wait, how come yours isn't green?" Jessica asked.

"I couldn't tell you if you put a gun to my head. I think I blacked out in that line. You run a bakery, right?"

"Yeah, but I already ate what I brought with me."

"Son of a bitch."

Jessica looked around. "Where's Evan?"

"Psh. Probably still asleep. She's never been an early bird."

"I take it you two knew each other before you came here?"

Meghan sipped her smoothie and her right eye twitched. "Damn, that could use some Sweet & Low. Yeah, we both just got promoted to partner at a law firm up in Seattle. The boss assumed we needed leadership training. One other person was promoted along with us, but for some strange reason *he* didn't need leadership training?" She feigned confusion. "I guess ol' Whittaker didn't want to seem as sexist as he is, so he said that being a female boss is a special challenge and he wanted to prepare us as best he could. I told him it's not that much of a challenge as long as we get to say and do the exact same things a male boss would without being disciplined for being 'rude' or 'abrupt,' but that went in one ear and out the other, and here we are." She took another sip of her smoothie and flinched, jerking her head back to glare at it.

Blinking off the taste, she returned her attention to Jessica. "Is it too much to hope that you're here to learn how to be a better leader so you can lead the estrogen revolution against men like Whittaker?"

"Uh ... yeah. I'm just here to figure out how to run my bakery."

"Hmph," said Meg, eyeing Jessica thoroughly, and, if

she wasn't mistaken, disapprovingly, but she didn't elaborate.

For the duration of the morning's digestive yoga, Jessica held out hope that there was something she was missing about the food options. Perhaps any minute now, the smoothie would kick in and she'd feel more full, content, and, hell, enlightened than she ever had. But when the group om-ed their last om and she was still jonesing for the next simple carb fix, she began to seriously consider the possibility that it was an intentionally cruel move, a break-them-down-to-build-them-up kind of strategy.

It was about halfway through the toxin release massage, where she lay facedown and naked on the table— less a product of being comfortable with the setup and more a result of being too weak to fight—when the masseuse, who insisted on being called a body guide or something along the lines of that, informed her that this could very well be the most painful detoxification process she ever went through. Jess wondered if the woman told that to everyone or just the ones that showed no clear signs of ever having struggled with a heroin addiction.

The massage was easily the most intimate encounter she'd ever had with anyone. Were all detoxes this sensual? She could see why so many people were in and out of rehab, if they were.

Things were going surprisingly well for how anxious Jessica had been about this part of the week. She felt herself begin to relax and think such obviously insane thoughts as, *Who cares if she sees a nipple?* and *My body is natural, not something to be embarrassed about.* So, it came as a complete surprise to her when the body guide began jabbing at her calf, and without thinking about it, Jessica blurted, "I miss muffins."

"Mm-hmm," crooned the masseuse. "We store our addictions in our bodies. Working out certain parts can trigger past patterns."

"My calf triggers muffins?"

"So it seems."

From then on, Jessica remained vigilant about what thoughts popped into her head and when. As far as she could tell, the arch on her left foot triggered butter cream, her right hamstring triggered kosher pigs-in-a-blanket, and a tiny, sinewy muscle in her right glute, unfortunately, triggered Jimmy Dean.

"Whoa," said the body toucher when she found the Jimmy Dean spot. "There it is."

"There what is?"

"The source of the toxins."

"My ass is the source of the toxins?"

"Yes. You store so much tension here. Tell me, what do you think about when I press ... here."

Jessica's eyes crossed as the thumb dug into her ass cheek. "Fighting you."

"Yes! I knew it would be aggression. Who do you want to fight?"

"You!"

The woman ground her thumb in farther. "No, not me. Who else?"

Jessica was pretty sure it *was* the body punisher she wanted to fight, but before she could reiterate, she spat, "Jimmy! I want to punch him in the fucking throat!" She slapped the bed, cringing through gritted teeth, on the verge of asking her Father for a little heavenly intervention.

Then the woman released the pressure and sighed. "Yes, there you go. Did you feel that release?"

Jessica did not. But she also didn't want to bring round two on herself if she could help it. "Yes."

"I don't know who that Jimmy is, but it sounds like he represents the patriarchy to you. Like I said, this will be a painful detoxification, but we've just dislodged the source, and it will start to move through your body over the next couple days. Don't be surprised if you end up thinking about Jimmy more than usual."

Jess lifted her head from the bed just so she could slam it down again. Great. Just what she needed. A whole glob of Jimmy plaque moving through her system. How that would help her run a bakery, she didn't know.

As the woman continued to activate Jessica's chocolate chip cookie muscle and her croissant flexors, she decided she could *really* use some comfort food.

Chapter Forty-Three

Her fork skewered the strawberry so hard, it chopped it clear in two. Jessica grunted and grabbed one half with her fingers, popping it into her mouth.

Someone slammed their plate down next to her, and a moment later, Evan sat and began stabbing at her fruit and pepitas salad. "Not even a real fucking meal."

"If I didn't want to starve to death, I'd throw this whole stupid bowl across the room," Jessica replied. "I've never hated fruit before, but now it just seems complicit."

"Thank you!" Evan said, slamming her fork down on the elaborate cloth.

Meg took her place across from them at the table. "You two look like your detoxification massage went about as peacefully as mine."

Jessica grunted.

"I swear to God, Meg," said Evan, "when we get back

to work, it'll be a miracle if I don't kick Whittaker right in his saggy old grandpa pants."

"Preaching to the choir."

Evan scoffed. "Idiot wouldn't have made us come here if he knew it'd only make us want to murder him." She turned to Jessica. "What'd you think about through the massage?"

"Mostly muffins."

"No people?"

"No," she said, mashing a piece of honeydew melon between her fingers, "one person." She considered throwing the squished honeydew back onto her plate, but she was too hungry. She tossed it into her mouth instead.

Meg nodded approval. "At least when you get out of here you can just go smite him, right?"

The melon fell out of her mouth, and she caught it just before it hit her brown linen pants. "What?"

"Sorry," said Meg quickly as Evan smacked her on the arm. "I've read about how you can smite things. It's true, right?"

But now Evan listened intently, and Jessica was just belligerent enough to be honest. "Yeah. But I don't do people."

"Shame," said Meg. "You would make an awesome assassin. Everyone would assume it was a just killing. You know, Jessica, I've been thinking about this since we met. I really don't understand why you refuse to ... oh for Christ's sake."

A slow rising hum filled the room, and Jessica shut her

eyes against the stupidity of this practice they had learned yesterday. The group om was the way the leaders got everyone's attention at the end of a meal, starting it themselves, expecting those who noticed them to join in until the whole damn place felt like living inside a gong. Had it bothered her so much *before* the bits of Jimmy had been dislodged from her ass?

Caren stood on the small platform at the front of the dome, if such thing could have a front, and waited until all eyes were on her to begin speaking. The robes she wore were ones Jessica hadn't seen before. While Jessica's closet was packed with a colorful assortment that felt like a celebration, only now, as Caren stood before them in head-to-toe white robes, looking like a Clorox poster child except for the ornate swirls of red stitching along the hems, did the lack of white in anyone else's wardrobe occur to Jessica.

An itch flared in the back of Jessica's mind. The Chief Galru's robes reminder her of something, but she couldn't—

Fuck. Jimmy. They reminded her of Jimmy.

BUT YOU'RE RIGHT. DEFINITELY NOT A CULT.

Shut up. It's just the detox that's making me think about him. They're nothing alike.

BLESS YOUR HEART.

A tingle moved through her that felt invigorating before turning into a thousand tiny pinpricks.

Stop that.

Clenching and unclenching her fists a few times to

work through the last effects of God's passive aggression, she refocused her attention on the front of the room.

Caren had each hand tucked in the opposite sleeve, giving her a monkish air of wisdom as she breathed in with her diaphragm, breathed out, breathed in ... It was hypnotizing like a lava lamp.

Finally, after nearly thirty seconds of silence, she spoke, "Sisters. I can feel the tension in the air after this morning's detoxification. I promise once these slights and hurts work their way from your body you'll feel fresh and new again."

Jessica doubted that. The moment she saw Jimmy again, she was sure her glute would clench right back up. No amount of work she could do on herself would make Jimmy less of a pain in the ass.

"We hold in our anger because society shuns us for expressing it. We're told to be good girls, to do what needs to be done no matter the cost to self. And do it all with a smile!" The shit-eating grin she plastered on her face reminded Jessica of the expression gorillas wore prior to a fight. "So we hold it in our bodies, store it away until it poisons us, turns to depression, anxiety, cancer. And how are we supposed to lead others when our own bodies have turned against us?"

Meg leaned toward Jessica and whispered, "I thought she was full of crap, but I'm starting to like her."

"And while our own bodies are turned against us, so are the bodies of others. Men view our bodies as their property to regulate, control, and use ..."

Her mind jumped to the stalker. He viewed her as his property for sure, something he should dominate and control by making her afraid to leave her bakery, and then by making her afraid to be inside it alone. He'd desecrated her sacred space one too many times, and now she was here, having fled from the one place she used to feel a sense of control.

Well, somewhat of a sense of control.

"And when we stand up for ourselves, they call us hysterical and disparage us for finding our voice until our voices hold no credibility with those in power."

Jessica's glute clenched.

Caren continued, "They hurt us, they control us, they legislate us, they *rape* us ..."

A BIT ONE-SIDED, DON'T YOU THINK?

Jessica ignored Him. She was enjoying the heady rush of indignation too much to let Him try to drag her down.

"We all have these stories, don't we?" Caren asked.

Meg was among the first to shout a wild affirmative, and Jessica, who'd felt like slapping someone since the body prodder found her Jimmy Dean muscle, settled on slapping her own hand again and again until her palms stung.

"I'll tell you why they do it!" Caren declared. "Because they're scared. They're scared of *us*. They're scared of our sacred feminine power! They blame us for their own weakness, going back to the Garden of Eden!"

Whoa.

That itch in the back of her mind became a flashing

red light, but she threw a blanket over it and continued clapping because it felt *amazing.*

"You hear it again and again. Men claim any woman who is tired of the mistreatment simply wants to lock all men underground and use them for their seed. Who here has heard that line before?"

Most of the room raised a hand.

Wait, what?

OH YES, IT'S QUITE COMMON.

How have I not heard that before?

YOU DO NOT FREQUENT THE INTERNET ENOUGH.

"However, this hyperbolic fear is simply another male fantasy. To sit around doing nothing while women bring them to orgasm again and again and then skirt the responsibility of child rearing?" She shook her head in disgust. "Don't you see? We're subjected to the toxic fantasy of men nonstop, even in their dismissal of our right to equality."

"Yeah, fuck them!" came a shout from the crowd.

Caren pointed to the shouter. "You. Come up here." She motioned her closer, and the woman was more than happy to jump up and join on stage.

Caren was easily a foot taller than the round Latina in purple pants and an orange top, and she put an arm around the woman's shoulder, facing her toward the crowd. "Tell them your story."

And so began a string of testimonials, one after the other, different verses of the same song, not unlike Jessica's visit to the Nu Alpha Omega house. At the conclusion of each, Jessica joined in with the raucous applause and even indulged herself in shouting "Screw him!" a few times. Jessica felt herself get swept up in the brash expression of emotions. It was unlike anything she'd ever felt, to be able to share in a common sense of misery and triumph, to let everything she felt flow through her and *out* rather than holding it back—fifty-eight hundred dollars was a steal for this.

But when one woman shouted, "You shoulda torn his dick off and fed it to him!" The stretching band of ebullience in Jessica's chest snapped, and already on a roll with shouting everything that came to her head, she shouted, "Whoa there!" and looked around for the source of the particularly horrifying yell. When she couldn't locate it and realized even more violent things were flowing forth from the mouths of women who had seemed quite pleasant just minutes before, Jessica's buzz was officially killed. She looked at Meg for a sign of recognition that *maybe* that was a little much.

Nothing.

She looked at Evan.

Still nothing. Any resistance to the ritual these women might have had before had been buried by bloodlust.

Okay. This has gotten out of hand, hasn't it?

IT HAS.

Should I try put a stop to it?

HELL NO. THEY'LL TEAR YOU APART.

Then what should I do?

WHATEVER YOU FEEL LIKE DOING.

Well, she certainly didn't feel like yelling anymore. Not if it made her sound like some of these psychopaths.

"Castrate the pig!" shouted Evan at the conclusion of another woman's testimony.

Oh. Shit.

MORE LIKE 'OH SLOP.'

This is ... how did this ...?

Never would she have believed she'd find herself on this side of the fervor, yet here she was. Or here she had been. She'd come close, but she hadn't become completely carried away. She easily could have, and probably would have, if not for the fact that she'd been the recipient of similar hate for, oh, most of her life. She guessed it was that fact that kept her tethered while the women around her flowed freely in the emotional currents.

Caren's warm radiance and charisma became almost frightening when held up in this new context. The way she engendered trust with her audience, played to their emotional weaknesses, gave them permission to lose themselves completely ...

I'm just being oversensitive because of my detox. Jimmy got dislodged from my ass and now he's running through my bloodstream. I need to stop projecting.

The spirit of the room was unnerving, but it wasn't as bad as White Light. Not yet.

She let herself settle into it a bit more. What did the shouting hurt, anyway? It wasn't like they were going to stampede out of the place and hunt down every last man in a hundred miles. And it wasn't like Caren had dragged an eleven-year-old child up in front of everyone to be their emotional whipping boy, unlike *some* people.

After thanking the last speaker and gently ushering her toward her seat with a hand on her lower back, Caren returned to the stage. "Can you feel that? That heat rising in your veins? That desire to destroy, to crush, to maim?"

Jessica did nod along with everyone on this, because, oh hell yeah, she could feel it, even if she were wary of it. She wasn't even sure if it was hers or the people next to her's, but it was there, like a molten blanket draped over all the women, connecting them even as it burned their flesh.

Caren lowered her voice. "That's not yours. That's the toxic self-loathing you've been force-fed your entire life seeping from the deep parts of your soul, working its way through your bones, your organs, your muscles. The rage might feel like yours, but it's only a side effect of your body trying to dispel years of self-hatred you've ingested, condensed, and stored away. Our vessels are made for peace and love, not bitterness, not anger. The wounds are open now—force out that which does not belong to you!" The scream that followed would have churned Jessica's stomach if she'd eaten anything heavier than fruit. The rest of the women followed suit until the dome became an echo chamber of agony.

Jessica gave it a shot, blurting out a quick wail that made her feel like a real idiot. She tried again and it felt less insane. On the third attempt, she started to understand the appeal. When was the last time she'd allowed herself to be this loud? When was the last time she wasn't worried about being noticed? Even with Jameson, when she was supposed to be embracing the attention people paid her, she hadn't felt entitled to be *loud*. What an indulgence!

The shouting died down once Caren motioned for someone to bring her a chair and took a seat on the stage. More than a few women were weeping, and Caren allowed them to continue as she spoke again, much softer this time, like she was telling a bedtime story. "You may not believe this, but I used to be married to a man who refused to work a steady job, who stayed home all day and didn't lift a finger to help raise our three children. And I'd gobbled up so much of the patriarchal lies that I didn't even know there was another way. I would drop the kids off at school, work full-time at the tech company I ran—this was back in the dot-com gold rush—pick up the kids from school, cook them dinner, and put them to bed. Sound familiar? I was living the life of a single mom while a man leeched off me day and night. He might as well have been locked underground and milked for his semen." When she chuckled, the audience allowed itself one as well. "And to top it off, he was cheating on me. Quite prolifically, I might add.

"I didn't have this retreat to escape to, but you know what I did have?" She paused. "I had love. Not self-love, oh no. Hank had fed me so much poison that I actually thought I had won the lottery when I'd married him. What saved me, oddly enough, was a man from out of town dropping into my life, reflecting back to me my own value, and urging me to chase after what I deserved." She paused, beaming out at the crowd. "I know, you didn't expect that. It was a *man* who started my transformation, who liberated me from the ignorance and captivity. I'm still baffled by that myself. But it goes to show that love is the antidote. Period. This man worshipped my body, if only for a short time, and that love of another planted the seeds for self-love to grow." She sighed. "He wasn't perfect by any means, and as you can tell, he didn't stick around. But if we want to be healthy leaders, we must learn how to accept the good and reject the bad without tossing the whole of them aside for a few faults. We must be discriminating.

"This next part is important: It's not *men* we hate, but a twisted idea of masculinity so many worship. It's a small but important difference there, and if we're not careful, our anger will blind us to the subtleties of it. Which is why we must not move on from here while that poison remains within us. Beings of the moon like us can just as easily absorb the lies of toxic sun energy and use it against our sisters."

The crying had stopped, and the room was silent like a grave.

OKAY, SHE LOST ME A LITTLE BIT THERE.

"Who here has ever been in love?"

Hands raised tentatively around the room, and Caren nodded, closing her eyes gently. "Yes, you know, then. You know how love can make you feel worthy. And that's why we must show it to the people around us.

"Love from a man was what freed me to finally leave

my husband behind. It freed me up to sell the business just before the crash, which freed me to move outside of the city and to buy this ranch and start this retreat, which brought all of you here today. One single act of love from the least expected place."

IT WASN'T A SINGLE ACT, I CAN TELL YOU THAT.

Jessica could hardly begrudge Caren an affair. If she were in that position and some charming Casanova came along and offered to bang her brains out, she couldn't say definitively that she wouldn't be all-in.

"You may be tempted to hold on to this anger you feel now—it feels like power, doesn't it?—but you have to let it go. Only then will you have room in your body to accept the love you need and to give the love that could make all the difference to the life of another."

Okay, this sounded more acceptable. She didn't understand all the moon and sun stuff, but there was no one shouting about human castration, so she could get on board with it.

And yet, when Caren stood, raised her hands, and began to lead the room in a group om, Jessica couldn't shake the lingering fear that the *om* would change into a *sooie*.

Chapter Forty-Four

Jessica's calf twinged the moment she caught a whiff of fresh-baked muffins. Her knee bounced anxiously as she sat cross-legged on the handwoven alpaca rug, waiting for the plate to move around the ten-woman circle. What muffins had to do with discovering her spirit animal, she had no clue. Nor did she care. Because muffins had everything to do with her own happiness. It was one of the things she'd discovered in this retreat for self-discovery, and by day three of the thing—day two of no simple carbs—she didn't even give two shits if that muffin was entirely bran.

Her head had stopped spinning from the day before after a good night's sleep, and she'd woken up, drank her smoothie like a good little camper, felt slightly less awkward about farting loudly in digestive yoga (everyone did, which was why they kept the doors open for a cross breeze), and, prior to entering into this teepee, had begun to wonder if she was finally losing her craving for baked goods.

"Just one piece," said the leader of the exercise when the plate made its way to her and she tried to take two. "Trust me, one piece is all you'll want."

Bullshit it was. The cravings came back with a vengeance, and she scoffed at her earlier thought that she'd moved on.

"Don't eat it yet," the leader, Gloria, a silver-haired woman with tan, freckled skin, instructed.

Are you kidding me? Jessica stared longingly at the fluffy treat pinched between her fingers. It was definitely blueberry. Praise whoever!

"This journey is going to feel abrupt. That's just the nature of it. But I guarantee you're perfectly safe, and there are no risks involved. Unless, um ... is anyone pregnant?"

A woman raised her hand, smiling pleasantly.

"O-kay," said Gloria. "You gotta go." She thumbed toward the door. "And leave the muffin."

That was an especially cruel thing to do to a pregnant woman, Jessica decided. If anything, they should give the woman the rest of the plate to go.

Once the mother-to-be had left the teepee, Gloria resumed her instructions. "Keeping in mind that you are perfectly safe, I want you to avoid resisting the journey. Just go with it. That's the only way to ensure a peaceful encounter with your spirit animal."

Evan raised her hand before speaking. "Do some people have violent encounters with their spirit animal?"

"Yes."

"And what happens to them?"

Gloria opened her mouth to speak, then thought better of it, paused, and said, "Just don't resist the experience, and you won't have to worry about it." She inhaled, setting her hands, palms up, on her knees, and on the exhale, she spoke again. "Now you're free to eat your portion of the muffin"—Jessica popped it in her mouth right away, hardly chewing before she swallowed it down—"whenever you're ready to embrace the ayahuasca journey."

Only a small bit of mush remained in Jessica's mouth. "Ayahuasca?"

The guide nodded. "Yes. It's an ancient medicinal—"

"I know what it is. It was *in the muffin?*"

"Yes, just a small dose. I can see you're considering fighting it, Jessica. You really, *really* shouldn't. It'll be fine."

Jessica's eyes were wide, her pupils dilated, and the drugs hadn't even hit her blood stream yet. "Bet it won't." She didn't know much about the particular drug, but she hadn't forgotten about the mushrooms and the burning cactus and Danny on top of her ... "Is this anything like mushrooms?"

"Somewhat. But much stronger."

Jessica tapped her fingers on her knees and fought the urge to run. "Fuck, fuck, fuck." She wanted to question the legality of it, but then she remembered the iffy jurisdiction and figured she had her answer.

Gloria crawled a few steps across the circle, leaning close to Jessica's ear. "If you can't calm down, I'm going to have to ask you to leave the circle. You'll ruin the collective vibrations."

Jessica nodded. It was probably too late to vomit this back up, and honestly, she could still taste the muffin and preferred that over the sour acidity of bile. "Yeah, okay. I'm fine." She addressed the rest of the women. "We're fine. We're all fine. I'm gonna meet my spirit animal and it will all be okay!"

She knew the second the drugs laid into her because it was the second her eyes rolled back in her head and she fell onto her back, staring up at the top of the tent which was now the night sky.

She rolled her head from side to side, taking in a Saharan sunset more vibrant than anything she'd seen in her nature shows. Was her spirit animal nearby? It must be, and the fact that she was in Africa held a lot of positive potential for the discovery.

As she pushed herself to standing, the stars began falling from the sky, flying past her from a single origin. She scanned her surroundings and found it, that bright star. She was supposed to walk toward it, so she did. The sound of hoof beats began to rumble the ground beneath the dry grasses, and Jessica squinted toward the horizon for the source. It came closer and closer, then finally she saw it clearly. A herd of giraffes sprinting toward her.

"Fuck yes!" she cried, pumping a fist into the air. "Best spirit animal ever!"

The giraffes moved with the steady flow of the stars, and she planted her feet to let them come to her. Which one of these beautiful orange beasts was hers? She wanted to meet her, to hug her, maybe even to ride on her back if that wasn't totally offensive to spirit giraffe customs.

When the herd reached her, still running at full speed, they split, passing her on either side.

None stopped to say hello like she'd hoped. She whirled around, hollering after them. "Wait! I'm one of your spirit humans! Come back!"

But they didn't. They kept running on with the flow of falling stars. Shitballs.

Maybe there were more giraffes ahead. She pushed on. But what she encountered next was no giraffe; it was the reason the giraffes were running.

A lean lioness appeared from behind a thick tree trunk, and stalked over to Jessica.

"What's up?" the lioness said.

Jess waved her hands in front of her, "No, no, no. You can't be my spirit animal."

"Why's that?" asked the lioness.

"Because spirit animals don't say 'what's up.'"

"We sure as shit do."

"No! You're not supposed to curse!"

The lioness sat straight, facing Jessica. "And why the hell not?"

"You're supposed to be majestic!"

She swiped a gigantic paw at her. "Please. I'm majestic as fuck. Just look at the light glint off my fur!" She turned her head to the left and right, and sure enough, there was glinting.

"You're right."

The lioness stood and prowled closer. "Don't you want to know my name?"

"Is that important?"

"Don't be a dick. Of course it's important. You want me to just call you 'girl'? No, I didn't think so."

"Fine, fine. What's your name?"

"Asha."

Jessica shook her head. "No, you're making that up. That's the name of my stuffed giraffe at work."

"Nah, bitch. *You're* making it up. This is all happening in your mind."

Jessica flinched. "I could use some more creativity then."

"You said it, not me."

The flow of stars was beginning to slow, and Jessica figured that meant she didn't have much time left. She took a seat and Asha laid down across from her. "I guess I should ask why you're a lioness."

"I'm not the one to ask. I don't know why I am what I am. Pretty sure it's your job to obsess about this weird-ass encounter for the next thirty years of your life."

"I don't know if I have that long."

The lioness bopped Jessica on the forehead with her massive paw. "Not this shit again. Listen. If you really want to figure out why I'm a lioness, maybe ask yourself what a lioness represents to you, okay? Jesus. I'm really not supposed to give you such obvious hints, but I guess I feel sorry for you."

"Thanks."

"Come here." Asha waved her closer and she remembered what Gloria had said about not resisting it. Asha already seemed agitated. Probably best not to prod her further.

When Jessica scooted closer, Asha got up and adjusted to lay her head in Jessica's lap.

"Am I supposed to pet you?" Jess asked.

"This will be kinda awkward if you don't."

So Jessica did. And as the final few stars fell from the sky, Asha left her with these parting words of wisdom: "Randy tasted like pork."

* * *

Jessica was especially grateful for the vegetarian diet at Camp Mindfuck after her conversation with Asha, even as she raked at the baked spaghetti squash with her fork.

"I can't believe mine was a penguin," Evan moaned. "I don't even like the cold."

"Yeah, that sucks," said Meg, whose spirit animal was a wild Arabian horse. "What was yours, Jessica?"

She paused before answering. Her mind hadn't truly left the encounter since she'd found herself staring up at top of the teepee, a mostly catatonic mess with drool slipping from each corner of her mouth hours before. "A lioness." She clawed at the squash. "A foul-mouthed lioness."

It wasn't Asha who Jessica had been fixated on, though, but Randy McAllister, the pervert demon with a fat doughnut around his middle who had tried to lure Jessica into a sex trap before stumbling backward, thanks to the mighty hand of God, falling into the lion's den at the Dallas Zoo, and being summarily torn to bits.

He tasted like pork.

God still wasn't cool with people eating pork, but clearly lions eating human that tasted like pork was fine, or else He wouldn't have given Randy the little love tap.

Sumus omnes porcos ...

Jessica shuddered.

"A lioness is a pretty badass spirit animal," Meg conceded. "I think it means you're strong and fierce."

"And I eat demonic perverts," she mumbled.

"Come again?"

Jessica paused, her fork hovering ahead of her lips. "Nothing. Sorry. Those drugs really did a number on me."

She'd seen Randy fall, seen the lionesses close in around him, and she even remembered rooting for Team Mega Cat. But she hadn't witnessed the gore because Mrs. Thomas had pulled her away.

Mrs. Thomas. How had she found her? Was it angel radar? There was so much of that day that Jessica simply couldn't remember, but she supposed that was how trauma worked. She ought to put the whole thing out of her mind.

"It's so cool, it's almost cliché," said Evan. "I mean, the

whole lioness spirit animal thing seems kind of obvious, right? Powerful feminine energy, the females being the most capable of the pride, blah, blah, blah."

Meg rolled her eyes and jabbed her fork at Evan to punctuate her words. "Bitterness does not become Penguins."

But Jess's mind stayed on a loop. She'd seen the lioness in its enclosure, sleeping peacefully against the glass when she and Randy had first arrived. She remembered thinking that it was just a cat. Yes, a powerful one, but still just a cat. As people knocked on the glass and shouted at her to move or do something interesting, the lioness remained asleep. She didn't want to eat anyone. Poor girl just wanted her beauty sleep. Everyone thought she owed it to them to be entertaining. And yet, when the time came for action ...

Those idiots got their entertainment in the end.

Jessica chuckled.

"Boy," said Meg. "You really are losing it. Laughing to yourself?"

"Just remembered something."

"Care to share?"

Oh hell. Why not? It was like what Jameson said. Retreats allowed you to try things on for size with no lasting consequences. She might as well try blunt honesty about her past. "When I was eleven, I went to the zoo on field trip and my group leader tried to ... well, he touched my ears, but looking back on it now, I'm pretty sure he was going to molest me."

Meg and Evan gaped in horror, clearly searching for the humor.

"Anyway, before he could, he tripped and fell into the lion pit. They jumped on him and ate him before the zookeepers could help him."

Evan took a swig of water from her wooden cup and waggled a finger at Jessica. "Yeah, okay, I see why that's funny."

"Weren't you traumatized?" asked Meg, showing uncharacteristic concern.

"Of course she was," Evan answered. "Why the hell do you think her spirit animal is a lioness? Clearly it imprinted on her."

"It wasn't that bad," Jessica said. "Also, it's fine because he was a demon."

Meg and Evan exchanged a quick look of concern. "A what now?" said Meg.

"A demon. Well, he wasn't a demon himself, but he let a demon inside him."

"O-kay," said Evan, taking the strangeness in stride easier than Meg appeared to be.

"I didn't see the actual goring. My teacher found me and made me look away. She's an angel, so I guess she could sense it or something."

Evan ran her tongue over her lips, nodding stiffly so her entire body rocked forward and back somewhat insanely on the bench. "An angel found you?" Before Jessica could respond, Evan's gaze sharpened and she said, "Wait, didn't she send you off alone with that creep in the first place?"

"Well, yeah, but I don't think she knew he was a creep when she agreed to let him take me to see the lions."

Meg set down her fork and smoothed her napkin on her lap as she inhaled deeply through her nose. "No. Doesn't matter. Anyone who sends a child off alone with a man they hardly know has some seriously fucked judgment."

"But ... no. Mrs. Thomas has great judgment. Way better judgment than me."

"The fact that she went looking for you tells me she knew something wasn't right from the start and sent you off anyway. Shit. It's a good thing public schools can't afford field trips anymore."

Evan was insinuating some rather damning things, and Jessica was unable to sit still until she came to her teacher's defense. "She felt bad about it, I promise. And everyone makes mistakes. She's actually the one that suggested I come here."

Meg stared forlornly down at her spaghetti squash and said, "Verdict's still out on whether that was a blessing or a curse."

Chapter Forty-Five

Hard Conversations 101 seemed to Jessica like the most intimidating name they could have given this seminar. She would have felt much less apprehensive going into Easy Conversations 301 or Intermediate Conversations 201. But no, she was shoved right into the hard stuff along with everyone else at the retreat.

With the morning's digestive yoga wrapped up, she found a spot on the mats in the center of the sanctuary, crossed her legs, and stared up at Caren, who explained the need for hard conversations.

It was the first genuinely leadership-focused activity provided since Jessica had arrived, and she wondered why they saved it until day four of five.

"A hard conversation is the best gift you can give someone you care about. Whether that's in a romantic, platonic, or business capacity, it remains true. Hard conversations are often unpleasant, but by engaging in one anyway, you're telling the person they matter, that it's worth the discomfort to do what needs to be done to clear the air and address the issue. It also shows your belief in a possible resolution. There are a million ways to *burn* bridges, but an honest, straightforward conversation is people on both sides of the divide working together to rebuild one."

Already, Jessica knew she would hate this.

"The trick to conducting a hard conversation is simple: know what you will and will not accept going in."

Simple? How was that simple? Jessica had no idea of what she would and wouldn't accept until someone had shoved it at her and she either found herself saying, "Thanks!" or "Ew, get it away!"

"We're going to start by providing our partner with an honest observation about them while you look them in the eyes. This first one should be neutral, like 'your eyes are blue' or 'your hair is brown.' Just make sure to stay away from debatable or relative observations, for example, someone who might seem tall to you is not objectively tall, they're relatively tall in comparison to yourself. Okay, now partner up."

Dread washed through Jessica. It was like reliving the worst moments of middle and high school all over again. "Partner up" had always meant "see who you're stuck with or if you're actually the odd one out because even Gary 'Busty Cats' Higgins has someone who wants to be with him."

Jessica already knew Meg and Evan, who were sitting

to her left, would pair up. So she turned to her right and found ...

A bunch of paired-up people.

For fuck's sake.

"Raise your hand if you don't yet have a partner," Caren instructed.

Swallowing the shame, as always, Jessica raised her hand. And so did one other person.

Jessica hadn't met the woman yet, but she'd smelled her the day before.

The woman, who had thinning bleach-blonde hair, sun-damaged skin and the worst case of halitosis Jessica had ever encountered hurried over and squeezed in close.

"Hi. Harmony."

That was unfortunate. Jessica's new goal was to steer their conversation away from any words that included aspirates.

"Jessica."

"I know."

"Now, looking each other in the eyes, take turns exchanging a neutral honest observation. Remember, not subjective."

Harmony smiled. "I'll go first. Your cheeks are pudgy."

Jessica blinked. Not neutral, sort of a touchy subject, but okay.

Now it was her turn. Instead of "your face is gaunt," or "your breath is atrocious," both of which were objectively true, Jessica went with, "Your eyes are green."

"Actually, they're hazel," said Harmony.

Like hell they were.

"Okay! Next up, I want you to make a positive observation about your partner, keeping that eye contact. Take turns. Go!"

Harmony started again. "You have a Northern European nose."

Again, a strange one. Not a positive observation, exactly ... "Thank you."

"You're welcome."

Great. Her turn. She scanned Harmony quickly, trying not to frown too openly. "Your neck is ... lean." Jessica was digging on that one, and she knew it.

"Thanks!" said Harmony. "I do exercises every day to keep it that way."

It was then that Jessica decided this would not, under normal circumstances, be someone she would bother having a hard conversation with.

"Very good!" said Caren. "I could tell that one was easy for some, difficult for others. That's okay! Even saying positive honest things can be difficult. It makes us vulnerable to rejection if the observation is debated. Now comes the moment you've been waiting for. I want you to give honest negative feedback to your partner."

This felt rushed and unproductive, and Jessica struggled to keep from jittering. How could she give Harmony any negative feedback other than "Your breath smells like I imagine a Florida sinkhole would"? She couldn't see past that one thing to find anything else worth mentioning.

Harmony went first again, grinning gently. "Your flat chest gives you a boyish figure in these robes."

"The hell is your problem?" Jessica snapped.

Harmony feigned shock. "It's just the exercise."

Gritting her teeth, Jessica composed herself and then went for it. "Okay, my turn. Your horrendous breath is a real issue that should be medically addressed."

Jessica rolled to the side just in time. Harmony flopped face first onto the hard tile floor of the dome after being unable to adjust the trajectory of her lunge. Jessica jumped up, ready to flee, but there was no need. Caren hurried over and asked what was the problem while Harmony was still tripping over her loose pants, trying to get her footing.

"She tried to fight me," Jessica said as calmly as she could.

What would inevitably come next was Caren's request for an explanation of what had transpired. This was a goddamn "learning opportunity" for the seminar if she ever saw one. She hated learning opportunities anytime she was the cause of them.

But instead, Caren nodded and said, "Well, not everyone is ready to hear honesty. Let's ... have you two split up."

When it was done, Jessica had joined Evan and Meghan, who seemed unimpressed by the exercise in general.

"Okay, next up: a role play," Caren said, like it wasn't everyone's nightmare. "You're going to pretend the other person is someone who you've been meaning to have a hard conversation with. Think up an opener, and keep this one rule in mind: do not pad the blow. Your instinct is to provide a compliment to soften the blow of honesty, but then you simply end on a sour note. Instead, cut right to it, speak as objectively as possible, and end with a genuine compliment that explains why it's important to you to have this hard conversation. I'll demonstrate first." She pulled up one of the other teachers and the two stood only a foot from each other as they looked directly into each other's eyes. "Kimberly, you have been taking longer than anyone else to complete your portion of the laundry lately, and it has been slowing down our routine and cutting into our morning meditation time. You're an invaluable asset to our cabal, and I'm confident you can work to improve this. If there's anything I can do to help you accomplish your tasks faster, please let me know."

Kimberly tilted her head, accepting the honesty. "There is. If we could invest in an electric washer and dryer instead of the washboards—"

"See?" Caren said, turning to the class. "I cut right to the chase with the problem, didn't call names, didn't say there was anything wrong with her, only her *results*, and then ended with the reason why it is important to have that conversation with her. I even offered to help her figure out how to solve the problem, which is a nice way to ease tensions if you sense the person you're speaking to isn't receptive to the conversation. Make them feel like you're in it together, that it's not all up to them."

Evan went first, looking at Meg. "Mr. Whittaker, only

sending the women to a dumbass leadership retreat looks like you possess a bias that women are less inclined toward leadership than men, which isn't supported by science. Because we found the leadership retreat so incredibly helpful, I believe it makes sense for Bradley to attend one as well. I enjoy working here, and I would hate to file a complaint against the company for workplace sexism. Let me know if you would like help looking up appropriate men's retreats that aren't, you know, just for gay swingers." She cocked her head to the side, and Meg nodded her approval.

"I think that will go over swimmingly. Why don't you give it a try, Jessica?"

She considered who she needed to have a hard conversation with and immediately came up with an obvious choice. But even just rehearsing a conversation like that with Mrs. Thomas would be Hard Conversations 301, and Jessica wasn't there yet.

She took a deep breath before diving in. "Jimmy, your obsession with making a buck off of me is causing me undue stress and distracting me from my bakery. I think you're a superb con man, and I want to see you succeed at that in another state if not continent. Please let me know what I can do to help relocate you."

Evan, who'd been Jimmy's stand-in, bowed her head. "Well done. I can tell it was really hard for you to call him a con man. You're so brave."

Meg, though, wasn't sharing in the amusement. "My turn," she said quickly, facing Jessica. "Jessica, I've wanted to say this to you all week. Your reluctance to be the female role model my eight-year-old daughter could really use has lasted too long. I know you don't want to lean into it, but that's a selfish decision, and you need to get over it and start thinking about all the little girls who need to see you crush Jimmy Dean's ass into the ground with the heel of your boot. And all the grown-up women who need to see that too. I know you're capable of it because I've been internet stalking you for years. Sorry I didn't mention that sooner. Let me know what I can do to help you stop running from this and own it."

Jessica's eyes were dry from not blinking, and heat infused her cheeks.

That was ... not a role play.

"Oh. Okay." Caren hadn't explained the proper way to receive a hard conversation, and Jessica wasn't sure what to say. "Thanks." That would do.

Meg relaxed her spine. "I mean it. You seem cool, and it's great that you're here and all, but who gives a shit about a bakery? You're God's daughter, right?"

"Yeah. And you believe it?"

"Not really. I just think you're a cool chick. I'm Jewish."

"That's awesome! I love Jews!"

Meg shook her head minutely. "Don't say that. It's weird. My point is that so long as you think you're God's daughter and all these other women and men think the same, you have a responsibility to act like it."

"Don't I have a say in what I do with my life?"

"Clearly. You're running a bakery and at a bullshit women's retreat in the desert. You have all the say. Doesn't mean any decision you make is the right one."

"So, I'm not supposed to consider what I want to do?" She sounded petulant and hated it, but she couldn't stop.

"I suspect that's all you're considering," Meg said. "And here you are. So tell me: are you living your dreams, Jess?"

Of course she wasn't! Who the hell actually got to do that? "Would you rather I give up everything I have and go get crucified instead? Women mature quicker than men, after all. Why should I have to wait until I'm thirty-three to get publicly murdered?"

"Talk about climbing up that cross ..." Evan mumbled.

Jessica snapped her head toward her. "You agree with her?"

"I think everyone with half a brain does, Jessica," said Evan. "Except, you know, Jimmy Dean. I'm sure it makes him extremely happy that Lady Jesus spends all her time baking in the kitchen rather than calling him out on his lies and burning the patriarchy to the ground."

"I have no obligation to burn the patriarchy to the ground. I'm not even entirely sure it's flammable. And I've tried to take on Jimmy's lies before. He just doubles down and lies harder and everyone assumes, 'no one would make such an outrageous statement if there wasn't a little truth to it!' and then I end up being yelled at by my publicist."

If she was hoping for pity from the others, which she was, she was disappointed. Evan looked at her

467

apologetically, but more in a "sorry you're so incredibly wrong," way. And Meg continued staring with her arms folded across her chest, her eyebrows floating skeptically mid forehead.

"Yeah," said Meg, "doing the right thing is hard. I'll give you that."

"You don't know," Jessica said, spinning away to face the front.

She thought they would take the hint that the conversation was over, but they didn't. "I like you, Jessica," said Meg. "I know I've only known you a few days, but in that time—and the years of cyberstalking—I can tell that if anyone can do this, it's you. I want to hear your story. And not from Jimmy, but from you. I'm just so sick of our stories coming from the mouths of men, I think I'll tear my hair out if I hear another one."

"I understand," Jessica said, trying her best to sound convincing.

Neither said anything else right away, and that was just fine, because being close to Meg and Evan had become excruciating. She needed space.

She got to her feet suddenly, saying, "I'm gonna go do a little digestive yoga on my own." And then she left the sanctuary.

Chapter Forty-Six

Of the sacrifices Jessica had made in her life, skipping ovarian acupuncture the previous night to sulk in her dome ranked toward the bottom. It was day five of the retreat, and that meant a farewell breakfast, digestive yoga, and then her departure from the commune to rejoin real life. Was she excited? Was she ready for this experiment in self to come to a conclusion?

"Jessica," called a voice as she made her way toward the sanctuary.

She spotted Caren gliding over in no hurry at all.

"Good morning," Jessica said.

When they met where her walkway intersected the main path, Caren rested a gentle hand between Jessica's shoulder blades, guiding her in the opposite direction of the sanctuary. "I saw you leave early from Hard Conversations 101 yesterday and I was informed you missed ovarian acupuncture later that night. Did the episode yesterday rattle you? I spoke with Harmony and she has been properly censured."

"No, it wasn't that. I was just tired and thought I would take some sleep where I could. I don't get much when I'm back home."

"Oh, Jessica," Caren said breathlessly, "you really must make time for sleep. It's crucial to keeping your chi flowing."

Super helpful. Obviously all Jessica needed to conjure up more hours for sleep was someone to tell her she needed it!

PERHAPS YOU SHOULD HAVE ATTENDED OVARIAN ACUPUNCTURE. YOU SEEM A LITTLE HORMONAL.

Not now.

But He was right and she knew it. Not right that she needed a bunch of needles stuck in and above her bush, but that she was a little hormonal. Not thunderstorms-and-electrocuted-pedophiles hormonal, but a week shy of it.

"Can I help you unburden your mind?" Caren asked. "Anything you'd like to talk about?"

"No." She paused. "Yeah, okay. One of the women accused me of using the bakery as a way to avoid doing something bigger, and, you know, maybe she has a point. Or maybe I'm playing too small with just running *one* bakery. Maybe I ought to be thinking bigger in general. I don't know. I feel so overwhelmed just doing this one thing, and to be told it's not enough ..."

"I can see why that would be difficult to hear. Do you

mind my asking what this woman thinks you should be doing instead?"

Would this all get back to Mrs. Thomas? She was friends with Caren, after all. If Mrs. Thomas heard Jessica was considering anything the than running the bakery forever, would she call in the loan? No. Mrs. Thomas would never do something drastic like that, but she would probably be incredibly disappointed. She was the only one who'd remained consistent in her belief that Jessica was in no way obligated to be acting daughter of God. Sure, Destinee supported the bakery *now*, but Jess knew her mom would drop it in a heartbeat to help her pursue something bigger, more connected to her literally God-given line of work and with a fervor Jessica had only ever witnessed when Destinee was talking about sex.

"She thinks, or rather, both of them think that I should be stepping into my role as ... um, a female role model."

"You're a business owner, Jessica! You're already a wonderful role model for young girls. Would I be correct in assuming the thing you're dancing around is your proclaimed lineage as the daughter of God?"

Nothing about Caren's tone gave an indication whether *she* believed that to be true, so Jessica proceeded cautiously. "Yeah, that's what they meant."

"And is that something that one can make a living from? I ask because I have no experience in that arena."

Was she being sarcastic? As a new-age guru, Caren was closer to a female messiah by profession than Jessica was. And judging by the luxury of this place and the cost to attend, Jessica assumed Caren knew *exactly* how to make a buck off it.

"I don't know. I mean, Jimmy Dean makes money off of me. He didn't for a while, but now he does."

"Indeed, the Reverend came from humble beginnings like yours and has now built quite an impressive empire for himself."

The crunch of gravel underneath her feet fell away as Jessica homed in on something that sounded remarkably like admiration in Caren's tone. "Right. And with any luck, it'll come crumbling down soon. You've read about the scandal, I assume."

A tiny smirk tugged at the corners of her lips. "I've read about it, but I'd hardly call it a scandal."

"What would you call it?"

The woman shrugged serenely, her hands clasped behind her back as they walked. "Oh, just a media frenzy. Trust me, I've seen my fair share of men using their power to sexually abuse women, but I think it's crucial to our cause not to shout fire every time we see a candle burning."

"But he rounded up a bunch of underage girls into a barn and told them the end of the world was coming." Maybe Caren hadn't heard the details.

"Yes, I know. He believed he was saving their souls, taking them with him to heaven. It may seem misguided to you and me, but his intentions were good."

She disagreed so strongly, she worried her retinas might detach, but she didn't say anything. Caren was wiser than she was, so she forced herself to listen with an open heart or whatever the fuck they'd said half a dozen times over the week.

"There's no one in this world that you'll agree with one hundred percent of the time," Caren continued. "Think about a disagreement you've had with someone you love. Did you accuse them of evil, of perversion, of ignorance, or were you able to allow them to continue coexisting with you while holding a belief you didn't share because you'd seen their soul and given them the benefit of the doubt?"

"Well, sure, but that's only with people I trust."

"Love does not have to be complicated, Jessica. We become our best selves when we can extend the love we reserve for a select few to all beings who walk the earth alongside us."

There was an allure to that, something that resonated with her, or at least felt really good to imagine, but ... "Seems like a quick way to let people screw you over."

Finally, Caren seemed to agree when she rocked her head forward slowly. "Yes. But you can't control what others choose to do. All you can control are your own thoughts and actions. Those who wish to do you ill will likely do so whether you show them love or not. If anything, a small offering of compassion and understanding at just the right moment will dissuade them from committing the unfavorable act they had planned."

The unusual November heat had left the night before, and now the air around them was crisp. No longer shielded by the densest cluster of domes, the wind swirled around them and found its way up Jessica's baggy sleeve, sending a chill down her spine. She shivered it off before saying, "I'm willing to consider that on the drive home, but I don't quite buy it yet."

Caren laughed, and it sounded like a dove taking flight. "I'm pleased with that."

"I can't promise I'll ever not want to put a boot up Jimmy's ass, though."

"You may be surprised what mercy and compassion your heart allows when you simply loosen the cords of anger that bind it."

The path they'd taken formed a U, and as they walked the bend and headed back toward the sanctuary, Caren said, "In my family, cooking has always been a way to show love. Running a bakery that not only provides food as delicious as yours, but caters to those who are often underserved due to dietary constraints, can be an act of love worthy of your time if you make it one. If you keep believing you should be doing some mysterious, grander thing, and you lose sight of what you have around you, you'll never find happiness. Misery is simply the difference between what we have and what we wish we had. Close that gap, and you'll find an inner peace, no matter what you're doing."

"Hmm ..." That sounded a lot like lowering expectations. But it also meant she was off the hook for being some sort of wise public figure like Evan and Meg (and so many more) thought she should be. So, she'd take it.

"That makes a lot of sense. Thanks."

"We can lead in many ways. It doesn't mean we must

be the best of our profession, the top dog. It simply means that we treat those who choose to follow us in a way that doesn't cast them aside." They reached the entrance of the sanctuary, and she placed her hand on the door before leaning close and adding, "For what it's worth, you make one hell of a lemon poppy seed muffin. Almost as if you were put on this earth to do it." She winked, and Jessica laughed. The notion that God had gone to all the trouble of having another kid just so she could make a specific kind of muffin was one of the dumbest things Jessica had ever heard.

But it still made her feel better.

When they entered the sanctuary, many of the tables were already full of breakfasters, and Caren parted ways with her to make final rounds among the fat-campers with the lower-ranking galrus.

Jessica's eyes found Meg's face in the crowd, and a wave of embarrassment crashed over her for the way she'd acted the day before. So childish. She couldn't even handle that sort of basic criticism? She'd heard so much worse.

She looked away and kept her head down through the smoothie line.

When she looked back up, though, Meg waved her over, grinning. So Jessica set her jaw, returned the smile, and decided to try bravery on for size.

"You feeling better?" Evan asked once Jessica had a seat next to her.

"Yes. Thanks."

"Hey," said Meg, "sorry about coming down on you so

hard yesterday. I guess I needed ovarian acupuncture more than I realized."

The three of them laughed, and the tension disappeared. "Don't worry about it. I was oversensitive. And you were just being honest."

"And I was right."

"Eh, I don't know about that. But I tell you what: I'll add it to the list of things to consider on my drive home later."

It was quite a long list now, but she had hours and hours to do nothing *but* think.

She settled into a comfortable conversation with the women, mostly about how sad they were to go back to bras (but regardless, they all would).

Her head was swimming by the time she said her final goodbyes just past the arch, now in her jeans and a light blue It is Risen T-shirt.

As she loaded up the car, a moment of panic washed over her: *I've learned nothing.*

But a few yoga breaths calmed her enough to change that thought to: *I can't wait to discover what I've learned.*

She started her car, caring a lot less that it was the dumpiest in the lot, and assured herself that she would be wiser by the time she arrived in Austin. She had to have learned something.

Things will click into place when the dust settles. I just need a little alone time and a lot of distance. That gave me a lot to think about.

FIVE DAYS AND FOUR NIGHTS IN THE

DESERT IS AN EXTRAORDINARY FEAT. YOU MUST BE SO MORALLY EXHAUSTED.

What ... in the hell are you going on about?

She pulled out her phone, which she'd shut off to conserve battery, from her purse, and powered it up before pulling out of the lot and onto the road into town.

NOTHING. JUST, YOU KNOW, YOUR BROTHER SPENT FORTY DAYS FASTING IN THE DESERT WHILE BEING TEMPTED BY THE DEVIL.

He did? She wondered how many times he'd called the Devil a meanie.

YES. HE HASN'T MENTIONED THIS?

Nope. I guess he didn't want to use it against me as much as you do.

ALL THE LORD IS SAYING IS THAT IF WOMEN WANT TO BE TREATED EQUAL TO MEN, THEY SHOULD BE PREPARED TO GO THROUGH THE SAME TRIALS.

Where did she even start? Ah, she had a place.

How long is the average female menstrual cycle?

TWENTY-EIGHT DAYS, FIVE HOURS, TWENTY MINUTES, FORTY-NINE SECONDS, AND THREE HUMMINGBIRD HEARTBEATS.

More specific than I was looking for, but okay. Now riddle me this, Mr. All That. Did Jesus have his period while he was in the desert?

WELL, NO, BUT THAT'S BECAUSE—

Until you level the playing field by giving men the blood-loss equivalent of a period, I don't want to hear your bullshit. Also, he lived two thousand years ago. In the Middle East. Before sewage systems. Going out into the desert where he didn't have to smell the unfiltered shit of the city was probably a step up.

IT WAS, BUT DON'T TELL ANYBODY. SORT OF RUINS THE STORY. ALSO, DURING THAT FORTY DAYS, A SERIOUS STOMACH BUG SWEPT THROUGH HIS NEIGHBORHOOD AND KILLED, LIKE, EVERYONE.

Is that why you sent him to the desert?

PARTLY.

Man, you aren't kidding about the food sanitation issues back then.

THE MORE IMPORTANT REASON I SENT HIM TO THE DESERT WAS TO CONFRONT THE DEVIL'S TEMPTATION.

Thanks for not dumping that hot tub of crap in my lap, I guess.

EHH ...

Although, I guess—wait.

Was someone at the retreat the Devil? She ran a quick test, thinking, *Is Caren the Devil?*

As usual, inconclus—

NOPE. NOT HER.

"Wait, what?"

CAREN IS NOT THE DEVIL, SO SPAKE THE LORD.

"But ... You usually open up a fissure on the other side

of the planet every time I so much as think about the devil!"

YEAH. SO THIS SHOULD BE A BIG FAT HINT

Hint? For what?

I PROMISED NOT TO DO A SPOILER ON THIS ONE, REMEMBER?

... Yes.

SO I STEERED CLEAR.

Right.

YET HERE I AM, NO LONGER WORRIED ABOUT SPOILERS.

And?

WHAT DOES THAT TELL YOU?

She didn't have a chance to piece it together before she came back into cell range and her phone exploded with notifications.

Chapter Forty-Seven

She pulled onto the narrow shoulder too quickly, her wheels kicking up rocks that attacked the undercarriage of her junky sedan, and when she tried to compensate by braking harder, the front tires locked up and she skidded on the thick dust to the side of the highway. She didn't think twice about it, though. Not after glimpsing her notifications to find forty-eight missed called, twenty-three voicemail messages, and seventy-nine texts waiting for her.

Oh yeah, something had gone horribly wrong.

They were all from the last twenty-four hours, and at least she could rule out the people who'd bombarded her as those who'd possibly died. Because someone had to have died, right? Or maybe a tornado hit Austin. Or—oh no— someone had set fire to It is Risen.

She started with the text messages, browsing the senders. Chris, Destinee, Dr. Bell, Wendy, Judith, and

Jameson. Shit, that left a lot of people who could have died in the last day or so.

Wendy would cut to the chase with whatever this was about, so Jessica started there. She had to scroll back, back, back through a long, irate monologue, searching for where it all began. As she scrolled, words and phrases like "contract," "ALL GONE," and, finally, "Dolores" gave a new shape to Jessica's fog of dread.

Wendy's correspondence grew more riddled with typos the farther down Jessica read, but she hardly noticed that.

Blood pounded deafeningly in her ears and every new detail of this catastrophe made it more difficult for her to hold onto her phone as the strength drained from her muscles.

Wendy referenced her lawyer multiple times, and by the end of the string, the tone had changed from shocked to defeated.

Jessica's eyes burned. "How could she do that?"

She didn't mean the publicist.

YOU SHOULD ALWAYS READ THE FINE PRINT.

"WELL NO SHIT!" She punched the roof of her car, pretending God could feel it, then caught up on Dr. Bell's texts. They started with: *Jessica, please call me as soon as you get this.* And ended with: *I'll keep looking for a way out of this, but I'm not sure there is one. I'm sorry I didn't voice my concerns sooner. I knew you were close and I didn't want to say anything until I had proof.*

Proof. Ha! If ever there were proof ...

Hoping for a bit of comfort, she checked Chris's next: *"Don't worry not broken. I'll be out for two weeks tho."* What the hell was he talking about?

Since it didn't relate to her world crashing down on her, she couldn't make sense of it and she moved on.

Jameson's texts assured her that if she needed money, he would help and that she could stay in the condo as long as she wanted. Small comfort. At least she wasn't homeless.

The accompanying realization that the homeless were about to be without their daily gluten-free baked goods hit her, and it felt like someone had put a plastic bag over her head. No matter how hard she sucked in for air, she couldn't get enough. She wanted to cry and scream, but she couldn't fight the crushing weight force of everything crashing *in* on her.

Destinee's texts were all caps from the start and mentioned a shotgun, shovels, and a cousin of hers who'd just gotten out of prison after thirty years.

If Mrs. Thomas—oh fuck that. *Dolores.* If Dolores fucking Thomas wasn't already in hiding, she better get there quick, because Jessica wasn't going to tell her mother to put down the gun this time, and she sure as hell wouldn't resurrect the woman.

No, not *the woman.* The Devil.

The transition was too sudden, and thinking of her mentor in this new role drove a sharp blade of excruciating sadness between her ribs. She grabbed at her side, feeling like she might vomit up the morning's smoothie.

There was too much to rectify, too many records to go back through and reevaluate. The interior of the car spun around her. "How?" she squeaked.

HOW WHAT?

"How did I not see it this whole time?"

YOU WEREN'T LOOKING. IT'S BEEN RATHER OBVIOUS FOR A WHILE.

"I thought I was supposed to fight the Devil! To confront her and see if I could defeat evil! I thought that was how it was supposed to go!"

LET ME GET THIS STRAIGHT. YOU THOUGHT THE DEVIL WOULD GIVE YOU A FAIR FIGHT?

"Oh, fuck off!"

The last unread message was from Judith: *So ... I guess I should find another job?*

The added guilt that her stupidity had just put Judith, as well as her mother and NAO sisters, out of a job, pushed her over the edge into a blind rage. The edges of her vision went fuzzy, and the pulse of blood in her ears roared.

She twisted around and threw the phone against the back seat as hard as she could, hoping it would break—she really needed to break something—while also really hoping it wouldn't break. It didn't. It skipped off the seat, hit the back rest, and then ricocheted into her nose before she could blink. Her hands flew up to her face. "Motherfucker!" She felt the rush of warmth immediately and pulled her hands back to reveal fresh blood on her palms. "You did that!" she yelled at the ceiling, more concerned with having a clear direction to aim her vitriol than the fact that God was not, in fact, in the sky.

JUST TRYING TO KNOCK SOME SENSE INTO YOU.

"Couldn't you have done that years ago? Maybe have a meteor crash into that goddamn taco shop to keep me from ever signing that contract?"

I TRIED.

"What do you mean *you tried*?" As the blood from her nose ran in front of her mouth, the last word sent it spattering across the steering wheel.

I TRIED TO STOP YOU FROM SIGNING.

"Like hell you did!"

I LITERALLY SENT JESUS TO KEEP YOU FROM SIGNING IT. YOU KNOW HOW MANY PEOPLE WOULD KILL FOR JESUS TO SHOW UP AND STOP THEM FROM MAKING THE BIGGEST MISTAKE OF THEIR LIFE?

Oh crap. She remembered that now. She hadn't known he was Jesus at the time. She thought he was just a creeper.

"Did he know she was the Devil?"

HEAVENS NO. HE WOULD NOT HAVE KEPT IT A SECRET SO YOU COULD BATTLE THIS YOURSELF.

"And if he'd told me, I wouldn't have believed him anyway," she said miserably. She put her head on the steering wheel. "I wouldn't have believed anyone. I'm so stupid. So incredibly stupid."

Bits and pieces of her entire life began surfacing in confusing vignettes, as all the nice things Dolores had ever done for her came into question again. But of them all, one that was already fresh rose to the top.

"She called him an idiot."

God knew who she meant. *HE WAS. HE HAD ONE JOB: TO SCAR YOU, TO TRAUMATIZE THE DAUGHTER OF GOD AT SUCH A TENDER AGE THAT IT WOULD ALTER THE COURSE OF YOUR LIFE AND PUT YOU OFF TRACK. HE WANTED TO TAKE SOMETHING FROM YOU IT WOULD TAKE YEARS FOR YOU TO FIND AGAIN, IF YOU EVER DID.*

But instead, you pushed him into the lion pit.

AND LOVED EVERY SECOND OF IT! WOO!

How many more moments like that are there?

HUNDREDS.

So, He'd been helping her more than she'd thought. She wanted to stay mad at Him, but her nose began throbbing, and she suspected He wasn't actually enjoying this. So she leaned across the car, pulled out a stack of fast-food napkins from the glove box (she'd known she was keeping them around for *some* reason), and began dabbing up whatever blood she could find around the cab. She tore the last one in half and shoved one piece up her nostril, using the other to wipe what she could from her hands.

Her It is Risen shirt was ruined, the light blue now a dark, muddy purple down the front.

The truth began to settle in, and she was grateful she

was out here when it did. She needed space to feel so ashamed, so devastated, so angry.

The bakery was gone. Dolores now legally owned it.

Jessica thought about pulling it up on her phone and looking over it for the first time, but what was the point? Smarter women than she had already done it and come to the same conclusion: Jessica had fallen too far behind on payments and had automatically defaulted on the loan. And now it all belonged to Dolores, a consequence Jessica would have known in advance if she'd read the fine print of the contract. Or read the contract at all. Instead, she'd let that bitch summarize it for her.

But she said it was okay. I asked her and—

Of course. She'd asked her over the phone. So much of their negotiations had been in person or over the phone, none written down.

In the quiet of her car, the scene came easily to mind: the two of them at the table, Dolores serenely jotting down the contract, Jesus leering at her disconcertingly. Never in a million years would Jessica have guessed that someone could put so much evil fine print down on paper so quickly and with such airtight legal jargon. How had Dolores done it off the top of her head like that?

Oh right. She was the Devil. She probably had a lot of evil clauses and addendums memorized. Including the one Wendy was most concerned about involving the ownership of Jessica's personal brand. What did that even mean? She was sure it wasn't good.

After an unknowable amount of time where her brain

spiraled down, down, down through her fond memories with Satan, Jessica could take no more. Not right now. She sighed. "I'd better text some people."

She started with Destinee: *Just found out. Please don't shoot Dolores yet. Just stay away from her. She's the devil.*

Then, figuring clarification might be necessary: *The literal devil. Satan. I'll explain later.*

A text came in right away, but it wasn't from her mother.

Quentin Jones: Everything okay? I just had this feeling that something might be wrong.

She'd text him back once the bulk of the shitstorm had dissipated.

A message to Wendy was next: *Just saw your texts and calls. I'm so sorry. I'm on my way back. If you can come to Austin tomorrow, we can meet and figure it out.*

Another buzz.

Kate O'Henry: Hey girl. You okay? Hope the retreat went well. Call me if you need anything. The Texas Tech NAOs are looking forward to this Saturday!

Shit. She'd have to cancel the visit to Lubbock. No way she could speak to a bunch of bright-eyed girls about anything right now, let alone answer all their sexual consent logic puzzles.

Dr. Bell probably required a call—after all, these were

some of the first texts Jessica had ever received from her, and it seemed weird imagining the professor texting. But calling right now was out of the question. She didn't have the faintest idea of how to fix any of this and was pretty sure it couldn't be fixed. But she needed to press pause on the frenzy for the next seven hours while she made it back to Austin, so the call would have to wait. In the meantime, a text would have to suffice: *I'm so sorry. I guess you sent the contract to Wendy, too. Thanks. I'm on the road, and I'll call you when I get a chance. I'm a fucking idiot.*

Another text notification popped up, and curiosity caused her to open it more than anything.

Jeremy Archer: Dad just told me. Chin up. Believe me, the Devil is the biggest meanie there is. You'll get her in the end. I believe in you, sis.

Jesus really needed to get his own cell phone.

Chris, Jameson, and Judith could wait a few hours before they got a response. She needed to get back on the road. Her organs were getting antsy, like they might take off at a sprint and test the cohesion of her skin and bones.

She ignored the steady stream of texts as she crossed New Mexico and finally returned to Texas.

Being on home turf wasn't close to the comfort she'd hoped it would be. But maybe nothing could comfort her right now. And why should she allow it? Her stupidity had blinded her to the obvious, and while she was so caught up being angry at men for all they'd done to her, a woman had gone and outshined them all with her devious long game.

Not a woman. Satan. Does that even matter?

She didn't know it was possible to operate a motor vehicle while being so deeply miserable. She drove in silence, sinking into the sound of the road under the tires and the occasional vibration of her phone on the passenger's seat. What if she just drove off the road? It would save everyone she cared about the trouble of trying to help her when she was clearly a lost cause. She could just take her hands off the steering wheel, close her eyes, and let her misaligned tires take it from there ...

IF YOU HOLD ANY EXPECTATIONS THAT I WILL TAKE THE WHEEL, THAT'S NOT REALLY MY THING.

Don't worry. I'm not relying on you to step in. Seems like you passed the buck along to Original Mistake a while ago.

I RESENT THAT.

What, you want credit for this clusterfuck?

She wasn't being entirely fair to Him, especially now that she knew about all His minor interventions when Dolores was trying to send more demons after her to screw her up. But still. He could have done something about this, about the big one.*NO, I'M GOOD. OH, AND WHAT'S ABOUT TO HAPPEN ... UH, YOU SHOULD KNOW THAT WILL ALSO NOT BE MY DOING.*

What will not be your doing?

The car lurched and a frantic tapping echoed from the

hood. Jessica cursed and glanced at her dashboard for a hint. The oil light came on.

A metallic *thunk* turned the tapping into a deep grinding. The check engine light came on a moment before the accelerator stopped working. "No! Noooo!" She screamed, searching around for her emergency flashers. "What's happening?!"

THE LORD IS NOT A MECHANIC, BUT I WOULD GUESS BEING FIFTEEN THOUSAND MILES OVERDUE FOR YOUR OIL CHANGE IS A FACTOR.

She'd been busy. Sure, she had never taken the car to get the oil changed since she'd bought it used, but she'd figured the "every five thousand miles" thing was just a ploy to make more money off of oil changes.

She managed to pull across I-10 onto the shoulder. The only small mercy, as her AC shut off, was that it was November and not August. She likely would have died from exposure if it were August.

Stay calm. You have roadside assistance. You can handle this. It took her ten minutes to find the number for roadside assistance through an unsteady 4G network, but she finally did, felt grown-up as hell for having done it, and made the call.

"Hello, roadside assistance. If this is an emerg—"

Silence.

She yanked the phone away from her ear and stared down at the screen.

Of course. She hadn't charged her phone all weekend,

and she must have been in and out of range on her drive back. With the screen lighting up every time a new text came in, it made sense why the battery was dead.

But wait!

She held her hands over the phone and closed her eyes, summoning her power forth.

DOESN'T WORK FOR BATTERIES.

"Shit!"

She leaned her head back against the headrest. "I'm going to die out here." And part of her thought, *Good.*

Chapter Forty-Eight

Jessica passed a miserable hour in the front seat, her windows rolled down to allow for circulation, before the crunch of tires on loose gravel nearby caught her attention. She glanced in the rearview mirror and spotted the black-and-white cruiser.

The trooper took his time exiting his vehicle and approaching hers on the passenger's side window. She saw the weaponry on his belt before he leaned down, peeking through the window. "Afternoon, Ms. McCloud."

Hearing her name stunned her, then she remembered the car was registered to her, and he'd probably looked it up before approaching. "Afternoon, sir."

"Problem with the car?" He removed his sunglasses and only then did she realize how young he was. Possibly only a few years her senior. His chocolate eyes made a quick sweep on the interior.

"Yeah, the engine. I probably need a tow, but my cell battery died."

"That's unfortunate. Where you headed?"

"Austin."

He whistled. "That's quite a tow."

She nodded, already having considered the substantial cost and inconvenience this would lead to, and accepting that she would now have to borrow the money from someone else to pay for it, since her already meager earnings were cut off.

"Tell you what. I know a place about forty miles east along the highway that can take good care of your girl. Would you like me to call a tow for you?"

A clamp in her chest loosened at the small kindness. "Yes. That would be amazing."

"And I reckon you need a ride back to Austin, huh?"

"Yeah. I'm sure I can call someone and they'll come get me."

He cleared his throat. "You're aware I'm a state trooper, right?"

Oh shit. Had she just suggested something illegal? "Yes, sir."

"Meaning, my jurisdiction extends throughout the state."

She nodded, waiting for him to spell out the charge.

"I'm happy to give you a ride back to Austin, is what I'm saying."

She blinked. The generosity amid such catastrophe should have been a beacon of hope for her, but she knew better. "That's a lot of trouble to go to for me. It's probably five and a half hours each way."

"Sure, if you're going the speed limit. But I figure we'll be going quite a bit over, and I just started my shift, so I can be back before it ends."

Her mental energy depleted, she didn't have anything left for this game. "What's the catch?"

"No catch, ma'am. You're stranded on the side of the road, and it's my job to keep folks safe on this great state's highways. Also, you're God's daughter, and I'm an angel. If I don't follow this little voice inside telling me to help you, I think I might start, I don't know, vomiting? I don't really want to test it out."

"Oh." The last bit seemed highly unprofessional, but she decided to overlook it. "How do I know you're a good angel?" she asked. "Forgive me, Officer..."

"Trooper."

"Trooper ...?"

"Michaels."

"Trooper Michaels."

"You can call me Gabriel."

"Gabriel Michaels?" Oh, for shit's sake. She felt silly finishing the question now, but went ahead with it, "The reason I'm here, stranded on the side of the road with my phone dead, is because a not-good angel screwed me. Not literally. Figuratively. So just because you're an angel doesn't mean I can trust you."

He squinted at her. "An angel screwed you over? That doesn't make sense. There's only one angel I can think of who would leave you in this kind of situation, and he's—"

"She's. She is the Devil. I'm aware ... now."

"Why don't you ask your Father, then? He'll vouch for me."

"I would, but he rarely helps me out like that. For some reason he thinks it's best if—"

FOR GLORY'S SAKE, TAKE THE BLESSED RIDE, YOU HOLY IDIOT.

She snapped her mouth shut. If she didn't know any better, she might think God had actually intervened by sending this guy.

She grabbed her bag off the seat next to her. "Okay, Gabriel, we're good to go."

Riding in the front seat of Trooper Michaels' Crown Victoria was so far outside of how she could have imagined her drive back to Austin that it was almost enough to make her never bother imagining anything ever again. What was the point when she could end up being so far off? Waste of energy, really.

Gabriel had the right kind of charger for her phone plugged into his dashboard computer, and he was more than happy to let her use it. As the notifications began flooding in again, she turned her phone to silent.

"You feel much like talking?" asked Gabriel as they whizzed down the highway.

"Not much to talk about. I just spent the last five days at a women's leadership retreat only to find out everything I've worked for has been stolen from me by the Devil."

Gabriel was silent for a minute, then he said, "To be clear, you said there *wasn't* much to talk about?"

A voice came through the radio, speaking in code Jessica didn't understand, and Gabriel reached forward and turned the volume nearly all the way down.

"I did. But maybe what I meant was that there was too much to talk about."

He nodded. "Yeah, I understand that. I used to be El Paso PD. Too much to talk about in that job, so I switched to this one. Much less to talk about."

She thought about Officer McBride, and a long-forming question surfaced. "Do you work with a lot of angels?"

He nodded. "Oh yeah. Law enforcement is full of them. But it also has plenty of plain humans who want to do good. And I've encountered the occasional demon in the department."

She jerked her head around. "What? You work with demons?"

"Not if I can help it. But usually I don't have control over the fact. They find ways to work under humans who wouldn't believe they were demons, even if I or other angels pointed it out. If we're lucky, there's an angel higher up who finds a reason to fire the bad ones, but that's not always possible." He sighed. "Just part of power, I guess. People come to this line of work for all kinds of reasons. Mostly, they're good ones."

"When did you realize you were an angel?"

"When I figured out I wasn't gay," he said. "I think I was eighteen."

"Don't fully understand that, if I'm being honest."

"I grew up in a small border town. Very religious. There was this boy, Jamie, who had this glow around him all the time. No one else saw it, but I did. I figured that meant I was in love with him—I didn't know much about gays at the time. And then I found out that he saw the glow around me. We didn't know it was just run-of-the-mill angel auras, so we thought we were destined to be together. Then we tried it and … nah. Pass. Just not for me. I read online a few months later that seeing auras was an angelic ability. Followed that rabbit hole all the way down. There's even a subreddit for that now."

"There *are* gay angels, you know."

He nodded quickly. "Oh, I know. Like I said, the subreddit. There are all *kinds* of angels according to that."

"And only one is evil?"

He snuck a glance at her, but she couldn't make out his eyes through his large sunglasses. "Yeah. You want to tell me about her? Promise I won't put it online."

"You can if you want. I don't care anymore." And then Jessica, figuring they had a bit of time still, launched into the story of her long-time relationship with Dolores Thomas, pausing every so often to interject an "Oh shit," or "that makes more sense now," or "I'm such an idiot."

They stopped only once on their way back to the capital city, and that was to get Jessica a double bacon cheeseburger, fries, and an ice cream cone.

* * *

Trooper Michaels' business card remained clutched in Jessica's hand as she watched his cruiser's taillights disappear around a corner three blocks down. She didn't want to turn around yet. She'd glimpsed the storefront from the passenger's seat and had cast her eyes away when she felt the dagger of regret pierce her left lung.

Tucking his card into her pants pocket, she clenched her teeth and forced herself to face the bakery, the front lit only by a nearby streetlamp. The lights were off inside, and the sign was flipped to closed. Even though she'd done that herself days before, it felt like an intentional detail to mock her.

Would Dolores continue to let Jessica work at the bakery?

More importantly, would Jessica be able to stand working at the bakery if it was owned by the Devil?

Not a chance in hell.

She'd get her laptop, a few other personal items she kept in the kitchen, and her stuffed giraffe, and then she would leave It is Risen behind and ... what? Start another bakery? There was no way. She had nothing to do now. She was just an unemployed messiah, and there was little more pathetic and detestable than that.

After digging her keys out of the bottom of her bag, she stuck the appropriate one into the lock.

It wouldn't even go in all the way.

"Oh, you're fucking kidding me."

But, no, this made sense. Of course, that didn't mean she wasn't livid. Changing the locks was pouring salt directly into the wound then rubbing it around, really grinding it in there. Did Dolores think Jessica would come back and set fire to the place, burn it to the ground so no one could have it? Even at her most vengeful, Jessica couldn't imagine doing that to the place she'd built.

Maybe the Devil hadn't changed the locks on the back door. It was unlikely, but worth a shot. What else did she have to do for the rest of her miserable existence?

She left her suitcase on the sidewalk and hurried around to the back. But when her key refused to do its sole job once again, and that tiny thread of hope was ripped away from her, her head began to pound. Nausea welled up in her core, a heady mixture of self-loathing, contempt, and futility. And then, wait, she felt something else. Something coming not in a small waves, but in one single tsunami of holy fury, only meters out from shore ...

The bitch had locked her out of her own business! The laptop was hers! Asha was hers! That evil bitch had taken things too far.

She wiggled her fingers to try to diffuse the swell of power building in her core as she stomped around toward the front to grab her suitcase and call her mother for a ride home. Destinee's own prolific rage was the only thing Jessica wanted around her right now. Sure, that meant eating quite a bit of crow over the coming days and months when it came to admitting Dolores was as bad as Destinee had always thought, but she knew her mother would wait until the anger wasn't so fresh before saying I told you so.

Thou shalt not smite ... thou shalt not smite ...

The dumpster was looking mighty tempting just then, and while she wasn't keen on burning the bakery to the ground, she wouldn't be opposed to covering it in exploded trash. Before she could decide that, yes, it was a go with smiting the dumpster, Jessica rounded the corner and froze in her tracks. Her suitcase was open and someone was rifling through it. No, not just someone.

First, she recognized that hat. That stupid Houston Texans hat! Her gaze flickered to the front door where a letter was taped. It hadn't been there just a moment before. "Hey!"

The man looked up, a pair of her unused underwear in his hand, and for a moment, neither moved. Her mouth fell open when she saw the weak chin, penis nose, and watery eyes that were fully dilated. "You sick fuck," she muttered, marching toward him. "You sick fucking fuck. Drop my panties, Donald!"

"You remembered my name," he moaned. "I knew you felt what I did. You just needed prodding."

She was only ten yards away now, closing in. *"Thou shalt drop my goddamn panties!"*

Still, he didn't do as she said, and, channeling her mother, she reared back, and socked him right in his punchable face. His head snapped back, and she realized two things instantly:

Punching someone hurt one's hand quite a lot.

And punching someone didn't diffuse her indignation, but only fanned the flames.

Holding his nose, he stared up at her wide eyed, but for some strange reason, it didn't look quite like fear. "Yes, my queen! Put up a fight! I lust for the struggle." His hands dropped from his nose as a trickle of blood ran down his cupid's bow. She felt no regret. This contemptible worm had tried to control her for months, and he'd been watching her at work for even longer, the whole time thinking that she somehow belonged to him, that he deserved to own her and he'd get his way whether she wanted it or not.

When his right hand went for his pants, she didn't wait to see where this freak show was headed. She couldn't have waited even if she'd wanted to. The wrath flowed through her in a flash, a wave of satisfaction crashing against her mind more so than it had for the grackle, the watermelons, the fire hydrant, the juniper tree ...

He exploded like a tomato dropped from a skyscraper, sending minute splinters of bone and the finest spray of blood and tissue in all directions.

HOLY MOTHER OF JESSICA!

Her breath caught in her chest, pinned there like it'd sprung a bear trap. The world around her was silent except for her heartbeat in her ears.

She blinked away the blood from her eyes, but her hands were too coated to rub anything away from the rest of her face. She gaped at the indentation in the sidewalk where her stalker had just stood, and the word that repeated itself over and over in her head was simply, *Whoops*.

Something gooey and with a bit of bulk to it slid from her hair down onto her shoulder.

Her stalker was gone. She had ...

Had anyone ...?

She managed to move again just to search the street for any openmouthed witnesses. She saw none, but did that matter?

She'd finally crossed a line. A big one. And all she felt was ... nothing.

Maybe it was shock, or maybe it was a case of stepping in dog shit while you were already knee deep in sewage.

Blood and guts dripped down the front windows of It is Risen, soaking the last letter her stalker would ever leave her.

A car passed by but didn't slow, and she wiped her right hand off on the back of her jeans, which had been spared the gore, and carefully pulled out her cell phone from her pocket.

She lowered herself to the cement of the sidewalk and calmly called 911.

Chapter Forty-Nine

"It's not usually my job to doubt a voluntary confession," said Officer McBride half an hour later, "but I feel like I'm missing something here."

Jessica leaned against the trunk of the police cruiser, arms folded cross her chest as she stared down the road, wondering how law enforcement became such a big part of her life.

Cars crept by, drivers alerted to something interesting by the flashing red and blue lights and rewarded when they saw a woman covered head to toe in blood and a storefront looking no less drippy.

"I smote him," Jessica explained. "It was the stalker. You can check the footage, if you can get inside. I can't because the biggest asshole in creation changed the locks. Anyway, he reached for his pants and I smote him."

"Yeaaah," said Officer McBride slowly, tapping her pen to her pad. "I think that's the part that's hanging me up.

When you say you smote him, what exactly are we talking about? A ... bomb?" She glanced over her shoulder at the scene, where homicide detectives were busy laying down evidence markers.

"Not a bomb. Smiting, like in the Bible. I can smite things. Just aim my anger at them and poof, obliterated. Like I said, it should be on the security footage. It's not pretty, though. I can tell you that."

"Right."

Jessica snuck a peek at the notepad where Officer McBride wrote the word smote in quotation marks.

"So, you're claiming you murdered someone by smiting him, is that right?"

"Yes."

McBride tucked the notepad into her breast pocket and stuck the pen beside it. "Murder is obviously a big deal. But I'm not sure exactly what to charge you with. I reckon the courts will have a hard time with it, too. Smiting could be manslaughter, or it could be first degree. You sure you want to confess to this? He was ..." she paused before mumbling, "kind of a scum bag." She quickly checked to make sure the other law enforcement on scene hadn't heard her.

"Maybe they'll let me off without the death penalty then," Jessica said.

McBride sighed. "You don't have to worry about that. To be honest, you'll probably be let off on self-defense. He was going for his pants! He could have been going for a knife or a gun."

"I think he was going for his dick," Jessica said honestly.

"Ah. But you know as well as I do *that* can be used as a weapon. It'll still be a pain in the ass to deal with the legal system, though. Could take up the next two years of your life."

Jessica picked at some dried blood on her arm. "That's fine. I don't have anything else to do."

"You being sarcastic?"

"Nope."

Jessica explained the events leading up to the murder, and McBride listened patiently.

When she was finished, the officer said, "That's some crap, right there. And now I get why you can't go inside. Stay here."

McBride spoke briefly with the homicide detectives, then disappeared around the side of the building. One of the detectives kept a casual eye on Jessica as she remained against the trunk. She tried to make it clear she wasn't going anywhere. If she was going to run, she would have done it an hour ago, *before* she called in her own crime.

The lights inside It is Risen flicked on, and McBride emerged in the cafe and unlocked the front door, pushing it open and hollering out. "Why don't we get that footage now?"

After a stop by the bathrooms to clean off her hands, Jessica logged into her laptop and pulled up the footage.

It was even grosser the second time around.

"I'll be damned," said McBride. Then she pulled her

eyes from the screen and said to Jessica, "Ms. McCloud, I don't even know if I can arrest you in good conscience."

"What?"

She gestured back toward the screen. "I'll run this by homicide, but look at it! You don't shoot him. You're three feet away from him and you just point at him then he explodes. Unless the law is going to arrest you on suspicion of superpowers, I'm pretty sure we don't have a case."

"But ... you have to. I promise you, I murdered him. I—"

"Smote him. I heard you the first dozen times." The look the officer gave her hinted that if Jessica *did* end up locked away, it would be in a facility with white, padded walls. "Tell you what. Gather up what you need from this place, and I'll grab Detective Langley. We'll see what he has to say about this."

They really weren't going to arrest her? Shit! What more did a girl have to do to be locked away for murder?

The fact that McBride had kicked the back door off its hinges was a small consolation to this complete mess. Dolores would have to pay to get it fixed now. And suddenly, the idea of wrecking the place didn't seem so unthinkable.

But first, she needed to gather her things.

Just as she grabbed Asha from the front counter, careful not to transfer blood onto the stuffed animal, McBride called her back into the kitchen. Detective Langley, a petit man with a boyish face and salt-and-pepper hair, scrunched up his nose as he leaned over the laptop. Jessica guided him through the video again. "There he is taping the letter to the door, and then he opens the suitcase. And there I am. I see him, we exchange words, and ... I punch him in the face—that should at least be assault—then he goes for his pants and I"—she let the footage roll—"smite him."

"Can you zoom in on that?" Langley asked, and Jessica was happy to comply. "Yeah, see?" he said. "You're not touching him, and there's no indication of you possessing a weapon. Besides, the only thing that could cause so much damage would be a bomb, but something of that power would have undoubtedly injured you, too, but you don't show any signs of injury. No shrapnel, and I'm pretty sure once we run this by ballistics, they're going to come up empty-handed, too." He straightened and stared up at Jessica's face. "Miss, I'm just not sure what to say. The man is dead, and even as I see it happen, I can't explain a cause. I'm afraid—"

"Uuugh, don't say it."

"I can't arrest you on murder."

"Oh come *on!*" Why was this so hard? She was a stupid idiot who'd been duped by the Devil and had lost control and killed a man. Was there no justice in this world? Her self-punishment alone didn't even come close to what she deserved.

"If you're really set on being arrested, I can take you in on assault."

She heaved a sigh. "Yes. Thank you. That'll do for now."

Langley glanced at McBride who shrugged then pulled her cuffs from her belt. "Sorry, but I gotta cuff you if you're going in the back seat. It's policy."

"Of course. One quick request? Could you disable the security system before you lead me out there? I'd rather not risk it getting out."

The detective nodded respectfully.

As McBride steered Jessica toward the broken back door, Langley gathered Jessica's small pile of things and followed.

She'd started the day in such a good place, but that walk with Caren around the property seemed like ages ago now. In the span of a single day, Jessica's life had been ruined.

Chapter Fifty

It hadn't been a difficult decision who to call from jail.

The only other time Jessica had tried to get herself arrested, following the hit-and-miracle-and-run of Mrs. Wurst during Jessica's senior year, she'd failed. She'd almost failed again, except the punch had saved her.

Destinee had been waiting for a call like this her whole life. Jessica's very first assault charge. At least among the rest of the horrifying day, she'd managed to make her mother proud.

Jessica's knuckles still ached as the jail door clanked shut behind her.

The phone conversation rang in her ears: Destinee asking Jessica to repeat herself, Jessica doing so and then finally begging Destinee not to attempt to break her out.

She belonged here. It was punishment for a life of stupidity, of allowing herself to be manipulated, of trusting the wrong person, of asking others to trust her.

Another woman occupied the jail cell, but she was pretending to be asleep, curled on her side on the bench, knees hugged to her chest. But Jessica hadn't missed it when the woman snuck a covert glance at her new roomie. And she also hadn't missed the way the woman's eyes widened when she saw the blood down Jessica's front.

The light blue T-shirt was for sure stained beyond the abilities of a good dry-clean now.

After extended conversation between Langley, McBride, and a Detective Primtree, murder charges had finally been brought against her. McBride assured her they wouldn't stick, but that didn't matter. It meant Jessica was in here for a good long while. She wouldn't find out until they presented it to a judge the next morning what her bond would be set at, but it didn't matter; she couldn't afford to pay it if it were any higher than $100, and she hoped for the sake of the justice system and public safety, that bond for murder was always set higher than triple digits.

The night stretched on, and Jessica lay on the unforgiving metal bench, staring up at the dusty ceiling tiles.

It was almost impressive how entirely she'd ruined everything. Because this *was* all her. No point blaming the Devil for being evil. That was the whole point of the Devil, wasn't it? Which meant that there was no one else to blame, no one to wallow with her disappointment and misery, besides herself. And wallow she would.

After all, Dolores hadn't killed someone. Jessica had.

She had smote another human being, taken his life because he made her a little uncomfortable.

HE WAS STALKING YOU.

So? He has the right to do that.

... NOT LEGALLY OR MORALLY SPEAKING.

Still, is it worth killing him over?

CLEARLY.

And is he ... Where is he now?

ALL OVER THE FRONT OF YOUR SHIRT.

Why did she even try with Him?

I don't mean that. I mean, what happens to someone's soul when I smite them?

YOU REALLY WANT TO KNOW?

Yes.

YOU'RE NOT GOING TO LIKE IT.

Good.

OKAY THEN, MISS MASOCHIST. WHEN SOMEONE IS SMOTE, THEIR SOUL GOES TO ... LET'S CALL IT "HEAVEN."

Hold up. Everyone I smite goes to Heaven? So, if I went around smiting awful people, I'd be rewarding them?

THE LORD HAD NOT THOUGHT ABOUT IT LIKE THAT, BUT YES.

You mean that jerk is now hanging out in the clouds stalking people who earned their way there?

HEAVEN IS NOT IN THE CLOUDS.

But you get my point.

YES. YOU ARE STILL WRONG. WHEN YOU SMITE, YOU CLEANSE THE SOUL OF ITS EVIL IMPULSES, SO IT NEEDS NO FURTHER PUNISHMENT. ALSO, THERE IS NO HANGING OUT IN HEAVEN BECAUSE SOULS HAVE NO PHYSICAL FORM. THEY'RE ALL SPREAD OUT AND MIXED TOGETHER.

She shook her head and stuck the butt of her hands into her eye sockets. *Stop there, please. I don't want to know any of the secrets of the universe right now.*

Perhaps because He felt sorry for her, He did as she requested, and she was left to spiral down into darker funnels of thought.

After silent hours, though, the self-flagellation grew a little dull, and as heated emotions thinned, her mind was able to pierce the fog and grasp at a few inconsistencies that had been politely tapping her on the shoulder since the moment it finally made it through her thick skull who Dolores Thomas really was.

What about all the times Dolores had helped her? She'd saved her from bullies, given her special treatment, and even sparing her the trauma of watching Randy get torn to shreds seemed very un-Devil-like.

Why would she do that?

I UNDERSTAND WHY YOU WOULD WANT THE DEVIL TO BE OBVIOUS IN HER EVIL DEEDS. BUT THAT WOULDN'T HAVE MADE HER EFFECTIVE, WOULD IT?

Can the Devil do good? Is that even possible?

DOING GOOD AND BEING GOOD ARE DIFFERENT THINGS. ANYONE CAN DO GOOD FOR THE SAKE OF EVIL, JUST AS ANYONE CAN DO EVIL FOR THE SAKE OF GOOD.

Which one is better?

INTERESTING QUESTION. BUT BEFORE WE GET INTO IT, THE LORD HAS A QUESTION FOR YOU: YOU STILL HAVE THAT GET-OUT-OF-JAIL-FREE CARD, CORRECT?

What?

The lock on the cell clanked and Jessica bolted up straight, surprised she hadn't heard the guard approaching. The door opened and he waved her toward him wordlessly. When he didn't place handcuffs on her, she knew something was up. "Where are you taking me? Oh, hell. Don't tell me they dropped the charges."

"Nope. But your bond was posted a few hours ago and someone paid your bail."

"What? Who?"

He shrugged, of course. What did he care who did it?

"Do you know what it was set at?"

He shrugged again. "Someone's here to take you home."

They passed through a door and Jessica spotted her mother waiting at the other side of the intake desk. When Destinee's mouth fell open, reminding Jess that she was still covered in dried blood. "Holy hell, baby!" An officer stopped her mother before she could pass the desk, and she only swatted him a few times before behaving herself.

Once Jessica had collected her things, handing Asha to her mother to make sure the giraffe didn't end up with too much of her stalker's DNA, the two McCloud women left the jail, stepping to into the bright outdoors. "I woulda brought you a new shirt and pants if I'da known."

Jessica squinted against the sunlight. "What time is it?"

"Nearly ten in the morning. You hungry?"

"Not exactly."

"Right. Let's get ya cleaned up, and I'll fix some pancakes."

As they arrived at Destinee's relatively new Nissan in the parking lot. Jessica asked, "Did you pay my bail?"

"Nope."

"Any idea who did?"

"Not a clue. Just got a message from McBride saying someone had and you might need a lift."

"A message?"

Destinee unlocked the car door. "Yeah. On Facebook." She slipped into the driver's seat and Jessica hurried in on her side.

"You're Facebook friends with Officer McBride?"

"Well, sure. It's hard as hell to make new friends when you're my age. Gotta take 'em where you can."

Destinee started the car and Jessica said, "Mom, I'm sorry I didn't know—"

"Not yet, baby. We ain't even left the property. Let's get the guts off you and get you a proper shower, some carbs, and a bit of sleep, then you can needlessly apologize to me for trusting someone who's been grooming you since you were a child and had everyone else fooled as well." She snuck a sideways glance at her daughter before reaching over to grab a pinch of Jessica's stomach. "Damn, baby. I thought it was a leadership retreat, not fat camp. You're gonna need a lot of goddamn pancakes."

Chapter Fifty-One

Jessica's ears rang as she laid on the couch of her condo, staring up at the ceiling and wishing half-heartedly she were back on the stainless steel bench in the jail. At least there she was safe from the text messages. At least there she felt like she was serving out a penance. Here, though, in the temperature-controlled room surrounded by luxury she hadn't paid for, she felt layer upon layer of guilt settle in her stomach.

She thought about going to bed, but she didn't deserve the comfort of that memory foam. And retreating into her bedroom seemed somehow final, while lying on the couch felt like a temporary break. Granted, it was one she didn't deserve ...

How did she feel like she had so much to do and yet had nothing to do?

You knew this was coming. You've known since you were eight. And you just pretended it was no big deal, like if you ignored it long enough it wouldn't happen, and now here you are.

Of course you couldn't run the business well—look at everything else about your life! You fail at everything you try.

You're just another college dropout. Stop pretending it was to start the bakery. You just didn't want to go to class anymore, so you found an excuse. And then you got everyone you know to give you money so you could keep pretending.

You deserve this. You took her money. You deserve every second of this.

She left her phone on vibrate so she knew damn well every time someone had something to say to her about the events of the last few days.

Wendy and Dr. Bell thought she was an idiot. Cash had sent her the most passive-aggressive text thanking her for putting them out of a job.

And that was just the people who'd come forward to explain what an asshole she was.

The others had been kinder in stating how her major failure had screwed them over.

Maddy, Tamara, and Jade, who she'd only just hired, were all out of a job.

Jesus would have to do without the food for the homeless, and that would quickly make the local population restless.

Jameson would undoubtedly need to distance himself from her, now that she was penniless and a murderer. He'd been kind enough not to mention it to her, though. Not yet, at least. Maybe he was giving her a day, or maybe the news hadn't reached him yet, but she doubted that, considering they shared a publicist.

Judith was out of a job, too, but outside of the text she had sent over the weekend, Jessica hadn't heard from her.

Then there was the next generation of NAOs, who were suddenly supporting a killer, and everyone who had helped her open the bakery only to see their time and money be thrown away because she hadn't demanded to see a copy of a freaking contract.

And in a way, she felt she'd let down God, though obviously that didn't matter so much.

She turned on the TV to drown out the buzzing in her head, and the station it was set to was covering none other than the ongoing scandal of Jimmy Dean. How did he get to make so many mistakes, do so many insane and harmful things and still find himself raking in the dough from White Light? And to top it off, he was now an elected official. It wasn't fair. One tiny mistake of signing a legally binding deal with the devil, and everything she'd ever worked for came crumbling down in a weekend. He'd started a cult, published a memoir full of lies, and who knew what other shady dealings, and he was just fine, smiling at the cameras even as the ticker below flashed phrases like, "Reverend Ruined" and "Possible Indictment Ahead?" And all of his glory built at her expense, built off the back of her birth and expanded around her gospel as told by Jimmy.

Then a strange idea hit her. If she'd ruined her own reputation, which was pretty obvious, she'd also made herself useless to Jimmy Dean. No doubt he would try to spin it in his favor, but as long as she remained down, he couldn't even get solid "Antichrist" mileage out of her. She was a nothing. No longer was she an ambitious business owner. If she stepped back, disappeared from the public eye, she'd be taking away Jimmy's biggest weapon: her.

IF THE LORD IS NOT MISTAKEN, YOU HAVE TRIED THAT BEFORE.

But not like this.

PRETTY MUCH LIKE THIS.

You're saying it won't work?

YES.

Then how do I keep Jimmy from using me?

YOU STOP LETTING HIM.

A knock on the door made her jump, and she steadied herself, feeling lightheaded as she stood, before going to answer it.

But she wasn't a complete idiot, and she looked through the peephole first.

She pulled opened the door. "Jameson. Aren't you supposed to be in Vancouver?"

"I had a couple days off and knew I had to come see you. I heard what happened. I can't even imagine."

His sympathy drained her. "Thanks. For coming to check on me, I mean."

He shook his head vaguely, staring at her like she was a puzzle. And then he leaned over in a rush and kissed her, wrapping his arms around her waist and pinning hers to her sides. When he let her go and stepped back, they stared at each other a moment. Jessica was the first to cringe, and Jameson piped up with, "Yeah, that didn't feel right at all."

"No. I'm too sad."

"I don't know why I thought this should be romantic."

"What movie are you shooting?"

"I'm starring in *Passion's Last Goodbye*. Why do you— Oh. Yeah, that's probably it."

"Come on in." She stepped to the side and he settled himself on the couch, turning his attention briefly to the news coverage, which had moved on to something far juicer.

Or at least bloodier. When Jessica saw the still image of her being led into the station with blood covering her front, she couldn't even muster the energy to be upset. She turned off the TV and pretended she hadn't noticed the horror on Jameson's face.

"What can I do to help?" he asked, tossing his baseball cap onto the coffee table.

"Nothing." She sat on the opposite end of the couch and pulled her knees to her chin, facing him. "Well, you can break up with me so your career doesn't go down the crapper, but more importantly, so Wendy doesn't go into early retirement."

"We don't have to break up," he said. "I'm not worried about my reputation."

"Don't be dense. You should be. Your career *is* your

reputation. Listen, if you want, we can go with the story that we broke up before I went to the retreat and this was all a downward spiral caused by my deep sense of loss."

He grimaced. "That's really good."

"Don't be ashamed. It's all yours if you want it."

But he continued to grimace, perhaps from the suggestion, but maybe also from the bloody shirt balled up on the expensive living room rug. "Is there anything else I can do? Hanging you out to dry doesn't exactly feel like helping."

"I think you've done enough, Jameson."

He frowned. "What do you mean? The condo?"

It wasn't hard to figure out who had financed her release. It had to be the same one who'd offered to help her out financially time and time again.

"No. Or yes, that, too. But I mean the bail money." Destinee had informed her that her bond was set at $100,000, which meant whoever had paid bail had shelled out a solid ten grand and was seriously hoping she didn't skip town. Perhaps that was why he'd come by, to make sure she wasn't a flight risk.

But one of his eyebrows levitated up his miraculously wrinkle-free forehead as he torqued his head to the side. "I didn't pay that, though. Don't get me wrong, I offered to as soon as I heard, but someone beat me to it."

She was confused for only a second before the truth hit her. She shut her eyes against the horror and put her head in her hands. "Oh no. I think I know exactly who did it."

"You do?"

She raised her head just enough to look up at him. "The Devil."

"The ... Devil?"

"Yes. Dolores Thomas is Satan. And I bet she paid my bail so I was even more in debt to her."

He held up a hand. "Back up. Your former teacher Mrs. Thomas? The one who helped you start your business and got you out of trouble a half-dozen more times —she's the Devil?"

"Yep." She considered mentioning another conclusion she'd come to in the state trooper's car that involved a bullet and his face, but there was no need to go into that right now.

"I don't think you're in debt to someone if you didn't ask for help and they helped you anyway."

"That's because you're not Lucifer. And let me be clear how happy I am that you're not."

"Did you think I was?"

"I might've considered it a few times."

"Fair enough.

"You want a drink?" She nodded to the fridge.

But he stood. "No, I'd better get going, actually. I have a flight out first thing tomorrow. I just wanted to make sure you're okay. Or, not *okay* because that would be weird, considering, but not, like ..."

"Suicidal. I'm not. And even if I were, I'm pretty sure the Alpha O-meddler wouldn't let it happen."

"I guess that's good."

She considered it. "No, it's really not." Then she found

herself laughing, and Jameson, appearing less sure of himself than she'd ever seen him, chuckled along.

When she opened the door for him, he paused, and both stepped toward each other at the same time. He hugged her close to his chest and whispered, "We'll talk about a break-up scenario later, okay? We don't have to do anything yet, and Wendy will want to have her say."

She nodded, her ear and jaw rubbing against the soft fabric of his expensive T-shirt.

"Good luck on the rest of the shoot," she said as she waved goodbye and forced a smile. It wasn't the most difficult smile she'd ever forced, so there was that.

But as soon as she closed the door and the isolation of the condo set in, the crushing pressure returned, and she was back at the bottom of the ocean.

She went straight for the fridge and grabbed a beer, reconsidered it, then grabbed another. She would definitely need more than one, and the less she had to get off the couch, the better. It was just efficient.

Her eyes jumped to the baseball cap on the coffee table a moment before there was a knock on the door. She grabbed the cap and went to hand it back to Jameson.

In her haze of depression, she neglected to check who it was before she turned the knob and swung open the door. She nearly dropped the cap when she saw him. It wasn't Jameson.

Chapter Fifty-Two

Christopher Riley had a crutch under his right arm and soft brace around his right knee. "This is a bad time, isn't it?"

"No. I mean, in general, yes, this is a bad time. Maybe the worst time. But it's not a bad time for you to show up." In fact, it might have been the best time. "Come on inside."

She ogled his injury as he passed on his way to the couch, where he promptly took a load off. "You expecting someone else?" He nodded at the two beers.

"No. Just been that kind of day. That kind of life."

He popped the cap off the unopened bottle and groaned as he leaned back. "Just passed Jameson on the way up. He said it was fine if I saw you one-on-one. For a movie star, he's really not that bad." Took the first sip and studied the bottle appraisingly before looking up at her quickly and adding, "If I'm interrupting anything—"

"Not even a little. But why did you need Jameson to ...

Oh." She sighed and grabbed the beer, resuming her position on the couch. "Chris, we're not really dating."

"I mean, you can date whoever you want," he said quickly, tipping his beer way back.

"Why? Are you dating someone?" She tried to sound disinterested, but it just wasn't happening tonight. Her well of bullshit was dry.

"Not anymore. But let's not talk about that. I heard what happened, what you found out ..." His mouth remained open for more words, but none came as he shook his head.

She couldn't meet his eyes. "I'm sorry."

"Huh? For what?"

"For not believing you about her."

"Stop. I'm not here to tell you I told you so, even though, well, you know." He took a swig from the bottle. "Goddamn this is good. I haven't had a real beer in months. You get a little money and everyone expects you to drink craft beer. I can't tell you how many shit beers I've had to endure."

"I'm sorry for your loss," she said sardonically.

His head shot up and he said, "Oh god, I'm sorry. I'm such a—" before he caught her eye and she snickered.

He shut his mouth and glared playfully at her, and for a moment, behind the mask of a man, she could see little Christopher Riley. "I'm glad you came over," she said.

Nodding, he threw an arm across the back of the couch, his hand open. She took it.

Then Chris nodded at the TV. "Why don't you turn that crap off?"

She took his suggestion, and as she threw the remote back onto the coffee table, she said, "Was it you?"

And without asking what, he said, "Yeah. Rex called me after he heard about it."

"I can pay you back."

Chris chuckled. "No, you can't."

She shut her eyes. "You're right. I can't."

"Just don't run off anywhere."

"No plans to."

"If that changes, know that I'll track you down. I'm a Philadelphian now. I don't fuck around."

"Psh. Please. You'll never not be a Texan."

His squeezed her hand as he leaned forward, eyes wide. "They're so weird up there, Jess. They never smile at strangers and some of the things they eat ... They don't even have proper queso."

"Shut up."

"I'm serious. Don't take this too hard, but half the reason I flew down here today was so I could get some queso that wasn't just Velveeta and Rotel."

She let go of his hand as he leaned back against the armrest again. "I'm glad it was you who paid my bail."

"You are?"

"Yeah. I was worried it was Mrs. Thomas."

He adjusted to extend his injured leg across the couch. "Why would she help you out *now*?"

"Why has she ever helped me out?"

He fell silent, looking for an answer and frowning when he found none. "Yeah, that doesn't make sense. Have you tried to talk to her about it? Asked her what the fuck?"

"No!" she spat before pulling back. "No. Not that I haven't thought about it. Hell, I've spent most nights in bed fantasizing about tearing her a new one. But what would I even say if I had her on the phone? I feel like I would just start shouting at her and never stop, and what's the point in that? She's the Devil! It wouldn't change anything, and it's probably best if I keep my distance from her anyway." She sipped her beer, and when Chris remained silent, she added, "Even worse, I don't know if I *could* yell at her over the phone because she's Mrs. Thomas."

"Phew," he said, shaking his head. "That's ... Yeah, I don't envy you. For what it's worth, you're handling it way better than I would."

She laughed morosely. "Bullshit. It's impossible to handle it worse than I am. I'm broke, out of a job, letting down everyone I—"

"Yeah, yeah," Chris said, mercifully cutting her off. "I get the picture. Look, you got screwed by the Devil and you could use some help. Will you let me help you out?"

She hugged her knees closer to her, burying her toes under the middle seat cushion. "I don't know if I can now."

"I'm not going to do what she did."

"How do I know that, though?" She winced, feeling a new layer of guilt for suspecting him, but unable to keep from suspecting him.

"It's a fair point," he conceded. "I'm not sure how to

527

convince you. But I will say that I'm not the Devil, so at least you know that. And I'm not a demon—I'm pretty sure angels can't be. But I guess the most compelling argument is this." He tipped the lip of his bottle at his wrapped knee.

"Your knee? What does that have to do with anything?"

"I get injured the same week your world goes to shit? Suddenly I have a little free time away from training to come check on you?" He raised his eyebrows as though expecting her to follow along. When she wasn't, he added, "If this doesn't have His name written all over it, I don't know what does."

She jerked her head back. "You think God gave you an injury so you would come bail me out of jail?"

"Yeah," he said firmly. "That's what I think. If you don't believe me, just ask Him."

ANGEL BOY IS GETTING SMARTER.

Regardless of the fact that Chris was right on the money, she was reluctant to confirm it—she couldn't imagine he'd be big on the idea of her Father bestowing upon him a career-threatening injury just so he could be available for when she finally had to play her get-out-of-jail-free card. "He says it was Original Mistake, not him."

LIAR.

"Liar," repeated Chris without knowing it. "But I appreciate the idea all the same."

He understood.

He almost always did.

After a comfortable pause, he asked, "I'm not gonna

sugarcoat it for you, Jess. Your life is shit right now. And it's probably not going to get any better if you go to trial for murder. You got a raw deal here, and it's not fair. And don't hit me for saying this—yeah, your mom told me you decked the guy before you smote him, which we'll circle back to later because it's super hot—but you're going to have one hell of a time digging yourself out of this without a whole lot of help. You're out of money, no one's going to hire you, and you look like you've lost twenty pounds since I last saw you, but I know exercise isn't your thing, so I can only assume you can't afford to feed yourself."

She nodded somberly and mumbled, "I accidentally went to fat camp."

"So, what do you say? Will you let me help you out, no strings attached?"

She groaned and leaned back to stare up at the ceiling. "It's been a long couple of days. I'll have to think about it. I just— My mind is so screwed up about money and trust and ... I don't know, it seems kind of weird to let some man provide for me like that. But then again, I let a woman take care of me, and here I am, out of a job and so much more."

"First of all, I'm not just some man. I'm me. I'm Chris. I hope that matters."

She propped herself up again to address him. "It does. Like I said, I'll think about it." They finished the rest of their drinks in silence, and when Chris tipped back the last of his, he set it on the table and said, "I really thought it would be Jimmy."

"You did?"

"Yeah. He just does so many bad things."

"That's a little obvious, don't you think?"

"I suppose so. If it makes you feel any better, for as little as I always cared for Mrs. Thomas, I wouldn't have guessed who she was, either. Bitch sure is subtle."

And all the more dangerous for it.

"What are you going to do now?" he asked. "Any ideas?"

She had a few, but nothing concrete. "Probably get drunk and go to bed."

He grabbed his crutch and pushed onto his feet. "I'll get out of your hair, then."

"You don't have to."

"No, no. I already have a hotel room booked downtown. I just wanted to swing by and make sure you're okay and not—"

"Suicidal." Same as Jameson, then. Great, had she found a new way to be a burden to everyone? Was someone going to schedule shifts for people to visit to make sure she didn't kill herself?

But Chris blew off that notion with a flick of his hand. "Psh. No. God would never let you kill yourself. I wanted to make sure you weren't watching the news. And I accomplished that, so I'd better get going."

The idea of him leaving stirred an animalistic fear inside her. "I have more beer. You're welcome to it."

He cringed and scratched his head. "Nah, I'd better not."

She swallowed down her impulse to turn from trickery

to begging and kept her mouth shut as she walked him over to the front door.

Just as he crossed the threshold, he paused and turned toward her. Did they hug here? She wasn't sure.

He said. "If you're set on watching something, I heard there's a good special on channel thirty-six tonight. Should be on now, actually."

He hobbled off on his crutch without a hug goodbye, and when she turned the TV to channel thirty-six and she saw the giraffe with her young, wobbly calf grazing from a tall tree, the tears finally crashed in on her.

Chapter Fifty-Three

"That is some bullshit," Quentin said, catching her under-thrown pass. All her passes were under thrown tonight. It was one of the lesser talked about side effects of depression, as it turned out.

"Which part?" she asked, waiting for his pass and hoping it hit her right in the nose. It didn't. It was a beautiful spiral directly to her chest, and putting her face in front of it would have required initiative beyond her capabilities for the last two miserable weeks.

"'*Which part*'?" he asked incredulously. "The part where you had to beg the police officers to arrest you while you were covered in blood and some dude's spleen bits were painting the sidewalk!"

"Oh, that. And yeah. It was. I couldn't believe they wouldn't just do it when I asked." Her pass hardly made it halfway, and Quentin shook his head as he chased after the awkward bounce.

"Uh, no. That's not the bullshit part. The bullshit part is that you can commit murder, confess to it, and they're still like, 'I dunno, she doesn't *look* like a killer.'"

"Welcome to being a woman where everyone thinks they know you better than yourself."

"Didn't you say the officer was a woman?"

She grunted. "Well, yes. But still."

"I dunno, Jess," he said, jogging backward and tossing her the ball in a lofty, effortless arc, "I think I'd take that over the assumptions people have about me. And just for the record, I'm going to tell this story to all my black friends and they're going to lose their shit."

She gripped the ball, extended her arm back to throw a pass but decided partway through the motion that she just didn't have it in her. The ball dropped behind her shoulder, bounced, and hit her in the back of the knee, causing her leg to buckle. "Guhh!" She didn't have the energy or desire to fight it, and she went down.

"Oh, come on now, Jess." Quentin jogged over and knelt down next to her. "You don't want them to see you like this, do you?" He nodded over to the waiting paparazzi on the bleachers.

"I didn't want them to see me at all, *Quentin.*" She spoke his name like an insult. "But you dragged me out here. I told you I would be no fun. I told you—"

"Yeah, yeah. Your life is over, nothing matters, nobody deserves to be subjected to you. I heard you the first time. Why don't we just stretch for a while? I assume you've been spending a lot of time in the fetal position—your hip flexors could probably use a little attention."

"Shows what you know." She said it bitingly, though his suggestion did show quite a depth of knowledge about how she'd been living her life lately.

She rolled onto her back and hugged one of her knees to her, which served up her fetal position fix for the hour.

The setting sun caused the wispy clouds overhead to glow red and orange.

Like Hell. Like where Dolores comes from.

Quentin tucked an ankle toward him and stretched forward to grab his toes. "Callie dumped me."

"Huh?" Jessica rolled her head toward him. "Quentin, I'm sorry. I had no idea." No idea they were still dating, mostly. Because she never asked about his life. Because she was the worst friend.

This is why Miranda left and never came back.

"Nah, it's fine. She didn't dump me so much as get back together with her ex. That's not quite the same. Like, they had history and, you know ..."

"History isn't everything," she said, trying not to sound too bitter as her thoughts traveled to Chris and the last time she'd seen him. "You're not upset about it?"

"I am a little, but don't, you know, tell anyone that."

"Why are you telling me?"

He shrugged and switched legs. "I don't really know. Maybe I thought you'd like to hear other people were going through it, too."

"Because you think I'm being self-absorbed?" she snapped.

He rolled his eyes. "No, because I want to make you feel better. Damn, why do I even try with you?"

"I don't know. I think I was pretty clear back at my place that you shouldn't." His surprise visit hadn't been met with the warmest reception, and she was pretty sure an assault took place during the struggle to get her out, but she wasn't sure who assaulted who. She could already see bruising on her forearms from where he'd grabbed her, and she was pretty sure he'd taken an elbow to the sternum. But he had much more fight in him than she did—that had become clear almost immediately.

"Would it make you feel better to smite something?" he asked.

She bolted upright. "*No!*" How could he even suggest it? "Especially not in front of them! Before, that kind of thing would just be used against me online, but now it could be used against me in the court of law. Are you crazy?"

"Easy, easy," he said. "I'm glad to see you aren't a complete blob. You still got a little fire in you."

"Eh, what do you know?" She flopped onto her back again, arms and legs extended like a starfish. She wasn't even pretending to stretch now.

"Want to get a burger?"

"Why not? It's not my money, and clearly I *love* burning through everyone else's."

"You're really pushing it, Jess, but I'm gonna let this

one slide because I can tell it's about Chris, and you *still* haven't brought him up."

"What is there to say?"

"Did you two get back together?"

"No," she moaned. "He left town, transferred money to me the next day."

"At the risk of you chewing me out, I have to ask: Why don't y'all get back together? It seems perfect. You broke up because you never got to see each other, but now you don't have a job anymore, so you could move up there, right?"

"No, *Quentin*. It's not perfect, and I worry deeply about you if you think this"—she motioned to the full length of her body—"could play any part in something that was perfect." She tried to sigh, but it felt like an unnecessary effort for her lungs. "It wouldn't work."

"Why not, though?"

"Because I'm too depressed, all right?" she snapped. "Because ... why would he want to be with me? He doesn't deserve that sort of punishment. It's bad enough he has to pay to keep me fed. I think I'm enough of a financial burden without being an emotional one, too. I really am the fucking moochsiah!"

"He loves you," Quentin insisted.

"And you love Miranda, but you don't move out to California to be with her. What, they don't have tech firms out there?"

"She doesn't—" He pulled up short, snapping his mouth shut. "No, you know what?" He stood and pulled his phone from his pocket, his pointer finger flying across the screen.

Was he calling Miranda? Had she actually said something useful?

A momentary flicker of hope warmed her chest against the December chill until Quentin said, "You're my friend, Jessica. And I know you're going through a lot. More than I can imagine. And that's why I'm going home before you push me too far and I have to stop being your friend." He tucked his phone into his pocket. "Your ride will be here in three minutes. His name is Leo, he drives a light blue Honda Fit, and he has a four-point-nine-star rating, so you shouldn't be murdered."

And with that, Quentin grabbed the ball from the ground and marched off the field.

For a moment, she considered apologizing, asking him to stay and help her figure out how to move forward, where to go from here when everything seemed ruined. She was all out of ideas and Quentin always knew what to do.

But she remained silent and watched him go, suspecting that the request would only cause her loyal and longtime friend to stubbornly shit his angelic pants and keep walking.

Chapter Fifty-Four

"... Happy birthday, dear Jesus. Happy birthday, to you!"

Jesus feigned annoyance with a roll of his eyes, but his grin gave him away, and he blew out the candles eagerly.

The dining room at Destinee and Rex's home was larger than that of the old McCloud doublewide because it existed. Otherwise, it was tiny, cramped, and hardly qualified as a room. It was more of a hallway between the kitchen and the living room with large alcoves on either side. Once the dining room table was added, there was hardly enough room to get through. And yet, Rex, both the McCloud women, Jesus, and his manfriend Jeremy managed to squeeze in for the birthday celebrations.

"You make a wish?" Destinee prompted.

"Was I supposed to?"

"Yeah. You close your eyes, make a wish, and then blow out the candles."

"I wish for world peace."

Destinee cringed. "You're not supposed to say it or else it won't come true."

"Ah."

Jessica watched the exchange through a fog. It had been a month since her career—and life—came to a screeching fuck you, and though she was surrounded by her family—and Jeremy—she still couldn't access the happiness she knew she should feel on such an occasion. Add it to the list of emotions her mind denied her access to now.

The debate over what sort of a birthday cake to bake for Jesus had been a prolonged one. First and foremost, Jesus had insisted he didn't need one, since it wasn't technically his birthday. Destinee wouldn't hear it. "Plenty of people don't celebrate their birthday on the actual day. They wait until the next available weekend for it."

Rex had posited the notion of a menorah cake, since Jesus was Jewish after all, but the son of God had politely explained that wasn't how it worked. Jessica had vetoed the fruitcake after Destinee had suggested it and Jesus had agreed that it sounded delightful. Eventually, they settled on a simple Texas Sheet Cake.

The question of how many candles to put on it was decided more quickly. Though the sheet cake did provide a large surface for candles, even if it had been enough to hold over two thousand candles, the collective smoke would have set off the detectors in the rental house immediately. In the end, they went with five wax letter candles: J-E-S-U-S. He approved even though he explained that was not the correct spelling.

"I shoulda told you about the wish first," Destinee said. "That's my bad. Guess we'll just have to have another celebration for you on your real birthday."

"I'd like that. Then I can wish for world peace again!"

Destinee flinched. "Nope. Spoiled it again. Just in advance this time."

"You said yourself it couldn't exist," Jessica grouched, hating herself for cutting through the jolly mood but unable to stop herself from doing it.

"Doesn't mean I can't wish for it," he replied sulkily.

"Peace itself is a fantasy," added Jeremy, though she wasn't sure if he intended it as consolation or not. "So long as there are men who feel entitled to controlling others, peace can never exist."

"That's not true," said Jesus. "After all, Jessica has been tasked with bringing peace to the United States. And God wouldn't assign it to her if it was impossible."

She felt the gravity of the room shift toward her, felt eyes on her from all around the table.

"You never mentioned that," said Destinee. "Is it true, baby?"

Jessica mean-mugged Jesus. This was the last thing she wanted to think about. "That was a long time ago."

"You were fifteen," said Jesus. "I remember it well."

"Yeah, but who cares? It's impossible. Just like

everything I'm asked to do is impossible." The self-pity wrapped around her like a warm blanket and she nestled into it. "Cut the damn cake."

Rex and Destinee shared a concerned look, and then Jesus grabbed the knife and carved up a piece. It was nearly a quarter of the cake, and he plated it and handed it to Jessica. "Eat of your feelings, sister."

She didn't need his blessing to do so, but she appreciated the support all the same and dug in without a fight.

"How about some TV?" asked Destinee once the remaining cake had been divvied out.

They settled into the living room, which was far more spacious. Rex had splurged on a new L-shaped couch with his pleasantly large football stipend, and Jessica perched in the crook of it. Rex and Destinee cozied up under a blanket further down the wing, and Jeremy claimed Rex's favorite recliner, while Jesus, as usual, opted to sit on the floor.

Much to Jessica's annoyance, Destinee turned to the TV stations rather than finding something to stream and settled on *It's a Wonderful Life.*

The angel Clarence was already on screen, showing George what his life would be like if he'd never been born. Clarence needed to keep his nose out of other people's damn business. Let George kill himself if he wanted to. Who gave a fuck?

As the scenes progressed, Jessica struggled against her

impulse to point out all the factual inaccuracies of Clarence. The only reason she fought the urge was because she hadn't forgotten what Quentin had done. He'd left her. She'd pushed an angel to his limits and driven him away. She doubted she could drive Destinee, Rex, and Jesus away, but that was somehow worse because it meant they wouldn't leave her when they should. If she didn't watch it, her mere presence would become a form of torture they couldn't escape.

It's just fiction. The movie can have whatever angel rules it wants.

For fuck's sake, even *she* was getting sick of her moodiness.

The holidays provided her a slight break from her lingering misery, as everyone was too busy and seasonally depressed to keep pushing her on the question of "what now?" Judith had found holiday employment easy enough. Same with Destinee, who'd administered hundreds of flu shots in the last two weeks alone, working long hours while Rex, who was already on Christmas break, held things down around the house. Wendy had agreed to wait until after the new year to broker the break-up between Jessica and Jameson, and Chris ...

She still hadn't heard from him, outside of a text to let her know the transfer was going through and she could expect her money in one business day.

His knee was better, and he was back on the active roster. One more regular season game, and then he would begin the playoffs.

At least someone's career is going as planned.

OH GOOD. I THOUGHT I'D MISSED THE PITY PARTY.

Oh look. The family's all together now. How touching.

YOUR CAREER IS GOING BETTER THAN IT EVER HAS.

Oh, shut up.

THE LORD SHALL NOT.

I have no career. How is that better than having a career?

YOU HAD THE WRONG CAREER.

Not this again. Professional messiah isn't going to pay my bills.

AND THE BAKERY DID?

Too soon. Besides, it was within a year of making a solid profit.

NO, IT WAS NOT. BECAUSE THERE WAS NOT A YEAR LEFT IN IT BEFORE THE DEVIL BROUGHT ABOUT THE END.

But if the Devil hadn't put a stop to it—

IRRELEVANT. SHE DID. THE SOONER YOU ACCEPT THAT, THE HAPPIER YOU'LL BE.

I can't imagine how accepting that the Devil stole my business and my brand would ever make me happy.

THAT IS OKAY, FOR YOUR IMAGINATION IS EMBARRASSINGLY LIMITED. THANKFULLY THE REALM OF POSSIBILITY IS NOT LIMITED TO IT.

Did you wish your son happy birthday?

IT IS NOT HIS BIRTHDAY.

God, you're obnoxious.

She felt Him leave her head, and a second later Jesus grinned and whispered, "Thanks, Dad."

The movie cut to a variety of holiday-themed commercials—one with a child brushing his teeth with Crest toothpaste to impress Santa, leaving Jessica wondering who thought Santa ought to get close enough to sleeping children to smell their breath, one about how Tide is the best brand to remove the inevitable grease stains from your Christmas ham (Jesus gasped when he learned that consuming pork was a part of his birthday celebration), and one mind-numbing Old Navy commercial that simply showed a mixed-raced family in matching reindeer footy-pajamas break dancing around a Christmas tree.

"So many strange heathen traditions," muttered Jesus.

The screen cut to Connor Wallace, Austin's long-time bearer of bad news, grinning into the camera. "Season's greetings! Join us at ten to see how Austin has kept Christmas weird. And later: What we know about the breaking abuse scandal in one of Texas's fastest growing churches." A picture of Jimmy Dean appeared above Connor Wallace's shoulder ... followed by stock footage of a pig rooting in the grass.

The image disappeared and the movie returned, leaving Jessica gaping at the TV. "Was that pig supposed to be there?"

"That *was* a little weird," conceded Destinee.

"Probably a practical joke," said Jeremy. "They told the

new kid to queue up a picture of the female accusers, and he was bitter he had to work on Christmas and put up pigs instead. Maybe even a White Light member. You'd be shocked to know how often that sort of thing happens on the local news."

Jessica was already googling it, though, ignoring the movie completely.

"Holy … shit." She stared down at the headline then scrolled up to make sure she was on a credible news site. She was. Without anyone asking, she read it aloud.

"White Light Church Accused of Covering Up Widespread Bestiality." She glanced up, met her mother's eyes, and said, "Pigfuckers."

Destinee's face lit up, giving her the appearance of a long-scorned woman opening a giant gift of schadenfreude on Christmas, which was exactly what she was. "Praise be," she whispered.

MERRY CHRISTMAS TO ALL AND TO ALL A GOOD NIGHT!

"There's more," Jessica said, ruining the line God had clearly meant to close on. She read the article aloud in full, both delighted it existed and horrified by what it said.

"That is … yucky," Jesus declared at the conclusion.

"Does it surprise anyone, though?" Jeremy asked.

"Yes," said Jessica, Destinee, Rex, and Jesus.

"I honestly didn't expect the pig fucking," Destinee added.

"Oh. Well, it shouldn't. Think about it. He's basically

created a religion that is, to use a metaphor, a pig in a blanket, and not a kosher one," Jeremy added darkly. "The sausage is our supposedly porcine nature, and the blanket is the repression and shame he wraps each of his followers in. If I tell you not to think about a pig in a blanket, all you'll do is think about a pig in a blanket."

"Dammit," said Destinee. "Now I'm hungry again."

Rex jumped up from the couch quickly. "I think we have some kosher pigs in a blanket in the freezer, Des. Would you like me to heat up—"

"See?" said Jeremy, pointing.

Rex lowered onto the couch again as Destinee straightened her spine and pointed a sharp finger at Jeremy. "Now hold up, you. We're talking food here. I could listen to someone talk about fucking pigs all day and not want to fuck one myself."

Jeremy shrugged as if he weren't so sure.

"Is it too much to hope that this will ruin Jimmy Dean?" Jessica asked.

"Probably," said Destinee. "Who needs a drink?"

Everyone did.

LOOK AT YOU, DARING TO HOPE FOR THINGS AGAIN.

Has Jimmy Dean been having sex with pigs?

TECHNICALLY IT WOULD BE RAPING PIGS SINCE THEY CANNOT CONSENT, AND NO. JIMMY HAS NOT RAPED PIGS.

Did he know what was going on in his congregation?

IT IS AMAZING WHAT A HUMAN CAN KNOW WITHOUT KNOWING HE KNOWS IT.

Have you been drinking?

IF ONLY.

By the time the movie ended, God was the only one in the room who wasn't drunk or well on the way to it. Jessica was perhaps the most sober, having spent too much time alternating between the movie and her phone as she scrolled through one breaking news post on White Light after another. Jesus was the second soberest, but only because he drank beer in small sips, making a satisfied noise after each, or as Destinee described it, "like a little bitch."

As Destinee began flipping around for something else to watch, Jessica said, "I forgot how awful the end of that movie is."

"I think it's nice," said Destinee.

Jeremy said, "Is it the horde of people entering into his home uninvited or the fact that George is clearly having a manic episode?"

"Probably both," Jessica said.

"Aw, hell to that," said Destinee. "I wouldn't be pissed if everyone I'd ever met decided to bust down my front door and shower me with money."

Rex adjusted his belt to compensate for his expanding gut. "Shame it doesn't pass the Bechdel test. I used to like that one a lot."

"You can still like it," Destinee said. "I ain't gonna hold it against you."

Rex issued a conflicted grunt. "I don't know. Is it right to give the patriarchy a pass?" He sounded as if he honestly wasn't sure but would like to know the definitive answer so he could stop worrying about it constantly.

Jeremy nodded. "Everyone always does."

"And you know," Rex said, "Mary gets no credit in that last scene. Potter does all his bullshit, George takes a vacation to find himself, and in the meantime, Mary is the one actually *doing* everything, going around town, calling George's brother to come home. And somehow we're supposed to buy that George's angel vacation and personal journey is what made everything happen!"

"Dammit, Rex," said Destinee, smacking him on the thigh. "Why can't you just enjoy things?"

"Men always get the credit," said Jeremy. "It's true."

Jesus turned away from the TV to stare up at his roommate. "This conversation is making me a little uncomfortable."

"It should!" Rex said. "It should make all of us uncomfortable. I mean, look at Des—she raised one hell of a girl all on her own, and you know what they call Jessica? The daughter of God. Not the daughter of Destinee. But *that's* what she should be called."

"Sounds a little melodramatic," Jessica said, ignoring the fact that giving credit to God for her achievements thus far in life wasn't saying much.

"And daughter of God isn't?" asked Jeremy.

"Who raised you up?" Rex asked Jesus. "Was it God?"

"No, but—"

"Was it Joseph?"

"Definitely not. He was a dimwit, bless his heart."

(Destinee high-fived him for correctly using the idiom she'd taught him over dinner.)

"So, Mary raised you?"

"Yes."

"And how often are you called the son of Mary?"

"Very rarely, and only by Catholics."

Rex raised an eyebrow to drive home the point through moderately slurred speech. "You know, sometimes I think it'd be better if God were a woman. Take all us men down a peg, ya know?"

Jeremy squinted at Rex, chewing his lip and nodding slowly. "Yes, that has interesting implications ..."

"If the Devil can be a woman, and God's child can be a woman, then why can't He? What's He so afraid of?" Rex looked like he might fight God if the deity were to walk into the room at that moment.

"Women aren't exactly perfect either," Jessica said.

Rex shrugged it off. "I'd take a different kind of bad at this point, wouldn't you?"

Jeremy tapped a finger to his mouth, or at least he meant to, but the beer softened his aim. "There may be something to that. Can men fix the gross mistakes that our own blind spots created? Or do we need a fresh perspective to bring solutions to the table?"

It was all ridiculous drunken jabber, obviously. But then Destinee said something that gave the idea its wings: "It sure would make Jimmy Dean poop those white pj pants of his to find out Deus Aper was a woman."

The statement was objectively true. And it might be the only thing that *could* send Jimmy into a panic.

The claims from the women hadn't. The pigfucking scandal probably wouldn't. But if he found out that God was actually the thing he detested most in this world ...

You there?

OH YES.

I remember once, when I asked if you were a man, you said it was complicated. What did you mean?

JUST THAT. IT'S COMPLICATED.

Does that mean you're not a man?

NO. I AM A MAN.

But didn't you exist before there were men and woman?

AND BOOMERANGS, YES.

So why did you decide to be a man?

I DID NOT.

Okay, I see why you'd said this is complicated.

MY GENDER WAS ASSIGNED BY THOSE IN POWER DURING THE EARLY AGES. IT WAS, BY AND LARGE, AN EPOCH OF BRUTE FORCE, AND EVOLUTION GAVE THE EDGE TO MEN. AND IN THEIR HUBRIS, THEY DESIGNED ME IN THEIR IMAGE.

And it's been that way ever since?

YEP.

So does that mean ...?

THE BIBLE IS WRONG?

I already assumed that. Does it mean you're whatever gender people believe you are?

OKAY, PERHAPS IT'S NOT THAT COMPLICATED, THEN.

"Shut the fuck up!" shouted Jessica.

"What's it?" Destinee said.

"Shh!" She held her finger to her lips so she could concentrate. *If enough people believe you're a woman, you'll just become a woman?*

IT GOES EMPIRE BY EMPIRE, BUT YES.

Empire by empire? *Wait a minute! Is the United States considered an empire?*

OH BOY.

Is it?

YES.

This new development wouldn't have anything to do with how I'm supposed to bring peace to this totally fucked up empire, would it?

BINGO WAS HER NAME-O.

"Shit." She finished her beer and slammed the empty bottle on the cushion next to her.

Jesus eyed her closely. "Was it Dad? Is He talking to you?"

"Oh yeah," Jessica replied. "That son of a bitch just told me how to bring peace to the United States."

The room went silent except for the sound from the television, where Santa drove a BMW along a winding road on the edge of a canyon while blasting dubstep.

Destinee muted it. "Shouldn't that be good news, baby?"

"It should."

"Then ... why do you look so sick?"

"Because," said Jessica, "no one's going to like it, and it will probably get me murdered."

... AND TO ALL A GOOD NIGHT!

END OF BOOK 6

Author's Note

Phew! What a long book, right?

But I'd like to think it accomplished some stuff, story wise.

First and foremost, you know who the Devil is. You probably already knew or strongly suspected, maybe even since book 1. Here's a secret: I kinda meant for that to happen. The point was never to make it a whodunit, or, as it were, a whodamnit. The aim was to make it fairly obvious right away and then sow the seeds of doubt here and there. And to provide you a textbook display of gaslighting that made you want to shake Jessica a little bit at the end, huh?

When we get to play the observer, it all seems so obvious. But when we're in it, being exposed to the love bombs and shame spears, it can get murky quick.

I'm fascinated by psychopaths. They hold the same

morbid appeal as black holes, because that's what they are. Black holes in human form.

I always thought the cartoonish idea of the Devil being this menace who makes no bones about doing horrible shit made zero sense. No one wants to hang around that guy. What's the appeal? It's like, "Uh, no thanks, Evil. You a hot mess."

Another thing you now know is the general direction book seven is heading in. The plan is to make it the last of the series, but there's really no telling. For instance, I planned on making this entire series one book back in the day. I wrote to the midpoint of book 2, thinking it was still part of book 1 and then realized that a) it would be years before I had a finished book to sell, b) there were actually many smaller story arcs in Jessica's life that each deserved their own book, and c) who in the hell would buy a 3,000 page book by an unknown author that was priced at like $19.99?

Always one for a good and layered pun, I've thought about calling the next book *Transubstantiation*, but I won't. It's about 50/50 whether the transgender community would love it or come after me with pitchforks, and I'm not willing to roll the dice on it. I honestly can't say which way it would go. I could probably ask around, but then I'd have to set up the joke for each person, and that would be spoilers galore. Not worth it. Also, I have #NoH8 for and no desire to belittle in any way those who put the T in that acronym I always get out of order.

But isn't it a nice little pun? And just imagine I did

publish it under that title and it did cause great offense. I would have found a way, possibly for the first time in history, to upset both the trans community *and* the Vatican in a single blow. (Because I'm sure Pope Francis has been following this series closely.) That in and of itself seems like it would belong on my satirist CV.

And yet, I won't do it. Instead I'm going to show this thing called "restraint" and will only mention it in this here author note for those who are already so deeply complicit in supporting this series that if I go down you go down too, mofos.

Jessica and I have a lot of work ahead of us for the next in this series, so I'd better get to it.

See you at the end of book 7,
    Claire, 11/28/18

P.S. If you want to know as soon as the next book is out and would enjoy a funny story or two in the meantime, join the Collective, my email group. I don't have time to spam you, but I will tell you things I think you'd enjoy, like the story of when my dog got high (not my fault) and if I read a really funny book you should check out. Oh, and you get one of my books for free right away.

Go to www.hclairetaylor.com/collective

About the Author

H. CLAIRE TAYLOR has lived in Austin since the eighties (it's her hometown) and hasn't yet found a compelling reason to move away.

After being a Very Good Student™ of creative writing at Texas State University, she worked an assortment of unfulfilling jobs until her inner tortured artist could recover from four soul-crushing years of academia, at which point she held her nose and jumped into the muddy waters of writing comedy full time.

Now she shares a home with her husband and two black-and-white mutts and suffers from an unhealthy dependency on Post-It Notes that she can quit whenever she wants. Really.

Casually stalk her:
www.hclairetaylor.com
contact@hclairetaylor.com

Also by H. Claire Taylor

The Jessica Christ Series

The Beginning (Book 1)

And It Was Good (Book 2)

It's a Miracle! (Book 3)

Nu Alpha Omega (Book 4)

It is Risen (Book 5)

Kilhaven Police (w/Brock Bloodworth)

Shift Work (Book 1)

Same Old Shift (Book 2)

Wimbledon, Kentucky

A Single's Guide to Texas Roadways

See all at www.hclairetaylor.com

Find more funny books at www.ffs.media